Pacification

Mark Neocleous is Professor of the Critique of Political Economy at Brunel University London. He is the author of many books, including *The Politics of Immunity: Security and the Policing of Bodies*; *A Critical Theory of Police Power: The Fabrication of the Social Order*; and *War Power, Police Power*.

Pacification

Social War and the Power of Police

Mark Neocleous

VERSO
London • New York

First published by Verso 2025

Illustrations from Wikimedia Commons

1 3 5 7 9 10 8 6 4 2

Verso
UK: 6 Meard Street, London W1F 0EG
US: 207 East 32nd Street, New York, NY 10016
versobooks.com

Verso is the imprint of New Left Books

ISBN-13: 978-1-80429-401-7
ISBN-13: 978-1-80429-402-4 (UK EBK)
ISBN-13: 978-1-80429-403-1 (US EBK)

British Library Cataloguing in Publication Data
A catalogue record for this book is available from the British Library

Library of Congress Cataloging-in-Publication Data
A catalog record for this book is available from the Library of Congress

Typeset in Minion by Hewer Text UK Ltd, Edinburgh
Printed and bound by CPI Group (UK) Ltd, Croydon CR0 4YY

Contents

Acknowledgements

This book has benefited from a long-standing intellectual and political engagement with friends in the Anti-Security Collective. Their incisive questions, comments, prompts, snips of information and, most of all, thinking and writing have helped this book come into being. As always, I am grateful once more for the love and support of Debbie and Lola Broadhurst.

Introduction

> *It is questionable how far it is possible to develop something like a social theory for a society which has in essence become as irrational as ours, [but] this thesis should be supplemented by the opposite and complementary one: the issue of what today still constitutes the veil that conceals all this. In a world where in fact any child can see the absurdity of the current order of things, how is it possible that this arrangement is preserved and maintained not simply by means of sheer force, or by the power of bayonets, or rather of missiles, to put this in a more contemporary way, but also through the consciousness of the human beings which it has produced and which are themselves constantly threatened by it?*
>
> Theodor Adorno, lecture (12 July 1960)

How is it possible that a society so fundamentally irrational, so horrendously exploitative, so palpably absurd, is preserved and maintained? The thesis of this book is that any critical theory that seeks to answer such a question requires the concept of pacification.

Why pacification?

The starting point of the irrationality of modern society is that *separation* appears the norm, while *unity* appears as either accident or error.[1] The first and foremost separation is between labour-power and the

1 Karl Marx, *Theories of Surplus Value, Part I*, transl. Emile Burns (London: Lawrence & Wishart, 1958), p. 396.

conditions of labour. This presupposes the separation of workers from ownership of the means through which they can realize their labour. In contrast to pre-capitalist formations such as feudalism, in which the labourer and their means of production remained closely united, 'like the snail with its shell', to use one of Marx's terms, capitalist production requires the separation of the labouring class from the means of subsistence and the conversion of those means into capital. In historical terms, this involved the dispossession of workers from the means of production. The outcome was the making of a class of wage labour and the rise of private property; in other words, proletarianization, enclosure and commodification. This is what Marx calls the systematic colonization of the world by capital. At the same time, the dissolution of the feudal forms which connected the individual to the political community created another form of separation between the independent individuals of civil society. When the political forms of feudal society such as the estates, corporations, and guilds were dissolved, what emerged was a civil society of autonomous, egoistic individuals experiencing social life as yet another form of separation, a form of social alienation that replicates the alienation of their labour in the workplace. Finally, in modern society needs are separated from capacities.[2] Human needs go unsatisfied while the capacity to satisfy them exists but is withheld. Human beings are alienated from the wealth they have created. These forms of separation are what count as 'freedom' under capital, without which there is no capitalist accumulation.

The historical process that sees the dispossession of the workers from ownership of the means of production, the transformation of human beings and their means of subsistence into the subjects and objects of property, and the dissolution of civil society into a mass of independent egoistic individuals, is the same process which sees the rise of the modern state. State and capital are formed in one and the same moment, and the security of private property rests on a system of impersonal power distinct from the personal power of a prince, monarch, or emperor.

To maintain modern society as an order of separation, to make and remake the working class, to regulate the dissolute mass of autonomous

2 Geoffrey Kay and James Mott, *Political Order and the Law of Labour* (London: Macmillan, 1982), p. 1.

individuals, and to defend the system of private property, force must be constantly applied, and the application of this force must be regarded as legitimate. Historically, this entailed a *war* of annihilation against every non-capitalist form encountered by capital, forging vagabonds and paupers out of peasants and then forging wage labourers out of the vagabonds and paupers. It was a class war between a rights-based model founded on custom and providing the direct producers with some measure of immediate access to the means of production, and a model of absolute property giving the direct producers access to subsistence only through the mediation of the wage form. This is war in the widest sense possible: war as order-formation. It is war conducted through laws and statutes that enclose the commons and undermine, for the overwhelming bulk of the population, any means of subsistence other than the wage. In other words, it is a war conducted through the police power. This war as order-formation exercised through an expansive police power is what we call pacification.

The *Oxford English Dictionary* (*OED*) dates the emergence of 'pacification' in the English language to the period of the rise of capitalism and the state. The *OED* offers as a definition of pacification 'a process or operation . . . designed to secure the peaceful cooperation of a population or an area where one's enemies are thought to be active'. Citing as early examples the Edicts of Pacification of 1563 and 1570, the *OED* offers for 'pacify' the idea of 'reducing to peaceful submission'. In taking from the Roman tradition of imperial glory, in which *pax* implied 'pacification', the verb 'pacificate', now obsolete, also connoted the making of peace; 'peacekeeper' enters the language in the very late sixteenth century, and 'peacemaker' just a little earlier. 'Peace' itself is a word that derives from the Middle English and Old French *paix*, itself adapted from the Latin *pacem*, which was in turn derived from *pax*, and connected to *pācāre*, which together connote what it means to satisfy, content, gratify and be acceptable to, but also to *appease* in the sense of *reducing to peace*. The English word 'pacification' therefore has affinities with domination, but also reminds us that peace is a form of subjugation; hence the phrase 'dictating the peace'. Sir Thomas Elyot's *Latin–English Dictionary* of 1538 offers *pacifer* as 'brynger of peace', *pacificatorius* as 'that whiche dothe pacyfie', and *pacifico* as 'to pacifie'.

Roman accounts of pacification were rooted in their knowledge of the absolute power wielded over subjects of the Empire, the brutal violence involved in subduing the territories, the crushing of the succession of revolts against Roman domination, and the subsequent internal wars of attrition. These wars were *expansive*, incorporating civil wars, slave wars, and social wars, about which I shall have much more to say in Chapter 1. This was part and parcel of what the Romans understood as the need for their subjects to be permanently reminded of the consequences of resistance and rebellion. In ideological terms, it was important for these wars to be masked by the banner of peace, as Cicero puts it in the 'Twelfth Philippic', giving rise to the idea of pacification as the 'brutality of peace', as Tacitus puts it in his *Histories*.

At the same time, however, pacification was also meant as a productive and constructive process, in the sense that empires had to be *built*. In this context, the *pax* stood for the establishment of a concord within the Empire, to be built through the constitution of a people accepting the peace imposed through their subjugation. Yet the Latin term *pax* was also broad enough to encompass ideas about welfare and prosperity, and the old French *paix* also points to a certain assumption about a civic order free from civil unrest. A people conquered is a people pacified; conversely, a people pacified is a people conquered. Thus, 'pacification' is a key concept in the discourse of domination.

On the one hand, then, when 'pacification' came to the fore in early modern European languages and in the context of the rise of capital and the formation of states, it quickly found a home in the discourse of colonial conquest and empire-building. For example, 'pacification' was the term used by the Spanish military captain Bernardo de Vargas Machuca in his writings defending the dispossession and domination of the American Indians, *Milicia Indiana* (1599) and *Defense and Discourse of the Western Conquests* (1603). Hence the Edicts of Pacification from the late sixteenth century cited by the *OED* all use phrases such as 'to put an end to strife or discontent' or 'to reduce to peaceful submission'. On the other hand, pacification stretched well beyond the defeat of those conquered in the colonial projects, coming to connote subjection in a more general and systematic sense. Hence, many of the early Edicts of Pacification were aimed at European towns and cities. Blaise de Monluc, a Gascon captain who in 1543 led a troop of harquebusiers in an ambush of the imperial army in Piedmont, then became marshal of France in 1574 and a leading military strategist, had perfected through the sixteenth century a means of terrifying the people of various European cities in order 'to help to pacifie a Tumult . . . risin in the City'.[3] At the same time, monarchs would send officials into towns and regions to enforce the Edicts of Pacification, the officials being granted executive authority and given the task of encouraging people to see pacification as an ongoing negotiation about the contours of their peace, and not simply an authoritarian decree from the king.

Pacification was thus a driving force behind the development of the executive power of the monarchical state, but also a means for the state in general to enforce a sovereign demand for peace on the people. As suggested by Elyot in *The Governor* (1531), the multitude will 'serve and obey' if laws are severe enough, but if given any license they will 'refuse to be bridled' and will rebel against being 'pacified and brought again into order'.[4] Pacified: brought into order.

The centrality of the idea of pacification during the rise of capitalism and the state cannot be overstressed. A Google Ngram of 'pacification' shows a pronounced spike in the use of the word around the turn of the seventeenth century (along with a much smaller spike in the 1960s, the period in which it merges with counterinsurgency, about which I shall shortly have more to say). At the very least, then, pacification's presence in the political lexicon of modernity suggests it deserves the kind of attention that has been given to related ideas that come to the fore during the same period, such as sovereignty and the state. But what I want to do here is not simply to pay attention to pacification's historical rise, but to appropriate and radicalize the concept for critical theory.

We might consider this strategy through the history of a parallel term: proletariat. When Marx and Engels, in *The Manifesto of the Communist Party* (1848), tried to capture the historic struggles through which revolutions take place and out of which new social formations emerge, they pointed to the revolutionary warfare between oppressing and oppressed classes. The struggle continues in modern society which, Marx and Engels insist, has simplified class antagonisms 'into two great hostile camps, into two great classes directly facing each other – Bourgeoisie and Proletariat'. Thus begins a history in which the idea of

3 Blaise de Monluc, *The Commentaries of Messire Blaize de Montluc, Mareschal of France. Fifth Book*, transl. Charles Cotton (London: H. Broome, 1674 [1592]), p. 268.

4 Sir Thomas Elyot, *The Book Named the Governor*, ed. S. E. Lehmberg (London: Dent, 1962 [1531]), p. 7.

the proletariat takes centre stage in Marxist thought. Dictionaries of etymology tend to claim that 'proletariat' came into English and other languages in the nineteenth century, arising from a body of socialist literature, and there is some truth in this, to which Marx and Engels's use of the word attests. However, the idea of the proletariat comes originally from the Romans. In the sixth century BCE, during the reign of Servius Tullius, a census was undertaken which used the word *proletarii* to describe the lowest class. The *proletarii* were those whose propertyless status made them ineligible for full participation in the political community, but who were nonetheless 'free' and whose role was to produce offspring ('proles') and sometimes serve in the army. In England, during the rise of capitalism, some writers appropriated the term to describe a labouring class whose main purpose seemed to be the same as that described as the Roman 'proletariat'. Thomas Rogers's *A Philosophical Discourse, Entitled, the Anatomy of the Mind* (1576) notes that 'the Romanes had a company of men called Proletaries, upon whome was never any task or fyne set, but they dyd benefite, and pleasure theyr countrey with begettinge children'. In 1609 the English translation of Ammianus Marcellinus's fourth-century text *Roman History* offered the idea that the sovereign 'should gaine a number of proletairie subjects to multiplie and beget issue'. In 1628 Robert Burton, in the opening section of *The Anatomy of Melancholy* ('Democritus to the Reader'), described '15,000 proletaries slain in a battle'. James Harrington in *Oceana* (1656) noted one of the 'tribes' of Rome as 'proletary', those who 'thro their poverty contributed nothing to the commonwealth but children'. This tendency continued into the eighteenth century. In 1710, Gregory King's calculation of the population referred to 'Proletarys, for furnishing us with people'; and later in the century French thinkers such as Montesquieu and Rousseau also employed the term, the latter seeing in the Roman proletariat the predecessor of the modern worker who becomes a citizen. The word was also used during the French Revolution.

That said, the most consistent use of the word really came about among French socialists writing in the 1820s and 1830s, who politicized 'proletariat' by using it in a way that implied more than an impoverished mass. 'It's not as if some of you haven't heard tell of the people', Charles Béranger announced to the Chamber of Deputies in February 1831. But who are 'the people'? This term, he suggests, refers to 'all those who work, all those who have no social existence, all those who possess nothing. You know about whom I wish to speak: the *proletariat*.'[5] Most of all, Béranger warned the Chamber, the proletariat was rebellious. As the 1830s progressed, ever more French socialists used the word, usually distinguishing it from the proletariat's key opponent, the bourgeoisie (not the aristocracy). Étienne Cabet in *Voyage en Icarie* (1839), Louis Blanc in *Organisation du Travail* (1839) and Pierre-Joseph Proudhon in *Qu'est-ce que la Propriete?* (1840) all draw the fundamental line between the bourgeoisie and the proletariat, but also distinguish the latter from the older notion of the 'poor'. The proletariat is imagined as a class engaged in the new forms of industry, producing the wealth of society, increasingly organized, and likely to revolt.

By the 1830s, then, a radical innovation in political life and language had occurred, at the heart of which was the idea of the proletariat as an 'independent and self-conscious force in politics', according to Eric Hobsbawm. This new development, Hobsbawm adds, should not be confused with the long and noble history of collective groups and formations that revolted against intolerable hardship. Rather, what was new was a certain kind of 'class consciousness and class ambition' attached to this collective force. It was no longer a case of 'the poor' facing 'the rich', but a specific class, the labouring class, the *proletariat*, up against another class, the capitalists, the *bourgeoisie*.[6]

When Marx moved from Cologne to Paris in 1843, his work underwent a transformation as he immersed himself in French socialist literature while writing a series of essays on the theory of the state, the nature of private property, and the possibility of human emancipation. One such essay was a critique of Hegel's philosophy of right, and although that manuscript remained unfinished and unpublished, Marx worked up one section of it for publication as an article, namely the 'Introduction'. Towards the end of that article, Marx turns to the idea of the proletariat, but in a manner distinct from other socialist literature of the period. Having embraced the idea of 'emancipation' from his reading of various sources, Marx asks: Where is the possibility of emancipation?

---

5 Charles Béranger, *Pétition d'un Prolétaire à la Chambre des Députés* (Paris: Bureau de L'Organisateur, 1831), p. 3. Emphasis in original. Author translation.

6 Eric Hobsbawm, *The Age of Revolution, 1789–1848* (London: Weidenfeld & Nicolson, 1995), pp. 111, 117, 209.

> *This is our answer*. In the formation of a class with *radical chains*, a class of civil society which is not a class of civil society, a class which is the dissolution of all classes, a sphere which has a universal character because of its universal suffering and which lays claim to no *particular right* because the wrong it suffers is not a *particular wrong* but *wrong in general*; a sphere of society which can no longer lay claim to a *historical* title, but merely to a *human* one . . . and finally a sphere which cannot emancipate itself without emancipating itself from – and thereby emancipating – all the other spheres of society, which is, in a word, the *total loss* of humanity and which can therefore redeem itself only through the *total redemption of humanity*. This dissolution of society as a particular class is the *proletariat*.[7]

'Proletariat' appears as the name for a class whose suffering, and therefore character, renders it somehow 'universal'. It is not only the collective noun for workers, but denotes the agent of revolution, and thus the subject of history: a force that will liberate itself from its suffering, and in the process liberate the whole of humanity from the same. Moreover, it is in this period that Marx begins to articulate the idea that the bourgeoisie and proletariat are at *war*, and that for the bourgeoisie this war is carried out by the gamut of institutions through which the state *polices* civil society.

These points will be developed below. Here, let us note that, to describe a body of workers without which modern society could not survive, which produces the wealth of society but is itself dispossessed and exploited, Marx adopts and radically reconsiders a Roman word that had been utilized by the European ruling class and leading ideologues of early capitalism to describe the mass ('proles'), and then radicalized by nineteenth-century socialists. In other words, 'proletariat' was taken from the language of Roman power and European thought to become part of the Marxian lexicon for understanding bourgeois society.

What is the proletarian experience? Marx consistently argues that we should think of class as a social *process*. Might part of this process be

7 Karl Marx, 'Critique of Hegel's Philosophy of Right. Introduction' (1844), transl. Rodney Livingstone and Gregor Benton, in Karl Marx, *Early Writings* (Harmondsworth: Penguin, 1992), 256. Emphases in original.

captured by another Roman word: pacification? Might this be why 'pacification' retained its place in the prose of the European ruling class and its state officials long after the Roman Empire faded? This is indeed one reason why pacification proves to be such an intriguing term. As we shall see throughout this book, the language of pacification can be found in a mass of ruling-class and state documentation, including, inter alia, legislation; executive orders; official, semi-official and unofficial reports; confidential documents; committee minutes; official conference proceedings; government announcements; memos; dossiers; personal biographies; interviews; military and police manuals; books and articles written by security intellectuals and counterinsurgency thinkers; and in a whole host of other places, including some of the major works of political thought that have sought to legitimize and defend the state and capital. The history of capitalist modernity is a history of the ruling class documenting its dream of pacification, and such documentation provides much of the source material for the argument in this book.

What I am interested in, then, is what Brendan McQuade has called *the prose of pacification*.[8] I am interested in what this prose tells us about the social wars and police powers mobilized in the fabrication of order. It is a prose that captures the shared discourses, forms of expertise, and techniques of power through which the state administers civil society. It is a prose that explodes the liberal myth of a fundamental distinction between the war power and the police power, exposes liberal peace as a fiction, and takes us beyond the trite, formulaic and academic distinctions such as foreign/domestic, colony/metropole, coercion/consent, and destruction/construction. It is a prose that reveals the expansion of security as the supreme idea and ideal of bourgeois society, and hence the principle through which pacification is often carried out. I have pursued some of these issues and arguments in earlier work, most notably in *The Fabrication of Social Order* (2000), revised as *A Critical Theory of Police Power* (2021); *Critique of Security* (2008); *War Power, Police Power* (2014); and *The Universal Adversary* (2016). Here I seek to develop them further through a critical theory of pacification.

In *Security/Capital*, George Rigakos suggests that the main economic expressions of pacification in capitalist societies are *dispossession*,

8 Brendan McQuade, *Pacifying the Homeland: Intelligence Fusion and Mass Supervision* (Oakland: University of California Press, 2019).

exploitation and *commodification*, which converge in the fabrication of productive labour and the control of space, time, and labourers themselves. As Rigakos puts it, 'to understand pacification is to understand how capitalism itself is produced and reproduced'.[9] But dispossession, exploitation and commodification are never straightforward or easy. They produce resistance, conflict, revolt, rebellion. Even when these things are not immediately apparent, such economic expressions correlate with political expressions, and so, along with dispossession, exploitation and commodification, we need to address the ways in which pacification aims to constitute us as obedient subjects who acquiesce in our own subjection. Hence pacification is also *containment*. Such containment can function as a response to insurgency, rebellion and revolt (pacification as a *countering* of such things); but it is most successful if order is fabricated in such a way that such things do not occur in the first place. Capitalism needs to be *built*, but it needs to be built in such a way that challenges to it are always already being contained.

What I attempt here is a political appropriation and expansive repurposing of the concept of pacification to capture the ways in which capitalist order is constituted, wage labour fabricated, obedient subjects created, and domination policed, rendering the modern state a pacification machine. Pacification is the sine qua non of modernity, which is to say that the modern state is structured in such a way that it can contain and counter whatever it thinks needs to be contained and countered – even sometimes generating new enemies to contain and counter. Pacification is state power as counterpower. Inherent in pacification is the *counterinsurgent logic of the modern state*. In fact, given their uneven and then combined development, a better formulation would be that, in counterinsurgency, we find the pacificatory logic of the modern state.

Counterinsurgency is one of the ways in which we find the prose of pacification articulated, and I will turn to that shortly. First, let us identify four other ways in which pacification appears across several fields of writing and thinking, and why their limitations point to the need for a wider critical theory, as attempted here.

The first is in what might be described as historical sociologies of the nation-state and modern social power. Norbert Elias in *The Civilizing*

---

9 George S. Rigakos, *Security/Capital: A General Theory of Pacification* (Edinburgh: Edinburgh University Press, 2016), p. 6.

Process (1939), Anthony Giddens in *The Nation-State and Violence* (1985) and Michael Mann in *The Sources of Social Power* (1986) have all shown the extent to which the growth of commercial and productive economic processes, and the concomitant rise of towns and cities as centres of commerce, required a transformation in the structure and exercise of violence over a realm described as fundamentally 'peaceful'. This required the creation of 'durably pacified social spaces' and the 'inner pacification of society' (Elias), an 'internally pacified state' (Giddens), and new forms of administrative power for the 'internal pacification' (Mann) of the social realm. Along with a plethora of religious conflicts, newly developing urban centres were generating concerns over forms of behaviour made possible by urban life, such as gambling, drinking, adultery, sodomy and blasphemy. All required policing, and all had wars launched against them. More important, all such behaviours were frequently connected to the increase in the number of the 'wandering' poor – a group of 'masterless' people perpetually associated with rebellion, seemingly out of reach of the law ('lawless') and beyond the forms of coercive control that might keep them in place ('disorderly'). In other words: beyond 'law and order'. Worse, such people were thought to be behind the rise of popular disturbances throughout Europe, such that the disorderliness and criminality of the masterless was imagined to be connected to the idea of political rebellion. Hence, they would become, as they remain, a core object of pacification. Elias, Giddens and Mann all use the language of pacification to describe such a process, though without including any extended treatment of this concept or its meaning.

The second way in which pacification is articulated is in a body of scholarly work along the lines of *The Pacification of X* ('The Pacification of Vietnam', 'The Pacification of Palestine', 'The Pacification of Ireland', and so on), where 'pacification' is barely ever explicated as an idea. The 'pacification' in such accounts is largely taken as read, used to describe a certain kind of warfare, though often with some kind of qualifier: counter-guerrilla warfare, counter-revolutionary war, quasi-war, other war, persistent conflict, civic action, grey-area operations, state of belligerency, state of hostilities, effects-based operations, military operations other than war, and – a term about which I shall shortly have more to say – 'counterinsurgency'. For those working in this frame, the general tendency is to focus on the pacification practices in whichever country is the focus of discussion, with next to no analysis of what pacification might be other than a description of those practices.

A third use of pacification treats it as a euphemism or misnomer – an ideological corruption of language, in the sense that the violence of pacification is meant to be hidden by the word itself. 'Defenceless villages are bombarded from the air, the inhabitants driven out into the countryside, the cattle machine-gunned, the huts set on fire with incendiary bullets: this is called *pacification*', writes George Orwell in 'Politics and the English Language' (1946), an essay on the euphemistic nature of much political language. Or take Roland Barthes's essay 'African Grammar' (1979), on the ways in which official French reports on African affairs often functioned more as a means of intimidation than communication, not least by employing a standard tactic of bourgeois ideology – namely, giving something the name of its contrary in order to deny that it is happening. In the case of 'war', for example, two options are available, Barthes observes. One is 'to name it as little as possible', generating the kind of concepts noted in the previous paragraph. The second option is to give war *the meaning of its contrary*. 'War is then used in the sense of peace, and pacification in the sense of war'. This is the more cunning procedure, observes Barthes, and is at the basis of almost all the mystifications of bourgeois discourse. Like Orwell, Barthes is pointing to the fact that the violence of war is being passed off as something else, something that is meant to sound, well, pacifying. Both Orwell and Barthes are on to something, and some of those mystifications will become apparent as we proceed, especially in Chapter 3.

The fourth way in which pacification is used is as a descriptor for a certain kind of cultural hegemony. Take the phrase 'pacification by cappuccino', which appears in a well-known essay by David Harvey, 'The Right to the City', published in *New Left Review* in 2008 – although Harvey ascribes the phrase to Sharon Zukin. 'Pacification by cappuccino' captures the strategy of city planners to encourage the proliferation of shopping malls offering security in consumption (for those who can afford it). The phrase 'pacification by cappuccino' quickly caught on: there now appear to be close to 2,000 citations of the phrase, and this should not surprise us. It has an easy appeal, brimming with confidence in seemingly putting its finger on so many things at once: the gentrification of cities; the displacement of working-class communities and the effacement of their cultural habits; the rise of a certain type of café culture; the bourgeoisie at leisure. But, more than anything, it points to the idea that hegemonic social and cultural practices are enough to render us pacified. The same idea about the pacifying effects of everyday cultural practices appears elsewhere – for example, in Bernard Harcourt's *The Counterrevolution* (2018) where, rather than the pleasures of a milky coffee, it is Netflix and other forms of mass digital entertainment that are said to 'pacify the masses'.[10] Yet, as accounts of pacification, these suggestions do not tell us very much, especially if, as in the subtitle of Harcourt's book, we really want to understand a state's war against its own citizens. We all know, of course, that to enjoy swallowing the shit of capital (to use Jean-François Lyotard's phrase),[11] it must be made to taste like something else, and cappuccino will do as well as anything – especially if we can drink it while consuming products of the culture industry. But, in the end, these formulations tell us literally nothing about pacification, other than it can sometimes make us feel as though we are living a 'brighter and nicer new life' (see Chapter 3).

The final way in which pacification is invoked is in the work of counterinsurgency (COIN) experts. Here, a longer discussion is required, not least because the figure of the insurgent will appear throughout this book. As noted above, there was rise in interest in pacification from roughly 1960 onwards, thanks to its association with counterinsurgency. Given that one of the purposes of this book is to explore the prose of pacification as it appears in the kind of state documents listed above, we need to pay heed to the fact that, from 1960, these documents are often also about counterinsurgency.

Any mention of counterinsurgency these days is almost obliged to start with the US Army/Marine Corps *Counterinsurgency Field Manual*, issued in 2006. The importance of this *Manual* cannot be overstated. It was a work intended to be of profound doctrinal importance in the 'war on terror', but was also designed to fill a gap created by the absence of any major official American publication on counterinsurgency for two decades or more. Its importance was reinforced in 2007 with the publication of a cheap paperback edition by the University of Chicago Press,

---

10 David Harvey, 'The Right to the City', *New Left Review* II/53 (September–October 2008), pp. 23–40; Bernard E. Harcourt, *The Counterrevolution: How Our Government Went to War Against Its Own Citizens* (New York: Basic, 2018), p. 187.

11 Jean-Francois Lyotard, *Libidinal Economy*, transl. Iain Hamilton Grant (London: Athlone Press, 1983 [1974]), p. 116.

which became a surprise bestseller. The book contains a Foreword by Lieutenant Colonel John Nagl, one of the team that put the *Manual* together, and an Introduction by Sarah Sewall, director of the Carr Center for Human Rights Policy at Harvard University. Its huge sales meant that it found its way into mainstream debates about the contours of contemporary counterinsurgency, the liberal way of war, human rights in the war on terror, and the relationship between academia and the war machine.

I will return to the *Manual* at various points throughout this book. I raise it here simply because, in the context of radically rethinking *counterinsurgency* strategy, the authors of the *Manual* offer a short discussion of *pacification*. That discussion appears in a two-page section on the war in Vietnam (described as 'accelerated pacification' – the term used to describe the period between 1968 and 1972), but which is clearly also meant to indicate the overall thrust of what is being described in the *Manual*. The effectiveness of the earlier pacification programme is described as 'a function of integrated civilian and military teams at every level of society'. Despite the brevity of its discussion, the *Manual* informs us that the pacification process 'was generally led, planned, and executed well' and is therefore 'a useful model to consider for other COIN operations'.[12] Precisely why the *Manual*'s authors thought of highlighting a strategy that, thirty years previously, had resulted in a humiliating retreat, is not of interest to us here. What is of interest is the fact that a twenty-first-century reappraisal of counterinsurgency conducted at the highest levels of the world's leading military power felt the need to hark back to something it once called 'pacification'. The *Manual* thus offers a clue to something important: when counterinsurgency is being discussed, the idea of pacification is never far away. This is why advocates of sending in more troops to Iraq and Afghanistan in 2009 were often seen carrying around Lewis Sorley's *A Better War* (1999) – a revisionist work on the Vietnam War which contends that the war could have been won if only the commanders had stuck to a coherent

12 The manual is available as US Army/Marine Corps, *Counterinsurgency Field Manual: U.S. Army Field Manual No. 3-24/Marine Corps Warfighting Publication No. 3-33.5*, 2006 (Chicago, IL: University of Chicago Press, 2007), sections 2-52–2-53, pp. 73–5.

pacification strategy.[13] It is also why other reports that emerged around the same time as the *Manual* refer to 'COIN and pacification' at one and the same time.[14]

One clue to the connection between pacification and counterinsurgency can be found in comments made in an interview with Nagl about the writing of the *Manual*. In the interview, he suggests that, had it been possible, he and the other people behind the creation of the *Manual* would have simply put an American Army cover on a much earlier book by David Galula called *Counterinsurgency Warfare* (1964).[15] Galula had been a captain in the French army during the attempted pacification of Algeria between 1956 and 1958. He took up a post at Harvard University in 1962, and was commissioned by RAND to write up his reflections on his experiences in the pacification of Algeria, as well as in Greece, the Philippines and Malaysia. The text that emerged, *Pacification in Algeria* (1963) was drafted simultaneously with *Counterinsurgency Warfare*. The latter was written in English for RAND and published by Praeger in 1964. *Pacification in Algeria*, by contrast, was classified by RAND until 2006, when it was published by Praeger at the same time as their translation of another major text in the history of counterinsurgency, Roger Trinquier's *Modern Warfare*, together with a new edition of Galula's *Counterinsurgency Warfare*. The new edition included a Foreword by Nagl, and the French edition (2008) came with a Foreword by General Petraeus, who was then at the heart of the development of the *Counterinsurgency Field Manual*, as well as the war in Iraq. Petraeus also ordered 1,500 copies of the English edition of Galula's book, making it required reading for every student at Fort Leavenworth's Command and General Staff College. The Joint Special Operations University in Florida ordered 100 copies.[16] At one point, one lieutenant colonel suggested that

13 Fred Kaplan, *The Insurgents: David Petraeus and the Plot to Change the American Way of War* (New York: Simon & Schuster, 2013), p. 311.

14 For example, Angel Rabasa, Lesley Anne Warner, Peter Chalk, Ivan Khilko and Paraag Shukla, *Money in the Bank: Lessons Learned from Past Counterinsurgency (COIN) Operations* (Santa Monica, CA: RAND, 2007), p. xi.

15 Interview with Amit Prakash, cited in Amit Prakash, *Empire on the Seine: The Policing of North Africans in Paris, 1925–1975* (Oxford: Oxford University Press, 2022), p. 185. Likewise, see General David H. Petraeus and Lieutenant Colonel John A. Nagl, 'Préface' to David Galula, *Contre-insurrection: Théorie et Pratique* (Paris: Economica, 2008).

16 Kaplan, *Insurgents*, p. 178.

the Americans in the war on terror were simply testing Galula's teaching.[17] Clearly, the United States regarded Galula as highly as he regarded himself: as 'the Clausewitz of counter-revolutionaries'.[18]

Galula went immediately from writing a book on 'pacification' to a book on 'counterinsurgency'. What is at stake in both books is a third term, 'counter-revolutionary war', which also sometimes appears as 'civil war' (see Chapter 1). Precisely what is the difference? In the earlier book, Galula comments on the uncertainty surrounding the terms, and writes that the general directive he received for Algeria was to 'win over the population'. 'The order was to "pacify". But exactly how? The sad truth was that, in spite of all our past experience, we had no single, official doctrine for counterinsurgency warfare.'[19] How was pacification to be achieved? Through a counterinsurgency doctrine.

In contrast to the long history of 'pacification', 'counterinsurgency' as an idea only emerged in the early 1960s. The *OED* dates the first appearance of 'counterinsurgency' to May 1962, but we can find slightly earlier uses of the term. According to the *Pentagon Papers*, the idea of a 'counterinsurgency plan' developed during 1961 as the basis for expanding the US 'assistance' to Vietnam. The plan had been in progress through 1960, and was then finalized by the Kennedy administration. According to Roger Hilsman, who went on to become director of the Bureau of Intelligence and Research in the State Department, the first question the new president asked following his January 1961 inauguration was 'What are we doing about guerrilla warfare?'[20] His question was political as much as military. On 1 February 1961, at a meeting of the National Security Council, Kennedy asked after 'the development of counter-guerrilla forces'.[21] This

17 Lieutenant Colonel Dale Kuehl, 'Testing Galula in Ameriyah: The People are the Key', *Military Review*, March–April 2009.

18 Cited in A. A. Cohen, *Galula: The Life and Writings of the French Officer Who Defined the Art of Counterinsurgency* (Santa Barbara, CA: Praeger, 2012), p. 223. I will have more to say about some of Galula's arguments in Chapter 3.

19 David Galula, *Pacification in Algeria, 1956–1958* (Santa Monica, CA: RAND, 2006 [1963]), pp. 64–5.

20 Roger Hilsman, *To Move a Nation: The Politics of Foreign Policy in the Administration of John F. Kennedy* (New York: Doubleday, 1967), p. 413.

21 David W. Mabon, ed., *Foreign Relations of the United States, 1961–1963, Volume VIII: National Security Policy* (Washington, DC: US Government Printing Office, 1996); National Security Council, minutes, 'Military Budget and National Security Policy', 475th NSC meeting, 1 February 1961.

focus on the guerrilla was important, because the *guerrilla* melded into the figure of the *insurgent*, and needed to be *countered*. What emerged was thus variously called 'counterinsurgency operations', a 'counterinsurgency plan', or just plain 'counterinsurgency'.[22] Throughout 1961, several high-level and interdepartmental study groups and research projects on counterinsurgency were established, while training in counterinsurgency was offered by the Foreign Service Institute, War Colleges and service schools. Even the more 'civilian' agencies – including the Army's Finance School and its Cooks' and Bakers' School – established special courses on counterinsurgency. Other documents appeared indicating the scope of the meaning of 'counterinsurgency', such as National Security Memorandum 114, in November 1961, titled *Training for Friendly Police and Armed Forces in Counter-Insurgency, Counter-Subversion, Riot Control and Related Matters*.[23] It should be understood that what was described as 'counterinsurgency' was imagined from the outset as a means of countering 'subversion' and policing public disorder within the homeland.

Concern on this issue gathered momentum with the establishment of a Special Group (Counter-insurgency) (SGCI). In April 1962, RAND organized a symposium on counterinsurgency at the behest of the president, involving leading experts on pacification such as Galula and Trinquier from France, and Sir Robert Thompson and Frank Kitson from the UK. Reflecting on this many years later, Kitson wrote that, despite their different backgrounds, everyone 'spoke the same language', having 'worked out theories of counterinsurgency procedures at one time or another which we thought were unique and original. But when we came to air them, all our ideas were essentially the same.'[24] Or, as

22 'Chronology', in *Pentagon Papers*, 'Part IV.B.1: Counterinsurgency: The Kennedy Commitments, 1961–1963', p. 11; 'Counterinsurgency Plan for South Viet-Nam' (January 1961), in *Pentagon Papers*, 'Part IV.A.5: Evolution of the War: Origins of the Insurgency', p. 48; MAAG Vietnam, 'Geographically Phased National Level Operations Plan for Counterinsurgency', 15 September 1961, in *Pentagon Papers*, 'IV.B.3: Evolution of the War. Counterinsurgency: The Advisory Build-Up, 1961–67', p. 49. Unless otherwise stated, all references to *Pentagon Papers* here and in later chapters can be pursued at archives.gov.

23 National Security Memorandum 114, 22 November 1961, in Mabon, *Foreign Relations of the United States, 1961–1963, Volume VIII: National Security Policy*, Document 59.

24 Frank Kitson, *Bunch of Five* (London: Faber, 1977), p. 200; Stephen T. Hosmer and Sibylle O. Crane, *Counterinsurgency: A Symposium, April 16–20, 1962* (Santa Monica, CA: RAND, 1963).

Thompson put it in *Defeating Communist Insurgency*, whatever complications there were in countering insurgency in different contexts, 'the enemy was exactly the same' – communism.[25] Momentum towards a comprehensive counterinsurgency strategy was now so developed that a progress report from all agencies concerned with counterinsurgency activities in the previous year reported in July 1962 that approximately 50,000 officer-grade personnel had received training in counterinsurgency techniques.

What can be seen through 1961 and into 1962, then, is the emergence of a new concept. A term that barely existed in 1960 had through 1961 become a new keyword so dominant that, by the end of 1962, some were suggesting it was now 'almost a fetish'.[26] And this new fetish fed into debates about pacification.

'The basic concepts of pacification emerged from the counterinsurgency doctrine of the late 1950s and early 1960s', writes Richard Hunt in *Pacification: The American Struggle for Vietnam's Hearts and Minds*.[27] But this gets it the wrong way round, both historically and conceptually. Rather, the basic concepts of counterinsurgency emerged from pacification doctrine stretching back centuries. This is one reason why the more sustained analyses of counterinsurgency often fall back on the idea of pacification. Consider, for example, Douglas Blaufarb's detailed analysis of what he calls the 'counterinsurgency era' between 1950 and the mid 1970s. Blaufarb claims that 'pacification' came to be the more formally recognized term for what the United States called 'counterinsurgency' from 1965 onwards, in conjunction with what was also by then being called 'the other war'. When Blaufarb shifts his focus to 'the revival of counterinsurgency' in Vietnam in the late 1960s, his chapter identifies pacification as the core issue, and the documents he discusses were all part of a plan to 'get pacification going', in the words of Ambassador Henry Cabot Lodge in 1965. We are therefore introduced to the 'CORDS phase of pacification', the 'Program for the

25 Robert Thompson, *Defeating Communist Insurgency: Experiences from Malaya and Vietnam* (London: Chatto & Windus, 1967), p. 20.

26 Hanson W. Baldwin, military editor of the *New York Times*, in a book review on 11 November 1962, cited in Bernard Fall, *The Two Viet-Nams: A Political and Military Analysis, Revised Edition* (New York: Praeger, 1964), p. 337.

27 Richard A. Hunt, *Pacification: The American Struggle for Vietnam's Hearts and Minds* (Boulder, CO: Westview, 1995), p. 2.

Pacification and Long-Term Development of Vietnam', the 'Accelerated Pacification Program', and many more similarly named programmes and phases. In effect, despite the stress that was being placed on the new idea of 'counterinsurgency', the prose of pacification remained central. This explains why the main concept in Blaufarb's analysis of the 'era of counterinsurgency' remains that of pacification. The ultimate question asked by Blaufarb about the counterinsurgency era is 'Did pacification succeed or fail?'[28]

In slipping back and forth between counterinsurgency and pacification, Blaufarb's book reflects the general tendency to try to separate the two terms, to insist that the more recent term is far more important, significant and modern – but then view counterinsurgency through the lens of pacification and pacification through the lens of counterinsurgency, to the point where the two concepts merge once more. This reflects the literature from the period, in which one document after another treats pacification and counterinsurgency as more or less synonymous. Phrases such as 'counterinsurgency, or pacification' appear just about everywhere – in ARPA reports, army documents and memos to the president.[29] As Gabriel Kolko suggests in his *Vietnam: Anatomy of War 1940–1975*, pacification and counterinsurgency became essentially interchangeable.[30] More recent scholarship is thus also full of phrases such as '"pacification", as counterinsurgency was called then'; 'pacification, which is now often called counterinsurgency'; 'French counterinsurgency (or "pacification")'.[31]

28 Douglas S. Blaufarb, *The Counterinsurgency Era: US Doctrine and Performance, 1950 to the Present* (New York: Free Press, 1977), pp. 206, 223, 243, 276.

29 This precise phrase is from R. W. Komer, *Bureaucracy Does Its Thing: Institutional Restraints on U.S.-GVN Performance in Vietnam*, DARPA Report, R-967-ARPA (Santa Monica, CA: RAND, 1972), pp. xi, 127, 129, 143, 147. For examples of other versions, see Robert McNamara, 'Memorandum to the President', 14 October 1966, in *Pentagon Papers*, 'IV.C.6.a: Evolution of the War: U.S. Ground Strategy and Force Deployments: 1965–1967'; Admiral Grant Sharp and General William C. Westmoreland, *Report on the War in Vietnam (As of 30 June 1968)* (Washington, DC: US Government Printing Office, 1969); Chester L. Cooper et al., *The American Experience with Pacification in Vietnam, Vol. II: Elements of Pacification* (Arlington, VA: Institute for Defense Analyses, 1972).

30 Gabriel Kolko, *Vietnam: Anatomy of War 1940–1975* (London: Unwin Hyman, 1986), p. 131.

31 Respectively: Antonia Chayes, *Borderless Wars: Civil Military Disorder and Legal Uncertainty* (Cambridge: Cambridge University Press, 2015), p. 27; Andrew J. Gawthorpe, *To Build as Well as Destroy: American Nation Building in South Vietnam*

It is often said that 'the average general that came to Vietnam did not have a good concept'.[32] What he did have was one very old concept, pacification, one very new concept, counterinsurgency, and a few others that oscillated between these two, such as 'counter-revolutionary warfare' and 'containment' (see Chapter 4). Unfortunately, no one seemed to know what the terms meant – or, if each thought they knew, they could not agree with one another. Thus, regardless of the fetish for 'counterinsurgency' (and various other terms), the concept of pacification could not be displaced. Discussion and debate about counterinsurgency made constant reference back to the older concept to describe what was taking place in Vietnam, or what they meant by counterinsurgency. 'We tried to find a name to describe what we were doing, but nothing seemed to work . . . We finally decided on calling it *pacification* – and the term, which had been used during the French war, stuck.'[33]

'What are we trying to do?' asked Roger Hilsman in June 1962 in a 'Progress Report on South Vietnam'. The answer: 'devise an integrated and systematic military-political-economic strategic counterinsurgency concept and plan'. But this 'search for a strategic concept', as Hilsman describes it in his memoirs, kept rediscovering pacification. 'We searched around for another name than "pacification"', CIA director William Colby noted about his own experience in Vietnam, adding that he and his colleagues 'finally gave up' on the grounds that 'we could find no other simple word'.[34] This explains why the fleshing out of the idea of 'counterinsurgency' with the concept of 'pacification' occurs in one official document and report after another, to the point where even those writing the reports were never entirely clear what differences there were

(Ithaca, NY: Cornell University Press, 2018), p. 189; Fredrik Logevall, 'Foreword to 2018 Edition', in Bernard B. Fall, *Street Without Joy: The French Debacle in Indochina* (Guilford, CT: Stackpole, 2018 [1961]).

32 Colonel David H. Hackworth, who did a tour of duty in Vietnam but who later denounced the whole war effort, in *About Face: The Odyssey of an American Warrior* (New York: Touchstone, 1989), p. 776.

33 Rufus Phillips, interview and cited by Zalin Grant, *Facing the Phoenix* (New York: W. W. Norton, 1991), p. 113. Emphasis in original.

34 Roger Hilsman, 'Progress Report on South Vietnam', Memo to Governor Harriman, 18 June 1962, in *The Pentagon Papers: The Defense Department History of United States Decision Making on Vietnam, Vol. II. Gravel edition* (Boston: Beacon Press, 1971), p. 673; Hilsman, *To Move a Nation*, p. 424; William Colby, *Honorable Men: My Life in the CIA* (New York: Simon & Schuster, 1978), p. 256.

between them, if any. In the summer of 1965, Ambassador Lodge informed a meeting of senior officers that, in his opinion, the US military needed to be ready to handle the VC in small units. 'This gives counter-subversion/terrorism or pacification or counterinsurgency – I am not overly concerned with what we call it – a new urgency.'[35]

The real problem amid this constant rediscovery of pacification is complicated yet further by the fact that the meaning of pacification itself was never entirely clear. Describing the Honolulu Conference held in February 1966 – a major gathering at which key figures from Vietnam and the United States discussed the ongoing war – the editors of the *Pentagon Papers* wrote that the proponents of pacification 'were often in such violent disagreement as to what pacification meant that they quarrelled publicly among themselves'.[36] Richard Holbrooke, a member of staff in the White House, and the person who collated the volume of the *Pentagon Papers* called *Re-emphasis on Pacification: 1965–1967*, apparently reported in February 1967 that a visitor to South Vietnam could visit ten provinces and 'get as many concepts and methods for pacification; not field expedients being tested but just different concepts about what the program is about'.[37] As the official history of the US Army's role in counterinsurgency notes, there was a distinct 'lack of clarity' when it came to the meaning of the term.[38]

On the one hand, then, an agreed understanding of pacification eluded the political, military and security elites who were meant to be carrying it out. Thus, throughout the 1960s and into the 1970s no lasting position on pacification could ever materialize. As most of the war's historians note, discussion about the very meaning of 'pacification' continued through the entire war.[39] Was pacification a theory or a

35 Lodge cited in *Pentagon Papers*, 'IV.C.8 Evolution of the War 8. Re-emphasis on Pacification: 1965–1967', p. 9.

36 Ibid., pp. i–ii.

37 Holbrooke memo to Komer, 27 February 1967, cited from Komer's files by Gawthorpe, *To Build as Well as Destroy*, p. 60.

38 Andrew J. Birtle, *US Army Counterinsurgency and Contingency Operations Doctrine 1942–1976* (Washington, DC: Center of Military History, United States Army, 2006), p. 389.

39 For example, Kolko, *Vietnam*, p. 131; Frances FitzGerald, *Fire in the Lake: The Vietnamese and the Americans in Vietnam* (New York: Vintage, 1973), p. 462; Geoffrey Fairbairn, *Revolutionary Guerrilla Warfare: The Countryside Version* (Harmondsworth: Penguin, 1974), p. 253; Marilyn B. Young, *The Vietnam Wars 1945–1990* (New York:

practice? A form of war or a mode of policing? A strategy or a tactic? A doctrine or a concept? On the other hand, when they could come close to any kind of agreed meaning, it generally involved claims such as the one offered by Robert Komer in 'What is Pacification?', one section of a report called *Giving a New Thrust to Pacification* (1966). The answer: '"pacification" can be used to encompass the whole of the military, political, and civil effort in Vietnam'.[40] The *whole* of the effort incorporating the *full range of state power*. Likewise, pacification is 'a broad array of civil, administrative, and constabulary functions designed to establish or maintain governmental authority'.[41] Or, moving beyond Vietnam, recall the 2006 US Army and Marine *Manual*, cited above, defining pacification as a function of integrated *civilian and military* teams working *across all levels of society*. Pacification thus either lacks meaning, or, better still, possesses a meaning that defines it as *the exercise of state power in its myriad forms.*

We will return to counterinsurgency throughout this book (see especially Chapter 3). For now, pacification can be understood as an ambiguous, if not downright chimeric concept. This chimeric nature of pacification is in fact integral to both its longevity and its scope. The state seemingly enjoys the lack of clarity over the meaning of the term. After all, if pacification is the exercise of state power in its myriad forms, then it can be anything the state desires.

What the state also seems to enjoy is the ability of pacification *to generate enemies that need pacifying*. This can be illustrated by reference to the idea of the insurgent. The insurgent is obviously central to the idea of counterinsurgency. But the problem is that, once counterinsurgency was invented, its thinkers quickly developed a tendency to see insurgency almost everywhere.[42] The leading texts in the counterinsurgency field tend to define insurgency as an attempt to overthrow the

---

HarperPerennial, 1991), p. 145; Bernd Greiner, *War Without Fronts: The USA in Vietnam*, transl. Anne Wyburd and Victoria Fern (London: Bodley Head, 2009 [2007]), p. 60.

40 *Pentagon Papers*, 'Part IV.C.8', p. 66.

41 Birtle, *US Army Counterinsurgency and Contingency Operations Doctrine*, p. 4.

42 M. L. R. Smith and David Martin Jones, *The Political Impossibility of Modern Counterinsurgency: Strategic Problems, Puzzles, and Paradoxes* (New York: Columbia University Press, 2015), pp. 2–3, 6; Christian Tripodi, *The Unknown Enemy: Counterinsurgency and the Illusion of Control* (Cambridge: Cambridge University Press, 2021), p. 113.

government – usually by force, often illegally – through political factions or groups. This locates 'insurgency' within a certain tradition of warfare which has gone by many of the names cited above, such as counter-revolutionary war, irregular war, low-intensity war, and so on. But it also locates insurgency within a broader mode of state operations to counter 'subversion', 'sedition', 'rebellion', 'revolution', and related notions – all equally ambiguous. Fundamental to this *countering* is the desire to *produce* a social order in which insurgency does not occur. The outcome is a permanent application of the powers of war and police that is all-encompassing and never-ending. Yet the need to apply the powers of war and police to create social order and counter insurgency was, for a long time, precisely central to the prose of pacification.

In contrast to the relatively recent birth of counterinsurgency as an idea, 'insurgency' and related terms, such as 'insurgence' and 'insurgent', have much older roots, deriving from the word 'insurge'. 'Insurge' is traceable to the birth of modernity. Its root is in the Latin *insurgentem*, the present participle of *insurgere*, meaning 'to rise up, rise against, stand high and gather force'. In the sixteenth century, 'insurge' was understood to mean a 'rising' or 'upheaval', and was used as a verb to connote 'stirring up' or 'raising in tumult, hostility, or insurrection'. The noun 'insurgent' – connoting a person who 'rises in revolt against constituted authority', 'a rebel who is not recognized as a belligerent' – began to appear a little later, in the mid 1700s. The insurgent is thus one of modernity's key figures; the invention of counterinsurgency in the 1960s merely reinforces this fact. In other words, countering insurgency has a history much longer than that of counterinsurgency – a history that is central to pacification.

The insurgent is a figure against which wars must be fought (see Chapter 1), and against which police power must be ranged (Chapter 3). Without the insurgent, much of the fear that permeates our order and undergirds the security apparatus would be undermined (Chapter 2). Without the insurgent, the logic of containment makes no sense (Chapter 4). The insurgent is a figure of disorder among order, a chaotic threat to the system from within the system, an unruly rebel against sovereignty, a seditious threat to authority, and thus a challenge to capital and the state. What this also means is that insurgency must be continually reinvented so that it can be countered. The ambiguity of all of the terms used to describe the insurgent – 'rising up', 'gathering force', 'tumult', 'stirring', 'hostile', 'sedition' – is thus a gift to the state, as it deprives the insurgent of any definition other than that imposed on it by the state. What this means, in turn, is that 'anyone can be on the side of the insurgents.'[43]

This takes us to the heart of one of pacification's most fundamental distinctions, which turns out to be yet another liberal myth. On the one hand, those seeking to pacify never cease to insist that pacification involves a fundamental distinction between the People and the insurgents, the population and the enemy, good subjects and suspect communities. This provides the grounds for one of pacification's central principles: 'the permanent isolation of the insurgent from the population.'[44] Once the insurgent is isolated from the population, the population can be won over. Once the population is won over, an area is more easily *cleared* of insurgents, *held* in security, and a new order *built*. This generates a doctrine of 'Clear–Hold–Build', about which I shall say more in Chapter 3.

On the other hand, integral to the prose of pacification is the idea that insurgents live among the population. Despite their vehement anti-communism, pacification experts love to cite Mao's essay *On Guerrilla Warfare*, in which he famously claims that the guerrilla or insurgent operates like a fish in the water of the people.[45] The problem with this is obvious: the whole body of the water itself, not just the fish, becomes the object of pacification. In other words, targeting the Insurgent means targeting the People. In exactly the same way, targeting the various other identities and practices said to threaten the social order means targeting the People. The Parties of Order and Security never stop telling us that they seek to save society from the enemies of society. Enemies without, of course, but also enemies within, as every demand for even the simplest of reforms, couched in the most mundane democratic language, is treated as a threat to social order, an attack on society, and thus an

43 Massimiliano Tomba, *Insurgent Universality: An Alternative Legacy of Modernity* (Oxford: Oxford University Press, 2019), p. 19.

44 David Galula, *Counterinsurgency Warfare: Theory and Practice* (Westport, CT: Praeger, 2006 [1964]), p. 54.

45 In 1989, the US Marine Corps published Mao's text as 'FMFRP 12-18', in a new translation by a US brigadier. The Marine Corps claimed, rather sheepishly, that the text was 'not intended to become doctrine', but as of spring 2023 the text was still available on the Marines' website.

incipient insurgency, or even all-out rebellion, against the nation and state. War will always be declared against such movements – war that becomes coterminous with the wars declared against criminals and terrorists, radicals and revolutionaries, vagrants and travellers, beggars and itinerants, single mothers and absent fathers. The outcome is that the whole social terrain becomes a zone of war overseen by the police power.

What emerges is a position articulated by Galula in the 'Company Instructions' issued to his men in Algeria in October 1957, and reproduced in *Pacification in Algeria*:

> 1. EXTERIORLY. EVERY VILLAGER IS A FRIEND . . .
> 2. INWARDLY. EVERY VILLAGER IS A SUSPECT.[46]

Friend, but suspect – which is to say, a friend one cannot fully trust, and thus not really a friend at all, but in fact someone who might be the enemy, and should therefore be suspected of being so. This is the very position articulated in police discourse, and could in fact be a definition of community policing (see Chapter 3).[47] As Benedict Spinoza astutely observed in his *Tractatus Politicus* (1675–76), the sovereign power constantly conspires against its people because it suspects that they are constantly conspiring against it.[48]

In the prose of pacification, the People are both friend and enemy. Any member of the People can be an insurgent, and thus all are potential insurgents, and so the insurgency is always already within the People, regardless of efforts to separate one from the other. Insurgency is endemic, which means that it is less the insurgents that must be countered than the People itself. The birth of counterinsurgency out of pacification goes some way to capturing this, highlighting pacification as a counterpower, and reveals that the power being countered is the power

46 David Galula, 'Company Instructions, October 1957', reprinted as Appendix A in Cohen, *Galula*, pp. 282–3. Also cited, in a slightly different formulation, in Galula, *Pacification in Algeria*, p. 72.

47 Markus Kienscherf, *US Domestic and International Regimes of Security: Pacifying the Globe, Securing the Homeland* (Abingdon: Routledge, 2013), p. 114.

48 Benedict De Spinoza, *Tractatus Politicus*, transl. R. H. M. Elwes, in A. G. A. Balz (ed.), *Writings on Political Philosophy by Benedict Spinoza* (New York: D. Appleton-Century, 1937), p. 100.

of the People; the war against insurgency is a war against the People.[49] Much as the political project of bourgeois modernity and the liberal state treats the People as the source of power and the democratic grounds of the state, so it also regards the People as the fundamental problem. As we shall see in the chapters that follow, it is the People that must be prevented from questioning power; it is the People that is expected to live in fear despite the state's insistence that it provides security; it is the People that must be constituted anew in an orderly fashion; it is the People that must be contained; and it is the People that must be forced to live up to its neck in debt. Above all, as we shall see, it is the People that ends up lying in the shit.

Grappling with pacification means, first and foremost, understanding the extent to which the dream of police power is a dream of obedient subjects, their acceptance of sovereign power, their submission to the logic of security and law and order, their mobilization for work, and their subjugation to the money form – subjects, in other words, who are economically active and politically docile. Any challenge to the order of property ownership and state power, the structures of class, gender, and racial domination, are always already forms of insurgency, but the logic of pacification is not simply to counter insurgency, but to prevent insurgency from arising in the first place by fabricating social order – producing 'order out of chaos', as pacification expert Frank Kitson puts it – and constituting obedient subjects.[50] That said, insurgency will always be found, if only because it suits the state to find it, because nothing suits the state better than fighting one social war after another under its watchwords of property, law and order, and security.

This renders bourgeois modernity a condition of war without end. First, there is the class war. This is a form of war distinct from the kind of war that the bourgeoisie wants us to regard as war, between sovereign states. It is the social war. Second, this warfare spirals out into a series of social wars against the proletariat's social cousins, subaltern groups and suspect communities. These are wars taking place within and through civil society, the myriad 'wars on *x*' (crime, drugs, poverty, and much else that I will discuss). This very idea of 'social war' jars with us because

49 Jeff Halper, *War Against the People: Israel, the Palestinians and Global Pacification* (London: Pluto, 2015).

50 Frank Kitson, *Warfare as a Whole* (London: Faber, 1987), p. 59.

it undermines the idea that has been drummed into us over centuries, that civil society is a realm of 'peace and security' provided for us by state and capital. Yet this peace is a series of wars layered one on top of the other, intersecting with the class war to the point where it often becomes impossible to tell them apart.

Such wars require the *policing of civil society* by a range of institutions of both civil society and the state, and not simply by the professional police. Policing and pacification have an elective affinity, and the latter term captures the expanded nature and function of the police power, which will be developed here through the idea of a social police, coterminous with social war. The 'keeping the peace' that we are told is the raison d'être of the police power turns out to be the peace of perpetual social war. This is the peace of pacification.

1

From *Stasis* to Sovereignty to Social War

No mysterious 'invisible hand' is guiding society; it is 'regulated' by the relentless permanent social war.

Paul Mattick, 'How New is the "New Order" of Fascism?' (1941)

There is a text from ancient Greece that goes by the title *The Athenian Constitution*. After tracing the development of Athenian constitutions, the ordinances of Draco, and the ensuing strife between the classes, the author, generally thought to be Aristotle, pauses over the constitutional reforms enacted by Solon. The Athenians had long been troubled by the fact that democracy had been overcome by oligarchy at various points, not least in the rule of the oligarchs in 404–403 BCE, but also by the seemingly chronic crisis produced by the conflict between rich and poor. As a result, they turned to the revered figure of Solon, whose constitutional reforms in effect became the first ever 'democratic' constitution. Athenians thereafter often referred to their laws as 'Solonian'. At one point in the text, after describing how Solon dealt with different classes and distributed the magistracies, the following comment appears:

> Solon realised that the city was often split by factional disputes [*pollakis stasiazousan*] but some citizens were content because of idleness to accept whatever the outcome might be; he therefore produced a specific law against them, laying down that anyone who did not

choose one side or the other in such a dispute should lose his citizen rights.[1]

Some translations of this last sentence suggest that whoever did not take a stand in such factional disputes was to be expelled from the *polis* as an outlaw (*atimia*). The severity of the punishment draws our attention to the perceived wrong: a failure to choose sides in a conflict. It would seem to be a constitutional requirement that a citizen *take a stand* in factional disputes. Trying to stand apart or aside from the 'wars' within the *polis* – the term 'wars' here is not unproblematic, as we shall see – is antithetical to political life. The definition of the citizen, according to this part of Solon's law, lies in participating in the very στάσις (*stasis*) through which so much of the political activity of the *polis* is animated. Engaging in *stasis*, in other words making a judgment, assuming a position, or taking a stand, is both a requirement and a prerogative of a citizen.

Solon's law has been described as surprising, even shocking, to modern minds.[2] Writers stretching back to Cicero have questioned it, as we shall see. After all, the attempt to establish a democratic constitution based on Solonic (and hence ideologically 'ancestral') laws was intended to unify the *polis* and achieve reconciliation in the aftermath of oligarchical violence. And yet this measure concerning *stasis* would appear to encourage factions in a way that is fundamentally divisive. It appears to jar with the widely held view that the Greeks were so concerned with stability and order that they saw conflict as a fundamental evil. If order and stability were so important, why was *stasis* so integral to their understanding of politics? Why was one a citizen not solely through simple participation in politics, but through participation in the fundamental conflicts (*staseis*) through which the *polis* was constituted?

This book by no means intends to answer those questions, which have been addressed at length in several important studies. Rather, I want to ask a different question that might help us think about pacification: What happened to *stasis* as an idea in modern thought? Textbooks

1 Aristotle, 'The Constitution of Athens', transl. J. M. Moore, in Aristotle, *The Politics and the Constitution of Athens*, ed. Stephen Everson (Cambridge: Cambridge University Press, 1996), p. 216.

2 Nicole Loraux, *The Divided City: On Memory and Forgetting in Ancient Athens*, transl. Corinne Pache and Jeff Fort (New York: Zone, 2006 [1997]), p. 102.

inform us time and again that we find many of our modern political ideas in the so-called Greek invention of politics. The *polis* as 'city-state', and thus the grounds of our conception of state; the *demos* (people) and *kratos* (power) as the basis of 'democracy'; the idea of a tension between money and justice – all come to us from the Greeks. But what about *stasis*? If *polis*, if *demos* and if *kratos*, then why not *stasis*? What happened in the modern world to the Greek idea that waging *stasis* is accepted and expected? After all, *stasis* is such a rich term that several contemporary writers have sought to utilize it in various studies, including Costas Constantinou in *States of Political Discourse* (2004), Costas Douzinas in *Philosophy and Resistance in the Crisis* (2013), Giorgio Agamben on the idea of civil war (*Stasis*, 2015), Dimitris Vardoulakis on agonistic democracy (*Stasis before the State*, 2018), and Tatjana Gajić on Spanish political culture under Franco (*Paradoxes of Stasis*, 2019). An analysis of *stasis* will, I hope, prove useful in helping us unravel the original secret of pacification, which, I will suggest, lies in a certain kind of ideological erasure of *stasis* with the rise of liberal modernity and its theory of the state.

Insurgent citizens: *stasis* becomes us

Stasis is 'one of the most remarkable words to be found in any language', observes M. I. Finley. Its root sense is 'placing', 'setting', 'stature', or 'station', but its range of political meanings, and hence its political importance, stems from the range of other definitions. Liddell and Scott's *Greek–English Lexicon* offers for *stasis* the idea of standing still, or the posture of standing, or the state of arrest, close to one modern meaning of the English word 'stasis'. But the term also connotes partisanship in the form of 'taking a stand', rooted in the idea of making a judgment, which connects *stasis* to *krisis* and, therefore also connotes the very opposite of 'standing still'.[3]

The most conventional English translation of the word when it appears in major political texts such as Plato's *Republic* and Aristotle's

3 M. I. Finley, *Democracy Ancient and Modern, Revised Edition* (New Brunswick, NJ: Rutgers University Press, 1985), p. 44; Henry George Liddell and Robert Scott, *A Greek–English Lexicon* (Oxford: Oxford University Press, 1925), p. 1633.

Politics is 'faction'. Yet, as useful as 'faction' might sometimes be, it barely scratches the surface of a complex term, the connotations of which range from disagreement through to sedition, and then outright war. In his history of Greek philosophy, W. K. C. Guthrie observes that the background to *stasis* is a war which appears at first to be an inter-state battle, but which it quickly becomes clear is a conflict between cities unified by their 'Greekness'.[4] The conflict is therefore a war between factions inherent to the Greek world, and hence close to what some have called 'civil war'. In some texts, such as Plato's *Republic*, *stasis* is contrasted with *polemos* (war), or perhaps, to put it in stronger terms, Plato refuses to give the name *polemos* to what is clearly *stasis*. Plato reports Socrates as saying that when Greeks fight foreigners (barbarians), it is because they are natural enemies, and hence it is called war. 'But when Greek fights Greek we shall say that they are naturally friends, but that Greece is sick and torn by faction, hostilities between one's own people, and that the quarrel should be called "civil strife" [*stasis*].'[5] In contrast to *polemos*, *stasis* occurs within a political space shared by citizens as friends, hence the resistance to calling such civil strife 'war'. This is why *stasis* is sometimes understood as 'party', 'sedition', 'civic discord', 'division', 'dissent'. It is also why the opposite of *stasis* is *homonoia* (concord), whereas the opposite of *polemos* (war) is *eirene* (peace).

Stasis thus has a meaning that was well understood by the ancient Greeks, but which translations such as 'faction' do not quite capture, since this word does not grasp the 'civil war'-like character of what was at stake. Since war was *polemos*, a better translation of *stasis* might be 'revolution'. Yet 'civil war' and 'revolution' both have complicated meanings, the modern iterations of which I will turn to below. Either way, *stasis* is regarded as one of the most significant features of the *polis*. This is why Aristotle collected vast quantities of data about the workings of *stasis* within Greek states, and why, in Books 3 to 6 of *The Politics*, he outlines a taxonomy of its various origins, forms and degrees of intensity.

4 W. K. C. Guthrie, *A History of Greek Philosophy, Vol. III: The Fifth-Century Enlightenment* (Cambridge: Cambridge University Press, 1969), pp. 84–5.

5 Plato, *The Republic*, transl. Desmond Lee (Harmondsworth: Penguin, 2003), p. 187.

At the beginning of *The Laws*, Plato has the book's protagonists ask whether legislators should rule with a view to war or peace? They realize, however, that there is a distinction even more fundamental than the one between war and peace – namely that between *polemos* and *stasis*. Plato suggests that *stasis* is 'the last thing a man would want to see in his country', and therefore that legislators will pay far more attention to *stasis* than *polemos*.[6] In similar fashion, Herodotus in his *Histories* writes that *stasis* is in many ways worse than war, and Thucydides in his *History of the Peloponnesian War* treats *stasis* as the origin of all sorts of wickedness.[7] All told, although *polemos* and *stasis* are both crucial to ancient Greek political thought, *stasis* was generally regarded as somehow more of a problem for the *polis*, because it appeared to be both essential, and yet seditious and disruptive to the point of revolution.[8] This would appear to be borne out by Thucydides, who opens his *History* discussing the difficulty the Greek peoples had settling anywhere, partly due to attacks from land and sea, but also because when they did settle they had to deal with various *staseis* which eventually undermined them.[9] It is also borne out by the encyclopaedic inventory of 1,500 ancient polities across the Mediterranean world, produced by the Copenhagen Polis Centre, which contains a chapter on '*stasis* as an essential aspect of the polis' and the nature of '*stasis* as an everyday phenomenon'.[10] That *stasis* was a form of conflict distinct from *polemos* and endemic to the *polis* perhaps explains the Greek focus on the question of how it might be managed, and the fact that it had to be managed – because it could never be eradicated. The *polis* is always already in *stasis*. Finley suggests that the dividing line between politics and *stasis* was a thin one. But we might

6 Plato, *The Laws*, transl. Trevor J. Saunders (Harmondsworth: Penguin, 1975), p. 50.

7 Herodotus, *The Histories*, transl. Robin Waterfield (Oxford: Oxford University Press, 2008), VIII.3, p. 489; Thucydides, *The Peloponnesian War*, transl. Thomas Hobbes (Chicago: University of Chicago Press, 1959), p. 206.

8 M. I. Finley, 'Athenian Demagogues', *Past & Present* 21 (1962); Peter T. Manicas, 'War, Stasis, and Greek Political Thought', *Comparative Studies in Society and History* 24: 4 (1982)

9 Thucydides, *Peloponnesian War*, p. 2.

10 Mogens Herman Hansen and Thomas Heine Nielsen, *An Inventory of Archaic and Classical Poleis: An Investigation Conducted by the Copenhagen Polis Centre for the Danish National Research Foundation* (Oxford: Oxford University Press, 2004), pp. 124, 126, 1361–2.

make more sense of it if we register, instead, an alternative argument, made by Nicole Loraux in her extensive work on the ancient Greek political imaginary: that we should imagine *stasis* within the *polis* as a 'war' of sorts, but one without great deeds or trophies, a 'war' with no peace declarations at the end *because there is no end*. As Loraux puts it, because '*stasis* sleeps within the *polis*', the existence of 'warring' factions becomes the grounds of possibility for the state itself.[11] The polity is nothing less than a continuous conflict, revolt and counter-revolt, in which we should all be participating. *Stasis* becomes us.

But if this is the case, then written into the very foundation of the *polis* appear to be two important features that will come to play a role in the much more modern politics of pacification. First, there is a rather interesting figure, one not named by the Greeks but which it is impossible for our modern political minds not to imagine. As Loraux puts it: if the obligation and willingness to take sides, form factions, and even take up arms in social conflict is one criterion of citizenship, then *stasis* and its requirements appear to us now, in our world of 'peace and security' and 'law and order', as nothing short of scandalous. Why? Because it appears that there is nothing to distinguish the figure of the citizen from that of the insurgent. 'It is precisely insofar as one is a citizen that *one has the obligation to be an insurgent*', writes Loraux.[12] *Stasis* thus becomes us as citizens; but then, as citizens, it renders us insurgents. Insurgency becomes us.

Herein lies one of the dialectical oppositions within the concept of *stasis*. As standing, taking a position, and holding the position, *stasis* provides the 'sta' in the English word stability, with which the modern English notion of 'stasis' as 'static' is aligned. But as stance, and hence resistance, *stasis* is also the very opposite of stability, since it connotes the other meaning of 'static' as interference or, to put it more politically, insurgency and all the other things that this entails, from sedition to revolt, and from insurrection to civil war.

The second important feature concerns the idea of peace. In *The Laws*, Plato has Cleinias observe that law 'established every one of our

---

11 Loraux, *Divided City*, pp. 25, 40, 64–5, 108; Nicole Loraux, *The Invention of Athens: The Funeral Oration in the Classical City*, transl. Alan Sheridan (New York: Zone, 2006 [1981]); M. I. Finley, *The Ancient Greeks* (Harmondsworth: Penguin, 1966), p. 60.

12 Loraux, *Divided City*, p. 103. Emphasis added.

institutions, both in the public sphere and the private, with an eye on war'. But the 'war' in question is named by Cleinias's interlocutor, the 'Athenian', as *stasis*, most often translated as 'civil war'.[13] *Stasis* thus points to a radical uncertainty and instability in the *polis*, deriving from the fact that the law is always already liable to be challenged. It therefore also points to the figure that might make such a challenge: not the barbarian at the gate engaged in *polemos*, but the insurgent engaged in *stasis*, who appears now to be so structured into the *polis* that there is no possibility of the figure's actions ever ending. There seems to be no end to insurgency, no way out of civil war. This is one reason why there can be no *eirene* (peace) from such a 'war'. There can be no peace even when the rulers have declared one, and this is something that the rulers themselves know all too well. 'The legislator's position would be that what most men call "peace" is really only a fiction', says Cleinias.[14] But it is an important fiction, around which the story of pacification unfolds, along with the figure of the insurgent. To get to that story, we need first to make four further observations about *stasis*, concerning property, *psyche*, disease, and mobility.

It is clear from the Greek sources that one of the main causes of *stasis* is the division between wealth and poverty. For example, when Thucydides discusses the factions in Corcyra during the war between Athens and Sparta, on the one side are those favouring 'the political equality of the multitude'. For Plato in the *Republic*, the *polis* always contains at least two states, the rich and the poor, at enmity with each other over profit and property, generating a desire for revolution on the part of some and a desire for more power, land or resources on the part of others.[15] This argument is pursued at length by Aristotle. Aristotle's typology of constitutions in the *Politics* appears initially to be based on a type of rule (by one, by a few, or by the many), but it transpires that those types are based in turn on distinctions of property and wealth. 'What really differentiates oligarchy and democracy is wealth or the lack of it.' This means that, for Aristotle, the prime division within the *polis* is between rich and poor. Hence, although he identifies a range of causes of *stasis*, he returns time and again to the idea that 'inequality is

13 Plato, *Laws*, pp. 47–50.

14 Ibid., p. 47.

15 Plato, *Republic*, pp. 61, 122–4, 280.

everywhere at the bottom of *stasis*'. This, in turn, gives rise to the idea that the conflict underlying *stasis* is not simply injustice, but a sense of injustice that emerges from the use of political power to enforce domination and exploitation of one economic group over another. Even when 'faction' arises from 'small' or 'personal' issues, it usually points to what Aristotle calls 'large issues', such as struggles against poverty or the fight for justice and equality.[16] 'Those who are bent on equality resort to faction [*stasis*]', Aristotle claims, later adding that 'it is always the weaker who go in search of justice and equality'. Conversely, 'those who are superior in virtue hardly ever start a faction [*stasis*]'. Once they mobilize and act in the name of justice, the lower 'class' of citizens become a 'warring' faction, a 'hostile element in the state', and look as though they could be behind some kind of revolutionary change.[17]

This is the real basis of the idea of the *demos* as 'the poor' or 'the mob', rather than the more neutral 'the many' or 'the people', even in democratic regimes. Tensions and revolts arising from the subjection of the poor, from degrees of poverty and wealth, and from the question of what, if anything, might be done about this, undergird most discussions of *stasis*. Or, to put it in the terms laid out some time ago by G. E. M. de Ste. Croix, and reiterated by many others from very different political persuasions, when we read about *stasis*, 'we can be reasonably safe in concluding that the conflict was basically between social classes, even if our information about it is not explicit'.[18] The Greek *polis* is thus not

16 Aristotle, *The Politics*, transl. T. A. Sinclair (Harmondsworth: Penguin, 1992), pp. 123, 125–6, 191, 249, 298, 306.

17 Aristotle, *Politics*, pp. 203, 296, 300, 309, 367. See Jill Frank, 'Wages of War: On Judgment in Plato's Republic', *Political Theory* 35: 4 (2007); Andrew Lintott, *Aristotle's Political Philosophy in Its Historical Context: A New Translation and Commentary on Politics Books 5 and 6* (Abingdon: Routledge, 2018), pp. 11–18; Ronald Weed, *Aristotle on Stasis: A Moral Psychology of Political Conflict* (Berlin: Logos Verlag, 2007); Steven Skultety, *Conflict in Aristotle's Political Philosophy* (New York: State University Press of New York, 2019).

18 G. E. M. de Ste. Croix, *The Class Struggle in the Ancient Greek World* (London: Duckworth, 1981), p. 49. See also R. G. Mulgan, *Aristotle's Political Theory* (Oxford: Clarendon, 1977), p. 64; Ellen Meiksins Wood and Neal Wood, *Class Ideology and Ancient Political Theory: Socrates, Plato, and Aristotle in Social Context* (Oxford: Basil Blackwell, 1978); M. I. Finley, *Politics in the Ancient World* (Cambridge: Cambridge University Press, 1983), p. 2; Josiah Ober, *Political Dissent in Democratic Athens: Intellectual Critics of Popular Rule* (Princeton, NJ: Princeton University Press, 1998), p. 307.

simply an arena of conflicting interests, but one of *conflicting classes*, and, if we are to take seriously the idea of the Greek invention of politics, then we need to recognize it as, in some way, the invention of an image of a *polis* torn apart by a fundamental struggle over material resources and the means of subsistence. Insurgency is beginning to take on a social form.

One reason why some people seek a civil war over wealth and poverty is because *stasis* is a feature of *psyche* as well as *polis*. A person can have a '*stasis* within' which sets them 'at variance within themselves' and renders them incapable of action, Plato comments in *The Republic*.[19] When Aristotle lists the three sources of *stasis*, first on the list is a person's 'psychological inclination' or 'state of mind'.[20] A *stasis* within drives them to engage in *stasis* without. For Thucydides, *stasis* is caused by those driven 'without regard of justice or the public good', but rather 'by their own appetite'. Such factions as are 'governed with pride rather than modesty', and hence driven by the 'unruliness of their anger' (this is Hobbes's translation of Thucydides, about which I will shortly have much more to say), or 'violent passions', as some translations offer.[21] The term *ekstasis* captures a little of what is at stake. As Erwin Rohde explains in his account of the Greek concept of *psyche*, an *ekstasis* of the soul involved 'orgiastic conditions of excitement', a form of 'madness' that touched on the sacred, in that it was understood as the soul leaving the body. This is why the Greeks described such people as 'possessed', no longer 'at home' but 'abroad', or as 'having left their body'. Yet *ekstasis* also shades into what we now call ecstasy, and related terms such as 'mania', 'excess', 'frenzy' and 'derangement'.[22] Each of these terms also has political implications: the ecstatic person is less in control of themselves,

---

19 Plato, *Republic*, pp. 36, 153, 289.

20 Aristotle, *The Politics*, p. 300. This translation refers to 'conditions', which does not really capture the meaning Aristotle has here of 'state of mind' – see the translation by Benjamin Jowett and revised by Jonathan Barnes in *The Complete Works of Aristotle, Vol. 2*, ed. Jonathan Barnes (Princeton, NJ: Princeton University Press, 1984), p. 2067.

21 Thucydides, *Peloponnesian War*, pp. 204–6. For the alternative, see Thucydides, *The War of the Peloponnesians and the Athenians*, transl. Jeremy Mynott (Cambridge: Cambridge University Press, 2013), p. 215.

22 Erwin Rohde, *Psyche: The Cult of Souls and Belief in Immortality among the Greeks* (London: Routledge, 1925), pp. 259–60, 285–6; Michael A. Rinella, *Pharmakon: Plato, Drug Culture, and Identity in Ancient Athens* (Lanham, MD: Lexington, 2010), p. 36.

and therefore more susceptible to poor political judgement, leading to a 'frenzy of the masses', as Plato dubs it. In the individual, the struggle between the desires and between desire and reason is 'like a struggle between political factions', a form of 'civil war' between the elements of the soul.[23] In *ekstasis*, then, we find a 'revolting' character prone to externalize their character onto forms of political insurgency, culminating in a kind of collective madness.

These dimensions of *stasis* are connected to a third aspect of its meaning: disease. The image of the body politic creates a strong association between physiological disease and political disorder, to the extent that *nosos* (disease) became one of the most prevalent traits of *stasis*.[24] In *Imagining the State* (2003), *The Monstrous and the Dead* (2005) and *The Politics of Immunity* (2022), I have discussed at length the ways in which our image of the body politic has its roots in ancient Greek thought, and how that image shifts with changing ideas about order, movement, mechanism, system and technology. In Greek thought, there is little in the way of anatomical detail when the image of the body politic is invoked. Rather, any sickness or disease within the *polis* is normally labelled *stasis*.[25] The *nosos* of *stasis* is not a particular disease so much as a lack of balance, or instability in the body. This is connected to the meaning of *stasis* as 'standing', in the sense of the body standing still. This explains why, when 'stasis' enters the English language in the eighteenth century, it does so in medical dictionaries, and refers to the stagnation of the humours and problems with the circulation of the blood. For the Greeks, *stasis* captured the idea of a disequilibrium between the elements, but also stoppages in the body's normal circulations and movements. Plato in the *Timaeus*, for example, describes the body as composed of four elements – earth, fire, air, and water – and treats disorders and diseases as an excess or deficiency in any one of them. For Plato, this means that the lack of balance between these four elements causes both *stasis* and *nosos*. A problem such as bile will be expelled from the body 'like an exile in a civil war', as some translations have it, while the person who takes care of their body by moderating food and

23 Plato, *Republic*, pp. 148, 151, 153, 219.

24 Kostas Kalimtzis, *Aristotle on Political Enmity and Disease: An Inquiry into Stasis* (Albany, NY: State University of New York Press, 2000), pp. 15–22, 99.

25 Roger Brock, *Greek Political Imagery from Homer to Aristotle* (London: Bloomsbury, 2013), p. 69.

drink and exercising well 'will not leave foe ranged by foe to produce conflict and disease in the body, but friend by friend to produce health'.[26]

This idea of the arrest of the body, or the standing still of the body's movements, draws attention to the fourth observation to make about *stasis*, pertaining to movement. On the one hand, *stasis* is a kind of *immobility*. As immobility, *stasis* forms the root of many words that enter European languages, and which permeate the whole of the Western tradition, including *standing*, *stability*, *static*, *status*. The 'sta' of *stasis* is the root of the *stability* that will come to be said to be offered by the *state*. In discussions of the emergence of 'state' as a political concept, etymologists, philologists and historians of political thought all make a great deal of the word's Latin roots: 'state', *lo stato*, *l'état*, *der Staat*, and *el estado* can all be traced back to the Latin *status*. But the Latin *status* and *statio* have their own roots in the Greek *stasis*. The development of this cluster of meanings gives rise to the notion of the state as the body that *stabilizes* the people, grants them a *status*, and gives them *standing* as a political community. On the other hand, *stasis* as seditious faction, unrest, upheaval, insurgency, revolution, and even 'civil war' generates a further semantic cluster that appears to contradict the first by connoting movement and mobility, and hence instability, a *kinesis* that by definition appears to undermine the supposed stability of the *polis*.[27] Thus we seem to have a political concept which connotes a kind of motionless agitation, movement at rest, or flow of immobility. I will take up this question of movement in more detail in Chapter 4. Here, we can note that *stasis* captures and reveals a complex vision of the *polis* as a duality within unity: immobility and mobility, stability and instability, quiescence and unrest – all are part of the dialectical unity of order and insurgency.

Stasis is thus a peculiar concept indeed. Moshe Berent suggests that we think of *stasis* as peculiar to Greek society itself, due to the unique character of the Greek *polis* as a stateless community rather than a 'state', as we now understand that term. The application of violence in the Greek *polis* was not monopolized by any single agency; the ability to use

26 Plato, *Timaeus*, in *Timaeus and Critias*, transl. Desmond Lee (Harmondsworth: Penguin, 1977), pp. 112, 116, 120.

27 Carl Schmitt, *Political Theology II: The Myth of the Closure of Any Political Theology*, transl. Michael Hoelzl and Graham Ward (Cambridge: Polity, 2008 [1970]), p. 123; Dimitris Vardoulakis, *Stasis Before the State: Nine Theses on Agonistic Democracy* (New York: Fordham University Press, 2018), pp. 95–7.

force was distributed among an armed population. No separate armed force existed that could *police* the factions. But, by the same token, there was no armed force that could itself conduct internal war against parts of the social body.[28] To put it another way, since the Greek *polis* was not a state in the modern meaning of the term, and since there was no 'civil society' that the state was expected to police, the *polis* had no police power (nor standing army or bureaucracy), and no concept of a 'social' world that needed policing. Hence, it also had no concept of 'social war', in which the police would fight on one side.

Berent thus suggests that what kept the *polis* peaceful in the absence of a force imposing 'law and order' was, on the one hand, a vivid memory of the outcome of the last *stasis*, and, on the other hand, new constitutional arrangements that had emerged. This explanation makes some sense. And yet, as Loraux points out, it is somewhat of a historian's explanation, locating the problem deep within a particular period in Greco-European history.[29] In other words, the implication of it as an explanation is that *stasis* existed in ancient Greece but could be overcome once the modern state was invented, because then so too is 'police' as a specialist apparatus of security, an ideology of peace and law-and-order, and a more refined constitutional arrangement to manage these things. To put that another way: rebellion, insurgency, disorder, and ultimately anything that smacks of an 'internal' war, are precisely what the invention of the modern state is supposed to avert, managing the demands of different groups while appearing to favour no one group in particular, and keeping the labouring classes in 'a state of peace'.

Yet maybe this difference is not so fundamental. Consider, for example, some of the measures suggested to deal with this phenomenon. Aristotle proposes waging war against barbarians as a means of establishing a stable constitution, given that a fear of enemies 'encourages people to keep a firm hold on their own constitution'. Hence, those who have constitutional stability at heart should 'invent terrors so that all citizens may be on their guard'.[30] This political technique has a long history thereafter, as we well know. A further measure was to recast

28 Moshe Berent, '*Stasis*, or the Greek Invention of Politics', *History of Political Thought* 19: 3 (1998), p. 333.

29 Loraux, *Divided City*, p. 105. See also Gustave Glotz, *The Greek City and Its Institutions* (London: Kegan Paul, 1929), pp. 104, 113, 130–1.

30 Aristotle, *Politics*, p. 325.

political upheavals as forms of *polemos* by imagining them as having been fought against an 'external' enemy rather than fellow citizens, to enable the *polis* to be 'reconciled', as Plato puts it in a funeral oration.[31] This fundamental forgetting could then serve to reunite the *polis* through monuments, rituals such as amnesty, and civic practices such as the funeral oration.[32] As well as waging war against barbarians, inventing terrors to keep the population in fear, and recasting earlier *stasis* as though it were a war against foreigners, Aristotle also recommends further techniques for managing *stasis*, including governing through law; eliminating corruption; educating citizens in the spirit of their constitution; the growth of a 'middle' and therefore 'moderate' class who have a different temperament than those other classes who are more susceptible to faction; grounding the *polis* in friendship; and concessions to the poor.[33] Commentators have noted that the word Aristotle uses for many of the devices used to facilitate the like-mindedness required for stability is *sugkeimenois*. This is usually translated as 'trickery' or 'concoction'. Picking up on this, Kostas Kalimtzis observes that Aristotle's proposals amount to a series of 'restraining devices' that 'never allow for pathways to autonomous choices'. He adds: 'these devices are what today would fall under the rubric of pacification.'[34] But this is a large leap, which for us requires a few more steps to match – not least by establishing how such a 'rubric of pacification' came about.

Seditious blockheads and the giddy people; or, did somebody say 'civil war'?

The idea of an impersonal structure of power called the state, within which sovereignty is concentrated and through which civil society is policed, is now engrained in our way of thinking about politics. This

31 Plato, *Menexenus*, in *The Dialogues of Plato, Vol. II*, transl. Benjamin Jowett (Oxford: Oxford University Press, 1871), pp. 526–7.

32 Loraux, *Divided City*, pp. 42, 65; Andrew Wolpert, *Remembering Defeat: Civil War and Civic Memory in Ancient Athens* (Baltimore: Johns Hopkins University Press, 2002), pp. 75–9; Julia L. Shear, *Polis and Revolution: Responding to Oligarchy in Classical Athens* (Cambridge: Cambridge University Press, 2011), pp. 295–306.

33 Aristotle, *Politics*, pp. 111, 268; Aristotle, *The Nicomachean Ethics*, transl. J. A. K. Thomson (Harmondsworth: Penguin, 2004), p. 201.

34 Kalimtzis, *Aristotle on Political Enmity*, p. 180.

form of rule is understood as legitimate because the policing of liberty and administration of civil society are performed in the name of security and law and order. The idea that there is a social realm that requires policing lies at the heart of modern state theory as it emerged from the sixteenth century.

From the sixteenth to the eighteenth centuries, a political theory of the state emerged that included within it an analysis of sovereignty, property, contract and labour. The need for such a theory was rooted in the joint development of the establishment of the political state, on the one hand, and the dissolution of civil society into independent individuals, on the other. As Marx pointed out, building on insights articulated by Hegel, the *abstraction* of the state as such is the hallmark of modernity, along with the emergence of a capitalist order formed of 'private' individuals who enter contracts within civil society. At the heart of this theory was the idea of a social contract, in which the submission and obedience of subjects was to be the exchange for the security offered by the state. Within this theory, some form of 'social' contract serves to replace natural will with political will, violence with peace, the law of nature with positive law, and fear (or what will later be called 'insecurity') with security.

The *locus classicus* of such accounts is the work of Thomas Hobbes, whose theory of the state, despite its absolutist tendencies, is widely considered the first definitive statement of the theory of the state per se. For this reason, as well as for Hobbes's account of the absolute subject that lies at the heart of pacification, I will have much to say about Hobbes's arguments here and in following chapters.

The starting point for Hobbes is the condition of fear within the state of nature, rooted in the existence of a *bellum omnium contra omnes*. In a war of all against all, in which human beings seek self-preservation at all costs and are under no moral obligation not to harm others, there is no possibility of commerce, industry, property, navigation, arts, letters, culture, knowledge, or any of the other benefits that accrue from living in political society. It is a condition lacking any kind of security whatsoever, in which people live in permanent fear of violent death. It is a condition of liberty in which, Hobbes famously tells us, life would be solitary, poor, nasty, brutish and short. Not wishing to live in such a condition, and with an inclination towards seeking peace to help manage their fundamental fear, these 'masterless' individuals form a contract through which a sovereign power is constituted in the form of the mighty Leviathan, a 'power able to over-awe them all' (*Leviathan*) or 'to keep them all in awe' (*Elements of Law*), offering security in exchange for obedience. John Locke's contribution later in the century was to stress private property as the beating heart of political society, while Hobbes's friend William Petty, who recognized labour-power as the source of wealth, focused on how to get the 'masterless' creatures of Hobbes's theory to work.

Commentaries on Hobbes tend to claim that the Leviathan state resolves the problem of the war of all against all in the natural condition. This war appears to be overcome through the law of nature that commands people to seek peace, but also requires the constitution of a sovereign power monopolizing the means of violence. Such a monopoly secures us from the violence of others as well as from any relapse into a state of nature. In other words, a categorical 'no' to war is announced. The sovereign power has 'the Right of making Warre, and Peace with other Nations and Common-wealths', Hobbes tells us, recognizing that war is always a possibility between sovereign powers, which face each other as though in the equivalent of the state of nature. The law of nations between states is, in the final analysis, merely a version of the law of nature between humans prior to the creation of states.[35] The categorical 'no' to war is directed inwards, to political society itself. The sovereign power exists 'to prevent Discord and Civill warre'.[36] As much as Hobbes shows an interest in external war and what might go by the name of 'international order', and has been appropriated in various ways by the academic discipline that goes by the name of International Relations, his real interest lies in the power dynamics internal to the sovereign power and the political order over which it exerts its domination. Most of all, Hobbes is concerned with the ways in which groups within society might form factions in opposition to the sovereign, leading to rebellion, a breakdown of political order, and thus to war within the body politic. Such rebellion would signal the end of the commonwealth. War within political society must never be allowed to break out.

35 Thomas Hobbes, *The Elements of Law: Natural and Politic*, ed. Ferdinand Tönnies (London: Frank Cass, 1969), p. 190.

36 Thomas Hobbes, *Leviathan*, ed. Richard Tuck (Cambridge: Cambridge University Press, 1991 [1651]), pp. 126–7.

To put it in the Greek terms with which Hobbes was deeply familiar: *polemos* can and will break out, but *stasis* must be forbidden.

Yet, much as *stasis* must be forbidden, can it ever be truly eradicated? After all, was not that precisely the point for the Greeks, and the reason they distinguished *stasis* from *polemos*? And what does it say about a polity that treats faction as sedition, sedition as rebellion, and rebellion as civil war, and therefore seeks to shut down factions before they even begin? What might such a process be called, if not *pacification*? To answer these questions, and to start to unravel the nature of pacification as it emerges as an idea in modern thought, we must register the significance of what amounts to Hobbes's first major intellectual work: his translation into English of Thucydides' *History of the Peloponnesian War*.

In a prefatory note addressed to the reader of his Thucydides translation, Hobbes explains that he thought it important to translate the book 'immediately from the Greek'. An English version of Thucydides' book was already available, but it had been translated from the French, which had itself been translated from a Latin edition rather than the original Greek. Hobbes returned to the Greek original, all the while meticulously keeping an eye on the Latin version (literally, in that he used an edition which contained the Latin and Greek texts alongside each other on facing pages). In translating the text, Hobbes sought to give meaning in English to some key Greek concepts, with a keen eye on related Latin words that had already become part of the English language. The key Greek concept of *polis*, for example, is now widely translated and understood as 'city-state', or just 'state', but originally had strong connotations of 'fortress' or 'citadel'. It is only in modern translations of Greek texts, not least Hobbes's translation of Thucydides, that the 'statism' of *polis* comes to the fore. Such a translation probably tells us more about the salience of the idea of the state in the modern world than it does the nature of the Greek *polis*. Hobbes was also searching for a way to grasp the meaning of *polis* consistent with the Latin notion of *civitas*, which connotes the entire body of *cives* as 'fellow citizens'. Likewise, the Greek *asphaleia* is often translated as 'security' (see Chapter 2). More telling is that the translation of *polis* as 'city-state' or just 'state', implying a fundamental unity of people, is one of the ways in which *stasis* has been disavowed, since it sets the state against *stasis*, positioning the state as a force for stability against destabilizing forces interpellated as seditious, rebellious, or insurgent. The state is imagined, from the onset of early modern state theory, as a power designed to counter insurgency, and anything that looks like insurgency.

In the opening paragraphs of the *History* I have already cited, Thucydides gives an account of *polemos* and *stasis* as the reasons for the difficulties experienced by the Greek peoples in settling anywhere. The translations Hobbes offers are, respectively, 'war' and 'sedition'. Likewise, in Book 5, Hobbes's translation points to a 'sedition' in Messana (Messina).[37] Discussing the *stasis* in Corcyra in Book III, also cited above, Hobbes offers us 'sedition' and 'faction'. He stresses that 'all forms of death were then seen'. 'So cruel was this Sedition' that fathers killed their sons and men were dragged from temples and killed:

> Many and heinous things happened in the cities through this sedition [*stasis*], which though they have been before and shall be ever as long as human nature is the same, yet they are more calm and of different kinds according to the several conjunctures . . . War, taking away the affluence of daily necessaries, is a most violent master and conformeth most men's passions to the present occasion. The cities therefore being now in sedition and those that fell into it later having heard what had been done in the former, they far exceeded the same in newness of conceit, both for the art of assailing and for the strangeness of their revenges.[38]

In Book 6, Hobbes translates Thucydides' citation of Athenagoras to the effect that 'our city is seldom quiet, but subject to sedition and contention, not so much against the enemy as within itself'. Later in Book 6, the Syracusans are described as generating seditious factions, and in Book 7 we read of anti-Athenian factions driven out of the territory of Thurii for being seditious. He repeats the point, and uses for *stasis* the terms 'sedition' and 'faction' time and again, albeit in a way that plays on the meaning of terms used by later translations of Thucydides, such as civil strife, civil war, internal conflict and rebellion.

37 In both instances, other translators offer 'internal conflict' – for example, Jeremy Mynott's translation, Thucydides, *The War of the Peloponnesians and the Athenians*.

38 Thucydides, *Peloponnesian War*, p. 204.

In one sense, this can be interpreted in the context of what Hobbes regards as the 'seditious factions' that would feed into the 'civil wars' of seventeenth-century England, such as his much later account in *Behemoth*, where he stresses that such wars were caused by seditious factions such as Papists; those who called themselves ministers of Christ; those arguing for 'liberty of religion' such as Independents, Anabaptists, Fifth Monarchy Men, Quakers, and Adamites; those educated men who believed, with many Greek and Roman writers that liberty and democracy are superior to monarchy; and those in the major trading centres who sought to use their new commercial power to challenge the power of kings.[39] 'Hobbes makes of Thucydides a seventeenth-century Englishman,' notes David Grene in his introductory comments to the Chicago University Press edition of Hobbes's Thucydides translation. And yet, in another sense – and not least because Hobbes was translating the book in the 1620s rather than later in the century – perhaps he was drawing attention to wider factions being created by the modern world. Maybe the secret of pacification is being slowly revealed. 'The narration itself doth secretly instruct the reader,' Hobbes notes of Thucydides' style.[40] (Hobbes himself loved a little secret: *Leviathan* is full of references to secret arts, secret machinations, secret hatreds, secret thoughts, secret counsels, secret intelligence, and the secrets of the commonwealth.) Perhaps this is a wry allusion to the possibility that his own narration-as-translation is intended to instruct us secretly. And perhaps it is intended to instruct us about more than simply the problems facing England. What might they be?

Here is Hobbes's translation of Thucydides' description of the *stasis* in Corcyra:

> The cause of all this is desire of rule out of avarice and ambition, and the zeal of contention from those two proceeding. For such as were of authority in the cities, both of the one and the other faction, preferring under decent titles, one, *the political equality of the multitude*, the other, *the moderate aristocracy* . . . Both ventured on most horrible

39 Thomas Hobbes, *Behemoth, or, the Long Parliament*, ed. Ferdinand Tönnies (Chicago: University of Chicago Press, 1990 [1668]), pp. 2–4, 56, 63, 95, 109, 159.

40 Thomas Hobbes, 'On the Life and History of Thucydides,' in Thucydides, *Peloponnesian War*, p. 577.

> outrages and prosecuted their revenges still farther without any regard of justice or the public good, but limiting them, each faction, by their own appetite, and stood ready, whether by unjust sentence or with their own hands, when they should get power, to satisfy their present spite ... The neutrals of the city were destroyed by both factions, partly because they would not side with them and partly for envy that they should so escape.[41]

It is not just 'civil wars', English or otherwise, about which Hobbes is concerned. After all, if that was his concern, he would have used the category 'civil war' in his translation – but this is a category he uses in later works, to the point where it becomes central to his arguments. Hobbes's main concern seems to be those who seek the 'equality of the multitude', and who want nothing less than democracy. In his essay on the life of Thucydides that accompanies his translation, Hobbes insists that the Greek writer 'least of all liked the Democracy' and 'best approved of the regal government'. Truth be told, that form of government is hardly a major part of Thucydides' account of the Peloponnesian War, yet the importance to Hobbes of the Greek historian's dislike of democracy is clear from Hobbes's autobiographical poem written over forty years later, where he lists the authors who most influenced him throughout his life, and suggests none pleased him as much as Thucydides. Why? Because the Greek historian made it clear that 'Democracy's a Foolish Thing'.[42] Hobbes's concern, then, was to draw out from Thucydides the danger of the multitude becoming seditious, forming some kind of democratic faction that would in turn become a rebellion. Rather than turning Thucydides into an Englishman, it would be more appropriate to say that Hobbes turned him into a thoroughgoing Hobbesian.[43]

---

41 Thucydides, *Peloponnesian War*, pp. 205–6.

42 Hobbes, 'On the Life and History of Thucydides', pp. 572–3; Thomas Hobbes, *Vita Carmine Espressa* (1672–73), published as *The Life of Mr Thomas Hobbes of Malmesbury Written by Himself in a Latine Poem, and Now Translated into English* (London: n.p., 1680).

43 Richard Schlatter, 'Introduction', in *Hobbes's Thucydides*, ed. Richard Schlatter (New Brunswick: Rutgers University Press, 1975), pp. xxvii–xxviii; Robin Sowerby, 'Thomas Hobbes's Translation of Thucydides', *Translation and Literature* 7: 2 (1998), pp. 147–69; Ioannis D. Evrigenis, *Images of Anarchy: The Rhetoric and Science in Hobbes's State of Nature* (Cambridge: Cambridge University Press, 2014), p. 37; Kinch Hoekstra,

There is, in other words, a politics to Hobbes's translation of Thucydides, as he intended – maybe even a secret politics; and nowhere is this more apparent than in his translation of *stasis*. Rather than a citizen's freedom and duty, and hence an essential feature of the polity, *stasis* is now rebellion by internal factions, an enemy within, often emerging from the multitude and seeking some form of democratic rule. To take up arms in the manner of *stasis* is now translated and interpreted as nothing less than *sedition*.

'Sedition' had, by Hobbes's time, become an established word in the English language. Sir Thomas Elyot in *The Governor* (1531) treats sedition as 'a thing most pernicious', and blames the collapse of Greece and Rome on the 'sedition and perpetual discord' created by trying to rule with more than one governor.[44] He was far from alone during the period. Tracts appeared with titles such as *A Remedy for Sedition* (Sir Richard Morison, 1536) and *The Hurt of Sedition* (Sir John Cheke, 1541). 'Rarely, one imagines, had more sedition been spoken of by so many, so suddenly', writes one historian of Reformation England.[45] The gist of their arguments is captured in Chapter 44 of Thomas Floyd's *The Picture of a Perfit Common Wealth* (1600), where sedition is presented as disobedience to both God and state, corruption of all manners, and an illegitimate revolt against the law. Sedition, Floyd writes, is 'a hell to the mind, a horror to the conscience, suppressing reason and inciting hatred'. And in support of his point, Floyd cites Thucydides on *stasis*.[46] Influenced by the Anglo-Norman *sediciun*, meaning treachery, the English word 'sedition' thus connoted rebellion, uprising, revolt, or insurrection. Perhaps most importantly, Francis Bacon added an essay on sedition to the expanded edition of his *Essays*, published in 1625. Hobbes had been reading Bacon since roughly 1610, and in the first half of the 1620s (the precise dates are unclear), in the period leading up to the publication of Bacon's expanded edition of the *Essays*, Hobbes worked as Bacon's secretary,

'Hobbes's Thucydides', in A. P. Martinich and Kinch Hoekstra, eds, *The Oxford Handbook of Hobbes* (Oxford: Oxford University Press, 2016), p. 549.

44 Sir Thomas Elyot, *The Book Named The Governor*, Lehmberg (London: Dent, 1962 [1531]), pp. 9, 241.

45 J. J. Scarisbrick, *Henry VIII* (London: Eyre & Spottiswoode, 1968), p. 339.

46 Thomas Floyd, *The Picture of a Perfit Common Wealth* (London: n.p., 1600), p. 297.

even translating some of the *Essays* into Latin (though probably not writing them himself, as some suggest). The first edition of the *Essays*, published in 1597, included the essay 'Of Faction'. There, Bacon argues that policing factions was a key feature of sovereign authority, and presents a series of examples from ancient Rome which, he notes, are examples of faction as war. In the extensively expanded edition of the *Essays* of 1625, Bacon added an essay on sedition in which he argues that 'when discords and quarrels and factions are carried openly and audaciously, it is a sign the reverence of government is lost'. For Bacon, one of the causes of seditious factions is what he calls 'fame' – his name for what might now be 'popular opinion' – and this is connected to the fact that a further cause of sedition is poverty. The poverty of the multitude and their 'popular opinions' on political matters might encourage seditious factions. 'The repressing of seditions in their beginnings' is therefore required, to be brought about by military prowess and 'good policy': the war power and the police power combined.[47]

Hobbes's choice of 'sedition' as one translation of a word describing a practice that the Greeks thought perfectly normal, even if problematic, is indicative of the profound shift taking place in political thought, not least as it sought to make sense of the nature of the political formations developing across Europe: *stasis* must now be stopped. Those engaging in *stasis* were not practising the agonistic side of their citizenship but, rather, were seditious and rebellious factions – insurgents within political society. We might even want to call them 'revolutionaries', but this is a term which, for the moment, we shall keep to one side.

As Hobbes then goes on to detail at length throughout his major works, the whole point of sovereign power is to 'teach us how to avoid the close, dark, and dangerous by-paths of faction and sedition'.[48] In Chapter 2, I will consider the political importance of *darkness*. Here, I will focus on what the by-paths are, and why they are so *dangerous*.

47 Francis Bacon, 'Of Faction' (1597) and 'Of Seditions and Troubles' (1625), both in *Essays* (London: Dent, 1972), pp. 42–8, 152–3.

48 Thomas Hobbes, *De Cive* (1642), in Hobbes, *Man and Citizen*, ed. Bernard Gert (Indianapolis: Hackett, 1991), p. 98.

Hobbes defines faction as follows:

> I call a *faction*, a multitude of subjects gathered together, either by mutual *contracts* among themselves, or by the power of some one, without his or their authority who bear the supreme Rule. A *faction*, therefore, is as it were a city in a city: for as by an union of men in the state of nature a city receives its being, so by a new union of subjects there ariseth a *faction*. According to this definition, a multitude of subjects who have bound themselves simply to obey any foreign prince or subject, or have made any pacts, or leagues of mutual defence between themselves against all men, not excepting those who have the supreme power in the city, is a *faction*.[49]

The duty of 'those whose authority and power is entire' is to 'cherish obedient subjects, and to depress the factious', 'restrain the factious', even to 'dissolve and dissipate' them. Why? Because seditious factions are a sign that the members of political society are at war with one another – and such a war is nothing less than *the death of the commonwealth*.[50]

Sedition is most genuine and threatening when it takes the form of a political organization, a faction, constituting a political body within the body politic, a state within the state, and thus, by definition, a threat to sovereign power. This generates a figure that will run through Hobbes's thought, appearing under different names within the theory of the state thereafter, and which serves to provide a rationale for the exercise of the state's police power. Hobbes calls this figure the 'seditious blockhead'.[51]

The seditious blockhead refuses to accept the authority of sovereign power, organizes factions, seeks political change rather than peace and stability, and thinks that rebellion is permissible – or worse, preferable to obedience. The seditious blockhead is a tumultuous, insurgent, rebellious subject who has forgotten the reason for their subjection. The seditious blockhead is 'discontented . . . in their purposes against the State' and 'alwayes in the procincts of Battell'. This is a permanent problem for all political order. As Hobbes illustrates with the example of Adam in the Garden of Eden, even obedience to the simplest command of the

49 Ibid., p. 266. Emphases in original.
50 Ibid.; *Elements of Law*, pp. 72, 168.
51 Hobbes, *Behemoth*, p. 113.

mightiest of rulers – 'Do not eat from this tree' – is easily broken. After all, if 'the tongue of man is a trumpet of war and sedition', and if one of the things that distinguishes man from other animals is the ability to 'provoke one another by words', then rebellion will be likely so long as people within civil society communicate.[52] There will always be some seditious blockhead willing to blow the trumpet of sedition and start a civil war.

I have noted that Hobbes does not use the term 'civil war' when translating *stasis* in Thucydides' *History*. But, by the time of his mature writings, 'civil war' has become a major concept and theme, as it has within state theory in general. 'The greatest inconvenience that can happen to a commonwealth', Hobbes insists, is 'to dissolve into civil war'.[53] In many ways, this reflects his experience of the English Civil Wars. In *Leviathan*'s 'Review and Conclusion', for example, on the book's very last page, Hobbes describes the writing of the book as 'occasioned by the disorders of the present time'. Yet, even if Hobbes does have one eye firmly on the state of England, he has a more general argument that civil war is essentially a return to a state of nature, in the sense that 'in those places where there is a civil war at any time . . . there is neither laws, nor commonwealth, nor society'.[54] This makes civil war the 'quintessential Hobbesian theme', to use Deborah Baumgold's phrase, precisely because it signals the end of the state as a political entity.[55] In civil war, obedience has disappeared under the sway of seditious rebellion. Even when Hobbes refers to the English Civil Wars, he often makes this more general point. For example, in the 'Review and Conclusion', he writes that 'the Civill warres have not yet sufficiently taught men, in what point of time it is, that a Subject becomes obliged to the Conquerour; nor what is Conquest; nor how it comes about, that it obliges men to obey his Laws'. Every example of a civil war teaches a more general lesson: the people must understand their *obligation to obedience*, their *submission to the sovereign*, and that they have *forgone any right to rebellion*. The People must

---

52 Hobbes, *Leviathan*, pp. 72, 395; Hobbes, *De Cive*, pp. 169, 310–11; *Elements of Law*, 169; Hobbes, *Behemoth*, p. 2.

53 Hobbes, *Elements of Law*, p. 143.

54 Thomas Hobbes, 'The Questions Concerning Liberty, Necessity, and Chance' (1656), in *The English Works of Thomas Hobbes*, ed. Sir William Molesworth (London: John Bohn, 1841), p. 184.

55 Deborah Baumgold, *Hobbes's Political Theory* (Cambridge: Cambridge University Press, 1988), p. 127.

understand that civil war would be the dissolution of their own security. The People must understand that they 'can never be without some incommodity or other', but that to object to such a situation would place them in the greatest 'incommodity' of all, namely 'the miseries, and horrible calamities, that accompany a Civill Warre'.[56] Hobbes makes clear what is at stake on the very first page of *Leviathan*, in one of the book's many striking images, where he compares the state, an artificial body, with the human body, writing that, in such a body, concord is health, sedition is sickness and *civil war is death*.

The fact that civil war is a war *within* the political order makes civil war somewhat worse than war itself. Hobbes writes time and again of 'Quarrells, Factions, and at last Warre', and argues that a unified sovereign power is necessary 'or else there must needs follow Faction, and Civil war in the Common-wealth'. Teachers of false philosophies 'tend to disorder in Government, as countenancing Rebellion, or Sedition', resulting in 'not one independent Common-wealth' but 'independent' and 'unlawful' factions fighting a civil war. In this sense, *Leviathan* is in many ways an extended study of 'the most frequent praetext of Sedition, and Civill Warre', which becomes the basis for Hobbes's argument that the sovereign power must be absolute as well as unified, for 'without such Arbitrary government, such [civil] Warre must be perpetuall'. He makes the same point in other works, such as *De Cive*, where he writes that, because human ambition and desire for honour will never be thwarted, the role of sovereignty is to 'order it' such that 'men may know that the way to honour is not by contempt of the present government, nor by factions'. The danger is that the contest for honour gives rise to 'hatred and envy', out of which 'arise *factions* in a commonweal; and out of *factions*, seditions and civil war'. 'What is it that can be called public, in a civil war, without the King?', he has one of the speakers in *Behemoth* ask.[57]

All of which is Hobbes's reminder that the people must understand what it means to promise what the Romans called *imperata facere*: to take the orders, to carry out the commands, made of them. This is what

56 Hobbes, *Leviathan*, p. 128.

57 Hobbes, *Leviathan*, pp. 21, 46, 70–2, 126, 164, 225, 228, 322, 402, 471, 474; Hobbes, *De Cive*, pp. 168, 231, 265; Hobbes, *Behemoth*, p. 113.

it means to be *pacified*, he suggests.[58] In civil war, the people are no longer pacified. Pacification is the antithesis of civil war, but also therefore the antithesis of any kind of factionalizing, rebellion, tumult, revolt. Pacification is necessary so that such things do not occur. In chapter 29 of *Leviathan*, he makes clear what is required by repeating a point made by Bacon, that Greek cities were always suffering from factions due to their imperfect 'policy'. Get the 'police' right, and civil war will not happen. It was precisely such a pacification that Hobbes desired for England during that country's civil wars. Just a few years prior to the publication of *Leviathan*, in March 1647, Hobbes wrote to Samuel Sorbière from Paris, to the effect that the publication of *De Cive* in France would prevent him from returning to England, 'if it is permitted, when England has somehow or other been pacified'.[59]

Much as Hobbes's starting point is the famous war of all against all in the natural condition, the 'war' that worries him most is a kind of war that becomes possible *once the political order is created*. The generation of *civil society* creates the possibility of *civil war*. This becomes the explicit position of state theory thereafter which, regardless of its precise formulation (monarchic, absolutist, mercantilist, liberal, democratic), wants the multitude to consider a basic question: the state or civil war? The theory assumes it knows the answer. To assert the necessity of the state to political life is to disavow civil war.[60] Better still, more than disavowal, it is to declare the state itself as a war on civil war, or even the possibility of civil war. It is to imagine the state as always already in a war against the agents of civil war – such as the seditious blockhead, the insurgent, the rebel, the revolutionary.

Civil war is thus configured as something to be countered, despite the extensive historical examples through the preceding centuries showing precisely how difficult a task this is. The state comes to be defined in advance and justified time and again – 'legitimized', we might say – as a

58 Hobbes, *Leviathan*, p. 485; see also pp. 21, 68.

59 Hobbes to Sorbière, in Noel Malcolm, ed., *The Clarendon Edition of the Works of Thomas Hobbes, Vol. 6: The Correspondence, Vol. 1: 1622–1659* (Oxford: Clarendon, 1994), p. 158.

60 Michel Foucault, *The Punitive Society: Lectures at the Collège de France, 1972–1973*, transl. Graham Burchell (Houndmills: Palgrave, 2015), p. 13; Tiqqun, *Introduction to Civil War* (2009), transl. Alexander R. Galloway and Jason E. Smith (Los Angeles: Semiotext(e), 2011), p. 73.

countervailing force whose powers of war and police are interpellated as simply *countering* and *containing* threats to peace, security, or law-and-order. The state presents itself as a counter-violence, a counter-subversion and a counter-revolution. This is the state that will eventually be defined as *countering insurgency*, as we saw in the Introduction. This supposed neutralization of violence stresses the state's monopoly over the legitimate use of force. Such a monopoly requires that members of civil society subscribe to a social contract founded upon an agreement not to conduct acts of 'violence' themselves, especially for political ends, and to accept that such violence be concentrated in the state.[61] Which is to say, out of the fear of civil war, subjects must learn to embrace their duty of obedience to the state, to be in awe of the state, to love the state – and to fear the state too (see Chapter 2). This is their pacification.

We have not finished with this argument, and there will be plenty more to say about civil war that changes the argument's focus. First, however, the historical picture must be fleshed out a little more. In his contribution to this argument, Hobbes was building on a long history of translations of political thought going back to the Romans, and a thoroughgoing reinterpretation of Greek thought conducted by the Romans, one feature of which was a portrayal of the Roman Republic and its constitution as better able to manage the *stasis* that they believed undermined the Greek *polis*. A short detour through some of the contours of Roman thought is therefore necessary to help explicate the relationship between sedition, war, violence, and pacification.

The story is often told of an insurgency during the first years of the Roman Republic, from which we have been handed the famous fable of the belly of the body politic, as recounted by Livy in *The Early History of Rome*. Livy records the story of an old man, in soiled and threadbare clothes, who presents himself to the Forum and explains that he is a former soldier who fought to defend Rome, only to return and find his crops ruined and his house destroyed, yet he was still expected to pay taxes. This led him into debt, after which he was seized by his creditor, reduced to slavery, and then hauled away to prison. On hearing the former soldier's story, the crowd engage in an uprising, recognizing in the story a wider problem: first, people are required to defend the

61 Étienne Balibar, *Violence and Civility: On the Limits of Political Philosophy*, transl. G. M. Goshgarian (New York: Columbia University Press, 2015), p. 32.

freedom of the Republic as soldiers, and yet denied freedom themselves; and second, their overwhelming debts have left people feeling a permanent threat of becoming slaves. The former soldier's story is thus another tale of the 'internal discord of ever-increasing bitterness between the ruling classes and the masses'. This prompts a revolt, in which the plebs withdraw to the Sacred Mount and set up camp there. As told by Livy, the plebs did so 'without any officer to direct them': a collective force with no leader with whom the patricians might negotiate. Enduring for days, their encampment caused an immediate labour shortage in the city, and left it at risk from invasion. 'In Rome there was something like panic', records Livy. 'Clearly', he adds, 'the only hope lay in finding a solution for the conflicting interests of the two classes in the state: by fair means or foul the country must recover its internal harmony'. The Senate dispatched Menenius Agrippa to the Mount to convince the plebs to return. Out of this encounter emerged the fable.

Addressing the plebs, Agrippa tells them a story of the body politic and its belly. The story recounts how the various parts of the body begin to resent having to supply food to the belly, which appears to do little other than consume the things that the body's other members provide: 'So the discontented members plotted together that the hand should carry no food to the mouth, that the mouth should take nothing that was offered it, and that the teeth should accept nothing new to chew.' The fable recounts how the parts soon realize that refusing to feed the belly weakens not only the belly, but the whole body as well: 'they [the parts] themselves and the whole body wasted away to nothing'. Rather than cutting off the food supply to the belly, then, all the parts of the body need to consider themselves as one, whatever differences exist between them, and the belly recognized for the role it plays in nourishing the parts. In Agrippa's tale, the patricians are Rome's belly, while the plebeians make up the other parts of the body. For the plebs to refuse to work with and for the belly would be an end to the body as a whole. According to Livy, the plebs on the Mount hear the fable and agree to return. Rome is transformed because the rebellion leads to two new 'tribunes of the people', who were to defend the commons against the consuls, enabling a new unity. Out of disorder, a new order emerges. More to the point, a political solution is found to an insurgency that emerged out of a socioeconomic division that was so profound it threatened to break the polity. In Greek terms, *stasis* was acknowledged, expressed, and managed; in Roman terms, the people were *pacified*.

As we have seen, the Solonic constitutional reforms included the idea that anyone who did not choose one side or the other in *stasis* should lose their rights as a citizen. In the tenth of his letters to Atticus, Cicero questions the authenticity of Solon's law, and instead opts to 'neglect the law of Solon . . . who provided the death penalty for anyone who should not take one side in a revolution [*seditione*]'.[62] In this he is followed by others, such as Plutarch, in his *Life of Solon*, where he describes the law as 'very peculiar'.[63] This was part and parcel of a rethinking of the whole logic of *stasis*. At the beginning of Book 6 of *On the Commonwealth*, Cicero suggests that good political leadership requires foresight and preparation in order 'always to be armed against things which disturb the stability of the state'. The people might be tempted into the kind of discord that results from 'sedition' or 'faction'.[64] How then to avoid such temptation? How might such desires be pacified?

In Book I of *De Inventione*, Cicero writes that every controversial subject can be resolved by a debate 'about a fact, or about a definition, or about the nature of an act, or about legal processes'. He adds that the question from which the whole case arises is called *constitutio* or the 'issue'.[65] *Constitutio* in this passage is a translation of στάσις (*stasis*). This becomes central to 'stasis theory' in rhetoric – the *inventione* in Cicero's title refers to rhetorical invention – and the debate about which words should be used to describe an act, and how to classify that act in relation to others. The example Cicero gives concerns a sacred object purloined from a private house: Is the act a theft or sacrilege? Cicero is concerned with matters of controversy, which he believes can only be resolved by speech and debate about questions of fact, questions of definition, and questions about the character of an act or legal process. The precise nature of rhetoric and the history of stasis theory within it need not

62 Cicero, *Letters to Atticus, Vol. II*, transl. E. O. Winstedt (London: Heinemann, 1913), p. 275.

63 Plutarch, 'Life of Solon', in Plutarch, *The Rise and Fall of Athens: Nine Greek Lives*, transl. Ian Scott-Kilvert and John Marincola (Harmondsworth: Penguin, 2003), p. 74.

64 Cicero, *On the Commonwealth and On the Laws*, transl. C. K. Ziegler (Cambridge: Cambridge University Press, 1999), p. 92.

65 Cicero, *De Inventione*, transl. H. M. Hubbell (Cambridge: Harvard University Press, 1949), p. 21.

detain us here, other than to note that Cicero's example of the theft reminds us that he is thinking through the rhetorical ploys for considering questions of law, which is one reason why 'stasis theory' in rhetoric is very much about the rhetoric of law. Suffice to say, at this point, that Cicero translates *stasis* as *constitution*, and focuses this word on the taking of a *stand* in a debate through which the disputing parties can find resolution.

In Book VI of his *Histories*, written during the second century BCE, Polybius restates the types of constitution outlined by Plato and Aristotle, noting the tendency of constitutions to degenerate into corrupt forms, and possibly even mob-rule. But he adds that the Romans sought to 'mix' the best of the various constitutions. He describes the Roman constitution as containing 'three elements, each of them possessing sovereign powers', with their respective share of power in the whole state, 'regulated with such a scrupulous regard to equality and equilibrium, that no one could say for certain, not even a native, whether the constitution as a whole were an aristocracy or democracy or despotism'.[66] The outcome is a concept of constitution incorporating the conflicts between factions and enabling their expression in a new form.[67] 'Constitution' is imagined here as a process to institutionalize conflict, manage rebellion, and even suppress revolution, eradicating *stasis*, or at least somehow erasing it ideologically. Polybius, like other commentators on Roman politics, is beginning to develop an argument in which *stasis* could be deplored, but also recognized as a reality that needed to be – and could be – managed through the laws and dynamics of constitution. In other words, constitutionalism is emerging as a way of managing and simultaneously downplaying, or even disavowing, the existence of fundamental conflicts that might otherwise tear apart the polity. The constitutionalized conflict becomes the grounds of a peaceful balance between oppositional forces.

In *On the Commonwealth*, after a summary of Plato's account of how political regimes fall apart through lack of balance and unity, Cicero

66 Polybius, *The Histories of Polybius, Vol. 1*, transl. Evelyn S. Shuckburgh (London: Macmillan, 1889), p. 468.

67 Andrew Lintott, 'The Theory of the Mixed Constitution at Rome', in Jonathan Barnes and Miriam Griffin, eds, *Philosophia Togata II* (Oxford: Clarendon, 1997), pp. 70–85; Benjamin Straumann, *Crisis and Constitutionalism: Roman Political Thought from the Fall of the Republic to the Age of Revolution* (Oxford: Oxford University Press, 2016), p. 152.

articulates his preference for a monarchy over other forms of government, but also expresses approval of a government formed of a compound: of 'having something outstanding and monarchic in a commonwealth; of there being something else assigned to the authority of aristocrats; of some things being set aside for the judgment and wishes of the people'. This structure also has a certain degree of equality and solidity, which helps avoid those tendencies in which 'a master arises in place of a king, a faction in place of aristocracy, a confused mob in place of the people'. He adds: 'There is no reason for revolution when each person is firmly set in his own rank, without the possibility of sudden collapse.' For Cicero, one of the greatest dangers in any commonwealth is that certain individuals, through their wealth or connections, form a faction and seek to control the state.[68] To counter this, the constitution is expected to be moderate, decent and calm. The first and most important provision is: 'let there be no violence', for nothing is more contrary to law and the constitution, and hence destructive to states, than the use of violence in public affairs in a duly constituted commonwealth. By bracketing violence out in this way, 'the law ordains obedience' and 'no sedition can take place'.[69]

In contrast to his Greek predecessors, who assumed a natural inequality among humans, Cicero postulates a moral equality. Yet he also still offers a powerful voice to the Roman culture of private property, with its inegalitarian nature.[70] Hence, like the Greeks before him, Cicero holds that the most fundamental factions are those organized around property ownership and the distribution of wealth. During the rise of Rome, a 'conflict of the orders' had developed pitting the plebeian against the patrician class (*classis*), as detailed in accounts such as Livy's, both classes being aware of the proletariat below them. Like other Roman thinkers, Cicero faced the need to seek some kind of accommodation between the classes, so that property and order might be protected. One sees this in the ways that Cicero suggests that those who present themselves as being on the side of the people, seeking to legislate against landholders and releasing debtors from their debts, undermine the very

68 Cicero, *On the Commonwealth*, pp. 31, 66.

69 Cicero, *On the Laws*, p. 173.

70 Neal Wood, *Cicero's Social and Political Thought* (Berkeley: University of California Press, 1988), p. 90.

foundations of the political community. This is captured in some of the phrases he uses, such as *concordia ordinum* ('concord of the orders'), *consensus bonorum* ('consensus of good men'), and *cum dignitate otium* ('leisure with dignity'). Concord, he claims, 'cannot exist when money is taken from some and bestowed upon others', and fairness resides in everyone 'keeping that which is his'. In Cicero's view in *De Officiis*, 'the proper function of a citizenship and a city is to ensure for everyone a free and unworried guardianship of his possessions'.[71]

For this reason, the use of 'constitution' for *stasis* was supplemented in Cicero's writings by one of the word's derivatives, 'status'. In *Topica* – a rethinking of Aristotle's *Topics* into Roman rhetoric and an attempt to incorporate them into the oratorical skills thought appropriate for Republican debate – Cicero writes that judicial inquiries are divided into accusation and defence. Someone is accused of a crime, and the counsel for the defence makes one of three replies: either the crime was not committed, called *infitialis* (denial) or *conjecturalis* (based on inference or conjecture); or, if it was committed, it has a different name, a question of *definitiva* (involving definition); or that the crime was justified, and hence a question of *juridicialis* (involving right and wrong):

> The proper arguments for these cases, selected from the topics which we have enumerated, have been developed in the rules for oratory. The reply to the accusation which constitutes the denial of the charge, may be called in Latin *status* since the Greeks call it *στάσις* (*stasis*): for this is the place where the defence takes its stand, as if it were coming to grips in a counter-attack.[72]

Within this idea of *stasis* as *status* is an emerging concept of the *state*. As we have seen, the Greeks could never move beyond the notion of the *polis* as synonymous with the community of citizens. Roman law encouraged a perception of a clearly defined public sphere in such a way as to imagine the state as a formal entity somehow distinct from the citizens it comprised. At the same time, a sharpening focus on private

71 Cicero, *On Duties*, transl. Margaret Atkins (Cambridge: Cambridge University Press, 1991), p. 95.

72 Cicero, *Topica*, in *Cicero in Twenty-Eight Volumes, Vol. II*, transl. H. M. Hubbell (Cambridge, MA: Harvard University Press, 1949), p. 455.

property was undergirded by a particular distinction between public and private that invited an understanding of *state* befitting such property. As Ellen Meiksins Wood points out, Cicero 'sets himself the task of conceptualizing the relation between public sphere and private in such a way as to maintain the sanctity of private property while stressing public duty'.[73] This is why, despite his distance from Plato and Aristotle, he shares some of their key anti-democratic positions, not least when it comes to the lower orders.

If discord is *seditio* – an attack on the very stability of the state, against which the citizen must be armed and willing to go to war – then what would it mean for the polity to go to war against sedition? Here, we find Cicero, along with many other writers, introducing a further conceptual development: civil war.

The term *bellum civile* appears in a speech of Cicero's delivered in 66 BCE, in which he tries to convince his audience that Pompey is the best general in Rome. 'What type of war can there be in which the fortune of the state has not made use of him? Civil, African, Transalpine, Spanish . . . slave, and naval wars'.[74] Cicero also refers to the role Pompey played in the first 'civil war' that Rome experienced, the Sullan war of the 80s. That he felt no need to explain the term suggests that it was already in use, but certainly 'civil war' came to be widely used thereafter, and then also applied retrospectively to earlier conflicts. Much later, Appian would claim in his *Civil Wars* that, when Sulla marched on Rome, a battle took place 'between political enemies which was the first conducted in Rome not under the guise of civil dissension [*stasis*] but nakedly as war [*polemos*].[75] In the 'Twelfth Philippic', Cicero claims that, although some people have described Antonius as 'only an adversary', he himself has 'invariably called that man a public enemy', because, although the sedition appears to be 'only a tumult', Cicero has 'always pronounced this to be a war'. Stressing this distinction again in the first book of *De Officiis*, a compilation of advice to his son Marcus on leaving

73 Ellen Meiksins Wood, *Citizens to Lords: A Social History of Western Political Thought from Antiquity to the Middle Ages* (London: Verso, 2008), p. 140.

74 Cicero, 'De Imperio Cn. Pompei' ('On the command of Gnaeus Pompeius') (66 BCE), in Cicero, *Political Speeches*, transl. D. H. Berry (Oxford: Oxford University Press, 2006), p. 119.

75 Appian, *The Civil Wars*, transl. John Carter (Harmondsworth: Penguin, 1996), p. 32.

Rome to study in Athens, Cicero suggests that *stasis* was 'the reason for serious strife in Athens', but that in Rome they 'have caused not merely sedition [*seditiones*] but even a disastrous civil war [*bella civilia*]'. Civil war, he adds, is an event so serious that every serious citizen will seek to avoid it.[76]

It is not uncommon to find *stasis* translated as 'civil war' in modern translations of Greek texts, but such a translation is somewhat anachronistic. The Greeks could never imagine *stasis* as 'civil war' because, as we have seen, they had no 'state' as such, and no distinct 'civic order' or 'civil society' within which political unity could be imagined, constituted, and policed; as we have seen, *stasis* was not *polemos*. The Romans, beginning to work with a new set of concepts, could imagine a *bellum civile* (along with other forms of internal war, to which I shall turn shortly). The Romans imagined their internal dissensions as fundamentally different to those suffered by the Greeks, but also as different to foreign wars. To understand them, they invented the term 'civil war'.[77] Hence, when Caesar crossed the Rubicon in 49 BCE, beginning a conflict that would last four years, the Romans understood this as *bellum civile*, and the following centuries saw a plethora of texts with 'civil war' as the main theme, such as Caesar's *Civil War* (known by that title due to his observation in Book II that 'it was a civil war, they said'), Lucan's epic poem *Civil War*, and Appian's *Civil Wars*.

The term *bellum civile* was understood to be paradoxical, in that *bellum*, normally understood to be a war against external enemies, was now taking place within the polity. 'Make us enemies of each and every people – just turn away civil war', one grieving mother cries in Lucan's *Civil War*. In another episode in the poem, Brutus asks Cato which side he might be taking in the war between Caesar and Pompey, hoping that Cato's position is the same as his own: 'Will you keep peace . . . or have you resolved to join the leaders in crime, the raving people's ruin – to absolve the civil war?' The injunction to avoid taking sides is not just to avoid the raving madness of the conflict, but to avoid civil war. Cato knows the absurdity of choosing but refuses simply to be a spectator,

76 Cicero, *Philippics*, transl. Walter C. A. Ker (Cambridge: Harvard University Press, 1957), p. 523; Cicero, *On Duties*, p. 34.

77 David Armitage, *Civil Wars: A History in Ideas* (New Haven, CT: Yale University Press, 2017), p. 45.

and takes a *stand* with Pompey.[78] As Shadi Bartsch points out in her account of Lucan's poem, Cato's choice is for *stasis* as civil war rather than *stasis* as stability.[79] For us, we might say that one word, *bellum*, is beginning to have to do a lot of work, used to depict what would once have been closer to *stasis*, and that *bellum civile* is essentially *stasis* in every sense of the word. The Romans had a Greek word rich in nuance, but they experienced what the Greeks designated with that word in a very different way, rendering *stasis* as far closer to *polemos*, to the point that taking a political stand was now akin to announcing that one was at (civil) war.

Even those Romans writing in Greek, such as Josephus and Appian, came round to this position, as is evident from their major works, Josephus's *The Jewish War*, written in the 70s of the first century, and Appian's *The Civil Wars*, written in the middle of the second century. Josephus was a Jewish priest of royal descent and Pharisaic persuasion, who took a leading part in the anti-Roman revolt of 66–73 (recounted in *The Jewish War*). He witnessed the fall of Jerusalem and the burning of the Temple, eventually became a Roman citizen, and spent the second half of his life as a Jew living in Rome writing historical works in Greek. *The Jewish War* sets out its position from the outset: 'I shall . . . distinguish the sufferings and calamities of the people, and how far they were afflicted by the war, and how far by the faction, and how far by famine, till at last Jerusalem was taken.'[80] *Polemos*, *stasis* and famine: three great misfortunes that can befall a city.[81] Yet *stasis* overtakes *polemos* as the key theme and interpretive tool in the book, appearing to be a far worse misfortune. This is reinforced by Josephus's extensive use of *stasis*-related concepts such as *zelotai* ('zealotry'), *sicarii* ('assassins'), *lestai* ('brigands'), *neoterizontes* ('innovators', 'insurrectionists' or 'revolutionaries') and *stasiastai* (fomenters of civil strife). For Josephus, those engaged in *stasis* are engaged in rebellion, insurgency, civil war, civic strife/disorder, uprising, insurrection, secession, defection, lawlessness,

78 Lucan, *Civil War*, transl. Matthew Fox (Harmondsworth: Penguin, 2012), pp. 31, 37.

79 Shadi Bartsch, *Ideology in Cold Blood: A Reading of Lucan's Civil War* (Cambridge: Harvard University Press, 1997), pp. 59–61, 73.

80 Josephus, *The Jewish War*, 'Preface', in *The Works of Flavius Josephus, Vol. IV*, transl. William Whiston and A. R. Shilleto (London: George Bell, 1890), p. 6.

81 Ibid., p. 333.

fratricide and sin.[82] So prevalent are the figures of rebellion and accounts of civil war that *The Jewish War* often reads like a polemic from the canon of modern counterinsurgency thinkers.

One aspect of *stasis* is the 'bitter contest between those that were enamoured of war and those that desired peace':

> At first this quarrelsome temper attacked persons in families who could not agree among themselves, and afterwards those people that were dearest to one another broke away from one another, and every one associated with those who held his own opinions, and already began to range themselves on different sides throughout the community. And *stasis* was everywhere.[83]

In effect, 'the city was infested on all sides by plotters and rabble, [and] the people of the city, between them, were like a great body being torn to pieces'.[84] To be sure, at various points Josephus makes it appear as though the *stasis* includes the struggle against Roman imperial power – but it is ultimately the *stasis* among the Jews that is the truly devastating 'war', one which the Jewish people are fighting among themselves, not against the Romans: a 'civil war' among the people 'rampant not only throughout Judaea, but also in Italy', one so bad that many people 'earnestly hoped for an external war to free them from their domestic miseries'. Yet 'internal dissensions [*stasis*] did not cease', and, even after the first Roman attack, the people continued to fight with one another. 'I venture to affirm that faction [*stasis*] destroyed the city, and the Romans destroyed the faction [*stasis*]'.

Several decades later, Appian, a Roman citizen who also wrote in his original Greek language, was able to capture what the Romans thought they had achieved. In the Preface to his *Roman History*, he claims that 'neither famine, nor frequently recurring plague, nor sedition [*stasis*]' could have stopped the Romans achieving their present greatness and prosperity.[85] In *The Civil Wars*, Appian time and again uses *stasis* to

82 Ibid., pp. 228, 350; Josephus, *The Jewish War*, in *The Works of Flavius Josephus, Vol. V*, transl. William Whiston and A. R. Shilleto (London: George Bell, 1890), pp. 4, 31.

83 Josephus, *Jewish War*, in *Works, IV*, p. 304.

84 Josephus, *Jewish War*, in *Works, V*, p. 4.

85 Appian, *Roman History, Vol. 1*, transl. Horace White (London: Heinemann, 1912), p. 19.

describe what happened during the wars in question. In each case, opposition groups 'made war in theory against the rival faction, but in fact against their own country; they attacked it as though it were enemy soil'. The result was banishment, torture, massacre and the confiscation of property. The plebs and patricians were especially at odds with each other over the passing of laws, the cancellation of debts and the distribution of land, and during elections, but 'no sword was ever brought into the assembly, and no Roman was ever killed by a Roman, until Tiberius Gracchus, while holding the office of tribune and in the act of proposing legislation, became the first man to die in civil unrest'.[86]

> The whole nature of their misfortunes was unlike that of a civil conflict or a wartime occupation. It was not the case that . . . they feared members of the other faction, or the enemy, and put themselves in the hands of their own household; on the contrary, they were more in fear of the latter than of the death squads – not because they were like opponents in war or civil conflict [*stasis*], but because they were members of their household.[87]

Describing the moment when Sulla relieved the tribunate of its powers – an act later annulled as illegal – Appian writes that 'episodes of civil strife escalated from rivalry and contentiousness to murder, and from murder to full-scale war'. Figures such as Sulpicius and Marius were to be 'regarded as public enemies' because 'they had stirred up civil war'.[88] For Appian, then, *stasis* is a feature of Roman history, but it stabilizes rather than destroys the Empire, giving rise to a new political entity, unified and organized around the figure of the emperor, but very much the result of Republican virtues and constitutional arrangements.

All told, Roman thinkers writing in either Greek or Latin naturally used Greek terms to describe Rome's history, and *stasis* was understandably one of them. And yet the Romans understood themselves to be experiencing something new, something that *stasis* could not quite capture, especially given its distinction from *polemos*. The Romans needed a new concept, and found it in a new kind of *polemos*, a *bellum*

86 Appian, *Civil Wars*, pp. 1–2.
87 Ibid., p. 215.
88 Ibid., p. 34.

distinct from other kinds of *bellum*, nothing less than *bellum civile*. Having conceived of the 'civil', the Romans joined it to 'war', retaining a fundamental distinction between 'external' and 'internal' war, but using the same category, 'war', for both, distinguishing one from the other with the addition of 'civil'. The Romans adopted 'civil war' reluctantly, notes David Armitage. It was an unsettling notion, because it hinted at the possible subversion of the polity. Moreover, once the idea of civil war was invented, the Romans were then almost obliged to reread their own history as nothing less than a series of civil wars.[89] And yet, at the same time, and precisely because it was imagined as *civil* war, *stasis* was understood as something that should be overcome, in a way that was beyond the Greeks, and this overcoming was the task of Roman liberty, civic unity and constitutional order; the instability of *stasis* transformed into the stability of an order constituted by power: the people pacified, we might say.

We can now return to Hobbes and to the theory of the state in general.

Hobbes claims that the validity of the contracts on which modern political order depends 'begins . . . with the Constitution of a Civill Power, sufficient to compel men to keep them'. And, as we have seen, the Romans made a great deal of 'constitution'. The dominant liberal-democratic account of 'constitution' with which we are familiar is of relatively recent coinage, and obscures the reasons why the idea of 'constitution' first emerged and contained such force. The Roman idea of 'constitution' implied the setting up of something, forming it or fabricating it, which contemporary constitutionalism tends to bracket out. As Stephen Holmes notes, 'the original meaning of "to constitute" is neither to constrain political power for the sake of individual liberty nor to force government to obey universal moral norms. What "to constitute" signifies, in the first instance, is *to set up* . . . To constitute (*constituere*) a republic meant to found and organize it.'[90] The primary function of the ancient idea of constitution was not to limit pre-existing power through various constitutional checks and balances, but to *create power in the first place*. In other words, *constitutio* referred to a political *ordering*, and

89 Armitage, *Civil Wars*, p. 35.

90 Stephen Holmes, 'Constitutions and Constitutionalism', in Michel Rosenfeld and András Sajó, eds, *The Oxford Handbook of Comparative Constitutional Law* (Oxford: Oxford University Press, 2012), p. 194. Emphasis in original.

with it a *pacification of seditious tendencies and rebellious factions*. A power could only be *constituted as a state* if it was seen as a solution to the problem of seditious factions and insurgencies within the wider order – and for this to happen it had to be able to command the power to define factions and insurgencies as such. In other words, the *constitution* of the state was seen as an answer to civil war.

This idea finds its way into state theory prior to the liberal constitutionalism of the late eighteenth century. That is why Hobbes writes of there being 'constituted great Commonwealths' or of people with a 'Soveraigne Power constituted over them'. When he writes of 'the first Constitution of their Common-wealth' or 'the constitution of Soveraign Power', he is referring not to an object (a document called 'The Constitution') but to a process (the act of constituting), and he notes that this is how the Romans used the term.[91] Moreover, such 'constitutionalism' is pitched against constituent power, which it sees as a 'violent and expansive force' fundamentally 'tied to the notion of democracy as absolute power', to use Antonio Negri's words. In other words, constitutionalism treats the constituent power of the multitude as an *insurgency* of some kind, and defines itself as insurgency's *counter*. The constitutionalism that undergirds the modern state presupposes that there cannot and should not be any constituent power *outside* the constitutional machine.[92] Any such power is, by definition, insurgent.

The 'constitutionalism' that runs through state theory is essentially and necessarily regarded as part of the need for the state to *counter insurgency*, and is therefore, like the state itself, tied to the historical project of pacification. The peace of constitutionalism, rooted in the wider fiction of the social contract through which 'civil peace' is said to ensue, is the 'peace' of pacification. Such peace is itself rooted in the idea of the state possessing a monopoly over the means of violence. The state's violence becomes the only legitimate form of violence (forgetting, in the process, its own founding violence). All other forms are rendered illegitimate, and anything that threatens or even questions the state's authority and power in this respect is regarded as quintessentially

91 Hobbes, *Leviathan*, pp. 67, 101, 103, 125, 189, 232, 254.

92 Antonio Negri, *Insurgencies: Constituent Power and the Modern State*, transl. Maurizia Boscagli (Minneapolis: University of Minnesota Press, 1999 [1992]), pp. 10–11, 161.

insurgent. Constitution binds us, bringing with it the *stability* of the *state* and not the civil war of *stasis*.

By the time the state was becoming the crucible of political power, what was also becoming apparent was the state's commitment to pacifying the civil society with which it had emerged. Civil society was considered 'civil' only so long as it did not succumb to 'civil' war. 'Civil war' became a concept indispensable to the theory of the state and the state's project of pacification, because, from the birth of the theory of the state, civil war could be seen only as a threat to political order and sovereign power. Despite the comment above suggesting that Hobbes sees civil war as a collapse back into the state of nature, we do not really need to follow those commentators who argue that civil war, as a war seemingly of 'all against all', is precisely such a collapse. Why? Because one does not really need a conception of the state of nature to recognize the power held by the idea (and fear) of 'civil war', which carries with it the profound implication that pacification is not working.

Avoiding civil war is the very thing for which 'all Civill Government was ordained', Hobbes insists.[93] The issue is not so much the question of the state of nature as it is the divisions within the civil order that might generate civil war. 'In the time of Sedition, and Civill War . . . there are two Chiefe Commands made out of one.'[94] One obvious division, especially in the context of England in the mid seventeenth century, is between parliament and king. A second obvious division is between the spiritual and the civil power, church and state. Hobbes, who admitted to submitting to the Church of England only because it is the spiritual authority authorized by the secular sovereign power whose subject he is, opens Chapter 43 of *Leviathan* by claiming that 'the most frequent praetext of Sedition, and Civill Warre . . . hath a long time proceeded from a difficulty, not yet sufficiently resolved, of obeying at once, both God, and Man.'[95] In *De Cive*, he writes that the point of having one unified authority is because, without such authority, civil war between church and state is bound to follow. This very problem was the source of much discussion about the need for pacification during the seventeenth century – especially in work published during the 1640s, such as Henry Parker's *The*

93 Hobbes, *Leviathan*, p. 372.

94 Hobbes, *De Cive*, p. 182.

95 Hobbes, *Leviathan*, pp. 307, 402–3.

Oath of Pacification (1643) and John Saltmarsh's *A Peace but No Pacification* (1643).

As is clear from these two more obvious examples of divided power, just as the division between two sovereign powers leads to relations that are naturally hostile and generates the possibility of war between them, the same is true when one has divisions within the body politic: any states that permit factions within 'do as much as if they received an enemy within their walls.'[96] But beyond the divisions between the spiritual and civil power, and between king and parliament, might there be another, and even more fundamental division at stake, one that points to an even wider pacificatory project?

I cited above Hobbes's comment to the effect that man can never be without some incommodity or other. Here we might add the point he makes at the end of the passage: the greatest 'incommodity' that can happen to the people are 'the miseries, and horrible calamities, that accompany a Civill Warre; or that dissolute condition of masterlesse men, without subjection to Lawes, and a coercive Power to tye their hands.' Civil war is here intimately connected to a condition of masterless men, to the extent that they are effectively equated. After all, 'amongst masterlesse men, there is perpetuall war, of every man against his neighbour.' This is not the same as the war of all against all in the state of nature, because the fact that *some* are deemed 'masterless' implies that *some* form of mastery has already been brought into existence against which their masterless condition can be compared. A large part of their threat lies in the fact that the masterless live among the multitude of the poor, those 'needy men, and hardy, not contented with their present condition,' and who are 'enclined to continue the causes of warre; and to stirre up trouble and sedition.'[97] The fact that the masterless lack a coercive power binding them to law and keeping them pacified is the reason they can be imagined as one of the fundamental problems of political order. By virtue of being inherently disorderly, their 'masterlessness' is the most fundamental form of disobedience.

Hobbes's arguments draw on the historical experience of the pacification of the masterless people of England and Europe, generated out of the ruins of feudalism and yet not fully integrated (as workers) into the

96 Hobbes, *De Cive*, p. 266.
97 Hobbes, *Leviathan*, pp. 70–1, 149.

new society being formed from those ruins. On the one hand, such people have too much time on their hands, 'having little employment', Hobbes writes in *De Cive*, and 'are least troubled with caring for necessary things'. In *Leviathan*, he compares those who 'keepeth attent on their trades, and labour', with those whose 'sloth carrieth after their sensuall pleasures'.[98] It is the lazy but able-bodied that concern him – that is, those who can and should be working but who appear not to be doing so. One solution to this problem lies in forced labour: 'Such as have strong bodies . . . they are to be forced to work'. 'To avoyd the excuse of not finding employment, there ought to be such Lawes, as may encourage all manner of Arts; as Navigation, Agriculture, Fishing, and all manner of Manifacture that requires labour.' A further solution is transportation to the colonies and forced labour:

> The multitude of poor, and yet strong people still encreasing, they are to be transplanted into Countries not sufficiently inhabited: where neverthelesse, they are not to exterminate those they find there; but constrain them to inhabit closer together, and not range a great deal of ground, to snatch what they find; but to court each little Plot with art and labour, to give them their sustenance in due season.[99]

Here we have Hobbes dealing with a problem that is not the state of nature, but neither is it reducible to the English Civil Wars – yet is a problem that takes us to the heart of pacification.

By the time Hobbes was writing, the description of the able-bodied unemployed being 'masterless' was a common way of defining the vagrant or vagabond. The various laws against vagabondage and the statutes of labourers all confirm this. The Act for the Punishment of Vagabonds, and for Relief of the Poor and Impotent, was passed in 1572, and is known as the 1572 Poor Law. It allowed for the punishment of masterless people such as 'fencers, bearwards, common players of interludes, and minstrels (not belonging to any baron of this realm, or to any other honourable person of greater degree), wandering abroad without the license of two justices'. Such people could be whipped and burned through the right ear with a hot iron. Many other such Acts either simply

98 Hobbes, *De Cive*, p. 252; Hobbes, *Leviathan*, p. 236.
99 Hobbes, *Leviathan*, p. 239.

repeated such punishments, tweaked them into punishments anew, or added more. As I have argued at length elsewhere, vagrancy is a crime of status rather than action. The fact that it remains so to this day draws our attention to the fundamental centrality of vagrancy law to the modern state and its policing of the market. Vagrants can be arrested, disciplined and punished not because of something they have done, but because of what they are. And what the original legislation made clear is that they are *masterless*. Historically speaking, having thrown off the mastery of feudal bondage, the vagrant had failed to accept the new forms of mastery then coming into being: on the one hand, the mastery of capital, and hence their submission as waged labour in the new mode of production; on the other hand, the mastery of the newly emerging state that was required to police that new mode of production. The status of the 'masterless', therefore, was and remains an offence to bourgeois law and order: 'These that beinge ydle, without any occupation, without landes, fees, wages, doo nothynge but complayne . . . of theym that be gouernours of the realme: And thus eyther sow sedition amonges the people, or els be the feldes them selfe apt to brynge forth such fruites.' So claimed one text, the title of which reminds us of what was at stake: *A Remedy for Sedition*.[100]

When Hobbes, in the opening pages of *Behemoth*, lists the range of factions behind the civil wars in England that I mentioned above – from papists to Anabaptists, from Quakers to lovers of liberty – he also includes as a cause of civil war an unnamed mass of people who are able-bodied but unable 'honestly to get their bread'. This is a 'multitude of ignorant people', people 'ignorant of their duty', slothful, with too little employment. These are the ones susceptible to being influenced by seditious factions.[101] They are 'the Giddy Rabble', as he calls them in *Vita Carmine Espressa*, or the 'giddy people', as he describes them in the dedication of *De Cive*, 'invited by their vacancy' to the easy temptations of the seditious blockheads. Their 'easy reading of histories, politics, orations, poems, and other pleasant books' leads to 'disputation among themselves concerning the commonweal'.[102] On the one hand, Hobbes believes they are the multitude whose judgment can be dismissed, as he

100 R. Morison, *A Remedy for Sedition* (London: n.p., 1536), no pagination.
101 Hobbes, *Behemoth*, pp. 38–9, 41, 68.
102 Hobbes, *De Cive*, p. 252.

puts it in his Preface to his translation of Thucydides. On the other hand, the danger is always that they will become susceptible to the seditious blockheads. This latter point opens the space for a major theme in the prose of pacification: how to separate the insurgents from the people (in Hobbes's terms, the seditious blockheads from the giddy rabble). We might pause here on Hobbes's presentation of the people as giddy.

'Giddy' comes to us from the Old English *gidig*, meaning insane, mad, foolish and stupid, also with connotations of anger, and is connected to the Old Germanic *gudom* (God), hinting at the mind being possessed by God. By the time Hobbes was writing, it was widely used as a term of contempt for the multitude:

> Whilst the giddy people, or confused multitude are cried up, and placed in the Throne to judge their Judges, who can hope for no mercy from them, there being no such Tyrant as are the people, when once they can get the power into their hands.[103]

> If the common Vote of the giddy multitude must rule the whole, how quickly would their own interest, peace, and safety be dash't and broken? It is not *vox*, but *Salus populi* that is the supream Law.[104]

> The giddy multitude judge weakly, fancy strongly, and act passionately; and, unless restrain'd by wary and sober Laws, will drive on so furiously in a good cause, till they run their Religion into Folly and Faction, and themselves into tumults.[105]

As the tone of this last passage makes clear, even an anti-Royalist did not necessarily trust the 'giddy people' – although, as Hobbes suggests in *Vita Carmine*, King Charles had 'rul'd the Giddy Rabble without Law'. The giddy people are the rabble, the disorganized multitude, ignorant, uninformed, unreflective, often tumultuous, susceptible to the nonsense

103 Captain Jones, *Plain English: or, The Sectaries Anatomized* (London: n.p., 1646), p. 17.

104 Anon., *Salus Populi Solus Rex: The Peoples Safety Is the Sole Soveraignty, or The Royalist Out-reasoned* (London, n.p., 1648), p. 10.

105 Samuel Parker, *A Discourse of Ecclesiastical Politie Wherein the Authority of the Civil Magistrate Over the Consciences of Subjects in Matters of External Religion Is Asserted* (London, n.p., 1671), pp. 152–3.

spouted by the seditious factions. The giddy people are also liable to grow angry, becoming a *raging* multitude (see Chapter 4).

A 'multitude', for Hobbes, is 'naturally not *One*, but *Many*'. In other words, a multitude is not a people, nor can it form a commonwealth. 'The multitude, as the dirt and dregs of men', must be 'formed into a civil person'.[106] In the form of a civil person, the people is *one*, possesses *one will*, to which *one action* may be attributed. None of this can be said about the multitude, which can become a unity (a civil person) only by *sovereign power*; this is pacification's *building project* (see Chapter 3):

> A Multitude of men, are made *One* Person, when they are by one man, or one Person, Represented . . . It is the *Unity* of the Representer, not the *Unity* of the Represented, that maketh the Person *One*. And it is the Representer that beareth the Person, and but one Person: And *Unity*, cannot otherwise be understood in Multitude.[107]

A multitude is thus an affront to the people and to sovereign power. It can be made into one – into a person – but *cannot and should not consider making itself one*. To be made into one is its pacification; to act as one is tantamount to enacting a civil war.

Recall Hobbes's comment in *De Cive*, cited above, to the effect that a faction is a multitude of subjects gathered together, who have made a pact or league 'of mutual defence between themselves against all men'. This is the multitude as faction, and thus the enemy within, to be made subject to the widest police power possible. Such powers are diverse – including assassinations, for example. In *Behemoth*, the lead speaker in the dialogue claims that the death of some 100,000 persons in the English Civil War had been caused by factions, and asks whether it would have been better if the 1,000 or so seditious blockheads who had led them 'had been all killed before they had preached'. This would have been 'a great massacre', admits Hobbes ('I confess'), but still would have been better than civil war.[108] More generally, Hobbes recommends a widespread police intelligence programme. In *De Cive*, he advises his readers:

106 Hobbes, *De Cive*, pp. 224, 250; *Leviathan*, p. 118.
107 Hobbes, *Leviathan*, p. 114.
108 Hobbes, *Behemoth*, p. 95.

> for those who will not acknowledge themselves subject to the civil magistrate, and will be exempt from all public burthens, and yet will live under his jurisdiction, and look for protection from the violence and injuries of others, that you would not look on them as fellow-subjects, but *esteem them for enemies*.[109]

Much later in the book, Hobbes makes clear the extent of such a system. No security is possible 'without *spies*', who could 'be compared to spiders', forming webs 'which, extended on all sides by the finest threads, do warn them, keeping in their small holes, of all outward motions'. Such '*discoverers* to ministers of state, are like the beams of the sun to the human soul', and they should have the power to '*search into* and *discover* the counsels and motions of all those who may prejudice' the state.[110]

What emerges out of Hobbes's argument is a theme that will become a core issue within the theory of the state: the founding of the commonwealth ends the war of all against all in the state of nature by constituting a civil order, only then to find within that civil order one potential threat after another, and so one thread in the *logic of war* becomes transposed onto such enemies within, to be *policed* in such a way that rebellion, sedition and revolt, do not happen. Yet, if they are being fought as enemies within, is this not a form of civil war? It would seem so. But has civil war not been banished? Is not the theory of the state a massive disavowal of civil war?

What kind of theory says 'no' to civil war, only to find one enemy after another within the polity against which wars must be fought? And what does this tell us about pacification? That it is deemed to bring peace only to discover that wars need to be fought within the very peace that it has constituted?

Answers to these questions cannot come from within the framework of civil war. Another concept is needed, one which will help us make sense of pacification and of the concept of police. That concept is social war. To understand why, we first need to outline some of the difficulties with the concept of civil war.

---

109 Hobbes, *De Cive*, p. 104. Emphasis added.
110 Ibid., p. 261. Emphases in original.

Social war

'Civil war' entered the modern world with a remarkable amount of 'accumulated awkward baggage', writes David Armitage.[111] As we have seen, the term played a key role in the bourgeois theory of the state that emerged with capitalist modernity. But it also became an indispensable concept for revolutionary movements, which came to treat capitalism itself as a form of civil war. In the *Manifesto of the Communist Party* (1848), Marx and Engels moved from the history of class struggle to the simplification of this history in modern society between two great classes, bourgeoisie and proletariat, engaged in a civil war that will culminate in revolution. The struggle between labour and capital is 'civil war in its most terrible aspect', Marx wrote in 'The June Revolution' later the same year. In *Capital* (1867), Marx described struggles over the working day as a 'protracted and more or less concealed civil war between the capitalist class and the working class', and, a few years later, he gave his pamphlet on the Paris Commune the title of *The Civil War in France*.[112] Marx is far from alone in using the category of civil war to describe the class wars raging across the European continent. From the other side of the political spectrum, Carl Schmitt brought together civil war and class struggle, and more recently it has been easy for writers to describe modernity as constituting one generalized and permanent global civil war.[113]

So, with a history running back to the Romans, connected to a rethinking of the logic of *stasis*, running through early-modern state theory, radicalized by Marx, and then applied hither and thither by various others in ways that add to the accumulated and awkward baggage,

---

111 Armitage, *Civil Wars*, p. 237.

112 Karl Marx and Frederick Engels, *The Manifesto of the Communist Party* (1848), in Karl Marx and Frederick Engels, *Collected Works, Vol. 6* (London: Lawrence & Wishart, 1984), p. 495; Karl Marx, 'The June Revolution' (1848), in Karl Marx and Frederick Engels, *Collected Works, Vol. 7* (London: Lawrence & Wishart, 1977), p. 147; Karl Marx, *Capital: A Critique of Political Economy, Vol. 1*, transl. Ben Fowkes (Harmondsworth: Penguin, 1976 [1867]), pp. 409, 412–13.

113 Carl Schmitt, *Theory of the Partisan: A Commentary/Remark on the Concept of the Political*, transl. A. C. Goodson (East Lansing, MI: Michigan State University Press, 2004 [1962]), p. 68; Giorgio Agamben, *State of Exception*, transl. Kevin Attell (Chicago: University of Chicago Press, 2005 [2003]), pp. 2–3; Michael Hardt and Antonio Negri, *Multitude: War and Democracy in the Age of Empire* (New York: Penguin, 2004), pp. 3–4, 69.

'civil war' nonetheless seems to be a concept that we can all grasp without much explanation.

But there is plenty that does need explanation and, more to the point, in relation to a critical theory of pacification, 'civil war' is a little problematic. To be sure, it at least points to *some* fundamental conflicts within the social order. But as a category, and notwithstanding the Marxist tradition, it tends to situate us firmly on a legal-military horizon; or, at least, it is legal-military discourse that has most successfully claimed and appropriated the concept. In this discourse, civil war is treated as presupposing armed groups (two opposing sides wanting to form a government), as an issue of international law (rather than internal policing), and feeds into the 'small wars' narrative so beloved of military thinkers. 'Civil war' in that sense has been claimed by the lawyers and military strategists. This is why, as soon as it entered the vocabulary of modern thought, 'civil war' was absorbed into the general framework of the law of nations. In Book III of *The Law of Nations* (1758), for example, Emer de Vattel notes the roots of social conflict in 'rebellion' and 'faction', and then connects these to 'civil war', before subsuming them under the framework of the laws of war:

> When a party is formed in a state, who no longer obey the sovereign, and are possessed of sufficient strength to oppose him, – or when, in a republic, the nation is divided into two opposite factions, and both sides take up arms, – this is called a *civil war*. Some writers confine this term to a just insurrection of the subjects against their sovereign, to distinguish that lawful resistance from *rebellion*, which is an open and unjust resistance. But what appellation will they give to a war which arises in a republic torn by two factions, – or in a monarchy, between two competitors for the crown?

Vattel suggests that we use 'civil war' to describe war between members of one and the same political society, or between factions of citizens and the sovereign to whom they owe obedience, adding that when the rebels acquire sufficient strength to be a serious opposition to the sovereign, the latter must necessarily submit to using the term 'civil war'.[114]

114 Emer de Vattel, *The Law of Nations*, transl. Thomas Nugent (Indianapolis: Liberty Fund, 2008 [1758]), pp. 644–5.

This subsumption of civil war under the general rubric of war, to which the rules of international law are said to apply, continues in later developments, such as the Lieber Code (1863). Formulated by Francis Lieber in the mid nineteenth century, and often treated as the precursor to the Geneva Conventions, the Code has its roots in Lieber's earlier thinking about rebellion, revolution and sedition. In some early notes from around 1850, Lieber worked his way through various terms that could be used to describe different species and degrees of revolution: 'Rising', 'Revolt', 'Riot', 'Insurrection', 'Sedition', 'Rebellion', 'Secession' and 'Civil War'.[115] As he developed what became the Code, arguing that the laws of war apply in civil war, Lieber continued to mull over his terms:

> There is this difficulty shrouding all civil war, that on the one hand the rebel or insurgent is besides being a warfarer, a belligerent, a criminal, that is to be punished or at any rate punishable by the lawful government, and that on the other hand the large number of the insurgents . . . precludes the lawful punishment and leads to those amnesties which are proclaimed while the criminality of the rebel may indeed be the greater.[116]

At this point, notes Armitage, Lieber did not make an especially clear distinction between rebellion and civil war, viewing the latter as possessing the features of both a 'true' or 'just' war and a police action against insurrection. Eventually, however, Articles 149–51 of the Lieber Code came to distinguish 'civil war' from both 'rebellion' and 'insurrection', albeit in terms of degree. The important point, however, is that civil war could be subsumed under the laws of war.

During the century that followed, 'civil war' came to be embraced by international institutions as something that falls under their auspices, not least as they sought 'humanitarian' and 'legal' ways of overseeing such conflicts. As a result, various attempts to rebrand 'civil war' took place, with terms such as 'non-international armed conflict' or 'international conflict of a non-international character'. In 1975, the Institute of

115 Armitage, *Civil Wars*, pp. 183–4.

116 Francis Lieber, 'Laws and Usages of War' (1861–62), cited in Armitage, *Civil Wars*, pp. 185–6.

International Law met at Wiesbaden to develop a statement on 'The Principle of Non-intervention in Civil Wars'. Defining 'civil war' as 'armed conflict not of an international character', the Principle of Non-intervention sought merely to stop such conflict escalating into international conflict, and permitted intervention only of a 'humanitarian' kind. Significantly, Article 1 makes clear that the term 'civil war' does not cover 'local disorders or riots' or 'conflicts arising from decolonization'. But, in that case, what kinds of conflicts are these last two? Moreover, what kinds of conflicts are the many other 'wars' of modernity in which so many lives are lost, and bodies and minds injured – those classic 'wars' declared by the state and carried out through the full range of police power, such as the war on crime, the war on vagrancy, the war on poverty, and the war on drugs? Defined as wars by the very authority that declares them, and with civil society as their main arena, they somehow manage not to fall under the label 'civil war'. Clearly, there is something odd going on.

It is this oddness, I think, that lies behind Michel Foucault's comment that 'civil war' is 'philosophically, politically, and historically, a rather poorly developed notion'.[117] And yet, despite this insight, Foucault goes on to use 'civil war' it in a way that seems . . . poorly developed. We should take a moment to understand this aspect of Foucault's work.

In a letter written in December 1972, Foucault commented that he was embarking on an analysis of power relations on the basis of 'the most condemned form of war: not Hobbes, not Clausewitz, not the class struggle, but civil war'.[118] He thereby quickly started to treat civil war as 'the matrix of all struggles of power, of all strategies of power, and, consequently, [as] the matrix of all the struggles regarding and against power'. This enabled him to start reading power, the law that it serves, and the myriad 'criminalities' that it combats as 'a particular way of pursuing civil war', and to treat society as the interplay 'between a permanent civil war and the opposed tactics of power'. Civil war is not the breakdown of power, but rather its exercise. 'Civil war and power are not mutually exclusive', he writes, adding that 'civil war takes place on

117 Foucault, *Punitive Society*, pp. 13, 24–8.

118 The letter was to Daniel Defert, cited in Defert, 'Chronology', transl. Timothy O'Leary, in Christopher Falzon, Timothy O'Leary and Jana Sawicki, eds, *A Companion to Foucault* (Oxford: Blackwell, 2013).

the stage of power'. To prove his point he makes a comment that, from our point of view, is quite telling: 'One thing is clear: we are in the midst of social war [*la guerre sociale*], which is not the war of all against all, but the war of rich against poor, of owners against those who have nothing, of bosses against proletarians.' Later in the same lecture, he contends that one example of civil war as the matrix of power is the *constitution of the peasantry as a social class* at the end of the Middle Ages. War? Of bosses against proletarians? Of rich against poor? Of the propertied against the propertyless? A war that constitutes the oppressed as a class? Surely, the term for this is 'class war'? The fact that Foucault refuses to go there – 'not the class struggle, but civil war' – is not the issue for us here, though I will return to the question below. Here, we can simply note that, for Foucault, at this point, 'power is not what suppresses civil war, but what conducts and continues it', and that politics is therefore 'the continuation of civil war'.[119]

It is significant, I think, that in the slightly later lecture course of 1975–76, published as *Society Must Be Defended*, and in *Discipline and Punish*, published in 1975, Foucault's critique of 'civil war' is pushed to the limit. Perhaps Foucault realized that, even in his own hands, 'civil war' would remain rather poorly developed. Either way, the word 'civil' was dropped from Foucault's argument, and politics is read simply as 'the continuation of war by other means', while 'liberal peace' is presented as a coded war. Or, as he puts it in *Discipline and Punish*, and repeats in *The History of Sexuality* (1976), 'politics' has 'been conceived as a continuation, if not exactly and directly of war, at least of the military model as a fundamental means of preventing civil disorder'.[120] I have argued at length in *War Power, Police Power* that the key category to bring into play here is 'police' – but 'police' is a concept Foucault keeps remarkably distant from his account of war. Rather than simply jettisoning the 'civil' in 'civil war', leaving us with only 'war', perhaps a better approach might be the one hinted at by Foucault in the telling passage just cited, to the effect that we are in a war that is

119 Foucault, *Punitive Society*, pp. 13–14, 22, 29, 32.

120 Michel Foucault, *'Society Must Be Defended': Lectures at the Collège de France, 1975–1976*, transl. David Macey (London: Allen Lane, 2003), pp. 15–16, 46–8, 50–1; Michel Foucault, *Discipline and Punish: The Birth of the Prison*, transl. Alan Sheridan (London: Penguin, 1977 [1975]), p. 168; Michel Foucault, *The History of Sexuality: An Introduction*, transl. Robert Hurley (London: Penguin, 1979 [1976]), p. 93.

not the war of all against all but between rich and poor, owners and the dispossessed, bosses and proletarians – what he calls *la guerre sociale*, but does not develop as an idea, no doubt worried that he might evoke a little too much the Marxism from which he always seeks to distance himself. Perhaps a better approach is to grasp the concept of *social war*. This might, in turn, help us make better sense of the idea of a *social enemy*, which, it could be argued, is the key figure in Foucault's work on the punitive society, and one that needs to be considered in conjunction with the idea of 'internal' ('civil'? 'social'?) war.[121]

In other words, why not *social war*? After all, if *social enemy*, then why not *social war*? If *social revolution*, then why not *social war*?[122] And if *martial law* – a concept that in its modern guise of 'emergency' has shifted from being a means of regulating the military to one of regulating the social order – then why not *social war*?[123] Might 'social war' be one of critical theory's lost concepts? And, if it is, could its recuperation help us get at something important in the prose of pacification? Might pacification be *social war carried out by the state*?

The concept of 'social war' has had a rather chequered history. The Romans certainly had such a term, as well as 'Servile Wars', referring to conflicts fought by or against slaves (*servi*), such as the Spartacus revolt in 71 BCE. The war between Rome and its Italian allies (*socii*) from 91 to 87 BCE is often known as the Social War, which is how it was described at the time – for example, by Cicero in 'Against Verres', and Appian in *Civil Wars*. Appian outlines how Gracchus's agrarian proposals created a problem between Rome and its 'allies', following which the Social War took place between the Romans and Italians who sought Roman citizenship.[124] But the 'social' nature of the war lay not just in the question of citizenship. As Marx points out, Appian highlights the economic dimensions of the conflict between the senators and the common people of Rome, and he offers a sympathetic treatment of the material grounds of

121 Foucault, *Punitive Society*, pp. 33–6, 44, 61–7, 149–50; Stuart Elden, *Foucault: The Birth of Power* (Cambridge: Polity, 2017), pp. 87–91.

122 In what is now a classic text, *States and Social Revolutions* (Cambridge: Cambridge University Press, 1979), Theda Skocpol has plenty to say about 'social revolution' and much to say about 'civil war'. But 'social war'? Nothing.

123 On martial law, see Mark Neocleous, *Critique of Security* (Edinburgh: Edinburgh University Press, 2008), pp. 42–59.

124 Appian, *Civil Wars*, pp. 20-29.

Tiberius Gracchus's attempted reforms – showing us, in effect, that what was ultimately at issue was the question of property and the possibility of what we might call a *social* revolution.[125]

We also find social war discussed by writers deploying far less 'materialist' arguments than Appian. Florus, in his *Epitome of Roman History*, gives accounts of social war and servile war alongside foreign war and civil war. Book 2 of the *Epitome* has chapters on the various seditions conducted by Tiberius Gracchus, Gaius Gracchus, Apuleius and Drusus, but also describes social wars against allies, servile wars against slaves, and specific wars within these, such as the war against Spartacus (the *bellum Spartacium*, not the *seditio* of Spartacus). Florus also makes clear how they slip and slide into one another: 'though we call this war a social war [*sociale bellum*] . . . if we are to tell the truth it was a civil war [*civile bellum*]'.[126] Ampelius, in *Liber Memorialis*, written in either the second or third century, discusses four kinds of wars: Gentile, against foreigners; Social, against allies; Servile, fought against fugitive slaves and their leaders, such as Spartacus; and Civil, between citizens.[127] In Book XVIII of his *Etymologies*, Isidore of Seville identifies four kinds of war: just, unjust, civil (between fellow-citizens), and 'more than civil' (between kinfolk). He cites Lucan's *Civil War* and adds that 'wars are therefore called internal, external, servile, social, and piratical [*interna, externa, servilia, socialia, piratica*]'.[128]

The idea of social war did not disappear with Roman power. In *The City of God*, St Augustine writes of Social Wars, Servile Wars, and Civil Wars (*bella socialia, bella seruilia, bella ciuilia*), but is keen to argue that it was the revolutionary activities of the plebs that caused the Social Wars.[129] In fact, if we fast-forward to the seventeenth century, we find references to 'social war' even during the rise of the theory of the state, albeit still somewhat merged with civil war. Hugo Grotius's little-read

125 Marx, *Capital, Vol. 1*, p. 888.

126 Florus, *Epitome of Roman History*, transl. Edward Seymour Forster (London: Heinemann, 1947), pp. 232–57.

127 Ampelius, *Liber Memorialis*, sect. 41, transl. Furius and Brady Kiesling, at topostext.org.

128 Isidore of Seville, *The Etymologies of Isidore of Seville*, transl. Stephen A. Barney, W. J. Lewis, J. A. Beach and Oliver Berghof (Cambridge: Cambridge University Press, 2006), p. 359.

129 Augustine, *City of God*, transl. Henry Bettenson (Harmondsworth: Penguin, 1972), pp. 104, 124, 126, 890.

text on war in the Low Countries, *Annales et historiae de rebus Belgicis* (written in 1612 but published posthumously in 1657), sets out 'to describe a war, the most celebrated of our time, which you could call social, for good reasons [*quod sociale haud immerito dixeris*]', but adds that 'the war also took the form of a civil war once rival parties had emerged'.[130] Robert Filmer, in *Patriarcha*, written between 1631 and 1642, takes a moment to castigate 'the most flourishing democracy' that was Rome because of the regular dissensions between the nobles and the commons, which led to one sedition after another. 'Also the Gracchian, the Apulian and the Drusian seditions filled the market-places, the temples and the capitol itself with blood of the citizens. The Social War was plainly civil'.[131] Algernon Sydney, who wrote his *Discourses Concerning Government* in response to Filmer, suggests that many of the seditions in Rome were harmless and do not count as 'civil wars', but that this did not apply to 'the servile and gladiatorian wars': 'The gladiators were slaves also, and civil wars can be made only by those who are members of the civil society, which slaves are not. Those that made the *bellum sociale*, were freemen, but not citizens; and the war they made could not be called civil.'[132]

Pushing further into the eighteenth century, we find William Bollan, in *The Freedom of Speech and Writing Upon Public Affairs* (1766), castigating British politicians 'who seem to delight in blood, and are so solicitous to introduce a social war'. Bollan was writing about the relationship between the English polity and its American colonies. In making the point that the British politicians seem ready to bring about a social war, he reminds his readers that Rome 'was brought to the brink of ruin by the social war, occasioned by her refusal to communicate the Roman right'.[133] In similar fashion, Adam Smith refers to the Roman social wars when discussing the various factions in America at that time causing turbulence by their opposition to taxes.[134]

---

130 Hugo Grotius, *Annales et historiae de rebus Belgicis* (Amsterdam: n.p., 1657), p. 1.

131 Robert Filmer, *Patriarcha* (circa 1631–42), in Robert Filmer, *Patriarcha and Other Writings* (Cambridge: Cambridge University Press, 1991), p. 25.

132 Algernon Sydney, *Discourses Concerning Government* (1681–83), (Indianapolis: Liberty Fund, 1996), p. 154.

133 William Bollan, *The Freedom of Speech and Writing Upon Public Affairs Considered* (London: S. Baker, 1766), pp. 158–9.

134 Adam Smith, *An Inquiry into the Nature and Causes of the Wealth of Nations*, ed. R. H. Campbell, A. S. Skinner and W. B. Todd (Indianapolis: Liberty Fund, 1979), p. 622.

That Smith, Bollan and many others had recourse to the concept of 'social war' to make sense of their times, often referring their readers back to the Romans, is not without significance. As J. G. A. Pocock has shown, political thought in the eighteenth century underwent a profound disruption in the context of a debate over the political structure of the English-speaking Atlantic:

> This disruption involved civil war, but was fought over and within the 'empire' rather than the 'realm' – imperfectly distinguished as these terms were – and was therefore capable of being styled in Roman terms a *bellum sociale* rather than a *bellum civile*. The Social War in Roman history was not fought between Roman citizens, but between Romans and their confederates or *socii* who were subject to Roman *imperium* but enjoyed less *jus* than was accorded Roman citizens.[135]

As these examples show, the term 'social war', along with 'servile war', had a life beyond the Romans. And yet, the term never quite found a place in political thought, intellectual history or popular discourse. In contrast to 'civil war', which had and continues to have a great career, 'social war' has been widely abandoned.

In *SPQR*, her history of ancient Rome, Mary Beard suggests that the category 'social war' is decidedly 'modern'.[136] In one sense, this is not quite right. The *Oxford English Dictionary* has an entry for 'civil war', which it describes as entering the English language from the 1550s, but no entry for 'social war' at all, not even as a term that is obsolete, despite the term's clear presence in the English language, as I have noted. In another sense, however, Beard is on to something. The Greeks had no concept of a social realm, in the same way that they had no idea of a police power – a power with which to counter or pacify the 'insurgency' inherent in *stasis*. The Romans began to develop a concept of a social realm, which is how they managed to conjure up the idea of a social war, and this idea of a social realm within which forms of conflict might be played out continues through the centuries, as we have seen. However, it

135 J. G. A. Pocock, 'Political Thought in the English-Speaking Atlantic, 1760–1790: (i) The Imperial Crisis', in J. G. A. Pocock, ed., *The Varieties of British Political Thought, 1500–1800* (Cambridge: Cambridge University Press, 1993), p. 256.

136 Mary Beard, *SPQR: A History of Ancient Rome* (London: Profile, 2015), p. 217.

is only with modernity that the idea of 'the social' comes to the fore, especially through the eighteenth and then early nineteenth centuries. One might have thought this would have encouraged the idea of social war, but in many ways the opposite happened.

The integration into political thought of the idea of the social gave rise to the birth of sociological discourse, which took centre stage as an analysis of the social realm and an account of the 'social question' in particular – namely the question of poverty. What emerged in turn were 'social' versions of other disciplines (social geography, social psychology, sociolinguistics, social history, and so on), and 'social reformers'. The common thread of much of this work was an understanding of the state as designed to manage the social realm for some kind of progressive good (what in Chapter 3 I will discuss as 'social police'). In the event, what emerged was a concept of the social as a peaceful and civilized realm through which movements could emerge that would demand of the state progressive improvements, to which the state was expected to respond. 'The social' came with a 'halo of altruism', and was always already surrounded by a 'benevolent idealism'.[137] This meant that the social simply could not be imagined as a realm of war; war within the body politic once again had to be disavowed. But if we eschew the halo and such idealism, the idea of social war begins to have some mileage. To understand why, let us ask after the figure or figures which, if social war is to be imagined, serve in the role of the social enemy.

The obvious starting point is to note that 'social war' captures most explicitly the most fundamental war raging through the social order: class war. As we have seen, this concept often coincides with 'civil war'. This is one reason why 'civil war' is constantly combined with the idea of 'revolution'. Reinhart Koselleck has shown that, by the eighteenth century, the idea of civil war had 'become something of an abstraction', and was beginning to be supplanted by 'revolution'.[138] In early-modern state theory, such a shift had not been possible. Hobbes, for example, certainly used the concept of 'revolution' in his work in the natural sciences based on his reading of Copernicus, Galileo and Kepler – yet in

137 Respectively: Richard M. Titmuss, *Social Policy: An Introduction* (London: Allen & Unwin, 1974), p. 27; Peter Squires, *Anti-Social Policy: Welfare, Ideology and the Disciplinary State* (New York: Harvester, 1990), p. 9.

138 Reinhart Koselleck, *Critique and Crisis: Enlightenment and the Pathogenesis of Modern Society* (Oxford: Berg, 1988 [1959]), pp. 2, 160–1.

his more directly political texts 'revolution' rarely appears. The 'disorders of the present time' in England, for example, are treated as 'civil war' or 'rebellion', as we have seen, but not 'revolution'. 'Revolution' makes one appearance in *Leviathan*, in the very last lines of the book, where Hobbes mentions 'the revolution of states'. The word also appears in the subtitle of *The Elements of Law, Moral and Politic: With discourses upon moral heads: as of the law of nature; of oaths and covenants; of several kinds of government; with the changes and revolutions of them*, but not in the text itself, even in the long discussion of 'rebellion'. The meaning of these limited uses of 'revolution' can be construed from Hobbes's one use of the word in *Behemoth*, also in the very last lines of the book: 'I have seen in this revolution a circular motion of the sovereign power.'

Hobbes's use of 'revolution' to describe a circular motion is hardly a surprise. This is how the word was originally understood in the natural sciences, and it remains one of its meanings. The decidedly modern idea of 'revolution' as a forward and almost irresistible momentum of politics – its 'pathos of novelty', to use Hannah Arendt's phrase – cannot be found prior to the late eighteenth century. Likewise, the word 'revolutionary' to describe the agent of political revolution also cannot be found prior to that period. Through the eighteenth century, the intellectual tradition known as the Enlightenment increasingly held that its values of progress, civilization and liberality would leave no room for civil war, which was considered antithetical to the enlightened 'revolutions' taking place in science, technology, arts, culture and politics. Koselleck explains that this paved the way for a progressive philosophy of history without civil war but with revolution – though the latter was imagined as steady, civil, liberal, progressive and enlightened. That is, revolution was fine so long as it was bourgeois. Into the nineteenth century, however, 'revolution' increasingly connoted the idea of a process of constant change, in this respect taking at least some of its impulse from the idea of civil war. This contrasted with pre-modern political language, in which, as we have seen, there were plenty of terms to describe the uprising of subjects against a ruler, but no single term that could capture a change in which the subjects might seek to become rulers themselves. Such was one of the possibilities captured by 'revolution' as the concept developed into the nineteenth century.

With a sense of historical (and revolutionary) purpose, this possibility came to underpin many of the debates about 'civil war' (and even war in general).[139]

These developments helped to attach 'revolution' to an anti-capitalist politics, to forms of class struggle, and to the question of poverty as the social question. Concomitantly, as we shall see, 'counter-revolution' could then emerge as a political doctrine, which would coincide in various ways with pacification – until, in the 1960s, 'counterinsurgency' was invented as a concept that brought both together.

By focusing on the question of poverty, the social question shone a spotlight on a condition which for centuries had been considered essential for capitalism to survive and thrive. The assumption had long been that poverty, in the form of the absence of any means of subsistence other than the wage, was necessary to get people to work in order to obtain that wage. 'Banish poverty, you banish wealth', as Bentham put it in his 1796 work on the poor laws.[140] However, as well as being a necessity for getting people to engage in wage labour, poverty, at least in its extreme forms, increasingly came to be seen as a certain kind of social distress, which the new forms of political administration might do something to ameliorate. At the same time, though, poverty also came to be regarded as the material grounds of a new social force – a social movement that might fully radicalize and thereby realize the revolutionary demands inherent in the revolutions of the late eighteenth century. This was the emergence of that entity discussed in the Introduction, the class whose poverty was deemed necessary for wealth to be produced: the proletariat. Thus, social conflicts of all types came to be interpreted in terms of 'class' – the idea of a fundamental *class war* was in place, as was the idea that what was being *policed within the social* was being policed in *class terms*.

Marx's abiding hope was that the modern age would see the radicalization of the class of poverty to the point where it might act to abolish

139 Ibid.; Reinhart Koselleck, *Futures Past: On the Semantics of Historical Time*, transl. Keith Tribe (New York: Columbia University Press, 2004 [1979]), pp. 56–7, 250; Hannah Arendt, *On Revolution* (New York: Viking, 1963), p. 34; John Dunn, 'Revolution', in Terence Ball, James Farr and Russell L. Hanson, eds, *Political Innovation and Conceptual Change* (Cambridge: Cambridge University Press, 1989).

140 Jeremy Bentham, 'Essay 1: Definitions and Distinctions', in *Writings on the Poor Laws, Vol. 1*, ed. Michael Quinn (Oxford: Clarendon Press, 2001), p. 3.

the conditions of its own existence, and thus the generalized human poverty of bourgeois society. This was the basis for Marx's own concept of 'the social', developed against the bourgeois class's concept of 'civil society', and which, as I argued in *Administering Civil Society* (1996), Marx used as a critical rather than a descriptive concept. He used it to begin imagining collective labour as sensuous human activity and the grounds of a *socialized humanity*. The task of revolution, then, is for human beings to organize their forces as *social forces*, to achieve a *socialized freedom*. The outcome is an argument that the only real solution to the social question lies in the revolutionary abolition of the capitalist mode of production. Buttressed by such an argument, by the impetus of the French Revolution, and by the influence of socialists such as Lorenz von Stein – who, in books such as *Socialist and Communist Movements Since the Third French Revolution* (1848), and *The History of the Social Movement in France* (1850), had introduced the idea of the *social movement* (and, within that, of social *movements* struggling for political recognition and gains) – 'revolution' could take on the air of a world-historical event. The agent of this revolution, the proletariat, must fight a war over the social question and abolish its own condition of absolute poverty. That is, the proletariat must fight the social war – the fundamental war of modern times, the war between exploiting and exploited classes. The social war is the class war. Unfortunately, the history of pacification is a history of the various ways in which the ruling class has since the dawn of modernity been one step ahead in this war.

Marx never made much use of the category of 'social war', remaining happy with 'civil war', which he uses even more than 'class war' – not least because he was at pains to try and link the class struggles taking place across the world with struggles understood as 'civil war', such as the one taking place in America in the 1860s. Engels was also happy to describe class struggle as 'civil war'. Yet, at the same time, and probably because he was steeped in military knowledge, Engels also seems to have sensed that 'civil war' was perhaps too close to the military mind, and thus opted to consider the class struggle through the category of social war. In *The Condition of the Working Class in England*, Engels describes a society which pits us against one another, as though we are threats and dangers to each other, in the manner of Hobbes's state of nature. But, under conditions of capitalist manufacture, any such 'war of all against all' takes a decidedly modern, industrial shape, creating a world of 'social warfare' that is openly carried on by the bourgeoisie, which nevertheless seeks to conduct it 'hypocritically, under the disguise of peace'. The war is really a form of 'social war'. 'Everywhere social warfare, every man's house in a state of siege, everywhere reciprocal plundering under the protection of the law, and all so shameless, so openly avowed that one shrinks before the consequences of our social state.'[141] Other Marxists followed Engels in using the phrase 'social war' in this way, but often without saying much about it other than to equate it with class struggle. Examples include Plekhanov in the 'Introduction' to an 1898 Russian edition of *The Manifesto of the Communist Party*; Karl Kautsky in *The Road to Power* (1909) and *Terrorism and Communism* (1919); Victor Serge in *Year One of the Russian Revolution* (1928); Emma Goldman in the second volume of *Living My Life* (1934); Amadeo Bordiga in *Proletarian Dictatorship and Class Party* (1951); and Paul Mattick in the essay cited as an epigraph to this chapter.[142]

The idea of 'social war' is not a rhetorical flourish or metaphor, but a way of understanding real class struggle and the campaign of violence carried out by state and capital, draped in law, conducted under the guise of peace. Viewed from the perspective of capital, social war is nothing less than the operationalization of the police power in the name of pacification. Such war is the fabrication of wage labour and class formation, in which the proletariat is produced through its own engagement in the war, and reproduced through the permanent policing of social order that ensues.

This is why, from the perspective of the ruling class and its political institutions, the proletariat is Social Enemy Number 1 – so dangerous that even demands for reform (the franchise, a ten-hour day, the right to form unions, wage rises to match the cost of living) appear revolutionary. This is an enemy forged within the social order due to the necessities of capital itself; but its exploitation, alienation, misery and degradation mean that it will always be fighting back. This is an enemy whose

141 Frederick Engels, *The Condition of the Working-Class in England* (1845), in Karl Marx and Frederick Engels, *Collected Works, Vol. 4* (London: Lawrence & Wishart, 1975), pp. 329–31, 427, 502, 509, 512, 553–4; Frederick Engels, 'Speech at Elberfeld', 8 February 1845, in Marx and Engels, *Collected Works, Vol. 4*, p. 248.

142 In an important essay – 'Marxism and War', *Radical Philosophy* 160 (2010) – Étienne Balibar comments on Marx's conceptualization of class struggle in terms of a 'civil war' or a 'social war', but it is the former that gets all the attention.

existence is both necessity and threat. As a threat it might be exterminated; but as a necessity it needs to be treated rather than killed: more patient than corpse. It is an enemy within that cannot be expelled or eliminated, since to do so would be the end of the capitalist polity, and it therefore becomes an enemy which must be policed through the mechanisms of law and administration – an enemy, that is, that must be pacified.

Yet this form of the social enemy goes only some of the way in helping us understand the plural social wars of pacification. When revolutionaries and critical theorists discuss 'class war', they tend to do so in a way that points to the fundamental split between classes. But we also know that capital and the state secure their power through myriad other wars, broken down along lines of race, gender, culture, sexuality, religion, and general notions of normality, orderliness, and acceptability – all of which intersect with the class war in countless ways. The profound fear of resistance, revolt and revolution experienced by the ruling class, as it engaged in the historical transformation of the masterless rabble and disorganized multitude into a disciplined working class, also generated a series of equally profound fears about the disorderly, degenerate, disobedient and criminal lives of that class. It continues to do so, in such a way that, just as class war continues to dominate the bourgeois imaginary – contra the regular refrain that class war is over, or that only leftists are interested in such a war, one never has to wait too long for yet another announcement along the lines of 'elite gathering reveals anxiety over "class war" and "revolution"'[143] – so too do the myriad associated wars through which pacification takes place. These are the social wars of modernity, the protracted wars of attrition that generate an image of the social as containing 'social disorders', 'social scourges', 'social menaces', 'social dangers', 'social deviants' and 'social problems'. The same imagination points to the need for a series of political interventions directed towards these defects, interventions grand enough to be imagined as wars – never completely independent from the class war, though the ways in which they are collocated and intersect with the class war are as manifold as the wars themselves. Such wars are a further reason that

143 Andrew Edgecliffe-Johnson, Lindsay Fortado and James Fontanella-Khan, 'Elite gathering reveals anxiety over "class war" and "revolution"', *Financial Times*, 2 May 2019.

'civil war' fails as a category, since these are wars fought largely by one side – the ruling class – through the police power, in order to discipline and punish those considered disorderly or a threat.

All of these – and, more than anything else, the 'social question' of which these other social problems are often considered a part – are assumed to require intervention, regulation, discipline, and sometimes eradication, generating an image of the social that undergirds the project of *social police*. This is why war and police so frequently coincide in the social world: social war as social police, seeking to fabricate good, upstanding, law-abiding, hard-working (wage-labouring) human subjects. This is also why they so frequently coincide in the various police wars through which the working class is managed. Some of these, such as the war on drugs and the war on crime, I have already mentioned, but an exhaustive list is probably impossible. It would include, inter alia, the war on poaching, the war on pauperism, the war on vagrancy, the war on begging, the war on sloth, the war on scroungers, the war on the undeserving poor, the war on hooligans, the war on yob culture, the war on immorality, the war on deviance, the war on illegitimacy, the war on degeneracy, the war on delinquency, the war on feeblemindedness, the war on strikers, and on it goes. To give a couple of examples from outside this standard list in order to illustrate the point, we might make note of the 'war on sodomy' and the 'war on moronism'. In the case of the former, many of the first laws against such acts appeared in statutes for the policing of vagrancy in the urban centres of early modernity, enabling the sodomy police to be most frequently mobilized against working-class men. In the case of the latter, the figure of the moron was invented in 1910, immediately said to constitute a national emergency, and then had war declared against it a few years later. In both cases, the problem was said to exist partly because of the condition of the working class, the propensity to criminality possessed by these figures, and their propensity to cause disorder.[144]

We have arrived at what appears to be an essential, if somewhat intriguing, feature of the modern age: that it explicitly disavows civil war

---

144 Respectively: Christopher Chitty, *Sexual Hegemony: Statecraft, Sodomy, and Capital in the Rise of the World System* (Durham, NC: Duke University Press, 2020); Gerald V. O'Brien, *Framing the Moron: The Social Construction of Feeble-Mindedness in the American Eugenic Era* (Manchester: Manchester University Press, 2013).

and avowedly pursues peace, yet seems to believe only in the reality of war, declaring one social war after another and often going so far as to invent a problem in order to declare war on it.

Central to many such wars is the figure of the criminal, not least because it is this figure that connects many of these wars back to the class war, and to the wars against the criminal's myriad social cousins. A major theme found throughout the early-modern theory of the state, police science and penal theory is that crime is one of the most fundamental breaches of contract, and an affront to private property per se. The criminal trespasses against property, and thereby commits an act of war against bourgeois order. The criminal is at 'War against all Mankind', as Locke puts it.[145] Discipline and punishment are the state fighting back. The criminal as a *social enemy* is transcribed into the theory of the state, along with the outlaw, the pirate, the brigand, the bandit, the fugitive, the hoodlum, the gang member, and many more – all of whom double-up as avatars of rebellion as well as criminality, all of whom must be the target of that most fundamental of war powers, the police. The pre-eminence of the social enemy in such a conception of the state not only helps emphasize the unity of the people (as 'friend') constituted through the power of the state itself, but also facilitates the exercise of the powers of war and police against the seditious blockheads and insurgents (as 'enemy'). State power essentially comes to be defined as a *permanent war on crime*, in which the criminal law operates alongside labour law and administrative law at the heart of the social wars of modernity. This is penal power as war and police, which is to say, as pacification.

The war on crime is the most prominent of the modern state's myriad wars against social disorders, but none of these wars can be permitted to fall under the rubric 'civil war'. The categorical 'no' to civil war coincides with an even more categorical 'yes' to social war. Indeed, not just a 'yes', but a 'yes please', for nothing captures the state's desire more than to fight a war on yet another enemy within. Pacification, then, is a process in which violence in the form of civil war is disavowed and forced from the political theatre, only for violence then to reappear centre stage in the form of one social war after another. Capitalism is governed through a

145 John Locke, *Two Treatises of Government* (Cambridge: Cambridge University Press, 1988), p. 274.

relentless series of permanent social wars, which is to say it is governed through police power. Pacification thus figures as peace *and* war – even peace *as* war. This is how police power comes to be defined as 'keeping the peace' while fighting war after war. This is also why war is woven into the social fabric of the so-called 'liberal peace'. And it is why the prose of pacification, like the prose of police power, is replete with the language of war.

Social wars have no end. Individual wars might come to an end: one hears very little these days about the 'war on morons'. Others have died a quiet death with new forms of liberalization: the gradual emergence of the good homosexual subject has facilitated the demise of the figure of 'the sodomite', and few people outside the theological far right these days want to fight a war on sodomy. But some wars look like they are here for the *longue durée*: there is no sign of a let-up in the endless war on drugs, while the wars on crime and vagrancy are integral to the essence of capitalism itself. Far from being any kind of intellectual aberration or strategic error, wars with no end are a deliberate political strategy, constituting a form of low-intensity warfare carried out by a formless, all-pervasive police power in the name of security. For the Parties of Order and Security to continue to exist, they must insist on society's need for wars of security, and that only they as Parties of Order and Security can save society from the enemies within. For this to work, new social enemies will be invented. And, for new enemies to be invented, nothing works better than playing on fear and making security the supreme concept of bourgeois society.

2

Securitati Perpetuae: Death, Fear, and the Cunning of Security

> *If we knocked on the graves and asked the dead whether they would like to rise again, they would shake their heads . . . With true instinct the ancients put on their tombstones:* Securitati perpetuae.
>
> Arthur Schopenhauer, *The World as Will and Representation* (1859)

It is not clear whether, in making this statement, Schopenhauer had in mind the satirical inscription to which Kant refers at the beginning of his famous 1795 essay on peace. The inscription in question, 'The Perpetual Peace', is said by Kant to have been seen on a Dutch innkeeper's signboard along with the image of a graveyard. In an essay known for its argument for a global community of lawful states and the implicit idea that such a community will lead to 'peace', Kant begins by hinting that *perpetual* peace really comes only with death: you will get peace when you finally Rest in Peace; but, in the meantime, you should commit to law. We might also observe that Kant's title, *Zum ewigen Frieden*, could easily be translated as 'Toward Eternal Peace', rather than the standard 'On Perpetual Peace' – an alternative that has very different connotations indeed, especially given that, just a year previously, Kant had written an essay called 'The End of All Things', which begins with the image of a dying person passing from historical time into eternity.

The politics of *perpetual peace* in Kant's essay, then, perhaps really requires us to think about death rather than law. In that sense, Schopenhauer's twist, substituting perpetual *security*, might simply be a cheeky nod towards Kant. But Schopenhauer was not known for his cheekiness, and although, philosophically speaking, his suggestion that the ancients might have got it right by putting *securitati perpetuae* on their tombstones is unremarkable, politically speaking the idea is completely antithetical to security's status as the supreme concept of bourgeois society, to the extent that the claim might seem nothing less than scandalous.

The claim that security is the supreme concept of bourgeois society is made by Marx in his early work. Working through the late-eighteenth-century declarations of the rights of man and the ideas of liberty, equality and security, Marx notes the contradictions: liberty is oppression, equality is inequality, and security is insecurity. This is why the police power is necessary. Security, as the supreme concept of bourgeois society, is synonymous with the concept of police. For Marx, this is because security functions as the assurance of the egoism of bourgeois society. Marx pursued this in indirect ways through his later work, spelling out the extent to which capitalist modernity generates a global workhouse in which the constant change and uninterrupted disturbance of all social conditions 'does away with all repose, all fixity and all security', while constantly insisting on the value of security.[1]

In previous work, I have pursued Marx's astute insight in different ways, arguing that a *critique of security* needs to be central to critical theory. Security undergirds liberal thought, takes priority over every other liberal value, underpins the powers of war and police, and is always the fallback whenever a thinker is trying to defend capitalism. Security is fundamental to the fabrication of social order and of the legitimation of the powers of war and police.[2] If, today, the world wants to be deceived, then it wants to be deceived in the name of security. *Security is pacification.*

'Fundamental to pacification is security.' Such is the observation made by General William C. Westmoreland, reflecting on his experience

1 Karl Marx, *Capital: A Critique of Political Economy, Vol. 1*, transl. Ben Fowkes (Harmondsworth: Penguin, 1976 [1867]), pp. 617–18.

2 Mark Neocleous, *Critique of Security* (Edinburgh: Edinburgh University Press, 2008); *War Power, Police Power* (Edinburgh: Edinburgh University Press, 2014); and *A Critical Theory of Police Power* (London: Verso, 2021); The Anti-Security Collective, *The Security Abolition Manifesto* (Ottawa: Red Quill Books, 2024).

conducting American pacification efforts against communism. His observation was far from unusual. Robert McNamara, US secretary of defense during the same efforts, once described the war in Vietnam as a 'pacification security job', and Robert W. Komer, US special assistant for pacification, suggested: 'security is the key to pacification.'[3] Everywhere we look, we find the same thought reiterated. 'The prerequisite is security', commented General Thang of the Vietnamese National Government at the Honolulu Conference in 1966, on which I touched in the Introduction.[4] 'Area security (or pacification)', one RAND document reported during the same period.[5] So prevalent was this idea at the time that some writers started to debate the 'new security' inherent in pacification. 'The debate over the meaning of security is most intense', observed one commentator on pacification as 'the link between security and politics'. This was a 'new security', beyond protection, and stretching to include the establishment of commerce and industry.[6] We find 'security' articulated as the grounds of pacification, and pacification justified in the name of security everywhere we look. Jump forward from the attempted pacification of communism in the 1960s and 1970s to the pacification programme known as the war on terror and one finds RAND reports describing 'one of the key elements of pacification – the provision of security', and the claim that pacification is 'best thought of as a combination of security and development'.[7] Or, to give a very different example, when Brazil launched its Unidades de Polícia Pacificadora (UPP – 'Police Pacification Units') in 2008 to clear the favelas, it was

3 General Westmoreland, *A Soldier Reports* (New York: Doubleday, 1976), p. 68; Robert McNamara, 'Memorandum to the President', 14 October 1966, in *Pentagon Papers*, 'Part IV.C.6.a: Evolution of the War: U.S. Ground Strategy and Force Deployments: 1965–1967', p. 85; Robert Komer, 'Memorandum to the President', April 1966, in *Pentagon Papers*, 'Part IV.C.8: Re-emphasis on Pacification, 1965–1967', p. 66.

4 General Thang of the Vietnamese National Government, Speaking to the Honolulu conference, 1966, *Pentagon Papers*, 'Part IV.C.8', pp. 38–9.

5 F. J. West, *Night Pacification Patrolling* (Santa Monica, CA: RAND, August 1969), p. 1.

6 Allan E. Goodman, 'South Vietnam and the New Security', *Asian Survey* 12: 2 (1972), pp. 122–3, 128.

7 Respectively: Angel Rabasa, Lesley Anne Warner, Peter Chalk, Ivan Khilko and Paraag Shukla, *Money in the Bank: Lessons Learned from Past Counterinsurgency (COIN) Operations*, RAND (Santa Monica, CA: RAND, 2007), p. 33; Austin Long, *On 'Other War': Lessons from Five Decades of RAND Counterinsurgency Research* (Santa Monica, CA: RAND, 2006), p. xi.

coordinated through Rio de Janeiro's Security Department, and the Brazilian state claimed to be introducing a *new model of public security*.[8]

Security structures reality in ways that pacify the people subjected to the measures announced in the name of security. Given the place of security as the supreme concept of bourgeois society, and the extent to which we are disciplined into desiring, cherishing and valuing security above all else, as though it were all we could ever hope for, pacification becomes total.

It would be very easy to pursue this argument concerning security as pacification in the most obvious way, by laying out in detail new security measures, new security procedures, new security products and new security policies. But the literature on such things is now immense, and there is really nothing useful to be added to it, just as there is also nothing useful in arguing that these things should be democratized, humanized or better regulated. Rather, I want to take the idea that security is pacification in a different direction, through an argument about fear, insecurity and death.

One of the questions heard many times in response to the critique of security is whether this implies the critic is somehow in favour of *insecurity*. The backdrop to such a question lies in a common refrain concerning contemporary 'insecurities'. It is a remarkable feature of contemporary political discourse that 'insecurity' now figures as predominantly as 'inequality' in the standard criticisms made of capitalism. According to the catalogue of the British Library, over 500 books have been published in English since 2000 with 'insecurity' in their title – almost three times as many as had been published in the previous four hundred years. At the end of 2022, the *Collins Dictionary* announced that its 'word of the year' was 'permacrisis', defined as a period of extended insecurity. This is our world: permanent crisis, extended insecurity.

There is no doubt, then, that we are living in an 'Age of Insecurity', as is suggested by the many books that have that exact phrase as their title. And yet we also appear to be living in an 'Age of Security', according to the same metric. It seems that the more we talk about security, the more

8 I shall have more to say about the UPP as well as the attempted pacification of Vietnam in Chapter 3.

insecure it seems we are becoming. Perhaps this is no surprise. The age of security brings forth insecurity; the age of insecurity undergirds the security industry. A learned insecurity now features as a core political feature of a system that has security as its supreme concept. The volatility that accompanies the dynamism of capitalism creates insecurity after insecurity: vulnerability for the growing mass of proletarianized workers; precarity caused by ceaseless shifts in market forces that we are told are uncontrollable; increasing levels of debt, much of which is literally unpayable (see Chapter 5). Each of these, individually and in combination, are added to the political insecurities we are encouraged to experience day after day, whether in the form of the next crime, terrorist attack or emerging virus, and a culture industry that often appears to have only one message: above all, be afraid.

We have become *securotic* subjects, fabricated as such by the security industry, because the securotic subject is precisely what that industry wants. The securotic subject is the pacified ideal.[9] This is how pacification and security merge, through our own internalization of the fears and desires that underpin the anxiety of security. The security industry follows us in all our actions, thoughts, hopes, and especially fears. Exhibit or express a particular insecurity, and the industry will offer something as a solution. Fail to exhibit or express a particular insecurity, and the industry will suggest that you really should have it, because everyone else does. It will quickly follow up by suggesting that the industry has things to help. Either way, we are inexorably dragged under the security industry's power. The extent of insecurity is untold in an age of security – and the extent of security measures is inexhaustible in an age of insecurity. To repeat: security is insecurity.

'We can never think security without insecurity, and *vice versa*,' observes Mick Dillon, pointing to the 'unified agonal relationship of mutual definition' between the two words. 'Modern usage proposes that there is a state of affairs – insecurity – and the negation of that state of affairs – security.' To this end, Dillon relies heavily on the formulation '(in)security'.[10] The radical ambivalence of this term has led it to become

9 The concept of the securotic subject is developed in Anti-Security Collective, *Security Abolition Manifesto*, pp. 55–74.

10 Michael Dillon, *Politics of Security: Towards a Political Philosophy of Continental Thought* (London: Routledge, 1996), pp. 120, 122, 127.

central to something that goes by the name 'critical security studies', which has become, in effect, a kind of '(in)security studies', the guiding idea of which is that 'society is no longer focused on achieving perfect security', but rather on managing the fact that 'insecurity pervades all'.[11] '*Security* and *insecurity* do not constitute a binary opposition', writes Ole Wæver. 'Both conditions share the security problematique.'[12]

In one sense, the point made by Dillon and Wæver feels right, which is why it has had such mileage in writing about contemporary insecurities. Once security is ensconced as the supreme concept of bourgeois society, and the police power fully operationalized to ensure that security retains that status, a certain *cunning of security* becomes clear. A great deal of cunning has always been required for domination to work, and insecurity is one form of cunning through which security becomes so dominant, whereby we are encouraged to believe that our terror before the abyss of never-ending insecurity is to be removed by an open-ended commitment to security, and thus the security industry. On one side is a cunning that runs through the message of the state: 'more security with the next security measure'. Feeling insecure about terrorism or crime? Accept these security measures, police powers, expansive laws and unrestricted emergency powers. On the other side is a cunning that runs through the message from capital: 'better security with the next security commodity'. Feeling insecure about your body, mind, personality, home? Buy this deodorant, take yoga classes, learn resilience, fit this new surveillance system. It is a cunning that peddles insecurity in order to sell security. Viewed in this way, our orientation to security is the modern world's version of Pascal's wager, at least as reformulated by Louis Althusser. Pascal thought that it was prudent to believe in God, to the extent that one might want to wager that God exists just in case he does exist, and therefore act in ways appropriate to such a belief – to the extent that in the end one really does believe: 'Kneel down, move your lips in prayer, and you will believe.'[13] Security is rather like that: 'Kneel down, repeat the mantra of security, and you will believe.' And inducing

11 M. J. Williams, '(In)Security Studies, Reflexive Modernization and the Risk Society', *Cooperation and Conflict* 43: 1 (2008), p. 66.

12 Ole Wæver, 'Securitization and Desecuritization', in Ronnie D. Lipschutz, ed., *On Security* (New York: Columbia University Press, 1995), p. 56.

13 Louis Althusser, *On the Reproduction of Capital: Ideology and Ideological State Apparatuses*, transl. G. M. Goshgarian (London: Verso, 2014), p. 186.

us to kneel, pray and repeat the mantra requires us to experience something that goes by the name 'insecurity'. Insecurity must be imposed on and experienced by the subject, such that security can be reinforced – but its reinforcement merely generates new or more intense insecurities, making us worry that what is secure is always insecure. The ultimate product is the pacified subject.

In another sense, however, there is something not quite right with the claim that we can never think of security without insecurity. 'Security' in fact existed for a long time before 'insecurity' was coined. In other words, people were for centuries *more than capable of thinking security without thinking insecurity*. Thomas Hobbes, for example, is taken within critical security studies as 'the classic source of modern wisdom about security'.[14] This is one reason why Hobbes appears throughout this book. But, as we shall see, Hobbes has absolutely nothing to say about *insecurity*.[15] What Hobbes does say a great deal about when discussing security is *fear*, especially fear of *death*, which is why these topics will be a central feature of this chapter and those that follow. To think of 'insecurity' as always already unified with security, then, in the form of one single idea of '(in)security', is, at the very least, a poor engagement with historical sources, reading them a little anachronistically. It is also to ignore the centrality of fear and death to security and the prose of pacification.

But the more telling point – one that arises from the basic materialist point that forms of consciousness have no history independent of the material activity of human beings – is that insecurity does eventually emerge and become conjoined with security, but it does so *in the condition of bourgeois modernity*. To put one part of my argument in a nutshell: much as 'security' can be traced back to the Romans, 'insecurity' emerged as an ideological category under capitalism, such that life under capitalism is constituted as fundamentally insecure. Security is insecurity *now*. Bourgeois thought and the prose of pacification have developed a jargon of 'insecurity' that has become part of the cunning of security. Rather than being understood as an unalterable truth intrinsic

14 R. B. J. Walker, 'The Subject of Security', in Keith Krause and Michael C. Williams, eds, *Critical Security Studies: Concepts and Cases* (London: UCL, 1997), p. 67.

15 In retrospect, my earlier *Critique of Security* elides this very point, along with most commentaries on Hobbes.

to the human condition, 'insecurity' needs to be understood as the product of very specific historical circumstances, subsuming within it a long history of fear. For this reason, not only am I doubtful about the use of 'insecurity' as a critical concept, but also, and more pressingly, I want to suggest that if security is insecurity, and security is pacification, then the jargon of insecurity is integral to our pacification. The relentless pursuit of security renders us more insecure; the relentless desire to deal with one insecurity after another sends us in search of the illusion that is security – and fear is at the heart of such processes. Any sense of security we develop is always paid for by an even greater sense of insecurity, once we realize that we lack confidence in the security we think we have gained, leaving us fearful and obedient: pacified.

'In the name of lasting security the leading men and women of the nation states, particularly the most powerful ones, create a state of permanent insecurity', noted Norbert Elias, in an essay written towards the end of his own life. Reflecting on aging, Elias sought to connect some of his earlier and profoundly influential arguments about the civilizing process to the question of death.[16] This becomes clearer in one of his later works, a short book called *The Loneliness of the Dying* (1982), in which he makes the following observation:

> The greater pacification of developed industrial states and the marked advance of the embarrassment threshold in the face of violence gives rise in these societies to a usually tacit but noticeable antipathy of the living towards the dying . . . Thus, a higher level of internal pacification also contributes to the aversion towards death, or more precisely towards the dying. So does a higher level of civilizing restraint.[17]

Whereas pacification in his earlier work was examined through the shift in practices and behaviours that helped turn once dangerous territories into modern spaces of security, Elias here makes a clever move, suggesting that pacification involves a shift in our relationship to death. His book ends with a comment on the ways in which modern society closes

16 Norbert Elias, 'Changes in the We–I Balance' (1987), in Norbert Elias, *The Society of Individuals*, ed. Michael Schröter (New York: Continuum, 2001), p. 78.

17 Norbert Elias, *The Loneliness of the Dying* (1982), transl. Edmund Jephcott (Oxford: Blackwell, 1985), pp. 88–9.

off death, rendering it unknown and unknowable, repressed, placed behind the veils created for it by civilization, leaving death something to be *feared*.

If security is pacification, and if, as Elias suggests, pacification involves a certain kind of elision of death, then we need to consider the relationship between security and death, not least because, in one sense at least, death is for many the greatest fear, and hence the greatest 'insecurity'. The cunning of security as pacification lies in the fear of death in a condition of unfreedom. What is at stake is a fundamental fear of death that comes with living a life pacified in the name of exploitation and domination. Perhaps what is at stake in the jargon of security, then, is nothing less than the two things which we fear but from which we appear unable to escape: capital and death.

'Security some men call the suburbs of hell'

The English word 'security' comes from the Latin *securitas*, a complex word derived from *sine*, meaning 'without', and *cura*, meaning 'troubling; solicitude; carefulness', giving us *securitas*: to be without care and untroubled. As can be seen, there is an immediate ambivalence here, something untranslatable, in that *cura* can express something troubling – such as anxiety or fear – but it can also express something beneficial, such as attentiveness or loving diligence.[18] So, *securitas* as the removal of *cura* can be either beneficial or harmful.

The idea that *securitas* is beneficial is found in the late Roman Republic, in the work of writers such as Cicero and Seneca, the former being the most likely candidate to have coined the term. For Cicero, the *cura* that is cancelled in *securitas* means that *securitas* itself tends to be associated with the *beata vita* ('blessed life') and *tranquillitas animi* ('peace of mind'). 'How can anyone be in possession of that desirable and much-requested security (for I now call a freedom from anxiety a security, on which freedom a happy life depends) who has, or may have, a multitude of evils attending him?' asks Cicero in the *Tusculan*

18 The untranslatability of *securitas* is why it appears as an entry (by John Hamilton) in Barbara Cassin, *Dictionary of Untranslatables: A Philosophical Lexicon* (Princeton, New Jersey: Princeton University Press, 2014), pp. 936–8.

Disputations.[19] The peace of mind that Cicero calls *securitas* refers to an internal stability and feeling of peace. 'We must empty ourselves of every agitation of the spirit – desire and fear, of course, but also sorrow and excessive pleasure and anger – in order to gain that tranquillity of spirit, that freedom from care [*tranquillitas animi et securitas*], which ensures both constancy and standing.'[20] Avoiding being controlled by the passions, most notably fear and desire, was a central tenet of the Stoic attitude, and Cicero stresses the point about fear later in Book II of *De Officiis*. In Book I of the *Tusculan Disputations*, he more explicitly argues against the fear of death, especially if such fear deters the wise person from considering what is best for the Republic. In one of the 'fragments' of *De Officiis*, he comments that 'death will bring us to a condition that is either better than life or at least no worse'. But note that this beneficial aspect of *securitas* makes it a highly personal thing, a question more of moral psychology than of political order, which is itself quite remarkable given how deeply political a thinker Cicero is. For Cicero, the notion of *securitas* tends to apply to the 'private' realm, as distinct from *salus*, with its connotations of safety or protection within the city: hence the expression made famous by Cicero, *Salus populi suprema lex*, refers to the *safety* of the people as the supreme law. He does also refer to statesmen doing well to possess *securitas*, but this is still in reference to a 'tranquillity of mind and freedom from care'.[21] John Hamilton expresses the distinction well: 'Self-therapy produced *securitas*; state therapy engendered *salus*.'[22]

With the collapse of the Roman Republic, however, the earlier Republican distinction between *salus* as public 'safety' and *securitas* as personal 'peace of mind' began to break down – although, in some languages, it never really developed in the first place; Spanish (*seguridad*), German (*sicherheit*) and Italian (*sicurezza*) all combine safety with security – and *securitas* was increasingly employed in a decidedly public fashion.[23] Some authors, such as Seneca in *Epistulae Morales*, increasingly

19 Cicero, *Tusculan Disputations*, transl. W. H. Main (London: W. Pickering, 1824), p. 244.

20 Cicero, *On Duties* (Cambridge: Cambridge University Press, 1991), p. 28.

21 Cicero, *On Duties*, p. 95.

22 John T. Hamilton, *Security: Politics, Humanity, and the Philology of Care* (Princeton, NJ: Princeton University Press, 2013), p. 59.

23 Ibid., pp. 58–9, 186.

connect the idea of an inner security with the idea of the security that is provided by the state. 'What is the happy life?' asks Seneca. Answer: 'It is peace of mind, and lasting tranquillity [*securitas et perpetua tranquillitas*].'[24] Tacitus makes a similar point in his book on Julius Agricola, the governor of Britain in the second half of the first century.[25] During the first century, *securitas*, and even *securitas perpetua*, begin to appear on coins and medallions (along with *pax*), hinting at an increasingly public and political dimension to the concept, certainly in its connotations of imperial propaganda – but also, like *pax*, hinting at questions of *internal* security.[26]

All of this might be taken to suggest that *securitas* becomes political with the Romans and then stays with us, which would make for a nice and even story. Unfortunately, that is not the story. For the fact that *securitas* could imply the removal of a careful attention meant that it could also be seen as something negative, connoting a freedom from concern about danger, and thus a state of *carelessness*. This is what took place with the rise of Christianity, for which *securitas* remained a personal peace – but, crucially, this is a personal peace that comes through union with God.

Augustine, for example, understands security as a blessed state, but its blessedness points to the fact that *true* security is only possible posthumously. 'There is no security' except through God, Augustine claims in *The Confessions*.[27] In the *City of God*, he is even more explicit, suggesting that 'in this situation of weakness and these times of evil such anxiety is even not without its use in leading them [worshippers] to seek, with more fervent longing, that state of serenity [*securitas*] where peace is utterly complete and assured.'[28] Security, like peace, ultimately comes with eternal life. Herein lies the basis of Schopenhauer's observation about the inscription on ancient tombstones – *Securitati perpetuae*

24 Seneca, *Ad Lucilium Epistulae Morales*, Vol. II, transl. Richard M. Gummere (London: William Heinemann, 1920), p. 449.

25 Tacitus, *Agricola and Germania*, transl. Harold Mattingly (Harmondsworth: Penguin, 2010), p. 2.

26 Erika Manders, *Coining Images of Power: Patterns in the Representation of Roman Emperors on Imperial Coinage, A.D. 193–284* (Leiden: Brill, 2012), pp. 205–11.

27 Saint Augustine, *The Confessions*, transl. Henry Chadwick (Oxford: Oxford University Press, 1991), p. 32.

28 Augustine, *City of God*, transl. Henry Bettenson (Harmondsworth: Penguin, 1972), p. 864.

– and of Nietzsche's observation that the Christian's strength lies in the delusion of being secured by God.[29] What greater security could there be? The implication of this, however, is that, because security is a blessed state in the eternal realm of peace in which we are freed from the troubled nature of earthly existence, to claim security in this world is nothing less than an insult to God. One of the dangers on Earth is that 'one should sin with deadly security [*mortiferas securitas*]', Augustine claims in *Of Holy Virginity*.[30] Hence, to think of oneself as *secure in this world* – or as we might now say, to try and be *free from insecurity* – undermines the ideal of and desire for real security, which comes only with the perpetual peace of death. Here lies the centrality in the Christian tradition of Paul's first epistle to the Thessalonians (4:13–5:3): after some of the Thessalonians that Paul had converted to Christianity die, those remaining ask questions about the status of the deceased, and Paul insists that 'through Jesus, God will bring with him those who have died'. The trumpet shall sound, heaven will call, the dead will rise, and the living will witness the Second Coming. 'You yourselves know well that the day of the Lord comes like a thief in the night', Paul insists. In the meantime, if people say 'there is peace and security', then destruction will come upon them. Peace and security come at the end of time, not in the ways in which this world is ordered politically. Until that time, all we can do is remain alert and vigilant, wear a breastplate, don a helmet. Paul's comment is one which Hobbes will put to good use, as we shall see. One finds the point reiterated through the Christian tradition. In his *Exposition on the Book of Blessed Job*, written in the late sixth century, Pope Gregory I (Saint Gregory, Gregory the Great) comments that 'security is often the parent of negligence', and adds that 'to keep security from generating carelessness, it is written, *My son, in coming to the service of God, stand in justice and fear*.'[31] The last of Martin Luther's Ninety-Five Theses (1517) likewise exhorts us to be confident of

29 Friedrich Nietzsche, 'Notebooks of November 1887–March 1888', in *Writings from the Late Notebooks*, transl. Kate Sturge (Cambridge: Cambridge University Press, 2003), p. 235.

30 Augustine, 'Of Holy Virginity', in Augustine, *Seventeen Short Treatises* (Oxford: John Henry Parker, 1847), p. 348.

31 St. Gregory the Great, *Morals on the Book of Job. The First Part of Volume III, Part V and Books XXVIII, XXIX* (Oxford: John Henry Parker, 1847), p. 69. Emphasis in original.

entering into heaven 'through many tribulations rather than through the security of peace'.[32] For Luther, people who think of themselves as secure are those who no longer put their faith in God – a condition which renders them unable either to work or to pray; *fiducio*, like *certitudo*, is better than *securitas*.

All of this goes some way to explaining why it is that the early references to security in the *Oxford English Dictionary* are to a *negative* state: 'our vayne glory, our viciousness, avarice, ydleness, security' (1564); 'they . . . were drowned in sinneful securitie' (1575). Shakespeare in *Macbeth* (1606) has Hecate declare that 'security is mortal's chiefest enemie'. Security here is a careless, dangerous, and in most cases sinful confidence. But security also figures as just plain dull. 'Security some men call the suburbs of hell', says the malcontent Bosola in John Webster's *The Duchess of Malfi* (1612–13), pre-empting the connection Marx makes between security and the monotony of bourgeois life.[33] This is captured in the wider literature of the sixteenth and seventeenth centuries. For example, a 1585 sermon by Edwin Sandys, archbishop of York, has him commenting that 'we sleep as well in security as in sin'. Because the world is one of perpetual warfare against God's adversaries, 'there is no place of security left for a Christian soldier', and 'there is nowhere any place wherein it is safe to be secure'. People have in the past sought peace, but 'their peace bred plenty; their plenty, their security; their security, their destruction'. Hence the message: 'watch, therefore, and sleep not in security'.[34]

We find a similar message in many other texts: in John Stockwood's *A Very Fruitfull and Necessarye Sermon of the Moste Lamentable Destruction of Jerusalem* (1584), where the author exhorts us to avoid being 'lulled a sleepe in the cradle of securitie or carelesnesse'; in Johann Habermann's *The Enimie of Securitie; or, A Daily Exercise of Godlie Meditations* (1591); and in William Est's *The Scourge of Securitie; or, The Expulsion and Returne of the Uncleane Spirit* (1609). Likewise,

32 Martin Luther, 'The Ninety-Five Theses', in *First Principles of the Reformation, or The Ninety-five Theses and Three Primary Works of Dr. Martin Luther*, transl. Henry Wace and C. A. Buchheim (Philadelphia: Lutheran Publication Society, 1885), p. 13.

33 Karl Marx, 'Economic Manuscript of 1861–63', in Karl Marx and Frederick Engels, *Collected Works, Vol. 30* (London: Lawrence & Wishart, 1988), p. 309.

34 Edwin Sandys, 'The Eleventh Sermon' (1585), in *The Sermons of Edwin Sandys* (Cambridge: Cambridge University Press, 1842), pp. 210–12.

John Downame's *Guide to Godlynesse* (1622) has as part of its long subtitle the suggestion that it includes *A Treatise of Carnall Securitie*. That part of the book was published separately as a shorter book, called *A Treatise of Security*. Downame exhorts his readers to rise out of the 'lethargy of carnal security', and lists among the causes of security an ignorance of God, customable sinning, the impunity of sinners, and the neglect or contempt of the means of grace. Security, for Downame, is 'the mother and nurse of all other wickedness' and 'deprives us of eternal happiness'. This builds on his more famous work, *The Christian Warfare Against the Devil, World and Flesh* (1609–18), in which Downame writes of the dangers of people being lured by 'carnal security' and lulled into the 'cradle of worldly vanities'. Robert Burton, in *The Anatomy of Melancholy*, published in various editions between 1621 and 1651, suggests two pieces of advice for warding off a melancholy despair: first, rely on God's word, and second, reject 'perverse security'. Better to live in danger than in security, he writes. Better to accept the afflictions and tribulations of life, because 'by such like crosses and calamities we are driven from the stake of security'.[35] The theme continues into late in the century: a sermon published in 1672 called *Security Surprized, or, The Destruction of the Careless*, denounces those who go about in sin and 'horrible security'. 'Consider the evil of this security you are in . . . when you cry peace, peace to your selves in the midst of God's displeasure. It is an evil disease, a spiritual lethargy.' And the sermon makes clear that this applies to people, nations and kingdoms, all 'drowned in drunken security' and a 'spiritual Lethargy that leadeth to death'. Death was brought upon Sodom and Gomorrah precisely because of their security.[36]

Throughout much of Christianity, then, *securitas* is largely a pejorative term describing a sinful condition, a lethargy, an ignorance of God and a source of wickedness. One might *seem* secure, but this is highly deceptive, being a false security and thus undesirable. Rather than *securitas*, the Christians were interested in *certitudo*, certainty of faith, and nothing could be worse than to suffer from the carelessness

35 Robert Burton, *The Anatomy of Melancholy, Vol. III* (London: G. Bell, 1913), pp. 188, 469, 486–7.

36 The text is 'Sermon XII' in Martin Day, ed., *Thrēnoikos: The House of Mourning, Furnished with Directions for, Preparations to, Meditations of, Consolations at, the Hour of Death: Delivered in LVI Sermons* (London: John Williams, 1672), pp. 143–58.

of a security that leaves one even more 'insecure' (as we would now put it) than ever. The Christianization of the Empire therefore meant that the positive connotations of *securitas* found in authors such as Cicero more or less vanished from political and religious usage, making it difficult to find any positive connotations of *securitas* in the Christian tradition. Although some such connotations can be found in a few legal contexts, Hamilton notes that the term *securitas* was, in general, 'not explicitly employed as a political or philosophical concept in any sustained manner before the fourteenth century'. What we find instead is a range of other words closer to what we understand as 'safety' (*salus*), 'certitude' (*certitudo*), and 'peace' (*pax*). In that sense, the concept of security has only really entered European political thought when institutions that had historically claimed to offer stability and cohesion, most obviously the church, have begun to weaken.[37] When it has done so, the meaning of *securitas* oscillates between an inner, subjective sense of composure and an external, objective sense of a public safety, the two dimensions circulating around each other, becoming part of the cunning of security, and providing the grounds of its pacificatory nature.

'Let every man go about without fear'

With that in mind, let us pause for a moment on Ambrogio Lorenzetti's so-called 'Good Government' and 'Bad Government' frescoes from the early fourteenth century. Since this series of three large paintings has been described as offering 'the most famous artistic political allegory of the fourteenth century', and has been a major point of political discussion in the history of ideas, art history, and political theory, it is worth considering what they have to say about security.[38] At the same time, however, I want to use them to consider what they manifestly do *not* say about insecurity, but what they do imply about fear, death, and punishment. This will allow me to proceed into a discussion of the same issues in the work of Thomas

37 Hamilton, *Security*, pp. 63–4, 137.

38 William M. Bowsky, *A Medieval Italian Commune: Siena under the Nine, 1287–1355* (Berkeley, CA: University of California Press, 1981), p. 283.

Hobbes and Adam Smith, drawing out some of the points I want to make about death and pacification.

Lorenzetti's paintings occupy three complete walls of the Sala dei Nove in the Palazzo Pubblico in Siena. This room was the main chamber of the Council of Nine, the ruling officials of the increasingly dominant merchant oligarchy that governed Siena between 1287 and 1355. The frescoes were commissioned by the Council, and produced between 1337 and 1339.

There are three walls. On the northern wall, in the middle and hence centre stage, is Peace, the central figure of the central image. Alongside Peace we have virtues such as Faith, Charity, Hope, Justice and Concord. The figure in the middle appears to be a king, but since Siena was a republic the figure is seen by some as representing the 'Common Good', and by others as a representative of the type of *signoria* (a type of lordship that at the time represented a neutral form of power), that a city needs to elect if the dictates of justice are to be achieved.[39] On the western wall is what is taken to be Bad Government. Dominated by a figure called Tyrammides, who sits enthroned like a king, but carrying a dagger rather than any of the standard instruments of kingly authority. At the feet of Tyrammides lies Justice, tied up and looking forlorn and unkempt, and also being held on a leash by another figure, reinforcing her submission and defeat. This is in contrast to the image of Justice in Good Government, where she is serene and beautiful. Surrounding Tyrammides are a black, satanic goat and a black hybrid man-beast called Furor; Avaritia, a figure withered by her desire for money; Crudelitas, strangling a baby; Fraus (fraud), a seemingly human woman, but with clawed feet poking out from the bottom of her dress; Vaingloria, admiring herself in the mirror; Divisio, cutting her own wrist with a saw; Guerra, with sword raised. Over the city hovers Timor. In the city itself, the only activities appear to be those of people going off to war, a man being murdered, women being raped, people leaving the city. There are crumbling houses, buildings being destroyed, lifeless streets, shops closed except for the armoury. It is a city of fear and death. Outside the city is a sterile plain, with a few trees that look like they might be dying.

39 Nicolai Rubinstein, 'Political Ideas in Sienese Art: The Frescoes by Ambrogio Lorenzetti and Taddeo di Bartolo in the Palazzo Pubblico', *Journal of the Warburg and Courtauld Institutes* 21 (1958), pp. 179–207.

On the other side of the river are soldiers leaving a burning village – presumably the work of their own hands. Depicted here is an empty, suffering and fearful wasteland, notes Patrick Boucheron, adding: 'this is a dead land'.[40]

On the eastern wall is what is said to be Good Government. On one side of the city wall is the hustle and bustle of the city: people working, shopping, talking, dancing. On its other side is the land just outside the city, where we see a lady going off to hunt with servants and dogs, people tending their cattle and tilling the land – which is itself very fertile, unlike the countryside in bad government. Beyond the city wall there appears no apparent danger. People are at peace and at work on both sides of the wall. Some commentators have noted that, if one follows the line of sight of Peace in the middle fresco, then one discovers that she is looking directly at this image. In other words, this is literally the 'vision of Peace'.[41]

Overlooking the whole scene of Good Government is Securitas, hovering in the sky, overseeing town and country, and thus guaranteeing the good order of the city. Securitas holds a banner with the words:

> Let every man go about without fear
> And let every man sow
> While this lady rules the land
> For she has taken the power from all the guilty.

The city is under the rule of Securitas. Securitas enables work and leisure. Securitas oversees the peaceful and commercial city. Securitas ensures good order. Securitas appears as both the desire and the product of the rising merchant class whose ruling oligarchy would meet in this very room to discuss, under the sign of security, how best to manage the commercial order of the city.

---

40 Patrick Boucheron, *The Power of Images: Siena, 1338*, transl. Andrew Brown (Cambridge: Polity, 2018 [2013]), p. 61.

41 Uta Feldges-Henning, 'The Pictorial Programme of the Sala della Pace: A New Interpretation', *Journal of the Warburg and Courtauld Institutes* 35 (1972); Jack M. Greenstein, 'The Vision of Peace: Meaning and Representation in Ambrogio Lorenzetti's *Sala Della Pace* Cityscapes', *Art History* 11: 4 (1988); Hamilton, *Security*, pp. 138–46, 152–3.

Ambrogio Lorenzetti, *The Allegory of Good and Bad Government*, frescoes (1337–1339), detail of Securitas

In one sense, what we see represented is an image of a social order founded on an institutional imposition of security. It is worth noting in passing that the statutes of Siena, established in 1319–20, held that the Nine should be chosen from the merchant or 'middling' class. It is also worth noting that Siena itself is, at this moment, at a key stage in the history of police power, having become an experiment in policing. In this policing, there were a number of different forces in operation: the *quattrini*, charged with daytime custody of the city and numbering around a hundred; the captain of the people, with a small force of between ten and twenty; the force of the *Podesta*, the town's chief magistrate, of around forty, established by the constitution of 1337; the war captain's force, of between fifty and a hundred; and the force of the Nine, also around a hundred strong. William Bowsky calculates that, all told, by the mid 1330s there was one 'policeman' per 145 inhabitants of Siena – a proportion of police to population far higher than in other cities, such as medieval Florence, but higher too than modern states.[42] This tells us what the subsequent development of capitalism confirmed: a free circulation of goods and people and a thriving commercial class

42 Bowsky, *Medieval Italian Commune*, p. 120.

require a heavily policed city; a heavily policed city is always policed under the sign of security. 'Security' and 'police' are beginning to come together as the supreme concepts of bourgeois society.

Herein also lies the significance of the war that is depicted, since the city is not engaged in an aggressive war against other cities or fighting intruders. Rather, the war is internal. It is a social war being fought by police. It is important to note that, despite being known as an allegory of 'good and bad government', Lorenzetti was, in fact, commissioned to depict 'war and peace'. But what appears to be depicted is civil strife, of the kind that appeared to threaten the developing cities of Italy. That is, the frescoes do not depict good and bad government – but neither do they quite depict war and peace. Rather, they depict war within the city. The frescoes reveal not *polemos*, a war against an external enemy, but *stasis*, a war within.[43] This might, in turn, explain why it is that Lorenzetti places infantrymen and cavalry together. Bringing together two types of violence workers who, in the context of Italian city-states, traditionally operated apart, Lorenzetti has them working together and within the city itself, exercising a constitutive violence across the city. In that sense, we can say that what is being depicted is nothing less than the *pacification of Siena*.[44]

All of this takes us back to the question of security. Lorenzetti's images go some way to capturing what was happening to *securitas* in early modern Europe. Whatever theological tropes remain in the images, *securitas* has developed in three important and overlapping ways: it has started to take on decidedly positive connotations, despite the wider Christian background and context; it has started to connect the inner tranquillity of the soul with the public tranquillity of the city; and it has become increasingly secular and political. All of which is to say that security has started to become the sign of modernity, a policy objective as well as a personal goal within a rising commercial order.

But, even with that in mind, we can note something fundamentally odd about the images: *insecurity is not represented*. The frescos possess a range of opposites: peace versus war; charity versus avarice; concord

---

43 Boucheron, *Power of Images*, pp. 63, 119.

44 Rosa Maria Dessì, 'Il bene comune nella comunicazione verbale e visiva. Indagini sugli affreschi del "Buon Governo"', in *Il bene comune: forme di governo e gerarchie sociali nel basso medioevo* (Spoleto: Fondazione Centro Italiano Di Studi Sull'alto Medioevo, 2012), pp. 89–130.

versus discord, and so on. Yet, despite the formidable presence of 'security', 'insecurity' is not depicted. Insecurity *cannot* be depicted, because insecurity does not yet exist. Insecurity may well be 'talked into existence' through 'discourses of danger', as Jef Huysmans puts it, but at this point in history, whatever dangers existed (and there were plenty of them), 'insecurity' has not been talked into existence.[45] What most certainly does exist, however, is *fear*. The banner of Securitas proclaims loudly: every man should go about the city without fear, not without insecurity. One of the inscriptions proclaims *senza paura*: without fear. To reinforce the point, on the scroll of Timor on the west wall we find the following:

> Because all seek their own good alone
> Justice is in thrall to tyranny
> Thus by this path
> No one passes without fearing death
> Because everything shrinks away, inside and outside the gates.

This dominating presence of fear and complete absence of insecurity must be read in the light of both the final line on the banner held by Securitas ('she has taken the power from all the guilty') and what she holds in her other hand: a figure executed on the gallows. Security, like law, impresses the fear of death within the people.

This somewhat complicates the message that Securitas will allow us to go without fear, for that message now appears to have two dimensions. First, people can go about without fear because Securitas will punish those who commit crimes in the city. In contrast to Bad Government, under which killing takes place on the street because of the absence of security, in Good Government killing takes place on the gallows in the name of security, and by Securitas's hand. But, second, one's fears might now need to be directed towards Securitas herself. The gallows is a reminder that it is Securitas that now holds power over life and death. To reinforce this, we see, on the left of the painting of Good Government, an angel dressed in red alongside two kneeling figures: with one hand the angel is about to decapitate one of them,

45 Jef Huysmans, *The Politics of Insecurity: Fear, Migration and Asylum in the EU* (Abingdon, Oxford: Routledge, 2006), p. 7.

execution-style; but, with the other hand, the angel is offering to the second kneeling figure a reward. The message is clear: Securitas may reward you, but may also execute you. And on the right, we also see a line of men, hands bound as prisoners, under armed guard, also awaiting punishment, possibly of the same sort befalling the person whose decapitated head lies in the lap of the figure of Justice just above them. These executions are a reminder of the sovereign violence that can take place under *securitas*. It is the violence of justice and the violence of pacification. *Securitas* removes fear of one kind of violent death, then, only to replace it with another, reminding us to fear security itself, to fear *securitas* as an apparatus in which the death penalty is necessarily and permanently inscribed, to use Derrida's formulation about sovereignty.[46] For Good Government to persist, Securitas *must hold death in her hands*. This is why a person condemned to death is always condemned in the name of security, and never simply justice. To use the wry formulation of Georg Christoph Lichtenberg, responding to the inscription with which Kant begins 'Perpetual Peace': 'When we walk past a graveyard, we can at least say that its residents can now rest assured that they aren't going to be hanged, which is more than we can.' A similar point was made much later by the psychoanalyst Gregory Zilboorg, who observes that, behind the sense of insecurity, there is always a basic fear of death, which is one reason people so often read about executions, finding pleasure in an unconscious reaction that could be expressed along the lines of 'at least it wasn't me who was executed last night'.[47] We know (or, at least, we believe and hope) that there is nothing as secure as the dead in their coffins; but we also know that, in the name of security, the sovereign power could make us join them sooner than we wish.

Perhaps this is also one reason why cities so often retain the reminders of past executions. In January 1536, in the city of Münster, three Anabaptist leaders, Jan Bockelson, Bernhard Knipperdolling and Bernhard Knechting, were tortured and executed for their rebellious activities, and their bodies exhibited in cages. The Italian

46 Jacques Derrida, *The Death Penalty, Vol. 1*, transl. Peggy Kamuf (Chicago: University of Chicago Press, 2014 [2012]), p. 23.

47 Georg Christoph Lichtenberg, *The Waste Books*, transl. R. J. Hollingdale (New York: New York Review of Books, 2000), Notebook L (1796–99), no. 15; Gregory Zilboorg, 'Fear of Death', *Psychoanalytic Quarterly* 12: 4 (1943), p. 469.

collective Luther Blissett observes in *Q*, its novel set in Reformation Europe, that this was intended to be a 'warning to the whole of Christendom':

> Three cages hang from the bell tower. Empty.
> No one looks at them.
> Bockelson, Knipperdolling, Knechting.
> . . .
> No one looks at them.
> The past hangs right over their heads. And if they try to lift their heads too far, the cages are there as a reminder.[48]

The bodies were on display for fifty years, as a reminder. The cages are still there. As a reminder?

Cages in the city of Münster.

48 Luther Blissett, *Q*, transl. Shaun Whiteside (London: Heinemann, 2003 [2000]), p. 568.

One way to read Lorenzetti's paintings is through the lens of what has become a commonplace in the history of political thought – namely, that the image shows us the gradual installation of security at the heart of the conceptions of state and social order. This is, of course, the very story we are told when we are introduced to modern political thought, in which we are taught that security comes to form the underpinning dynamic of modern ideas about sovereignty, and that it does so because of the *insecurity* experienced by human beings. The insecurity of the state of nature leads us to create the social contract and the state, we are told; and it is the insecurity that remains, even after the creation of the sovereign, that leads us to accept the ongoing authority of the state. But there is a problem with that story. It is a complex problem that has several overlapping dimensions upon which I have already touched, and which are pertinent to my argument here: first, insecurity is not yet in the picture; second, what is very much in the picture is fear; and third, the key fear appears to be that of death. I want now to unravel this a little through a discussion of Hobbes, because he is widely regarded as the philosopher of security par excellence, as we have already seen. But I also want to use the work of that seemingly anti-Hobbesian liberal, Adam Smith, to extend the point to encompass capital as well as the state, and to explore further the politics of our darkness.

'Acknowledge your darkness'

As we saw in Chapter 1, Hobbes believes that the reason we would agree a mutual transfer of natural rights is for peace and security. The extent to which security is central to Hobbes's thought is evident from the fact that he oscillates between, but often combines, *securitas* and *salus*, along with other terms such as the New Testament Greek *asphaleia*, which refers to a firmness or stability, often in the literal sense of a 'security' against falling, but also sometimes in the civic sense of the stability of institutions. In his translation of Thucydides' *History of the Peloponnesian War*, Hobbes translates *asphaleia* as 'security', and extends it to include military practice rather than just personal security. So, Hobbes is certainly keen on pushing the logic of security for which his work has become well known. At the same time, he also rejects Cicero's position on tranquillity: there can be 'no such thing as perpetual Tranquillity' because 'Life it selfe is but Motion'. And the fact that life itself is motion means that human beings 'can never be without Desire, *nor without Feare*'.[49]

Yet what Hobbes does not have is the concept of 'insecurity'. The frequently quoted passages on the generation of Leviathan often describe it as a response to the insecurity of the state of nature, and our insecurity in relation to others. Yet 'insecurity' is, at this point, not a common term. The *OED* dates the first use of 'insecurity' to 1646, in Sir Thomas Browne's *Pseudodoxia Epidemica*, where it is used to describe 'the insecurity of truth', with no political connotations whatsoever. So, Hobbes might have been able to use 'insecurity', or could perhaps even have been at the forefront of developing the word himself, which would not have been a surprise, given how often his conceptual and linguistic innovations shaped the English language in the seventeenth century. But he does not do so. What he does say a lot about, however, is *metus*, a Latin word which for him is the closest we might find to the opposite of *securitas*, but is usually translated as 'fear'.

Nothing is more dangerous to sovereign power than a fearless subject. This is the reason for Machiavelli's injunction to princes that they should seek to be both loved and feared by their subjects, but that if they can be only one of these, it should be feared. This is also why the injunction becomes a general maxim of the impersonal state. Not only should subjects not be fearless – they should be reminded at every turn that fear is the reason we cannot expect security from others. Fear must be mobilized so that it can be administered politically. Fear is the glue that holds the security system together. Fear constitutes the individual. Fear is crucial in our pacification.

'The Passion to be reckoned upon, is Fear', Hobbes states. Specifically, the 'continual feare and danger of violent death'. In *De Cive* the reason given for why we cannot expect security from others is 'mutual fear' – a term he had already used in *Elements of Law* – which stems in turn from our 'mutual will of hurting'. In *De Homine*, 'security of future time' is set against fear of death as 'the greatest of all evils', and, in *De*

49 Thomas Hobbes, *Leviathan*, ed. Richard Tuck (Cambridge: Cambridge University Press, 1991 [1651]), pp. 6, 46, 135, 316. Emphasis added.

Cive, death is 'the chiefest of natural evils'.[50] What distinguishes humans from other animals is an ability to imagine our own death and, worse, to imagine it as violent. This generates a perpetual 'Anxiety of the Time to Come':

> It is impossible for a man, who continually endeavoureth to secure himselfe against the evill he feares, and procure the good he desireth, not to be in a perpetuall solicitude of the time to come . . . So that man, which looks too far before him, in the care of future time, hath his heart all the day long, gnawed on by feare of death, poverty, or other calamity; and has no repose, nor pause of his anxiety, but in sleep.[51]

The 'sleep' in question is not that experienced at night, since we know that, even then, and even with the extra security measures such as locking doors, the fear still runs deep (given the external darkness that encourages our darkness within). The 'sleep' in question is the eternal sleep of death.

A condition lacking in security, in which there is no industry, no cultivation, no navigation, no building, no transport, no knowledge, no arts and no society, is described by Hobbes not as a condition of 'insecurity', but rather a condition of continual fear of violent death – and it is this condition that pushes us towards the creation of a sovereign power. 'The Passions that encline men to Peace, are Feare of Death; Desire of such things as are necessary to commodious living; and a Hope by their Industry to obtain them.' The lack of security in the state of nature is intimately connected to our knowledge of our death. In the state of nature 'there can be no security to any man . . . of living out the time, which Nature ordinarily alloweth men to live'.[52] Sovereignty is founded on the 'Fear of Death and Wounds', and it is this fear, not insecurity, that undergirds Hobbes's philosophical system, because it pacifies subjects through their willingness to construct and obey a sovereign power that

50 Hobbes, *Leviathan*, p. 10; *De Homine* (1658), in Thomas Hobbes, *Man and Citizen*, ed. Bernard Gert (Indianapolis: Hackett, 1991), p. 48; Thomas Hobbes, *De Cive* (1642), in Hobbes, *Man and Citizen*, p. 115; Thomas Hobbes, *The Elements of Law: Natural and Politic*, ed. Ferdinand Tonnies (London: Frank Cass, 1969), p. xvi.

51 Hobbes, *Leviathan*, p. 76.

52 Ibid., pp. 89, 90, 91, 138.

offers some kind of security against violent death.[53] 'It is through fear that men secure themselves.'[54] And note that the power they create, the mighty Leviathan, is described in the Biblical book of Job (41:33) as having nothing on Earth that can compare with it, for it is *made without fear*. Hobbes's whole work is organized around this fundamental fear of death, which is why Leo Strauss stresses this aspect of Hobbes's work in *The Political Philosophy of Thomas Hobbes* (1936) – which, I think consciously echoing Hobbes, eschews the language of 'insecurity'. It is also one reason why Hobbes's work is so highly regarded by security intellectuals and counterinsurgency thinkers.[55] Fear of death at the hands of another is the very foundation of our obligation to obedience, and thus the grounds of our pacification.

At the same time, however, this fear *remains present in the very state that is erected to provide security*. Hobbes was himself a fearful man. Not only did he fear the seditious blockheads, the giddy people, the masterless men, rebellion, disorder, and civil war; he also feared for his life. Of course, in one sense this should not surprise us, since being regarded as on the side of monarchy during such a tumultuous period really did put one's life in danger. But fear also ran so intensely through his personal life that he regarded it as his personal twin. In his autobiographical poem, he quips that his mother gave birth to him upon hearing news of the Spanish Armada, and that she 'Did bring forth Twins at once, both Me, and Fear'.[56] His twin stayed by his side throughout his life. According to the sketch of Hobbes that appears in John Aubrey's *Brief Lives*, written towards the end of the seventeenth century, Hobbes would apparently lie in his room at night fearing what the darkness might bring. He also feared death strongly enough to play tennis into his old age and to sing every evening, hoping that such

53 Ibid., p. 70.

54 Hobbes, *De Cive*, pp. 112–13.

55 See, for example, an article in the quarterly journal of the US Army War College, *Parameters*, which takes as its starting point the Hobbesian idea that self-preservation in the face of a profound fear of violent death is the foundation stone of social order, and that is why a study of Hobbes is so useful in counterinsurgency: Raymond Millen, 'The Hobbesian Notion of Self-Preservation Concerning Human Behavior during an Insurgency', *Parameters: US Army War College Quarterly* 36: 4 (2006), p. 13.

56 Thomas Hobbes, Thomas Hobbes, *Vita Carmine Espressa* (1672–73), published as *The Life of Mr Thomas Hobbes of Malmesbury Written by Himself in a Latine Poem, and Now Translated into English* (London: n.p., 1680).

habits might keep him going that little bit longer. And when he drank alcohol with friends, he would leave the room to make himself vomit, because he either feared getting drunk (a state he compares to madness in Chapter 8 of *Leviathan*) or feared that the alcohol would kill him. The more general point, however, is that the imagination of death in the state of nature as the most telling detail of our fundamental fear as a fundamental equality – in that the ultimate equality lies in death – is carried over into an imagination rife with incalculable fears within a social order created for security.

In a note added to the later edition of *De Cive* to clarify the notion of 'mutual fear' that he had presented in the book's opening pages, Hobbes wrote:

> I comprehend in this word *fear*, a certain foresight of future evil; neither do I conceive flight the sole property of fear, but to distrust, suspect, take heed, provide so that they may not fear, is also incident to the fearful. They who go to sleep, shut their doors; they who travel, carry their swords with them, because they fear thieves. Kingdoms guard their coasts and frontiers with forts and castles; cities are compact with walls; and all for fear of neighbouring kingdoms and towns. Even the strongest armies, and most accomplished for fight, yet sometimes parley for peace, as fearing each other's power, and lest they might be overcome.[57]

Despite the creation of the Leviathan – despite Securitas overlooking the city – we still undertake our own 'security measures' in response to our fears. As Hobbes reminds us, the fact that we travel with swords and lock our doors is 'testimony of the distrust [we] have of each other'.[58] We all know, Hobbes believes, that people will turn to violence for mere 'trifles', such as a misplaced word, a crooked smile, a different opinion, or some minor sign of disrespect.[59] The natural fear of death takes on a stark social dimension with political repercussions: the knowledge that security is always already under threat, and that the police power is always already liable to fail, serves only to make us

57 Hobbes, *De Cive*, p. 113.
58 Ibid., p. 99.
59 Hobbes, *Leviathan*, p. 88; Hobbes, *Elements of Law*, p. 71.

even more fearful. To repeat: man is in his heart, all day long, gnawed at by the fear of death.

Yet Hobbes is not done with this litany of fears. The maintenance of civil society requires nothing less than that the sovereign power claims for itself 'the power of Life and Death', and thus possesses the right 'of inflicting greater punishments, than Death'.[60] The creation of a sovereign power to ease our fears generates . . . fear. It generates a fear of the coercive power that offers security and keeps us in subjection: man must 'be restrained through fear of some coercive power'.[61] Fear drives us to create the sovereign power, but then fear of that power restrains us. What 'manner of life there would be, where there were no common Power to feare'? Here, we come to one dimension of Securitas depicted in Lorenzetti's frescoes: the terror of punishment and the fear of death at the hands of the sovereign. In Chapter 1, we saw Hobbes note that even the simplest obedience is easily broken, and his example was Adam and Eve in the Garden of Eden. But this example can now be reconsidered in starker terms, concerning the punishment of death. 'God said to Adam, that on the day hee should eate of the forbidden fruit, he should certainly die', Hobbes notes, reciting the well-known story. Hobbes adds, more ominously, 'from that time forward he [Adam] was a dead man by sentence'.[62] Dare to rebel, and you are a dead man; accept your pacification, and such a sentence can be avoided – though you will also never forget that such a sentence is possible.

In *The Elements of Law*, Hobbes suggests that a person fears a death brought about by the 'displeasing of his superior', because behind this lies the 'fear of eternal death hereafter'. In *Leviathan*, the idea that 'there is no natural knowledge of man's estate after death' forms one of the grounds of political order, for the one way of 'gaining the secure and perpetuall felicity of Heaven' lies in satisfying contracts, and hence in a general 'security of performance'. To claim the power to preserve our life, the sovereign claims the power of death, and the rebel knows that to fail in the rebellion 'is to die the death of a traitor' at the hands of the mortal God. And this is the case even though Hobbes considers the fear of death to be so fundamental to human nature that he regards it as the

60 Hobbes, *Leviathan*, pp. 306–7.
61 Hobbes, *De Cive*, p. 99.
62 Hobbes, *Leviathan*, p. 431.

sole grounds for a subject to refuse the sovereign's command. Despite the fact that 'no Law can oblige a man to abandon his own preservation', the state can rightfully seek to enforce the punishment of death in the name of security, and the knowledge of such punishment is the root of the fear of breaking the law.[63] In effect, the fear that exists in the state of nature is replaced by the fear that exists within political society – but this latter fear is as much a fear of the sovereign as it is fear of others. To be successful in its offer of protection, then, *securitas* must itself threaten death. The gallows rope always dangles before us, the bodies of the executed exhibited in their cages: little reminders, lest they be needed.

It is clear, then, that Hobbes places the management of death at the heart of political power and the social order. Life (security) is only possible because it is policed by the sovereign, and the sovereign polices security (life) through a monopoly power over death and the right to kill. This is why *Leviathan* needs to be read not simply for what it says or implies about security in the first two parts of the book, 'Of Man' and 'Of Commonwealth', where Hobbes offers an image of man and political society, but also, and more pertinently, for what it says about security in the fourth and final part, a political theology concerning 'The Kingdom of Darkness' – itself a development of Part III, 'Of a Christian Commonwealth'. Parts III and IV of *Leviathan* really bring home the centrality of scriptural and religious questions to the book; taken together, the two parts are almost equal in length to the more widely read parts I and II, yet they are frequently ignored in discussions of Hobbes's work. As J. G. A. Pocock pointed out some time ago, the attitude of many scholars is either that the latter two parts are not there, or that Hobbes did not really mean them.[64] But they are there, and he did mean them.

In Chapter 1, I noted Hobbes's focus on the difficulty of obeying both God and Man at once, especially when their commands seem contrary to one another, and that this difficulty was in many ways the pretext for the writing of *Leviathan* itself. In the spring of 1646, Hobbes had intended to return to his book *De Corpore*. But, as he recounts in his autobiographical poem, an event took place which made him change his

63 Hobbes, *Elements of Law*, pp. 147, 168; Hobbes, *Leviathan*, pp. 102–3, 206, 208.

64 J. G. A. Pocock, *Politics, Language and Time* (London: Methuen, 1972), p. 160.

plans and turn instead to his work on *Leviathan*. The event was the appearance of the heir to the throne, Charles, in Paris in July, accompanied by a band of followers, full of news about the latest royalist defeats and, even more significant, the tendency of their enemies to regard their successes as signs of God's providence. Hobbes reports his horror at hearing such terrible crimes being attributed to the commands of God. He decided that, although he had prepared the materials for *De Corpore*, he would now delay it, as the priority was to write a book to 'absolve the divine laws'. It was at this moment, he claims, that he began to compose *Leviathan*. The fight for absolute sovereignty, then, is also a fight over questions of God's commands and general questions of belief. This is perhaps why Hobbes time and again insists that his arguments are consistent with the holy scriptures (such as in the 'Review and Conclusion' to *Leviathan*).

But the progress into the political theology of Parts III and IV of *Leviathan* generates far wider questions concerning death, fear, and the existence of all manner of imaginary forces. What happens is that the theological imaginary concerning fear comes to be deployed in the service of a political discourse of sovereignty and security. The philosopher of science enters the world of unnameable dread. Such dread casts a heavy shadow.

A hint of what was to come is delivered much earlier in the book, in Chapter 12, 'Of Religion', where Hobbes argues that the very nature of man's inquisitiveness and search for the causes of things generates an anxiety over the future so powerful that it pushes us into considering whether the punishment of Hell is worse than the punishment of death. For Hobbes, although we all die a corporeal death, our bodies will be resurrected for 'the Kingdom of God by Christ beginneth at the day of Judgment'. At that point, the righteous 'shall have their bodies suddenly changed, and made spirituall, and Immortall'. Their salvation is their security: 'to be saved, is to be secured'. However, the Reprobates will not be subject to eternal torments, as might be expected, but, rather, 'shall rise again to receive punishment for their sins'. What is the punishment? Nothing other than death once more. The Elect, having been made spiritual and immortal, 'can die no more'; but for the Reprobates there remains 'a Second, and Eternall Death' after the Resurrection. Moreover, between their resurrection and second death they receive their punishment and torment: 'many of them that sleep in the dust of the Earth, shall awake; some to Everlasting life; and some to shame, and everlasting contempt'. The latter suffer 'a grief, and discontent of mind, from the sight of that Eternal felicity in others, which they themselves through their own incredulity, and disobedience have lost'. From witnessing the felicity and obedience of the Elect, for every condemned man 'there is to bee a Second Death . . . after which hee shall die no more'.[65]

In the opening chapter of Part IV, on the 'spiritual darkness' that can stem from the misinterpretation of scripture, Hobbes imagines the Apostles, after Jesus's Resurrection, asking him whether he will restore the Kingdom of God. Hobbes offers us Jesus's answer:

> *It is not for you to know the times and the seasons, which the Father hath put in his own power* . . . Which is as much as to say, My Kingdome is not yet come, nor shall you foreknow when it shall come; for it shall come as a theefe in the night; But I will send you the Holy Ghost, and by him you shall have power to bear witnesse to all the world (by your preaching) of my Resurrection, and the workes I have done, and the doctrine I have taught, that they may beleeve in me, and expect eternal life, at my comming againe.[66]

Here Hobbes is lifting the passage from Paul's letter to the Thessalonians that I have already cited, and also referencing the more general Christian tradition I have also noted, to the effect that when people say 'there is security', then destruction will be upon them. Perhaps one outcome of acknowledging the kingdom of darkness is the realization that the security that is seemingly constructed through the erection of a sovereign power much earlier in the book is not real security. It cannot be real security, because man is still ultimately a wolf to man, each threating the other with death; because Behemoth, the monster of revolution, is always possible; because, despite the ever-present threat of the gallows, the obedience we learn is perpetually liable to dissipate; and because, after all, Leviathan is not the City of God. Indeed, the fact that Leviathan is a *mortal* God reminds us that it too could be destroyed, with the implication that the social

65 Hobbes, *Leviathan*, pp. 38, 314–15, 432–3.

66 Ibid., 427.

order could lose the very thing that keeps it orderly, human beings would fall back into the state of nature, and the fear of death would resume its original state.

This means that the picture is far more complicated than the one suggesting that, for Hobbes, the sovereign is created in order to provide security. The security offered by the sovereign is a kind of holding power during which human beings must learn to '*acknowledge their owne Darknesse*'.[67] As much as *Leviathan* is known as one of modern philosophy's leading texts on security, it could easily be argued that darkness is a far more prominent theme in the book. Acknowledging our darkness is central to the philosophy of security that underpins *Leviathan*, for it is in *the* darkness and in *our* darkness that fear finds its power and drives us into subjection under both mortal and immortal Gods. 'Have you seen the gates of deep darkness?' God asks Job (Job 38:17, a passage rendered in the King James Version of the Bible as 'hast thou seen the doors of the shadow of death?').[68] Hobbes wants us to understand that the deepest darkness is within, where our fears fester. This is the moment when statecraft becomes soulcraft.[69] It becomes soulcraft because Hobbes believes that this darkness generates fears about what he variously describes as 'Powers Invisible', 'Spirits Invisible', 'Invisible Agents', and 'Invisible Powers'. The fear of such powers, of things unknown and unnameable, is 'in every man, his own Religion'.[70] 'The natural Seed' of religion has four dimensions: 'the Opinion of Ghosts, Ignorance of second causes, Devotion to what men fear, and Taking of things Casuall for Prognostiques'. Such seeds have been cultivated by two kinds of men, one pursuing a more political road, the other pursuing God's commandment:

> But both sorts have done it, with a purpose to make those men that relyed on them, the more apt to Obedience, Lawes, Peace, Charity, and civill Society. So that the Religion of the former sort, is a part of humane Politiques; and teacheth part of the duty which Earthly Kings require of their Subjects. And the Religion of the later sort is Divine

67 Ibid., p. 418. Emphasis added.

68 The first translation is from The Standard Revised Version. Hereafter all translations from The Bible are from the King James Version.

69 Neocleous, *Critique of Security*, pp. 106–41; Neocleous, *Critical Theory*, 33–42.

70 Hobbes, *Leviathan*, p. 99.

> Politiques; and containeth Precepts to those that have yeelded themselves subjects in the Kingdome of God. Of the former sort, were all the Founders of Common-wealths, and the Law-givers of the Gentiles . . . by whom have been derived unto us the Lawes of the Kingdome of God.[71]

Hobbes is alluding here to the fact that the struggle for sovereignty is fought over the imaginations of human beings concerning a future that is unknowable. This assists 'the Governours of the Heathen Commonwealths to regulate . . . fear, by establishing that DAEMONOLOGY' from which there will emerge a 'Publique Peace' and 'the Obedience of Subjects'.[72] The sovereign and the prophet both have something to offer, just as they are both capable of invoking the fear of death to command our obedience.

In his discussion of Hobbes's fear of the dark, Samuel Denne notes that Hobbes was comfortable writing about matters pertaining to philosophy, science and religion, 'but no sooner was he obliged to descend into his own breast, than all his natural apprehensions returned'. This fear is of the darkness not only of the night, but also of the soul. So scared was Hobbes of such darkness, reports Denne, that he dreaded any discussion of death with friends, and whenever such a discussion arose Hobbes 'express[ed] a desire of finding a hole out of which he might creep out of the world'.[73] He was willing to acknowledge his darkness, just as he expected people to acknowledge theirs. If the lesson Hobbes wants us to learn is political, it is one that is underpinned by deep existential dread and dark fears: acknowledge your darkness; acknowledge the darkness within as well as without; acknowledge your fears about what is in the darkness; acknowledge such fears so that you will better appreciate the security being offered to you by the sovereign, despite knowing security is ultimately impossible, because this is a crucial step towards *acknowledging the pacification you need and want*. This, for Hobbes, is to simply acknowledge the human condition.

71 Ibid., 79.

72 Ibid., 441.

73 Samuel Denne, *A Letter to Sir Robert Ladbroke, Knt . . . With an Attempt to Shew the Good Effects Which May Be Reasonably Expected from the Confinement of Criminals in Separate Apartments* (London: n.p., 1771), p. 57.

Human fear has two general objects. One is the power of those who we might offend, about which I have already said a great deal. The other, however, is 'the Power of Spirits Invisible':

> This perpetuall feare, alwayes accompanying mankind in the ignorance of causes, as it were in the Dark, must needs have for object something. And therefore when there is nothing to be seen, there is nothing to accuse, either of their good, or evill fortune, but some *Power*, or *Agent Invisible*: In which sense perhaps it was, that some of the old Poets said, that the Gods were at first created by humane Feare.[74]

In particular, he adds, the fear of things invisible is so strong that it takes on a status equal to or perhaps greater than the fear of death: 'the fear of Darknesse, and Ghosts, is greater than other fears'.[75]

For Hobbes, those who think that there can be more than one sovereign in a commonwealth 'set up a *Supremacy* against the *Soveraignty*; *Canons* against *Lawes*; and a *Ghostly Authority* against the *Civill*'. Such people like to 'work on men's minds, with words and distinctions, that of themselves signifie nothing', but which point to the possibility of 'another Kingdome', nothing less than 'a Kingdome of Fayries, in the dark'. The potential clash between secular and religious authority is a distinction 'of *Temporall*, and *Ghostly* . . . Kingdomes':

> When therefore these two Powers oppose one another, the Commonwealth cannot but be in great danger of Civill warre, and Dissolution. For the *Civill* Authority being more visible, and standing in the cleerer light of natural reason, cannot choose but draw to it in all times a very considerable part of the people: And the *Spirituall*, though it stand in the darknesse of Schoole distinctions, and hard words; yet because the fear of Darknesse, and Ghosts, is greater than other fears, cannot want a party sufficient to Trouble, and sometimes to Destroy a Common-wealth.[76]

74 Hobbes, *Leviathan*, p. 76.
75 Ibid., p. 227.
76 Ibid., pp. 226–7.

The Invisible Powers have a 'Kingdom on Earth':

> This seed of Religion, having been observed by many; some of those that have observed it, have been enclined thereby so to nourish, dresse, and forme it into Lawes; and to adde to it of their own invention, any opinion of the causes of future events, by which they thought they should best be able to govern others, and to make unto themselves the greatest use of their Powers.[77]

In other words, one of the main mechanisms of political obedience is the fear of death at the hands of some unknown 'Invisible Agents'. Despite being a dyed-in-the wool materialist, Hobbes believes fears often centre on 'the Power of Invisible Things' such as witches, fairies, ghosts, and goblins. Whether this fear is of a presence or an absence is unclear, but it is certainly all the darker for being superstitious. This is how fear shades into security, and security into fear: there is always another fear to ground the politics of another security, as Nietzsche puts it in section 57 of *Dawn* (1881). Such is the cunning of the security industry, and perhaps the culture industry too.

In this regard, we might consider two of the key agents of the Invisible Powers: the witch and the ghost, both of which appear, remarkably, just a few pages into the beginning of *Leviathan*. I have discussed the figure of the witch at length in *The Universal Adversary* (2016), so will only pause here to note that, although Hobbes does not really believe in witchcraft – 'as for Witches, I think not that their witchcraft is any reall power' – he nonetheless thinks that 'they are justly punished, for the false beliefe they have, that they can do such mischiefe, joyned with their purpose to do it if they can: their trade being nearer to a new Religion, than to a Craft or Science'.[78] Hobbes would have been well aware of the arguments of Jean Bodin in both the *Six Books of the Commonwealth* (1576) and *On the Demon-Mania of Witches* (1580). Bodin, who did believe that witchcraft was a real power, argued that the witch is aligned with heinous crimes such as sedition, rebellion and civil war. Punishing the witch will therefore 'strike fear and terror into others', and the general persecution of witches is necessary so that 'the good can

77 Ibid., p. 75.
78 Ibid., p. 18.

live in security'.[79] For Hobbes too, this fear of invisible powers generates one security measure after another. In terms of the argument presented in Chapter 1, we might say that what emerges is the justification for yet another war against yet another enemy within – one which, despite the notion of 'invisible powers', is very firmly rooted in the materiality of women's bodies. But what, then, of the ghost?

According to both Pierre Bayle and Samuel Denne, Hobbes's fear of the dark lay in part in his fear of the spectral forces and invisible powers that might manifest themselves there, and Hobbes no doubt believes that we all suffer in the same way.[80] Moreover, the fear of ghosts is important in the struggle for the imagination that takes place between religion and the state, and hence important to the allegiance and obedience of subjects. It was a fundamental feature of the Enlightenment after Hobbes to seek to overcome dark fears, especially fears of invisible powers such as ghosts. The entry for 'Mort' in the mid-eighteenth-century *Encyclopédie*, the Enlightenment bible of reason and science composed between 1751 and 1780, includes the claim that 'men fear death as children fear the dark, and only because their imaginations have been frightened by ghosts that are as insubstantial as they are frightening'. Such science and reason are said now to be central to the rationality of the state and the forms of power it exercises in the name of security. And yet ghosts haunt the security imaginary.

'This subject of ghosts has been among the torments of my life', declared Jeremy Bentham, who knew a thing or two about security. 'Even now, when sixty or seventy years have passed over my head since my boyhood received the impression which my grandmother gave it, though my judgment is wholly free, my imagination is not wholly so.' Later in the same text, his 'Memoirs', he adds that his 'fear of ghosts, and of the visitations of spiritual beings, was strong'.[81] This

79 Jean Bodin, *Six Books of the Commonwealth*, transl. M. J. Tooley (Place of Publication Unknown: Seven Treasures, 2009 [1576]), p. 206; Jean Bodin, *On the Demon-Mania of Witches*, transl. Randy A. Scott (Toronto: CRRS Publications, 1995 [1580]), pp. 203–4.

80 Pierre Bayle, 'Hobbes', entry in his *Historical and Critical Dictionary* (1697–1702), in *Political Writings* (Cambridge: Cambridge University Press, 2000), pp. 90–2; Denne, *Letter to Sir Robert Ladbroke*, p. 57.

81 Jeremy Bentham, 'Memoirs', in *The Works of Jeremy Bentham, Vol. X*, ed. John Bowring (Edinburgh: William Tait, 1843), pp. 18, 39.

is remarkable given that the legal theory which underpins Bentham's political arguments is set firmly against legal fictions, which he considered to be falsehoods and swindles that undermine the rationality of legislation. 'The season of Fiction is now over', he declares in *A Fragment on Government*, his critique of Blackstone's *Commentaries*.[82] Legal fictions are designed to overawe us, he argues, making us imagine the law as an 'old Gothic castle . . . fitted up for a modern inhabitant', as Blackstone put it. For Bentham, legal rationality would remove such entities from the law. Bentham's horror at the possibility of legal fictions runs parallel with his horror at the possibility of ghosts. Both horrors 'can be shown to have played their part in determining the intensity and pertinacity of his researches', notes C. K. Ogden.[83] And yet so driven is Bentham by acknowledging the ghosts in his own darkness that they make their way into his constitutional code. 'Ghosts and other fabulous maleficent beings' are as important to discuss as monarchs and other figures of state, he claims. 'In no man's judgement can a stronger persuasion of the non-existence of those sources of terror have place than in mine; yet no sooner do I lay myself down to sleep in a dark room . . . than these instruments of terror obtrude themselves'.[84] For this reason, Bentham's fear of ghosts appears in some of his arguments about imprisonment, that form of security architecture with which he is often associated. In *The Principles of Penal Law*, he argues against solitary confinement on the following grounds:

> When the external senses are restrained from action, the imagination is more active, and produces a numerous race of ideal beings. In a state of solitude, infantine superstitions, ghosts, and spectres, recur to the imagination. This, of itself, forms a sufficient reason for not prolonging this species of punishment, which may overthrow the powers of the mind, and produce incurable melancholy.

82 Jeremy Bentham, *A Fragment on Government*, in *Works, Vol. I*, ed. John Bowring (Edinburgh: William Tait, 1843), p. 269.

83 C. K. Ogden, *Bentham's Theory of Fictions* (London: Kegan Paul, 1932), pp. ix–x.

84 Jeremy Bentham, *Constitutional Code* (1827), in *Works, Vol. IX*, ed. John Bowring (Edinburgh: William Tait, 1843), p. 84.

This, Bentham adds, is an effect of the 'darkness' which has 'a peculiar tendency to dispose men to conceive, and in a manner to feel, the presence of invisible agents'.[85]

In both his memoirs and the *Code*, Bentham clearly lays the blame for his own fear of ghosts on workers. His fear 'was not unknown to the servants', he admits, and they found it 'a permanent source of amusement to ply me with horrible phantoms in all imaginable shapes'. He later adds that the 'fear of ghosts had been implanted in my mind from earliest infancy by the too customary cultivators of that noxious weed, domestic servants'. In the *Code* he claims that 'the cause of these illusions were the stories told by servants in my childhood'.[86] Bentham was thus a good liberal, obsessed as all liberals are with security, afraid of ghosts and spooked by the workers. Might it be the very obsession with security that helps produce such fears?

It is a fascinating, if not very often noticed, feature of counterinsurgency literature that ghosts play a prominent role in it. 'The insurgents are ghosts', commented one *New York Times* report during the war on terror, adding that soldiers report seeing the ghosts, getting close to the ghosts, and, of course, destroying the ghosts. 'The best antidote for the menacing ghostliness of the ambushing enemy is killing and knowing you've killed them', claimed one soldier to the reporter. Journalism from the period was replete with comments along the lines that Western soldiers were up 'against a ghostly enemy'.[87] During the 1980s, Soviet conscripts also called Afghan rebels *dukhi*: ghosts. Everywhere we find similar claims: the terrorist is 'a ghost, a figure in the shadows', 'a faceless ghost heading anywhere and everywhere', a 'phantom', a 'spectral presence'. This is the prose of pacification as ghost story, evident from some of the volumes in the counterinsurgency library: *Ghost Wars: The Secret History of the CIA, Afghanistan, and Bin Laden, from the Soviet Invasion to September 10, 2001* (Steve Coll, 2004); *Chasing Ghosts: Unconventional Warfare in American History* (John J. Tierney, 2006); *Ghost: Confessions of a Counterterrorism Agent* (Fred Burton, 2008); *Chasing Ghosts: The Policing of Terrorism* (John Mueller and Mark G. Stewart, 2016);

85 Jeremy Bentham, 'The Principles of Penal Law', in *Works, Vol. I*, p. 426.

86 Respectively: Bentham, 'Memoirs', pp. 18, 64; *Constitutional Code*, p. 84.

87 Elizabeth Rubin, 'Battle Company Is Out There', *New York Times Magazine*, 24 February 2008; Peter Beaumont, 'US Sails against Ghostly Enemy', *Observer*, 23 November 2001.

The Ghost Warriors: Inside Israel's Undercover War Against Suicide Terrorism (Samuel M. Katz, 2016); *The Ghosts of Langley: Into the Heart of the CIA* (John Prados, 2017). The obsession with ghosts might also explain why security operations often involve 'ghost planes' and 'ghost detainees'. Maybe this also explains why the Vietnam war haunts subsequent acts in the pacification drama, as the same counterinsurgency library reveals, with books such as *Ghosts of War in Vietnam* (2008), *Ghosts of Vietnam* (2011), *Vietnam Shadows: The War, Its Ghosts, and Its Legacy* (1997), and *Vietnam in Iraq: Tactics, Lessons, Legacies and Ghosts* (2007). Both of these lists could go on and on.

The spooks are spooked, it seems – haunted by the ghosts of their previous dramas, fearful of the invisible powers of a spectral enemy, superstitious to the core, and unable to let the dead bury their dead.[88] The spooks are believers who hunt the ghosts to prove they exist, fearing that the rest of the population do not sufficiently believe in the ghosts, and hence lack the right level of fear. At the same time, the spooks express their own paranoia about who exactly is controlling things. The spooks are troubled by their inability to control the terrors they themselves have done so much to conjure up, perhaps troubled by the ghostly return of the enemies they have killed, or maybe even unable to give up the evil thoughts they have about the dead. And yet, as well as believing in ghosts and thinking they need to hunt the ghosts, security intellectuals are also genuinely frightened that the ghost will keep coming back. The ghost might be interpreted in many ways, from being a figment of the imagination to being a message from beyond; but, for security intellectuals, the ghost is the dead that will not die, carrying the threat of revenge that might overturn the power of security, thereby generating more insecurities, and hence reasserting the necessity of ever more security measures. More to the point, the ghost figures as a spirit that has the strength somehow to *withstand death*, which makes it even more threatening to those who prioritize security, for it is they who demand the right to manage death itself. 'Out, ghost!' But the ghost will not leave.

---

88 On these themes and the ways in which they might situate security intellectuals politically, see my books *The Monstrous and the Dead: Burke, Marx, Fascism* (Cardiff: University of Wales Press, 2005), and *The Universal Adversary: Security, Capital and 'The Enemies of All Mankind'* (London: Routledge, 2016).

The chasing of ghosts produces its own sets of fears and paranoias – when one fails to catch them, but even more so when one thinks one has killed them. This adds to their power to spook us, perhaps through the curses they cast against those who have killed them, their very existence a reminder of the damage done to them: killed by the security apparatus, but feared to have not been properly killed, surviving instead as an ineradicable ghostly power, a spectre of masterlessness, rebellion and return. The spirit of a terror that was supposed to have been destroyed generates a greater fear, or certainly a different kind of fear, of the undead, and hence yet more insecurity among those who believe in them. 'Present fears are less than horrible imaginings', as Macbeth puts it.

Because ghosts have no physiological or phenomenal form by which they might be distinguished, they either appear as one mass, the ghostly, in which they all look alike and which makes them impossible to eradicate, or they take on a phenomenal form, in the body of this or that figure. The point of the ghosts is not really to catch them so much as to make us believe in them, along with other such Invisible Agents. Just as the cunning of security once operated through the invention of witchcraft, so now ghostcraft is central to that cunning. A spectre haunts the minds of security intellectuals – the spectre of insurgency. War must be declared, and the police power mobilized. The security apparatus sees in the ghost a power without limit, which is precisely the kind of power that is claimed for the security apparatus itself. As Walter Benjamin noted astutely some time ago, 'a consideration of the police institution encounters nothing essential at all. Its power is formless, like its nowhere tangible, all-pervasive, ghostly presence in the life of civilized states.'[89] Yet the police power's own ghostly presence somehow never manages to kill, eradicate, banish or defeat the invisible powers. Such powers *must* go undefeated, so that pacification can continue, and their ghostliness is evidence itself of their undefeated status. The cries of Francisco and Bernardo in *Hamlet*: 'Who's there?' 'Nay, answer me: stand, and unfold yourself', are those of the security intellectual, because if nothing else they allow the reassertion of the line that follows, that most resolute reassertion of security as well as sovereignty: 'Long Live the King!' Exit ghost.

89 Walter Benjamin, 'Critique of Violence' (1921), in *Walter Benjamin, Selected Writings, Vol. 1: 1913–1926*, ed. Marcus Bullock and Michael W. Jennings (Cambridge, MA: Harvard University Press, 1996).

Hobbes's suggestion that human beings are gnawed at by the fear of death would seem to suggest that only in death itself will we be free from such fear. That is, only in the afterlife will one achieve real security. Such an account would play heavily on the Christian tradition of security with God. Yet this is not Hobbes's argument. Hobbes's point is not that subjects should seek perpetual security in a better life after death, but, rather, that they should offer obedience to a form of power that offers them as much security as is possible in this life. Given the nature of human beings, there is no such thing as an absolute and perpetual form of security; but there is such a thing as a partial and temporary form of security. To have subjects brooding and despairing over their own annihilation is one way to guarantee their submission to such security. This is also a reason why one must accept one's pacified status under security's rule: pacification rooted in anxiety and dread, fear and despair.

This is the real cunning of security. The danger in any security is that it might in fact diminish our fear of death, make us complacent ('at ease'), and hence less submissive in the face of power. Once we feel too secure, our fear of violent death might diminish, and we might lose our understanding of the political power that has offered us something called security in the first place. Subjects who do not fear death cannot be relied upon to accept the security offered them by the state. Since fear of death is the grounds of sovereignty, once human beings begin to allow their imaginations to subordinate the fear of death to some other passion, belief or superstition, the basis of sovereign power is destroyed, and with it the basis of any politics organized around the logic of security. The cunning of security, then, is to constitute us as fearful subjects, so that we might appreciate the security offered to us, however much we know, deep down, that it is an illusion.

This explains the fundamental discrepancy between the 'models of man' found in Hobbes's work: on the one hand, we find man as a rational human being committed to self-preservation rooted in an understanding of the world and its motions; on the other hand, we find man as an irrational creature falling into superstitions and ignorant beliefs. The latter model feeds directly into the book's theological and apocalyptic tone, which in turn has intensely political implications for the cunning of security. When security operates well, it assures not only the egoism of bourgeois order, but also that order's fundamental *cruelty*. 'Contempt, or little sense of the calamity of others, is that which men call CRUELTY;

proceeding from Security of their own fortune', Hobbes comments, in one of his starker Machiavellian moments.[90] Machiavelli's advice to the Prince, that cruelty is more efficient and effective than leniency in maintaining the obedience of his subjects, extends beyond the sixteenth century 'handbook to princes' style of writing, and finds its way into the theory of the state, the prose of pacification and the liberalism of fear, to use Judith Shklar's well-known phrase. Although cruelty appears superficially to be antithetical to liberal values, liberalism always puts security first, and putting security first means *putting cruelty first*.[91]

For security to function, fear must be presumed to be simultaneously resolvable and yet irresolvable, taking us into the very heart of the darkness that we are expected to acknowledge. Only in that darkness will we understand that security is achievable only through the Kingdom of God restored by Christ at the end of historical time. 'The Kingdom of God is a Civil Common-wealth, where God himself is Sovereign.'[92] Man is saved, and thus secured. In this context, the frontispiece of the first edition of *De Cive*, published in 1642 (the 1647 edition had a new frontispiece which is far less interesting), becomes just as compelling as the more famous frontispiece of *Leviathan*. The image has three sections, corresponding to the three parts of book: Liberty, Dominion, Religion. On one side of the image is 'Libertas', a 'natural' condition, presenting us with a forlorn looking semi-naked Indian holding a bow and arrow, with other Indians in the background hunting other humans as well as animals. On the other side is 'Imperium', a state of sovereignty, portrayed by the figure holding the scales of justice, bearing a sword and with work and industry taking place in the background. It is the interface between these two sides of the image, given the conditions they represent and the relationship between the two, from nature to the state (and possibly back), from natural liberty to sovereign order, that has attracted most attention. But, at the top of the frontispiece, above both Imperium and Libertas and stretching across the whole frame, is 'Religio', an image of the Last Judgement, with people heading for either the perpetual security of Heaven on Earth or the perpetual misery of Hell.

90 Hobbes, *Leviathan*, pp. 43–4.

91 Judith N. Shklar, 'Putting Cruelty First', *Daedalus* 111: 3 (1982), pp. 18, 23; Judith N. Shklar, *Ordinary Vices* (Cambridge: Harvard University Press, 1984), Chapter 1.

92 Hobbes, *Leviathan*, p. 311.

Frontispiece to Thomas Hobbes, *De Cive* (1642).

Lest much of the argument in the discussion thus far seem a little too, well, Hobbesian, let me flesh out some of the themes through the work of Adam Smith, as a liberal and supposedly anti-Hobbesian counterpoint to the 'authoritarian' tendencies found in Hobbes.

The first thing to note is that, a century after Hobbes, and despite the emergence of 'insecurity' in the mid seventeenth century, the word, as we have seen, had still not yet become common. The first book with 'insecurity' in its title did not appear in English until 1706 (*The Insecurity of a Printed Overture for an Act for the Church's Security*); and the second book, *Insecurity Against the Small-pox*, took another 100 years to appear (in 1806). It is therefore no surprise to find that 'insecurity' does not figure in Smith's work, in the same way that it does not figure in Hobbes's. In neither *The Theory of Moral Sentiments* (1759) nor *The Wealth of Nations* (1776) does 'insecurity' make an appearance, despite the former book being about human morality and the latter containing descriptions of the negative effects of the division of labour on society. 'Insecure' appears once in *The Wealth of Nations*, but only in relation to the situation of a sovereign who has lost support of the clergy. In the *Lectures on Jurisprudence*, delivered in the early 1760s, Smith refers to 'security' time and again in discussions of police, liberty and sovereignty, but 'insecurity' is nowhere to be found. In contrast to this complete absence of any interest in or use of 'insecurity' on Smith's part, fear and death are as integral to his work as they are to Hobbes's.

The fact that fear is central to the writings of a figure widely understood to be one of the leading classical liberal thinkers and political economists is telling. Perhaps even more telling is that, in contrast to Hobbes, Smith rarely ever appears in intellectual histories of fear, such as Corey Robin's *Fear: The History of a Political Idea* (2004), or Geoffrey Skoll's *Social Theory of Fear* (2010). Smith likewise rarely makes an appearance in cultural histories of fear, despite how much his main work concerning competition, work and sympathy resonates with key cultural tropes in the West. Hence Smith is largely absent from Frank Furedi's *Culture of Fear* (2002), Joanna Bourke's *Fear: A Cultural History* (2005), Barry Glassner's *The Culture of Fear* (1999) and Marc Mulholland's *Bourgeois Liberty and the Politics of Fear* (2012). This absence is rather strange, given the centrality of fear to Smith's political economy of liberty, and, more to the point, the centrality of the fear of death to his argument.

A notable feature of the account of sympathy in *The Theory of Moral Sentiments* is that it begins with and relies on an argument about sympathy with the dead. 'We sympathize even with the dead', he says, and are affected by the 'awful futurity which awaits them':

> It is miserable, we think, to be deprived of the light of the sun; to be shut out from life and conversation; to be laid in the cold grave, a prey to corruption and the reptiles of the earth; to be no more thought of in this world, but to be obliterated, in a little time, from the affections, and almost from the memory, of their dearest friends and relations.[93]

In a later chapter he comments on our sympathy for someone being oppressed by another, but this quickly turns into a discussion of death.

93 Adam Smith, *The Theory of Moral Sentiments*, ed. D. D. Raphael and A. L. Macfie (Indianapolis: Liberty Fund, 1982 [1759]), p. 12.

We sympathize with the injured party and rejoice when we see them attack their adversary. And yet, 'if the injured should perish in the quarrel, we not only sympathize with the real resentment of his friends and relations, but with the imaginary resentment which in fancy we lend to the dead, who is no longer capable of feeling that or any other human sentiment':

> We put ourselves in his situation, as we enter, as it were, into his body, and in our imaginations, in some measure, animate anew the deformed and mangled carcass of the slain, when we bring home in this manner his case to our own bosoms, we feel upon this, as upon many other occasions, an emotion which the person principally concerned is incapable of feeling, and which yet we feel by an illusive sympathy with him . . . We feel that resentment which we imagine he ought to feel, and which he would feel, if in his cold and lifeless body there remained any consciousness of what passes upon earth. His blood, we think, calls aloud for vengeance. The very ashes of the dead seem to be disturbed at the thought that his injuries are to pass unrevenged.

The example is telling, for it concerns a person who has been killed by another, and whose very death thus demands vengeance: 'the *ghosts* which, superstition imagines, rise from their graves to demand vengeance upon those who brought them to an untimely end, all take their origin from this natural sympathy with the imaginary resentment of the slain.'[94]

All this leads Smith to what he claims is 'one of the most important principles in human nature': the fear of death. This claim completes the opening chapter of *The Theory of Moral Sentiments*, and is perhaps more important than the general logic of sympathy for which the book is better known. It is important for several reasons. First, our fear of death generates a 'foresight of our own dissolution so terrible to us', generating a sympathy for the dead which in turn forms the foundation of all other sympathy. Second, we feel sympathy for the dead, yet also recognize that death is a 'safe and quiet harbour'. The *happiness* of the dead is not affected by their being dead. Why? Because of *the profound security of*

94 Ibid., p. 71. Emphasis added.

their condition. Hence, we identify with the dead, but we do so in a way that differentiates and distances ourselves from them. In particular, we *differentiate our own lack of security from the security of the dead.* When Smith says that we 'lodge' our 'own living souls in their inanimated bodies', it may well be their security we are seeking, for this security is something that we ourselves cannot have, in stark contrast to the dead. Third, our fear of death propels us in turn into new forms of security. 'Death . . . is the king of terrors', Smith says, in one of his many Hobbesian moments, invoking a phrase routinely used to describe the death penalty, and hinting at the ultimate sovereign power. This psychology concerning the terror of death pushes us into the hands of a power that might then appear to offer security, or at least some version of it: '[T]he dread of death [is] but the great restraint upon the injustice of mankind, which, while it afflicts and mortifies the individual, guards and protects the society'.[95]

Smith is on the terrain of security as both moral psychology and political strategy. This terrain is grounded not on 'insecurity', however, but on the fear surrounding death. Hence, into this picture comes the other dimension of fear, which we have encountered already: the fear of death at the hands of the state.

'[W]e both punish and approve of punishment, merely from a view to the general interest of society, which, we imagine, cannot otherwise be secured'. For Smith, as for Hobbes, it is the 'terror of punishment' that lies at the heart of social order. Recall the examples just given: those who have suffered a violent death at the hands of another demand vengeance, and we sympathize with their demand. The feeling that vengeance in the form of punishment is justice lies in the fact that resentment is a feature of the general sympathy around which Smith's theory of moral sentiments is organized. We readily 'sympathize with the natural resentment of the injured, and the offender becomes the object of . . . hatred and indignation'. The criminal, as 'the proper object of the resentment and indignation of mankind' must therefore accept the 'vengeance and punishment' that follows. Since punishment is 'the natural consequence of resentment', so mankind will always 'approve of the violence employed to avenge the hurt', *including the punishment of death*. Indeed, those especially 'detestable characters' guilty of 'dreadful crimes' can hope

95 Ibid., pp. 13, 239, 280.

only 'by their death to reconcile themselves, at least in their imagination, to the natural sentiments of mankind'.[96]

The punishment of death applies especially to those crimes that damage not a particular person, but, rather, the security of the whole society. 'Of this kind are all the punishments inflicted for breaches of what is called either civil police, or military discipline.' The 'severity' of the execution of these people who threaten the powers of war and police is 'just and proper'.[97] Here, Smith positions himself in the long line of theorists of sovereign power who highlight the executioner as a key representative of that power, going back to Hobbes and before him, of course, all the way to Lorenzetti and further still, but also including a whole gamut of right-thinking people, from the 'well-mannered', such as Shaftesbury ('I know too, that the mere Vulgar of Mankind often stand in need of such a rectifying Object as *the Gallows* before their Eyes') through to the thoroughly reactionary Joseph de Maistre: 'All greatness, all power, all subordination rests on the executioner; he is both the horror and the bond of human association. Remove this incomprehensible agent from the world, and in a moment order gives way to chaos, thrones fall, and society disappears.' Deprive the world of the executioner, and all order disappears.[98] All the virtues admired by these thinkers, regardless of some of their profound differences – over obedience, authority, law and order, police, army, and the whole architecture of security – are united in the executioner. Hence Smith's vision of punishment as one of the fundamental forms of police power. The significance of identifying the 'dread of death' as 'one of the most important principles in human nature' in the opening chapter of *The Theory of Moral Sentiments* is now abundantly clear: the key to sovereign power is policing the fear of death.

'The modern State manages death in a number of different ways', observes Nicos Poulantzas.[99] Nothing officially exists unless it is noted,

96 Ibid., pp. 84–5, 88, 90, 333.

97 Ibid., pp. 79, 83–4, 90, 118–19.

98 Earl of Shaftesbury, '*Sensus Communis*: An Essay on the Freedom of Wit and Humour' (1709), in *Characteristicks of Men, Manners, Opinions, Times, Vol. I* (Indianapolis: Liberty Fund, 2001 [1711]), p. 79; Joseph de Maistre, *The St Petersburg Dialogues. Or, Conversations on the Temporal Government of Providence*, transl. Richard A. Lebrun (Montreal: McGill-Queen's University Press, 1993 [1821]), pp. 20, 207.

99 Nicos Poulantzas, *State, Power, Socialism*, transl. Patrick Camiller (London: New Left Books, 1978), p. 82.

recorded and classified by the state, and this political administration extends to death. Whether you live or die is of no interest to the state. What is of interest is the who, what, when and how of death, and this the state claims the authority to determine. This is one reason why, from the onset of capitalism, political economists started counting the dead and the causes of their death. This would appear to be an outcome of the founding myth of the commonwealth as recounted by Hobbes and revised by Petty: we enter the state to avoid the fear of violent death but, once this occurs, we must acknowledge that our subjection to the state extends to the political administration of death. Moreover, as well as claiming the right to be the only power to cause death deliberately, reinforcing the centrality of capital punishment to sovereign power, the state also demands authority over that ultimate token of autonomy – namely, one's ability to choose the time and manner of one's own death.[100]

Whichever way you die, you are not dead until you are officially administered as a dead subject by the state. Only then can you consider yourself in perpetual peace and security. In the meantime, during the period in which the state polices us as the objects and subjects of political administration, the period from birth to death, the state also knowingly administers us as fearful subjects. It administers us as subjects whose greatest fear is death and all the darkness which surrounds it, including all the other fears that emerge from within our darkness. The message is clear: acknowledge your darkness, accept the offerings made in the name of security, and be grateful for your pacification.

'Death has us by the scruff of the neck' I: security

Despite important differences in their work, Hobbes and Smith are exemplary thinkers on the nature of a social order driven by 'possessive individualism', whether that possessiveness comes in the form of an aggressive and antagonistic search for honour and glory (Hobbes) or a self-regarding but sympathetic competitiveness (Smith). A fundamental feature of such an order for both thinkers is a sovereign power whose security industry reminds us over and over of our fear of death, and does so in large part by reminding us of the myriad threats we face:

100 See Mark Neocleous, *The Most Beautiful Suicide* (forthcoming).

threats from without, in the darkness, and threats from within, in our darkness. On such threats and fears security resides. The point appears to be the need for something that might act as a political condition of security, and might do so because of our darkest fears, most notably the fear of death, while also revealing that anything we might call 'real' security is possible only in death. These visions of politics consider both the public (political) and private (psychological) sides of security, but also, simultaneously, the impossibility of security other than in death. Harking back to the Christian tradition, security is still in some sense divine, but divine only by virtue of being a feeling achieved with the divine. In the meantime, all that we have is the temporary, uncertain, and even threatening security offered by the sovereign power. This security plays heavily on the concept that will much later become something called 'insecurity', but about which these writers have absolutely nothing to say.

All of which provides a kind of historico-theological backdrop to the political problem we face in thinking about security as pacification – a problem which, for a number of reasons, points to a fundamental bind, touched upon by Jean Baudrillard when he observes that 'our obsessional compulsion for security can be interpreted as a gigantic collective ascesis, an anticipation of death in life itself'. Security, he suggests, is some kind of pact devised in opposition to death, which is precisely why it has come to stand as the basis of sovereignty and aligns with political economy.[101] What, then, is the bind?

First, the peace and security of being in the arms of God was no doubt once highly reassuring, but we are in the rather unfortunate position of having disillusioned man so that he no longer revolves around God, without simultaneously abolishing the conditions of that illusion. God is dead. A new secular and mortal God has been created: *securitas*. Our liberation from a *theology* of perpetual security has been used to reinforce our belief in a *politics* of transitory securities, in the form of a secular state which likes to reassure us that it can perform the task of God, all the while knowing, and knowing that we too also know, that such a task is impossible. This may well be the greatest instantiation of the sly and crafty knowingness inherent in the cunning of security.

101 Jean Baudrillard, *Symbolic Exchange and Death*, transl. Iain Hamilton Grant (London: Sage, 1993 [1976]), p. 178.

Second, what this tells us is that security wants to dispossess us of our own death. 'Terror management' is the term used by psychologists to understand our 'insecurity' in relation to death (following Ernest Becker's path-breaking *Denial of Death*); but it is also a term that describes perfectly what takes place in security politics. These came together following the attacks on the World Trade Center in 2001: 'Our work has . . . suddenly been recognized to be relevant to current circumstances', noted the leading psychologists in the field of terror management in 2002.[102] The existential 'taming of terror' in the face of death coincides with the political 'taming of terror' offered to us by the security industry as the grounds of its power. To the extent that security wants to dispossess us of our death in this way, so it allows 'insecurity' to step in and consume our thinking. Instead of developing the critique of political economy, and with it the critique of security, we are instead expected to fall back on the constant refrain of 'insecurity'. But the cry of 'insecurity' is impossible to disconnect from a cry for security and an acceptance of the pacification conducted in its name. Aside from anything else, this is why 'insecurity' has absolutely no purchase as a critical idea.

Third, if there is one thing that might be said about security, it is that it is a death machine. This is why security undergirds modernity's social wars as well as its international order. Carol Cohn, writing about her experience of working with security intellectuals, comments that she came to see herself as 'a feminist in the house of death'.[103] Let us be honest: security is a system for the manufacture of corpses. Better still, with an eye on the chapter to follow, security is a system for the manufacture of the Enemy that figures as both patient and corpse. Securitas holding the gallows in Lorenzetti's fresco now takes the form of the images on our TV screens of piles of corpses created in the name of security. From the gallows to the drone: *I am security, I hold death in my hands*. And yet, surviving through the manufacture of death and thriving on the spectacle that this creates, security has an easy time insisting that what it is doing is necessary because of our purported insecurities

102 Tom Pyszczynski, Sheldon Solomon and Jeff Greenberg, *In the Wake of 9/11: The Psychology of Terror* (Washington, DC: American Psychological Association, 2002), p. 8; Ernest Becker, *The Denial of Death* (New York: Free Press, 1973), p. 145.

103 Carol Cohn, 'Sex and Death in the Rational World of Defense Intellectuals', *Signs: Journal of Women in Culture and Society* 12: 4 (1987), p. 691.

and fear of death. The terror before the abyss of death is to be administered by a consciousness of an abstract 'security', and then a series of concrete 'security measures'. Yet all that then transpires is a terrible fear in the face of those very same measures: security as the sublimation of death, reducing us to terror management.

'Death has us by the scruff of the neck at every moment', Montaigne once reminded us, as if we needed reminding. But he added that a person who has learned how to die has unlearned how to be a slave: 'to practice death is to practice freedom', he added, hinting at the work of many an ancient philosopher. Paraphrasing Montaigne, we could say that genuinely practising death might be a way of learning how not to be a slave to security, and hence might be the basis of our liberation from the jargon of insecurity and the pacification that takes place in its name. My paraphrasing here might not be so far off the mark, at least as regards Montaigne. According to Giovanni Botero's 1588 *Treatise Concerning the Causes of the Magnificency and Greatness of Cities*, the 'multitude of thieves and murderers' in France had led to an increasing number of 'confines, boundaries, ditches, hedges and enclosures', and the employment of large numbers of police officers ('watchmen') to oversee the security of private estates and property.[104] 'Fear [was] always and everywhere', Lucien Febvre remarked, following his reading of countless autobiographies written in the sixteenth century – not just fear of thieves and murderers, but also 'fear of spirits, whose exploits are constantly recounted by old wives; fear of the night, which is haunted; fear of the specks of dust dancing in a beam of light'.[105] Yet Montaigne employed one elderly doorkeeper and – contra Hobbes's knowing reminder to us of the everyday practices that are manifestations of our fear, such as locking our doors – Montaigne often did not lock his door, sensing perhaps that allowing such fears to dominate our imagination would push us into the banal world of security, and distract us from learning

104 Michel de Montaigne, 'To Philosophize Is to Learn How to Die', in *The Complete Essays*, transl. M. A. Screech (London: Penguin, 1987 [1580]), pp. 89–108; Giovanni Botero, *The Greatness of Cities* (1588), in Giovanni Botero, *The Reason of State* and *The Greatness of Cities*, both transl. Robert Peterson (London: Routledge, 1956), p. 279.

105 Lucien Febvre, *The Problem of Unbelief in the Sixteenth Century: The Religion of Rabelais*, transl. Beatrice Gottlieb (Cambridge, MA: Harvard University Press, 1982 [1942]), p. 409.

how to die. The thing to fear most is fear, especially fear of death, was Montaigne's position – for this is what underpins the cruelty of the rulers and the suffering of the rulers' victims. Practising death is thus not only a practice of freedom, but a practice of freedom from cruelty and from security, and from security as cruelty: it is security as well as death that now has us by the scruff of the neck. Perhaps this is because we have forgotten how to die. Perhaps this is the darkness we need to acknowledge, which a critical theory of pacification highlights. This would make such a theory a form of 'thinking that does not shy away from the horror of the world, the darkness, but looks it straight in the face, and thus passes over into a different kingdom, which is not the kingdom of darkness'.[106]

'The disturbed relationship with the dead . . . is one of the symptoms of the sickness of today', observe Theodor Adorno and Max Horkheimer. If we lived a genuinely fulfilled and non-pacified life, then perhaps we would be better positioned to embrace death without fear, even to the point of freely choosing the time and manner of our own deaths in an act of defiant autonomy. A society in which death is an instrument of pacification requires a destruction of the ideology of death itself, which, as Marcuse noted, would also be 'an explosive transvaluation of social concepts'.[107] To the extent that security seeks to take our future from us in this way, it colonizes any thinking about alternative futures, pacifying us under its power. The future comes to be appropriated by the supreme concept of bourgeois society and the security industry's myth of its own power, perpetuating the illusion of security through a jargon of fear, insecurity and terror.

'Do not fear death so much, fear an inadequate life!' one of the characters says in Bertolt Brecht's play *The Mother* (1931). The character, Pelagea Vlassova, is being visited by some religiously minded peasants who have come to console her over the death of her son, Pavel, a communist murdered by members of the security apparatus. The peasants see

106 Henri Lefebvre, *The Critique of Everyday Life, Vol. 3*, transl. Gregory Elliott (London: Verso, 2005 [1981]), p. 171.

107 Theodor Adorno and Max Horkheimer, *Dialectic of Enlightenment*, transl. John Cumming (London: Verso, 1979 [1944]), p. 215; Herbert Marcuse, 'The Ideology of Death', in *Philosophy, Psychoanalysis and Emancipation: Collected Papers of Herbert Marcuse, Vol. 5*, eds Douglas Kellner and Clayton Pierce (London: Routledge, 2011 [1959]), p. 128.

this as an opportunity to teach her that living a religious life is much better than fighting a communist life, but Pelagea responds that her son was willing to fight for communism because he was *not afraid to die*. More to the point, her son preferred to die fighting against our pacification by the state and its accumulation regime. Do not fear death so much, fear a pacified life.

3

The Art of Well Building

> *To maintain and transmit a value system, human beings are punched, bullied, sent to jail, thrown into concentration camps, cajoled, bribed, made into heroes, encouraged to read newspapers, stood up against a wall and shot, and sometimes even taught sociology.*
>
> Barrington Moore Jr, *Social Origins of Dictatorship and Democracy* (1967)

In *Leviathan*, Hobbes spells out for us the implications of living in the 'natural condition'. I have touched on many of them in the previous chapters, but here is the famous passage where he runs through them one by one:

> Whatsoever therefore is consequent to a time of Warre, where every man is Enemy to every man; the same is consequent to the time, wherein men live without other security, than what their own strength, and their own invention shall furnish them withall. In such condition, there is no place for Industry; because the fruit thereof is uncertain: and consequently no Culture of the Earth; no Navigation, nor use of the commodities that may be imported by Sea; no commodious Building; no instruments of moving, and removing such things as require much force; no Knowledge of the face of the Earth; no account of Time; no Arts; no Letters; no Society; and which is worst of all, continuall feare, and danger of

violent death; And the life of man, solitary, poore, nasty, brutish, and short.[1]

This paragraph has been subject to extensive analysis and cited many times, not least for the famous description of the natural condition as being a war of all against all in which life would be nasty, brutish, and short. Perhaps the least analysed part of the paragraph is Hobbes's comment that in the state of nature there would be no *commodious building*.

At the time Hobbes was writing, *commodious* had connotations of 'beneficial', 'advantageous', 'convenient' and 'profitable', from the Medieval Latin *commodiosus* ('convenient', 'useful') and *commodus* ('proper', 'fit', 'appropriate', 'convenient', 'satisfactory'), as well as the connotations it now possesses of 'roomy', 'spacious' or 'sufficiently large'. The word also hinted at a lifestyle that was free from hardship, as seen from Hobbes's comment at the very end of Chapter 13 of *Leviathan*, where he writes about 'commodious living'. The *building* Hobbes had in mind was not simply the construction of buildings, but of buildings that benefited other things, such as the arts, commerce and navigation, and perhaps also the building up of these things themselves, and maybe even the building of a political order that makes possible the very labour that produces these things. But, without a sovereign power, there can be no building of any kind whatsoever, whether commodious or otherwise. Political power is thus, for Hobbes, an 'art of well building'. This picks up on the meaning of 'constitution' discussed in Chapter 1 – namely, that what is being built is being *constituted*. In the founding act of creation, human beings sought to 'constitute Common-wealths' and establish some principles of reason 'to make their constitution . . . everlasting'.[2] What is being constituted is the state – but also the state as a power to *constitute social order*, and thereby give life and motion to civil society. The state is an artifice of people, a creation called the commonwealth; but those same people are in turn constituted as a People by the state. Once this happens, all sorts of other building and constituting can take place, of the kind listed in the passage cited. Hobbes wants us to

1 Thomas Hobbes, *Leviathan*, ed. Richard Tuck (Cambridge: Cambridge University Press, 1991 [1651]), p. 89.

2 Ibid., p. 232.

understand that, although man might well be a wolf to man, as indicated in invocation of the state of nature, in terms of creativity and production man is also a kind of God to man.

We might consider this in the terms laid out by Hobbes in Chapter 15 of *De Cive*, where he spells out the significance of sovereign power by using God's response to Job (Job 38:4), following Job's remonstrations with God that he, Job, has been a just man, and yet God has made him suffer so much. God's response is simple: Where were you when I surveyed the earth? Where were you when I mapped out its lines and territories? Where were you when I made possible the navigation of the seas? Where were you when I tamed the monsters? More than anything, *where were you when I laid the foundation of the earth*? Job has no answer. Recall, furthermore, that Job is God's servant, and yet God is implying that it is he who has performed the real work of creation. The message is clear: you, the worker, the menial servant, did nothing; I, the sovereign master, *built this thing*, and in so doing I *made everything else possible*.

If ever there was an art of well building, the bourgeois class has mastered it. One of the points Marx and Engels make in the *Manifesto of the Communist Party* is that the bourgeoisie, in its rise to power, sought the continuous destruction of those things considered 'premodern' and non-bourgeois – but that this destruction was part of the building of a new world, one which will in turn be rebuilt, over and over again. This is why, in bourgeois society, things are perpetually disturbed, even before they settle: 'All that is solid melts into air', as Marx and Engels famously put it. The modern world has been built by the bourgeoisie. It *forged* itself as a class, *brought into existence* another class to work for it for a wage, and *built* a world after its own image. The same class also continuously applies its creative powers, and does so by assiduously replacing, renewing, regenerating, reintegrating and redesigning its own world. The bourgeoisie has thus fulfilled a double mission: *destructive* in its annihilation of old societies, former modes of life and non-commodified forms of subsistence; but also *constructive* in building nothing less than the material conditions of a new world.

With this in mind, and developing an argument I have previously made about the powers of war and police in the fabrication of social order, we need to consider pacification as a *productive process*. Without losing sight of pacification's destructive nature, I will focus here on its constructive dimension: pacification as the art of well building.

Consider, to begin with, a propaganda statement from the heyday of the war on terror. It came in 2010, and followed the angry response by Afghans to the destruction by American rocket-propelled explosives and airstrikes of the village of Tarok Kolache, in the Kandahar province of Afghanistan. On hearing about the anger, one US spokesperson commented: 'Sure they are pissed about the loss of their mud huts . . . but that is why the BUILD story is important.'[3] 'The build story': an ambiguous phrase with multiple synonyms, as we shall see, each of which is equally ambiguous. Yet it is an interesting phrase, given the destruction to which it refers in this case, and also because the spokesperson clearly took it as read that the meaning of the phrase was clear. 'The build story' draws our attention to a central idea within the prose of pacification: that pacification is a process of construction and reconstruction (or at least imagined as such by those who preach it), its practitioners and thinkers inviting us into their world where they endlessly speak and write of building and rebuilding, creating and recreating, designing and redesigning, organizing and reorganizing, structuring and restructuring, constituting and reconstituting. The prose draws our attention to an absolute faith in social construction, the vagueness of which does little to undermine its centrality to the prose or its ability to unify the minds of counterinsurgency thinkers. This is pacification as the building of schools and clinics, the naming of peoples, the making of maps, the distribution of land, the collection of taxes, the determining of the official language, the planning of the school curriculum, the cultivation of land and crops, and the manufacture of commodities. It is pacification as political administration, the ultimate end of which is the fabrication of a social order in which insurgency is expected neither to thrive nor even survive. It is pacification as social police, as I will call it towards the end of the chapter, in unity with pacification as social war. This chapter therefore seeks to make good a claim made in the Introduction – namely, that to understand pacification is to understand how social order is produced.

3 The statement was from Paula Broadwell, one-time US Army Reserve lieutenant colonel, and then close confidant and biographer of David Petraeus. Cited Spencer Ackerman, '25 Tons of Bombs Wipe Afghan Town Off Map', *Wired*, 19 January 2011.

As the expression of a will to power and a desire to organize the conduct of conduct by forcing people to change their lives, adjust their behaviour, transform themselves as subjects and learn to desire their subjection, pacification is a war to build the world anew, again and again, in a project of continual improvement, forcing us to view the project of pacification through the lens of the third prong of its core tripartite logic: Clear–Hold–*Build*.

Clear–Hold–Build

In 2014, Rory Stewart talked about his experience of walking 6,000 miles through Afghanistan between 2000 and 2002, being sent to Iraq to administer two provinces and help write the country's new constitution during the war on terror, and then writing two bestselling memoirs about those experiences. He sought to capture some of the uncertainties surrounding the idea of 'counterinsurgency', comparing it to a kind of theological madness:

> Our entire conceptual framework was mad. All these theories – counterinsurgency warfare, state building – were actually complete abstract madness. They were like very weird religious systems, because they always break down into three principles, 10 functions, seven this or that. So they're reminiscent of Buddhists who say: 'These are the four paths', or of Christians who say: 'These are the seven deadly sins.' They're sort of theologies, essentially, made by people like Buddhist monks in the eighth century – people who have a fundamental faith, which is probably, in the end, itself completely delusional.[4]

Stewart was, no doubt, on to something. Certainly, reading counterinsurgency texts or working close to security intellectuals, one gets the strong sense of a religious cult. Counterinsurgency works! We believe! You should believe! And, in the light of the discussion in Chapter 2, it is a cult that worships the supreme concept of bourgeois society, the God called 'Security'. Open any text on pacification or counterinsurgency, and the

---

4 In Decca Aitkenhead, 'Rory Stewart: "The Secret of Modern Britain Is There Is No Power Anywhere"', *Guardian*, 3 January 2014.

prose is replete with one or another iteration of cult-like doctrine: 'Seven Pillars', 'Thirteen Points', 'Nine Rules', 'Five Basic Principles', 'Twenty-eight Articles', 'Four Laws', 'Eight Steps', among many others. One such doctrine even takes the form of a Holy Trinity: Clear–Hold–Build.

The US Army/Marine Corps *Counterinsurgency Field Manual* (2006) offers 'Clear–Hold–Build' as one of counterinsurgency's three strategies. Prior to the *Manual*'s publication in 2006, Secretary of State Condoleezza Rice informed the Senate Committee on Foreign Relations (on 19 October 2005) that the US strategy was to 'clear, hold, and build'.

> With our Iraqi allies, we are working to:
> - Clear the toughest places – no sanctuaries to the enemy – and disrupt foreign support for the insurgents.
> - Hold and steadily enlarge the secure areas . . .
> - Build truly national institutions . . . These Iraqi institutions must sustain security forces, bring rule of law, visibly deliver essential services, and offer the Iraqi people hope for a better economic future.

'Clear–Hold–Build' had come to Rice's attention via Philip Zelikow, a former official at the National Security Council. In preparation for his work on Iraq, Zelikow familiarized himself with literature on the Vietnam War, including Lewis Sorley's *A Better War*, which was being widely read at the time. Sorely's book discusses a 'clear and hold' doctrine. Writing the draft of Rice's testimony to the Committee, Zelikow included the phrase 'clear and hold', but General Odierno, having read the draft, recommended to Zelikow that the word 'build' be added to capture the wider nature of the campaign. 'Clear–Hold–Build' entered the war on terror.[5]

But its entry was by no means straightforward. Donald Rumsfeld was keen to avoid anything that looked like 'nation-building', and was apparently alarmed by this emphasis on Clear–Hold–Build.[6]

---

5 David E. Johnson et al., *The US Army and the Battle for Baghdad* (Santa Monica: RAND, 2019), p. 104; Lewis Sorley, *A Better War: The Unexamined Victories and Final Tragedy of America's Last Years in Vietnam* (New York: Harcourt Brace, 1999), pp. 7, 29, 75.

6 Fred Kaplan, *The Insurgents: David Petraeus and the Plot to Change the American Way of War* (New York: Simon & Schuster, 2013), pp. 196–7.

Nonetheless, just a week after Rice's comments, President Bush announced: 'Our strategy is to clear, hold, and build. We're working to clear areas from terrorist control, to hold those areas securely, and to build lasting, democratic Iraqi institutions.' Despite the sustained objections of Rumsfeld and others, and despite Bush himself insisting that the United States had no interest in nation-building, Bush continued to claim in speeches that US strategy had changed: 'Instead of coming in and removing the terrorists, and then moving on, the Iraqi government and the coalition adopted a new approach called clear, hold, and build.' Factsheets were prepared to accompany such speeches, with titles such as 'Strategy for Victory: Clear, Hold, and Build', and the 'Baghdad Security Plan' was designed to implement the strategy. By the time the *Counterinsurgency Manual* was published, the trinity had been formalized as doctrine: *clear* the area by eliminating or neutralizing insurgents, *hold* the area with security forces, and *build* a new social order. Such building is said to involve organizing a society and mobilizing its productive forces and energies in order to build capacities, build infrastructure, build security, build understanding, build objects of value, build trust, build cooperation, build confidence, build esprit. In effect, the aim is to legitimize pacification by producing consent, and to produce consent by building a new social order. There were various tweaks to the idea. For example, one Congressional Research Service report observed in 2008 that a major general in Baghdad had described the plan as 'clear, control, and retain' (clearing out insurgents, controlling those neighbourhoods that had been cleared, and 'retaining' the neighbourhoods) – though it conceded that this was in fact simply 'another paraphrase of "clear, hold, build"'. In 2009, debates were also taking place within the Department of Defense. Robert Gates recorded a plan to improve the ability to 'clear' and 'hold' some key areas in sufficient enough fashion to 'build' a social order immune to insurgency.[7]

---

7 President George W. Bush, 'Address to Joint Armed Forces Officers' Wives', Washington, DC, 25 October 2005, and 'President Discusses War on Terror and Operation Iraqi Freedom', Cleveland, Ohio, 20 March 2006 – both available at georgewbush-whitehouse.archives.gov; Catherine Dale, *Operation Iraqi Freedom: Strategies, Approaches, Results, and Issues for Congress* (CRS Report for Congress, 28 March 2008); Robert M. Gates, *Duty: Memoirs of a Secretary at War* (New York: Alfred A. Knopf, 2014), p. 341.

To put it bluntly, Clear–Hold–Build has come to be reasserted as the Holy Trinity of pacification in the twenty-first century. Clear–Hold–Build is NATO's 'preferred operational approach' in the *Allied Joint Doctrine for Counterinsurgency* (2011): the organization's 'Generic Reference Curriculum' for counterinsurgency training includes a course on 'Clear–Hold–Build', which it describes as a 'whole of government approach'.[8] The *British Army Field Manual: Countering Insurgency* (2009) cites one brigade commander on his work in Afghanistan in 2007: 'In essence it boiled down to a requirement to CLEAR, HOLD, BUILD where we could and DISRUPT, INTERDICT, DEFEAT where we could not . . . We were very clear that we were not going to CLEAR unless we could HOLD; and we're not going to HOLD unless we could BUILD.' The *Manual* adds some nuance to the general point, reflecting the wider interests among the Western alliance in tweaking the doctrine a little, for example into 'Shape, Secure, Develop' or 'Engage, Secure, Develop'. This played heavily on the 'Security and Development' couplet popular among academics, policy wonks and politicians – especially those who liked to talk of human rights and humanitarian intervention, but, as the British *Manual* puts it, the 'Develop' of 'Shape–Secure–Develop' is really just a euphemism for the 'Build' in 'Clear–Hold–Build'.[9] The International Security Assistance Force, the name of NATO's coalition in Afghanistan, offers 'Shape/Clear/Hold/Build', where the objective of all the building of relationships, institutions, continuity, stability, structures and mechanisms is ultimately to 'build a coherent Afghan state'.[10] In 2010, Anthony Cordesman of the Washington-based Center for Strategic and International Studies, asked whether such terms are merely buzzwords. 'The British have used the phrase: "Shape, clear, hold, and build" while senior US NSC officials have used the term "Clear, hold, build, and transfer". None of these terms have yet been defined in detail, or in the form of clear operational

8 NATO, *Allied Joint Doctrine for Counterinsurgency (COIN) – AJP 3.4.4* (NATO, February 2011), Section 5–13; NATO, *Counterinsurgency: A Generic Reference Curriculum* (NATO, n.d.), p. 56.

9 *British Army Field Manual, Vol. 1 Part 10: Countering Insurgency*, Army Code 71876 (2009), Sections 4-11, 4-17, 4-25, 4-26, 4-33.

10 General Stanley A. McChrystal, *Commander's Initial Assessment*, NATO International Security Assistance Force (Afghanistan: 30 August 2009), A-2, pp. 2–9.

plans and goals.' The fact that none of the terms were clearly defined or offered any clarity in terms of operations is reflected in the use of synonyms, the most obvious of which – despite Rumsfeld's concerns – is 'nation-building'. Cordesman, for example, suggests in the same document that the war in Afghanistan 'is an exercise in armed nation building and anyone who denies this is simply a fool or a liar'.[11] The US Army and Marine Corps' *Counterinsurgency Manual* reflects David Petraeus's belief in nation-building, and Sarah Sewell, in her Introduction to the *Manual*, insists that what is at stake is the development of 'operational capacities for nation-building'. Lieutenant Colonel John Nagl, one of the architects of the *Manual*, suggests that counterinsurgency is a project 'to change entire societies' – and plenty of other similarly placed commentators have repeated the point.[12]

Despite the frequent assertion that Clear–Hold–Build is a twenty-first-century doctrine, its roots lie deep in the prose of pacification. The Army and Marine Corps *Manual*, for example, finds the doctrine's roots in 'Search–Destroy–Clear–Hold–Secure' or 'Build–Secure–Clear' programmes during the attempted pacification of Vietnam. Indeed, the official history of the US Army's counterinsurgency operations describes 'clear-and-hold–type pacification operations' as the army's 'bread and butter', developed and employed most forcefully during the early 1960s.[13] Counterinsurgency manuals also often claim that doctrines used in Vietnam, such as 'Search–Destroy–Clear–Hold–Secure' are 'the doctrinal precedent of the modern Clear–Hold–Build approach'.[14] This focus on the roots of Clear–Hold–Build in Vietnam is one reason why

11 Anthony H. Cordesman, with Nicholas B. Greenough, *Shape, Clear, Hold, Build, and Transfer: The Full Metrics of the Afghan War* (Washington, DC: Center for Strategic and International Studies, 2010), p. 117.

12 Lieutenant General David H. Petraeus, U.S. Army, 'Learning Counterinsurgency: Observations from Soldiering in Iraq', *Military Review* 86: 12 (January–February 2006); Sarah Sewell, 'Introduction', in US Army/Marine Corps, *Counterinsurgency Field Manual: U.S. Army Field Manual No. 3-24/Marine Corps Warfighting Publication No. 3-33.5* (2006) (Chicago, IL: University of Chicago Press, 2007), p. xxx; John Nagl, 'Review of The Echo of Battle', *RUSI Journal* 153: 2 (2008), p. 83.

13 Andrew J. Birtle, *US Army Counterinsurgency and Contingency Operations Doctrine 1942–1976* (Washington, DC: Center of Military History, United States Army, 2006), pp. 252–4, 263, 314.

14 US Army Command and General Staff College, *Establishing A Suitable Tactical Design Model for Clear–Hold–Build Counterinsurgency Operations* (Leavenworth, KS: 2015), p. 25.

so many books on that war highlight the doctrine, such as Thomas Richardson's *Destroy and Build: Pacification in Phuoc Tuy, 1966–72* (2017), Andrew J. Gawthorpe's *To Build as Well as Destroy: American Nation Building in South Vietnam* (2018), and Robert J. Thompson's *Clear, Hold, and Destroy: Pacification in Phú Yên and the American War in Vietnam* (2021).

What we have, then, is a very powerful tradition of framing pacification as productive by describing it as a building project. Let us try to make sense of this by means of a vignette concerning French tactics during the Rif War of 1925–26, which appears in NATO's *Counterinsurgency* manual, cited above:

> The French governor was Marshall Lyautey, a pupil of French General Gallieni, designer of the soft colonisation concept and of the 'oil spot method' for counterinsurgency . . . The French plan consisted of three phases. First, they drove Abd el Krim's forces back into the mountains before the rainy season and coordinated with Spain. These operations *cleared* the area. Then Lyautey started the *hold* phase by taking advantage of the operational pause provided by the rains, undermining Abd el Krim's authority and support by using political and psychological operations against the tribes. Early in May 1926, a final push broke the remaining rebellion and captured Abd el Krim. Then, the *build phase* restored the Sultan's authority and administration over the whole country.[15]

Why would a twenty-first-century NATO manual refer to two French military leaders whose main work took place in the late nineteenth and early twentieth centuries?

In an essay on the colonial role of the army, published in 1900 in both a popular general-interest journal, *Revue des Deux Mondes*, and as a short pamphlet, Lyautey suggests that pacification cannot reside solely in destroying the people under a regime of terror: 'A country is not conquered and pacified when a military operation has decimated the inhabitants and bowed them under terror, because once the terror calms down it will germinate a mass revolt.' What is needed is construction: 'It must be remembered that in colonial struggles we

15 NATO, *Allied Joint Doctrine for Counterinsurgency*, 55. Emphases added.

must destroy only in the last resort, and . . . destroy only to build better.' The first responsibilities are 'to rebuild the village, create a market, establish a school. It is the combined action of politics and force that will result in the pacification of the country.'[16] Lyautey makes the point that what is needed to build in this way is not an *army in the colonies* but a *colonial army*. These are not the same thing. Why? Because a colonial army is engaged in pacification, and not simply military occupation. This idea alludes to what Lyautey, in an earlier essay, had called the 'social role of the officer'. Such a role includes a moral obligation to build and develop the social order being pacified. It requires soldiers to be leaders, teachers, gardeners, and any other roles necessary in the fabrication of social order. 'He who is only a soldier is a bad soldier', Lyautey liked to say, because pacification involves organizing the people, building markets and villages, creating a tax system and a money economy.[17]

Lyautey's arguments about the social duties of the soldier and the colonial army 'became part of the intellectual equipment of numerous "thinking" soldiers', notes Peter Paret. The arguments also resonated with liberal thinkers and the colonial reason exercised by the French state.[18] In 1893, French businesses formed the Union Coloniale Française, seeking to establish 'all measures necessary to support the development, the prosperity and the defence of various branches of Trade and Industry in . . . lands under French influence.'[19] Staunch believers in private enterprise and trade, their interest was in capitalist expansion, not military control – though there was a strong ideological convergence between these things. This convergence was captured in the idea of pacification as more than 'lines of operations' and 'invasion routes', but rather as a productive process towards nothing less than 'the

16 Hubert Lyautey, 'Du rôle colonial de l'armée', *Revue des Deux Mondes* 157 (1900), pp. 308–28; Hubert Lyautey, *Du Rôle colonial de l'armée* (Paris: Armand Colin, 1900), p. 18.

17 Hubert Lyautey, *Le Rôle social de l'officier* (Paris: Librarie Plon, 1935 [1891]).

18 Peter Paret, *French Revolutionary Warfare from Indochina to Algeria: The Analysis of a Political and Military Doctrine* (London: Pall Mall, 1964), p. 108; Paul Rabinow, *French Modern: Norms and Forms of the Social Environment* (Cambridge, MA: MIT, 1989), pp. 9, 114.

19 Cited in A. S. Kanya-Forstner, *The Conquest of the Western Sudan: A Study in French Military Imperialism* (Cambridge: Cambridge University Press, 1969), p. 206.

commercial path of tomorrow'.[20] New periodicals were launched to peddle such ideas, such as *La Politique coloniale* (1891), and lecture tours were arranged to gain public support for them.[21] More broadly, as noted by André Maurois, Lyautey sought to build on liberal accounts of the civilizing process as articulated in the work of liberals such as John Stuart Mill, whose work Lyautey spent many hours discussing with General Gallieni.[22]

'All this is Gallieni', Lyautey liked to say when describing his own work.[23] Much of Lyautey's essay on the colonial role of the army consists of quotes from the set of instructions on colonial rule issued in 1898 by General Gallieni, the governor of Madagascar and leading strategist of French colonial warfare, who appointed Lyautey as his chief of staff. 'The best way to achieve pacification in our new colony is to employ the combined action of force and politics', claimed Gallieni in 'Principes de Pacification et d'Organisation', written as part of his *Trois Colonnes au Tonkin, 1894–1895*. By 'force' and 'politics' he means 'destruction' and 'reconstruction', respectively. These go together, yet he insists that it is 'the political action that is the most important', for the political act of reconstruction derives its strength from a knowledge of the country and its inhabitants, which is then used in turn to better pacify the population.[24] Reconstruction of the country is intended to be a 'new mode of existence':

> As pacification takes hold, the country becomes more cultivated, the markets reopen, commerce resumes. The role of the soldier takes second place [and] that of the administrator begins. On the one hand, it is necessary to study and satisfy the social needs of the population and, on the other hand, extend colonization to enhance

20 Lyautey, *Du Rôle colonial*, p. 15. See also Hubert Lyautey, *Dans le sud de Madagascar: pénétration militaire, situation politique et économique, 1900-1902* (Paris: Henri Charles-Lavauzelle, 1903), pp. 300–10.

21 Kanya-Forstner, *Conquest of the Western Sudan*, p. 207.

22 André Maurois, *Marshal Lyautey* (London: John Lane, 1931), pp. 59, 155.

23 Hubert Lyautey, journal entry for 16, 17 and 18 March 1896, and letter to his sister, 30 September 1895, both in *Lettres du Tonkin et de Madagascar, 1894–1899, Tome I* (Paris: Librarie Armand Colin, 1920), pp. 237, 334; Lyautey, *Dans le sud de Madagascar*, p. 248.

24 Joseph-Simon Gallieni, *Trois Colonnes au Tonkin, 1894–1895* (Paris: Librairie Militaire R. Chapelot, 1899), p. 154; Lyautey, *Du Rôle colonial*, p. 16.

the natural wealth of the soil and open up markets for European trade.

The pacified subject 'will therefore have to overcome his laziness and resolutely set himself to work, either by increasing his crops and adopting more productive methods' or by 'lending' to the European colonists the colonial workforce. Pacification is deemed a success, according to Gallieni, when 'the country becomes more civilized, markets are reopened, trade is re-established'. Markets, trade, and production: *voilà, la pacification*, writes Lyautey.[25]

What emerges from claims such as these is the idea of pacification as the construction of an order in which insurgency will either not arise or will not gain enough support from the people if it does. What counts is not just *clearing* and *holding* a territory but *building* a new type of order: markets constructed; railway lines laid; telegraph lines erected; villages, streets and public buildings created; teachers, social workers and police officers trained – all towards a new social order organized around bourgeois notions of commerce, trade and work. Lyautey is said to have been fond of claiming: 'Un chantier vaut un bataillon' – a construction site is worth more than a battalion; though he also sometimes preferred *hôpital* to *chantier*.[26]

A hospital is worth more than a battalion. Hospitals are to be constructed at the very moment and during the same process as lives are being destroyed, bodies maimed, and minds fractured beyond belief. This is why Frantz Fanon situates the hospital at the heart of the French state's attempted pacification of countries such as Algeria, and why Michel Foucault identifies the importance of the medical aspect of the military management of space.[27] The hospital and the clinic operate as the institutional base of a medical police that not only helps develop a knowledge of the population, but reshapes that very population

25 Gallieni, *Trois Colonnes au Tonkin*, pp. 157–8; Lyautey, *Du Rôle colonial*, p. 20.

26 Gwendolyn Wright, *The Politics of Design in French Colonial Urbanism* (Chicago: University of Chicago Press, 1991), pp. 76, 340.

27 Frantz Fanon, *A Dying Colonialism*, transl. Haakon Chevalier (New York: Grove Press, 1965 [1959]), pp. 121–45; Michel Foucault, 'The Eye of Power: A Conversation with Jean-Pierre Barou and Michelle Perrot' (1977), in Michel Foucault, *Power/Knowledge: Selected Interviews and Other Writings 1972–1977*, ed. Colin Gordon (Brighton: Harvester, 1988), p. 151.

according to the exigencies of the pacifying power – that is, medical police as pacification. The power to treat and cure through the medical police goes hand-in-hand with the power to educate through the police of ideology. The prose of pacification is replete with comments and descriptions of building regular schools, vocational schools and agricultural schools.[28] Through education, 'we make population our first auxiliary', Lyautey comments, adding that it is through education that the population 'learns the beneficial aspects of our occupation.'[29] Perhaps the population might even be taught sociology, as Barrington Moore Jr might say.

On the one hand, building hospitals and schools is intended to legitimize the violence of pacification. On the other hand, through such institutions the behaviour and consciousness of the pacified subject is to be constituted anew, as a subject who learns how to be pacified. In pacification, then, the enemy is certainly to be attacked, injured, damaged or killed, but the enemy is also to be treated, cured, recovered and rebuilt. In pacification, the enemy may end up a corpse, but is sometimes treated as a patient:

> Cinema newsreel: the invasion of the Marianas, including Guam. The impression is not of battles, but of civil engineering and blasting operations undertaken with immeasurably intensified vehemence, also of 'fumigation', insect-extermination on a terrestrial scale. Works are put in hand, until no grass grows. The enemy acts as patient and corpse.[30]

The prose of pacification imagines the state as doctor, curing the population of its ills, eradicating diseases such as communism and treating disorders such as insurgency, just as it imagines the state as educator of the people instilling a new type of civilization, and as social worker bringing the giddy rabble to its sober senses in the world of wage labour.

28 Lyautey, *Du Rôle colonial*, pp. 18–19, 27; Lyautey, 'Letter from Hanoi, 5 February 1895', in *Lettres du Tonkin et de Madagascar*, pp. 112–13; Lyautey, *Dans le sud de Madagascar*, p. 253.

29 Lyautey, journal entry for 16, 17 and 18 March 1896, p. 334.

30 Theodor Adorno, *Minima Moralia: Reflections from Damaged Life*, transl. E. F. N. Jephcott (London: Verso, 1978 [1944]), p. 56.

Involving a whole gamut of forces that constitute the powers of war and police, pacification employs armies of workers through all the sectors of society, 'a reservoir of foremen, workshop leaders, teachers, gardeners, farmers'. Pacification is a 'providential mission to introduce industrial, agricultural and economic life, and also, yes, it must be said, a higher moral life, a more complete life'.[31] Pacification is a work of *social reconstruction*, *moral transformation*, and *economic development* towards a new social order. Is this a 'social art' (Lyautey) or an 'engineering feat' (Gallieni)? Perhaps it is both – an 'art of social engineering', we might say. Perhaps this is also why Lyautey came to be known as the 'builder' of French Morocco, following his stint as resident-general there between 1912 and 1925. 'There are more than twenty towns in the world of my own building', he liked to boast, while overseeing the destruction of everything deemed obsolete.[32]

Where should we begin in building a higher moral and more complete life? How about with taxation? The prose of pacification is thick with discussions of money, especially debt (see Chapter 5). But another major topic is tax. Among Gallieni's first acts in the pacification of Madagascar in 1895 was the imposition of heavy taxes.[33] One reason was said to be to cover the costs of the building taking place, but taxation was also meant to have a far wider remit. It was intended, for example, to teach people the value of wage labour, since to pay the tax one either had to grow cash crops, work for wages, or send one's children to work for wages. Wage labour could thus be constituted through a new tax regime, which could in turn monetize the economy, pacifying through the money form and the morality it was expected to inculcate. The French used the term *impôt moralisateur*: 'moralizing tax'.[34] Taxation is a means of creating productive wage labourers and active economic subjects in a monetized economy – 'intended to be educative rather than a source of revenue', in the words of one British expert, who added that it 'has the

31 Lyautey, *Du Rôle colonial*, pp. 20–1.

32 Maurois, *Marshal Lyautey*, p. 281; V. Lutsky, *Modern History of the Arab Countries* (1949–53), transl. Lika Nasser (Moscow: Progress, 1969), pp. 30–6.

33 Joseph-Simon Gallieni, 'Letter to Chailley, 8 February 1901', in Joseph-Simon Gallieni, *Lettres de Madagascar 1896–1905* (Paris: Société d'éditions Géographiques, Maritimes et Coloniales, 1928), p. 66.

34 Joseph-Simon Gallieni, 'Considérations général sur le remaniement' (1904), in Hubert Deschamps and Paul Chauvet, eds, *Gallieni pacificateur: Écrits coloniaux de Gallieni* (Paris: Presses Universitaires de France, 1949), p. 362.

effect of curbing lawlessness, of accelerating progress to a higher plane, and of stimulating industry'.[35] Moreover, refusal to pay taxes is then treated as an insurgency that needs countering. The same theme runs through the prose of pacification: the tax collector 'personifies . . . government, administration, and power' (David Galula, 1963); 'to the last breath a government will try to collect taxes' (Bernard Fall, 1965); 'the tax collector and the policeman are the central government's more prominent representatives' (Robert Thompson, 1967).[36]

Bernard Fall liked to tell the following story of his experience in Vietnam:

> I went with large-scale maps to the Vietnamese provinces. The Provincial Governors, after many periods of tea drinking, got down to business. I said, 'I'm a student of political science and I'm interested in provincial administration. All I would like to know is, how is your taxation system here? Do you collect taxes?' The reason for this question, gentlemen, was very simple . . . we do judge a government by its ability to collect taxes.
>
> The Vietnamese Provincial Governor said, 'You know, I have quite a bit of difficulty with taxes. I just collect taxes in this area and that area, etc.' Then I went back to the tax rolls in Hanoi . . . and found that 85 percent of the delta villages were not paying any taxes. They hadn't been paying any taxes for years. Therefore, I, on my own maps, charted out those areas which did not pay taxes as areas highly unlikely to be effectively administered by the Vietnamese National Government. But I needed a cross-check. The cross-check was indeed very simple. Another thing any government that is worth its salt will try to do is to keep the schools open and schoolteachers in them. So, I went over to the Office of Public Education for North Vietnam and went through the schoolteacher lists. And you guessed it; the same places that didn't pay any taxes didn't have any

35 The words of Sir F. D. Lugard, *The Dual Mandate in British Tropical Africa* (Edinburgh: William Blackwood, 1929 [1922]), pp. 234, 254.

36 David Galula, *Pacification in Algeria, 1956–1958* (Santa Monica, CA: RAND, 2006 [1963]), p. 107; Bernard B. Fall, 'The Theory and Practice of Insurgency and Counterinsurgency', *Naval War College Review* 17: 8 (1965), p. 28; Robert Thompson, *Defeating Communist Insurgency: Experiences from Malaya and Vietnam* (London: Chatto & Windus, 1967), p. 22.

> schoolteachers. With this information I went back to the Provincial Governors and we had it out in 10 minutes flat. 'Yes, Monsieur, this is a very unfortunate area. We have not been able to keep schoolteachers in that particular area.' 'Why?' 'They get killed.' 'And how about your tax collectors?' 'They, too, get killed.' So, I said, 'In fact, you don't administer the area, do you?' He said, 'Really, Monsieur, I do not administer this area' . . .
>
> Of course, anyone can quit paying taxes, but in a revolutionary warfare situation it does not mean that you quit paying taxes altogether; you just quit paying taxes to the legal government. The Communists operate according to the same principle: they need money, and they will put in schoolteachers. So, what actually happens, then, is that the Communists just as the legal government, need money, recruits, and supplies, etc. Therefore, whatever the government does not get, believe me, doesn't just simply disappear; somebody else is getting it.[37]

As well as a source of revenue, taxation is moralizing and educative; managed in the right way, under the right conditions, it works to counter insurgency. Taxation is a mechanism through which subjects learn to be pacified objects of political administration.

'Subversion is negative administration', Fall liked to claim. 'Administration with a "minus" sign in front.'[38] This is why pacification 'begins obviously with a thorough census', to gain intelligence on the population and administer it accordingly.[39] 'Algeria was grossly underadministered', and 'underadministration' creates the space for subversion: 'When a country is being subverted it is not being outfought; it is being out-administered.'[40] To be out-administered by an insurgency over basic forms of political administration, then, points to insurgency as the antithesis of political administration – nothing less than a threat to the most basic powers of social police. Pacified subjects understand

37 Bernard B. Fall, *Counterinsurgency: The French Experience* (Washington, DC: Industrial College of the Armed Forces, 1963), pp. 119–22.

38 Ibid.

39 David Galula, *Counterinsurgency Warfare: Theory and Practice* (Westport, CT: Praeger, 2006 [1964]), p. 82.

40 Respectively: Galula, *Pacification in Algeria*, p. 23; Fall, 'Theory and Practice', p. 34.

their obligation to be compliant by accepting the forms of political administration through which they are ruled. And a well-ordered commercial society will always involve taxation as a means of training the subjects on how to be good subjects, as well as to pay for the order being built for them.

All of this is what Gallieni describes as the 'progressive method' of pacification, introducing us to the oil-stain theory. I have already noted NATO's reference to this idea over a century after Gallieni proposed it. During the century between Gallieni's doctrine and NATO's reference to it, the 'oil-stain theory' came to operate as a fundamental tenet of pacification, being used across the globe from Algiers to Argentina, Baghdad to Buenos Aires, Hanoi to Harlem, Paris to New York, and many other places along the way. The idea of a 'progressive' method has a double meaning. On the one side, 'progressive' is taken to imply gradual change spreading like oil through the fabric of the territory, until the whole nation is fully 'stained' (pacified). On the other, 'progressive' is also intended in the liberal sense of a 'civilizing mission' focusing on imposing liberal forms of power and bourgeois codes on the people. The two sides are neatly captured by Lyautey: pacification advances 'like an oil stain, in a great band of civilization'.[41] Civilization advances, commerce grows, order spreads, property and security are enthroned as the supreme ideas. This is pacification.

'All this is Gallieni', we have seen Lyautey remark when he described pacification as building a new order. But he also liked to claim that his ideas about pacification were 'Bugeaud at his best', working as he was in the 'tradition of Marshal Bugeaud'.[42] Thomas-Robert Bugeaud was a well-known figure in French politics through the nineteenth century. He was appointed as Algeria's governor-general in December 1840 following active service there, and is widely recognized as 'the first to have applied, everywhere at once, the type of war that . . . is the only type of war practicable in Africa'. Those are the words of Alexis de Tocqueville, and they refer to the *chouannerie*, an eighteenth-century term for counter-revolutionary warfare. Others who lauded Bugeaud,

41 Gallieni, *Trois Colonnes*, p. 241; Lyautey, 'Letter from Hanoi, 5 February 1895', in Lyautey, *Lettres du Tonkin et de Madagascar*, pp. 112–13.

42 Lyautey, 'Letter from Hanoi, 5 February 1895', pp. 112–13; Lyautey, *Du Rôle colonial*, p. 23.

such as Colonel Charles Callwell in the British War Office, did so for Bugeaud's expertise in what they called *guerrilla* warfare, a term which has had more staying power than *chouannerie*.[43] The 'guerrilla war' concept was invented in 1808–09 from the Spanish diminutive of *guerra*. It was then used in English during the Peninsular War (1808–14), when Napoleon's troops needed tactics for the 'small' or 'little' wars fought by bands of Spanish peasants (the idea of 'petite guerre' having a longer history, stretching back to the sixteenth century). 'Guerrilla war' quickly came to be part of the prose of pacification, as the guerrilla was increasingly identified with the insurgent. In this context, many of those countering the guerrilla-insurgent sought to adopt their methods, and Bugeaud was one such person, claiming that he made his forces 'more Arab than the Arabs'. The fact that the key guerrilla-insurgent method was to have no 'centre of gravity' meant that tactics employed by states had to shift beyond the classic 'Napoleonic' and 'Clausewitzian' style. Large columns and orchestrated battles were not viable in fighting guerrilla wars. What was needed was a war of movement using mobile columns and light infantry, plundering the enemy's grain silos, raiding their flocks, destroying what crops could not be raided, and often decimating towns and villages.

When Bugeaud claimed that he had made his forces 'more Arab than the Arabs', he was referring to the *razzia*, which he placed on a doctrinal level equal to if not higher than anything emanating from Clausewitz. It was a technique adopted by the Russians in the Caucasus, by the British in India in 1857 and again during the Second Boer War (1899–1901), by the French in Western Sudan later in the nineteenth century, and by the Germans in south-west and east Africa at the turn of the twentieth century. The *razzia* as a technique included mass murder, extermination and violent destruction. One infamous event will suffice as an example. It concerns the death by asphyxiation of

43 Alexis de Tocqueville, 'Intervention in the Debate over the Appropriation of Special Funding' (1846), in Alexis de Tocqueville, *Writings on Empire and Slavery*, transl. Jennifer Pitts (Baltimore: Johns Hopkins University Press, 2001); C. E. Callwell, *Small Wars: Their Principles and Practice* (London: HMSO, 1899), pp. 128, 135, 145. COINdinistas have recently returned to Bugeaud's work in debates about 'swarming' during the so-called 'new wars': Michael Few, 'Interview with Dr John Aquilla: How Can French Encounters with Irregular Warfare in the 19th Century Inform COIN in Our Time?', *Small Wars Journal Blog*, 30 November 2010.

1,000 members of the Ouled Riah, in the Dahra mountains in June 1845, after they had taken refuge from French troops in a deep cave. The French troops built a fire at the cave's entrance and stoked it through the night, until those taking shelter were choked to death. But as well as employing such standard forms of colonial violence, the *razzia* was part of a wider set of claims concerning a *pénétration pacifique*, a 'peaceful' projection of power and control seeking cooperation with the people, the development of a commercial order, and the fabrication of obedient labouring subjects – what other thinkers at the time were calling the 'civilizing mission', and would later be termed 'progressive pacification'. Tocqueville saw the *razzia* as a necessity for 'real pacification' in a context in which the enemy is 'the population itself', rather than an army or government.[44] Hence Bugeaud's methods involved plans for rebuilding the decimated areas with new roads, new housing and new markets. It included establishing a Bureau Arabe to mediate between the French Army and the Algerian people, interacting with the indigenous population, gathering intelligence, monitoring religious activities, overseeing tribal affairs, and governing public morality. The Bureau was essentially a police mechanism – a precursor to more recent versions of it in the form of 'Psychological Action Bureaus', 'Human Terrain Teams', and 'Female Engagement Teams'. One of the Bureau's tasks was to combine politics with force: to build as well as destroy. This was captured in *De la Civilisation du Peuple Arabe* (1850), a book by one of the Bureau's leading figures in the mid nineteenth century, Charles Richard. The book has two parts: 'The Hammer' and 'The Trowel'. The destructive power of the hammer was to merge with the cultivating power of the trowel: smash with the hammer, cultivate with the trowel. Each part of the book begins with a quote from the Roman Vitruvius: Part I: 'To build on ruins, you must first demolish'; Part II: 'After having demolished, it is necessary to build'.[45] As is clear, French efforts in Algeria followed the same pattern we have seen, the violence of pacification being wrapped up in the idea of reconstituting the pacified as civilized, moral and labouring subjects. 'When the Arabs are subdued', Bugeaud liked to claim, 'I give them the

44 Alexis de Tocqueville, 'Essay on Algeria' (1841), and 'First Report on Algeria' (1847), in *Writings on Empire and Slavery*, pp. 70–1, 135, 146.

45 Charles Richard, *De la Civilisation du Peuple Arabe* (Paris, 1850), pp. 1, 17.

best possible treatment . . . and rule them with humanity'.[46] Hence, he spent a huge amount of time and effort allotting building materials, seeds, animals, farming equipment and land in new model villages. Decades before Lyautey became known as the builder of French Morocco, Bugeaud was known as the 'Great Head Gardener' of French Algeria.

The idea of sovereign territory as a garden has a long history, reaching back at least to the sixteenth century, as found in the famous 'gardening scene' in Shakespeare's *Richard II* (III.4) – perhaps even back to that ultimate sovereign space constituted as the Garden of Eden. The idea of the garden was also sometimes used by police scientists, such as English police reformer Henry Fielding, in his 'Charge Delivered to the Grand Jury' (in London on 29 June 1749). As I have discussed in *Critique of Security*, the garden offers an image of an enclosed space of territory and property, fenced off, bordered, and expected to offer some kind of security (although not as much as a house); even the Garden of Eden is presented as walled in many depictions. Etymologically, the origin of 'garden' lies in enclosure, which is how it comes to form an 'enclosed space'. This reminds us that gardens do not exist 'naturally', despite the intimations of nature they contain. Rather, they are constituted and cultivated through human intervention as an exercise of power and a form of order, control and surveillance. The garden is a fantasy of containment, to use a concept I will develop in Chapter 4. Hence, if we follow the suggestion of Zygmunt Bauman in *Legislators and Interpreters* (1987) and *Modernity and Ambivalence* (1991), building on Ernest Gellner's *Nations and Nationalism* (1983), the modern state can be considered a gardening state. The image of a Great Head Gardener in the prose of pacification plays heavily on the kind of cultivating power through which modernity in general has been ordered, and offers a strong sense of the right and responsibility of reproducing and policing the garden as a pacified space. As Lyautey puts it, picking up on the theme:

> When it comes to cultivating part of a land invaded by rank weeds, it is not enough to pull them up just to have to start again the next

46 Cited in Anthony Thrall Sullivan, *Thomas-Robert Bugeaud: France and Algeria, 1784–1849* (Hamden, CT: Archon, 1983), p. 105.

> day . . . It is essential that where the ground has been ploughed up, the conquered soil should be isolated, fenced, and then sowed with the good grain which alone will make it impervious to the weeds. The same applies to territory given over to brigandage: armed occupation, with or without fighting, is the ploughshare; the establishment of a military cordon fences it and isolates it; and finally the organization and reconstitution of the population, its arming, the setting-up of markets and various cultivations, the driving of roads, are like the sowing of the good grain, and render the conquered region impervious to brigandage.[47]

The gardening state pacifies; pacification requires cultivation.

Such cultivation applies well beyond the colonial context, to the process of the systematic colonization of the world in general. In the case of Bugeaud in the mid nineteenth century, he was helped by the fact that Algeria was not considered a distinct country but an administrative unit (a 'department') of France. In his mind, the two countries were one. But, more to the point, they were also as one because pacification is considered a universal process. In early 1848, Bugeaud was appointed commander of the Paris military garrison. He was already well known for his hatred of cities in general, viewing them as centres of ill-discipline, moral degeneracy and communist agitation – a position which earned him a reputation as 'the Achilles of the conservatives'. His contempt for radical republicans and intellectuals was also well known: he had once suggested that deporting republicans to Algeria, where they might be killed, 'would serve the country well'. Being appointed to the Paris garrison was an opportunity to use in urban France the methods and tactics that had been used to pacify the Algerians, and to revive his earlier role in the suppression of the Parisian insurgency of 1834. His first step in 1848 was to instruct his troops 'to employ extreme measures to re-establish order', which meant employing the *razzia* on the urban proletariat. 'You are to attack energetically the crowds and barricades', he commanded his men, urging them on in a 'vigorous offensive, one

47 Lyautey, 'Propositions Faites par le General en Chef au Gouverneur Général pour la Campagne D'hiver' (1895–96), in Lyautey, *Lettres du Tonkin et de Madagascar*. The same passage is largely repeated in *Du Rôle colonial*, pp. 11–12.

without compromises and without indecision'.[48] Using a classic police trope, Bugeaud announced that this was a 'war of the streets'. In *La Guerre des rues et des maisons* (*The War of Streets and Houses*, 1847), Bugeaud argued that such a war was necessary to crush urban unrest and counter political insurgencies. This involved taking key locations which could then be used as fortresses from which soldiers could move quickly in small groups and tight formation to break down barricades and take control of the streets.[49]

For Bugeaud, the 'war of the streets' in Paris was one and the same war as was taking place in Algeria. This much was pointed out by Marx in an entry on Bugeaud for the *New American Cyclopedia* in 1859, where he drew attention to the claim Bugeaud had made to his officers before their attack on the Parisians that he had never been beaten by the rebellious rabble on either the battlefield or in insurrections.[50] Liberals such as Tocqueville also made the connection between the pacification of Parisian workers in 1848 and that of Algerian insurgents. The image of the 'rebellious rabble' incorporated both the French proletarian as urban insurgent and the Algerian peasant as guerrilla fighter, uniting the war of the streets and the war of the plains into one and the same process.

Bugeaud's articulation of pacification thus not only captures the link between the guerrilla war in Spain under Napoleon and the somewhat different and vastly more successful campaign against the resistance in Algeria in the middle of the nineteenth century, but also demonstrates the connection of both with the pacification of the French proletariat throughout that century. This was a single war with multiple fronts, which culminated in the pacification of the Paris Commune and the national uprising in Algeria in the spring of 1871.

From 1853 onwards, Paris had been gradually rebuilt with the pacification of the proletariat in mind. The rebuilding had been overseen by Baron Haussmann, who possessed a hatred of the urban proletariat equal to Bugeaud's – which is no doubt also why he possessed a copy of *La Guerre des rues et des maisons*. 'The true goal of Haussmann's projects

48 Bugeaud cited in Sullivan, *Thomas-Robert Bugeaud*, p. 135.

49 Thomas Bugeaud, *The War of Streets and Houses*, transl. Eric Nylund, *Cabinet* 22 (2006 [1847]).

50 Karl Marx, 'Bugeaud', *New American Cyclopedia* IV (1859), in Karl Marx and Frederick Engels, *Collected Works, Vol. 18* (London: Lawrence & Wishart, 1982), p. 213.

was to secure the city against civil war', notes Walter Benjamin.[51] By the time of the Commune, it had become commonplace among the French ruling class and its military and police chiefs to link the Paris revolutionaries of 1871 not only with the revolutionaries of 1848, but also with the insurgency against the French state still taking place in Algeria. After all, Algeria had been the place to which France had banished workers after the revolts in 1848 and after the Bonaparte coup of 1851. The fact that the Commune coincided with a national uprising in Algeria in spring 1871 served to reinforce this understanding of one great unitary insurgency. By 1871, the continued pacification of Algeria now included the famine of 1868–70, a cholera epidemic that killed half a million people (nearly one-fifth of the population), and the active destruction of many Algerian villages. As well as seeking an end to such violent repression, the Republican Association of Algeria was by 1870 agitating for elected municipalities along the lines of 'communes'. This is the context of an insurgency in 1871 that stretched from Paris to Algeria. Writing about this insurgency, Vladimir Lutsky notes that insurgents in Algeria were aware of what was taking place in the Commune, and that French colonial rule was designed to serve the Parisian bourgeoisie. The promulgation of the Paris Commune occasioned an upsurge in demonstrations of solidarity in Algeria, the revolutionary press published detailed updates on the Commune's progress, and the Republican Association of Algeria sent delegates. Parisian Communards and Algerian peasants understood that they had the same enemy in the French bourgeoisie, notes Lutsky.[52] That said, we should also make the reverse observation that the French bourgeoisie saw in the Paris Communards and Algerian peasants one and the same enemy. The point is that pacification is a total process – one and the same war of dispossession and expropriation, one and the same process of systematic colonization, one and the same campaign to build a social order in which insurgency does not arise, or can be easily crushed if it does.

'To build, this is the goal', claims Lyautey, in the kind of phrase we have heard so many times already in this chapter.[53] It is a claim states

51 Walter Benjamin, 'Paris, Capital of the Nineteenth Century' (1935), in Walter Benjamin, *The Arcades Project*, transl. Howard Eiland and Kevin McLaughlin (Cambridge: Belknap, 1999), p. 12.

52 Lutsky, *Modern History of the Arab Countries*, pp. 266, 270, 273–4.

53 Cited in Wright, *Politics of Design*, p. 83.

like to make about their war machines and their police measures, rendering them more 'social' in the process, encouraging us to see them as essentially *benevolent*. In proclamations and instructions issued to his generals in late 1898, US President McKinley claimed the country was pursuing a policy in the Philippines that avoided the 'usual emphasis on brutality and atrocity' and was instead 'benevolent'. The bloody campaign of killing, torturing and maiming in an attempt to destroy opposition could then be known as 'benevolent pacification'.[54] As a result, we find reiterations of what we now know are key themes in the prose of pacification. The enemy is being treated as patient rather than corpse, cultivated rather than destroyed:

> Public works were undertaken and carried through, roads and bridges built, schools opened and attendance enforced, enlisted men being detained as teachers, and officers themselves often conducting classes. Streets were graded, towns drained, and a condition of sanitation introduced that, in the Philippine Islands, is only possible under military rule. The pueblos became models of neatness and a spirit of wholesome rivalry was engendered. Vaccination was made compulsory . . . Nor were these efforts spasmodic or confined to particular localities, but were general throughout the islands wherever and whenever the work of pacification permitted.[55]

This is language that could have been lifted straight out of Lyautey or Gallieni. Indeed, one historian writes: 'The Americans, having been in the Philippines less than three years at that time, were arriving at substantially the same conclusions outlined by Lyautey.'[56] The process was also to involve a policing of moral life through the regulation of prostitution and sale of alcohol, prohibition of cockfighting, closure of gambling houses and lotteries, discontinuation of contracts for sale of opium, and extended down to bourgeois table manners in teaching people to eat with knives and forks instead of their fingers. This was

54 Reynaldo C. Ileto, *Knowledge and Pacification: On the US Conquest and the Writing of Philippine History* (Manila: Ateneo de Manila University Press, 2017), pp. 261–2.

55 D. H. Broughton, 'How Soldiers Have Ruled in the Philippines' (1902), cited in John Morgan Gates, *Schoolbooks and Krags: The United States Army in the Philippines, 1898–1902* (Westport: Greenwood, 1973), pp. 140–1.

56 Gates, *Schoolbooks and Krags*, p. 280.

pacification, then, defined as an act of benevolence – but still governed by the same narrative: insurgents cleared, territory held, and a new order built, leading towards *a brighter and nicer new life*.

'A brighter and nicer new life'

In a speech delivered in November 1957 at Supreme Headquarters Allied Powers Europe (SHAPE), one of NATO's two strategic commands, General Allard of Canada spoke about pacification:

> In revolutionary war, pure military action, which is of prime importance in conventional war, gives way to psychological action; to propaganda; to intelligence gathering and processing, political as well as operational; to police measures; to personal contacts with the population; to social and economic programs.
>
> I shall classify these various missions under two categories:
>
> DESTRUCTION – CONSTRUCTION
> These two terms are inseparable, destroying without reconstructing would mean useless work; building without first destroying would be a mistake.
>
> 1. *Destruction*:
> This means first of all: uncovering, dismantling, and suppressing the politico-administrative armoury of the rebel, the very nervous system of the rebellion. The mass of the population, willingly or more usually by force – is taken in hand, separated into groups, indoctrinated, pressurized, terrorized; somehow caught in a tight net from which they cannot escape . . .
>
> This mission constitutes our first objective. It has more of the character of police than war. It requires the cooperation of all legal forces under a single command . . .
>
> 2. *Construction*:
> Destruction will serve nothing if we don't go beyond it. The rebel organisation would soon reappear if the population were left to itself. It's necessary, after destroying, to construct.

> Construction means building the peace, preparing for the establishment of a new order. *This is the mission of pacification*. It calls first of all for the re-establishment of personal contact with the people, protecting and helping them in all areas, and giving them back the confidence they had lost or were losing. [Pacification] means organizing the people, separating them into hierarchies.[57]

Such a position was by that point a key trope in the prose of pacification. A few years after Allard's speech, Robert Trinquier published *La Guerre moderne* (1961), in which 'modern war' turns out to be *revolutionary war*, and hence a *war of pacification*, in which pacification takes the form of 'an interlocking system of actions – political, economic, psychological, military'. These combine in 'a broad *social programme*', the objective of which is 'to give the people the material and moral assistance necessary to permit them to resume their normal activities'. For the French at this time, the pacification of Algeria remained a pressing issue, but merely one 'front' in the counter-revolutionary campaign against international communism from France to Indochina.[58] Other counterinsurgency experts, such as Frank Kitson and Robert Thompson in Britain, also equated pacification with a war against communism. For David Galula, too, 'insurgency' essentially meant communism, and we might learn a few things from pausing briefly on Galula's work.

As noted in the Introduction, Galula rose through the ranks of the French army before being recruited by Harvard University and commissioned by RAND to report on his experiences in pacification. This resulted in *Pacification in Algeria* (1963) and *Counterinsurgency Warfare* (1964). In the former book, Galula notes uncertainty about the meaning of pacification:

> The order was to 'pacify'. But exactly how? The sad truth was that, in spite of all our past experience, we had no single, official doctrine for counterinsurgency warfare. Instead, there were various schools of

57 'General Allard, Speech in November 1957', reproduced in Michel Déon, *L'Armée d'Algérie et la Pacification* (Paris: Plon, 1959), pp. 77–9. Emphasis added.

58 Roger Trinquier, *Modern Warfare: A French View of Counterinsurgency*, transl. Daniel Lee (Westport, CN: Praeger Security International, 2006 [1961]), pp. 5, 21, 24, 37.

> thought, all unofficial, some highly vociferous . . . At one extreme stood the 'warriors', officers who had learned nothing, who challenged the very idea that the population was the real objective, who maintained that military action pursued with sufficient vigor and for a sufficiently long time would defeat the rebels . . . At the other extreme were the 'psychologists', most of them recruited among officers who had undergone the Vietminh brainwashing in prisoner camps. To them, psychological action was everything, not merely the simple propaganda and psychological warfare adjunct to other types of operations, conventional or otherwise. 'You use force against the enemy', one of their leaders told me, 'not so much to destroy him but in order to make him change his mind on the necessity of pursuing the fight. In other words, you do a psychological action'. They were convinced that the population could be manipulated through certain techniques adapted from communist methods.[59]

For Galula, 'the military action is secondary to the political one'. The latter is 'constructive pacification work' through medical police and other 'pacification units' such as schools.[60] Like so many pacification experts before him, including those I have already discussed here, Galula also understood his work to apply to countering insurgency and communism in the metropole as well as the colony. In July 1958 he was recalled from Algeria to contribute his expertise towards the policing of Paris, as part of what was essentially a 'crisis group' within the National Defence Headquarters.[61]

This was much more than a case of what is often widely called 'hearts and minds', and more than simply a carrot dangled from the left hand while a stick is being brandished by the right.[62] Galula observed that the mere mention of the word 'pacification' often brought forth 'deriding smiles', as many 'seem to think of pacification as the distribution of candies to the children and smiles to the old people'.[63] The French had

---

59 Galula, *Pacification in Algeria*, pp. 64–5.

60 Galula, *Counterinsurgency Warfare*, p. 63.

61 A. A. Cohen, *Galula: The Life and Writings of the French Officer Who Defined the Art of Counterinsurgency* (Santa Barbara, CA: Praeger, 2012), pp. 140, 183.

62 David Galula, 'Notes on Pacification in Greater Kabylia' (1956), in *Pacification in Algeria*, p. 269.

63 Ibid., p. 269.

established a Psychological Action Bureau in Algeria in March 1955, but Galula disliked the name, believing that 'psychological' failed to capture the expansive political nature of the work he thought necessary. In 'The Technique of Pacification in Kabylia', a report for colleagues on the essentials of pacification, which formed the basis of what became the Challe Plan, Galula commented: 'It is a great psychological mistake to have labeled it "psychological action" ', when in fact it should have been a 'political bureau'.[64] Once again, the *political* nature of pacification was meant to capture the expansive and constructive nature of what was at stake. This is why Galula's writings are, like Bugeaud's, Gallieni's and Lyautey's, replete with tales of what was built, where it was built, and why it matters; over and over, we read sentences along the lines of 'I opened a dispensary', 'I also opened a school', 'I arranged for *x* to be built'. That is the key theme when, in *Counterinsurgency Warfare*, Galula attempts a succinct definition of pacification: 'Build (or rebuild) a political machine from the population upward.' Yet again, the prose repeats: on the one hand, the soldier must 'be prepared to become a propagandist, a social worker, a civil engineer, a school-teacher, a nurse, a boy scout', while on the other hand those very same figures within the social order – the administrator, the policeman, the social worker – are themselves fundamental to pacification. 'The counterinsurgent personnel who implement the strategy . . . are a widely mixed group of politicians, civil servants, economists, social workers, soldiers.'[65]

The question of how a modern society can be built animated a major 1962 symposium on social science research and the US Army's role in 'limited wars', organized by the American University in Washington, DC, and sponsored by the Department of the Army.[66] Again, the double-sided nature of the project was restated. Secretary of the Army Elvis Stahr argued in a keynote address to the conference that the Army should 'not only be a mailed fist to strike at any enemy'

64 David Galula, 'The Technique of Pacification in Kabylia' (1957), in *Pacification in Algeria*, p. 277.

65 Galula, *Counterinsurgency Warfare*, pp. 8, 59, 62, 95.

66 The question was posed this way by a leading political scientist in Lucian Pye, 'The Role of the Military in Political Development', in William A. Lybrand, ed., *Proceedings of the Symposium 'The US Army's Limited-War Mission and Social Science Research'* (Washington, DC: Special Operations Office, 1962), p. 168.

but should also be 'a helping hand to assist in the development of the nation'. 'Striking at the very roots of insurgency' requires the establishment of communications, the improvement of roads and trails, the construction of bridges, the operation of clinics, the provision of sanitary facilities, and many other civic and economic advancements.[67] The conference delegates all agreed that building and construction were the key. A few years later, in March 1966, President Johnson announced that the attempt by America to pacify Vietnam was now to be coordinated by Robert Komer, who was to assume a new position on the White House staff. Komer's official role, as per the National Security Action Memorandum 343, signed off a week later, was 'Special Assistant for Peaceful Construction in Vietnam'. The story goes that Johnson had earlier summoned Komer to the Oval Office to discuss the role:

> 'Bob', Johnson drawled when they sat together, 'I'm going to put you in charge of the other war in Vietnam'. Komer was unfamiliar with the term 'the other war'. 'Mr. President, what's the other war in Vietnam? I thought we only had one'. 'Well', the President replied, 'that's part of the problem. I want to have a war to build as well as to destroy'.[68]

The 'otherness' of this 'other war' has meant that it has often been dismissed as a sideshow to the 'main' military campaign, the term 'other war' often being used to differentiate pacification operations from the 'real war' of conventional destruction.[69] But the phrase would be repeated so often that dismissing it means we would be missing something important. After all, as was indicated in a report delivered by Komer to the president in September 1966, called *The Other War in Vietnam*, as a war to build as well as destroy, pacification is to take place on the 'civil side', carried out through 'Health, Education, and Welfare',

67 Elvis Stahr, 'Invited Address: The US Army's Limited-War Mission and Social Science Research', in Lybrand, *Proceedings of the Symposium*, pp. 3–8.

68 Cited from testimony in a later court case, Westmoreland v. CBS, by Frank L. Jones, 'Blowtorch: Robert Komer and the Making of Vietnam Pacification Policy', *Parameters: US Army College Quarterly* 35: 3 (2005), p. 104.

69 Austin Long, *On 'Other War': Lessons from Five Decades of RAND Counterinsurgency Research* (Santa Monica, CA: RAND, 2006), p. 2.

but also through inflation, pricing and the industrial base. Pacification is a war of electrification.[70]

The month before Komer's appointment, a major conference on the war in Vietnam was held at Honolulu. This conference is known as the one at which pacification became the key to US strategy, but also for the stress it laid on generating a radical policy of constructive change in Vietnam.[71] At one point, Secretary Freeman summarized for the conference the discussion about rural development, land reform, electrification and the training of officials, saying that the word 'pacification' might be better replaced with 'social construction'.[72] The *Pentagon Papers* record that it was decided to use the phrase 'social construction' in place of pacification, but that everyone then lapsed back into using 'pacification'.[73] Komer's report, *Giving a New Thrust to Pacification*, refers to pacification as encompassing 'the whole of the military, political, and civil effort', while *The Other War in Vietnam* uses the term 'revolutionary development'.[74] Similar labels were bandied around throughout numerous debates and policy developments, generating a range of synonyms to try to capture the nature of the project: as well as 'revolutionary development', we find 'rural construction', 'rural construction (pacification)', 'reconstruction', 'rural reconstruction', 'revolutionary reconstruction', 'provincial reconstruction', 'community development', 'civic action', 'civil operations' and 'rural edification'.[75] William Colby, who replaced Komer in Vietnam and later became CIA director, suggests that one reason so many people stuck to the term 'pacification' is because they could not quite find the right word to capture the developmental building project that was to take place in its name.[76] Writing in the late 1960s about the

70 US Department of State Bulletin, *The Other War in Vietnam: A Progress Report* (Washington, DC: Department of State, 1966).

71 R. W. Komer, *Bureaucracy Does Its Thing: Institutional Restraints on U.S.-GVN Performance in Vietnam*, DARPA Report, R-967-ARPA (Santa Monica, CA: RAND, 1972), p. 113.

72 *Pentagon Papers*, 'Part IV.C.8: Re-emphasis on Pacification, 1965–1967', p. 40.

73 Ibid., p. 43.

74 Ibid., p. 66; *State Department Bulletin* LV: 1424, 1425 (10 and 17 October 1966).

75 *Pentagon Papers*, 'Part IV.B.3: Evolution of the War. Counterinsurgency: The Advisory Build-Up, 1961–67', pp. 112, 113; *Pentagon Papers*, 'Part IV.C.8', pp. 3, 12, 13, 22.

76 William Colby, *Honorable Men: My Life in the CIA* (New York: Simon & Schuster, 1978), pp. 246–56.

problems faced by the United States in Vietnam, pacification expert Robert Thompson pointed to the 'unfortunate tendency to regard the war as being three wars – nation building, pacification and military operations'. In fact, he suggests, the military operations were a *defensive* and *destructive* programme, the nation building was an *offensive* and *constructive* programme, and the programme that linked those two was pacification, which was dependent on clinics, medical centres, schools, roads, canals and bridges, productivity and cash cropping.[77]

Underpinning these comments is a version of earlier pacification thinkers' ideas about a higher, moral and more complete life, which is why so much of the literature was, theoretically, little more than a reiteration of Gallieni and Lyautey's oil-stain concept of pacification.[78] What was perhaps new, however, was the shinier gloss put on the project than that found among earlier thinkers. 'The problem of building a new nation', one US handbook stated in 1970, is how to produce 'a free, peaceful and full life', generating a revolution aiming for 'a new life', as one province representative put it in 1966. 'A better life in a new society' is how General Thang described pacification at the Honolulu Conference that same year.[79] 'We are determined to realize a social revolution in rural area[s], aiming at destroying the present, gloomy, old life and replacing it with *a brighter and nicer new life*.'[80]

As anyone who has read anything about the American war in Vietnam knows, the constant stress on 'new life' activities in 'new hamlets' in furtherance of a 'new society' was itself renewed again and again, leading to layer upon layer of even newer projects. Strategic Hamlets, for example, were replaced by New Life Hamlets, which were in turn replaced by Really New Life Hamlets. Each was literally built

77 Robert Thompson, *No Exit from Vietnam* (London: Chatto & Windus, 1969), pp. 149–50; Thompson, *Defeating Communist Insurgency*, pp. 111–13, 125.

78 Robert B. Asprey, *War in the Shadows: The Guerrilla in History, Vol. 2* (New York: Doubleday, 1975), p. 1052.

79 *Handbook for District Senior Advisor, MAC-CORDS*, 1970, no pagination, available at vva.vietnam.ttu.edu; William A. Nighswonger, *Rural Pacification in Vietnam, 1962–1965* (Department of Defense, Advanced Research Projects Agency, 1966), pp. 305–6; Thang in *Pentagon Papers*, 'Part IV.C.8', pp. 38–9.

80 Ministry for Revolutionary Development, *11 Criteria and 98 Steps: Handbook No. 12017* (Saigon: RD Ministry, 1966), cited in Douglas S. Blaufarb, *The Counterinsurgency Era: U.S. Doctrine and Performance 1950 to the Present* (New York: Free Press, 1977), p. 228. Emphasis added.

directly on top of the ruins of the previous version, creating 'an archaeology of pacification going back ten, sometimes twenty years'.[81] The stress on such activities also underpinned the prose of pacification's incessant quantification of 'achievements', usually supported by one set of metrics and evaluation system after another, all 'developed by CIA analysts (with military input) to provide a means of measuring the progress of the somewhat nebulous concept of pacification'.[82] Everything that could be measured was to be measured – a position taken even further when Secretary of Defense Robert S. McNamara brought operations analysis and systems theory into the measurement of pacification.[83] The Hamlet Evaluation System (HES), for example, measured hamlets against eighteen indicators concerning health, education, welfare, economic development and administrative activities, generating a monthly average of 90,000 pages of reports.[84] As anyone who has read anything about the American war in Vietnam also knows, the volume of metrics produced was both repetitive and overwhelming, intended to impress us through the sublime nature of quantification. To give one example, from Birtle's two-volume history of the US Army's counterinsurgency actions: within the first seven months of the civil affairs/psychological operations programme established by the 173rd Airborne Brigade after its arrival in Vietnam in May 1965, the Brigade either built, refurbished, or began work on fourteen schools, a laundry facility, three latrines, five wells, a refugee settlement, two playgrounds, twenty-nine bridges, forty-three kilometres of roads, a church, and two medical facilities. It also administered 51,400 medical treatments, distributed 182 tons of food and clothing, donated nearly 200,000 piasters to local charities, and hosted ten parties for Vietnamese civilians. On the next page Birtle lists the US military's overall achievements by 1967: built or repaired 31,000 houses, 83 hospitals, 180 kilometres of irrigation systems, 200 churches, 380 dispensaries, 225 marketplaces, 72 orphanages, 1,052

81 Frances FitzGerald, *Fire in the Lake: The Vietnamese and the Americans in Vietnam* (New York: Vintage, 1973), p. 453.

82 Long, *On 'Other War'*, p. 39.

83 For an extended discussion of the politics of systems theory, see my *The Politics of Immunity: Security and the Policing of Bodies* (London: Verso, 2022).

84 Gregory A. Daddis, 'The Problem of Metrics: Assessing Progress and Effectiveness in the Vietnam War', *War in History* 19: 1 (2012), p. 93.

schools, and over 2,000 wells, while dispensing 10,286,677 medical treatments and 41,573 tons of food and commodities.[85] Report after report engages in the same kind of accounting. One document lists the work performed in the Mekong Delta between 1968 and 1970, including 'the rebuilding of 27 churches, 33 dispensaries, 37 market places and almost a thousand dwellings', providing '1,600,000 pounds of cement, about 1,600,000 board feet of lumber and 11,500 sheets of tin', and building or rebuilding 447 bridges and over 1,100 kilometres of road.[86]

This was pacification by numbers, intending to impress by the sheer volumes involved, along with their enumeration, categorization, and management. Such reports also opened space for highlighting the involvement in pacification of the various armies noted above: the civic workers, administrators, teachers, accountants, doctors, welfare workers, police inspectors, city planners, psychological warfare experts, counterinsurgency specialists, handicraft consultants, agricultural advisers, horticulturalists, pig experts, aid administrators and voluntary workers. Such administration, expertise and policymaking, focused towards a brighter and nicer new life, combined with an 'amorphous liberal rhetoric' (Gabriel Kolko's term) and 'touchy-feely domination' (Kurt Jacobsen's term), makes the attempted pacification of Vietnam 'sound like a program for the construction of a liberal welfare state'.[87] If so, might that also make us think of the liberal welfare state as pacification?

I will say more on that below. First, let us also note that none of this quantification of social reconstruction hid the destruction. Indeed, such destruction also had to be quantified. To give just one example:

> By 1968 there were 800 B-52 bombing raids a month, increasing to 3,150 per month by 1972, with each B-52 capable of dropping

85 Birtle, *US Army Counterinsurgency and Contingency Operations Doctrine*, pp. 396–7.

86 Lieutenant General Julian J. Ewell and Major General Ira A. Hunt, Jr, *Sharpening the Combat Edge: The Use of Analysis to Reinforce Military Judgment* (Washington, DC: Department of the Army, 1974), pp. 178–9.

87 James William Gibson, *The Perfect War: Technowar in Vietnam* (New York: Grove, 1986), pp. 281, 291; Gabriel Kolko, *Vietnam: Anatomy of a War 1940–1975* (London: Unwin Hyman, 1986), p. 236; Kurt Jacobsen, *Pacification and Its Discontents* (Chicago: Prickly Paradigm, 2009), p. 87.

> 60,000 pounds of bombs. During the most intensive periods of air warfare, a time which lasted eight years, the B-52s flew an amazing 124,532 sorties and dropped 2,949,000 tons. In all, the United States exploded 14 million tons of ordnance over South Vietnam, half on the ground, half from the air. Over one million tons were dropped on North Vietnam by airplane, 1.5 millions on Laos, and over half a million tons on Cambodia. By many times over, this was the most destructive physical force ever employed in the history of warfare.[88]

Pacification's destructive capacity extends to the earth itself ('scorched earth'), making it feel 'as though the very earth has been turned into an enemy', as Derek Gregory puts it.[89] In its destructive mode, pacification constitutes nothing less than *ecocide* – a term that is now widely used to capture the devastation of the world by capitalism, but which was coined initially to grasp the devastation of the world by capitalism *in the name of pacification*.[90] The whole of Earth is to be the patient, until it becomes a corpse.

Noting the extent to which pacifying powers like to talk up their productive capabilities and achievements, Aimé Césaire highlighted in 1955 the ideological double movement inherent in the prose of pacification:

> They talk to me about progress, about 'achievements', diseases cured, improved standards of living.
>
> *I* am talking about societies drained of their essence, cultures trampled underfoot, institutions undermined, lands confiscated, religions smashed, magnificent artistic creations destroyed, extraordinary *possibilities* wiped out.
>
> They throw facts at my head, statistics, mileages of roads, canals, and railroad tracks.
>
> *I* am talking about . . . millions of men torn from their gods, their land, their habits, their life.

88 John J. Tierney, *Chasing Ghosts: Unconventional Warfare in American History* (Washington, DC: Potomac, 2008), pp. 244–5.

89 Derek Gregory, *The Colonial Present* (Oxford: Blackwell, 2004), p. 131.

90 Barry Weisberg, ed., *Ecocide in Indochina: The Ecology of War* (San Francisco: Canfield, 1970).

> They dazzle me with the tonnage of cotton or cocoa that has been exported, the acreage that has been planted with olive trees or grapevines.
>
> *I* am talking about natural economies that have been disrupted . . . food crops destroyed, malnutrition permanently introduced, agricultural development oriented solely toward the benefit of the metropolitan countries; about the looting of products, the looting of raw materials.[91]

They say construction, we experience destruction. Yet our experience of destruction is precisely what they need and want in order to be able to stake a claim for construction. In the prose of pacification, the master-builders are master-destroyers. This is what it takes to build a nation.

'Nation building' was the term used in two 1970 RAND reports to capture pacification's 'constructive politico-economic' dimension.[92] The term was by no means new. 'The essential tasks of revolutionary development and nation building' is how William Westmoreland put it in 1966 – a phrase repeated in other documents of the period.[93] 'Nation building', as we have seen, was the very thing some senior figures in the US state apparatus wanted to avoid in the wars on Iraq and Afghanistan in the first decade of the twenty-first century. The connection is revealing, because 'few Americans in Vietnam consistently used the term "nation building" themselves, preferring to talk about "pacification" or "the other war" '.[94] At the same time, however, the term 'nation building' is entirely consistent with the idea that pacification was meant to be *modernization*.

91 Aimé Césaire, *Discourse on Colonialism*, transl. Joan Pinkham (New York: Monthly Review Press, 2000 [1955]), pp. 42–3.

92 R. W. Komer, *Organization and Management of the "New Model" Pacification Program – 1966–1969* (Santa Monica, CA: RAND, May 1970), pp. 120, 168, 257; R. W. Komer, *Impact of Pacification on Insurgency in South Vietnam* (Santa Monica, CA: RAND, August 1970), pp. 3, 5–6, 10.

93 William Westmoreland, 'Concept of Military Operations in South Vietnam', cable of 26 August, 1966, available at history.state.gov; Office of the Deputy Chief of Staff for Military Operations, Department of the Army, *A Program for the Pacification and Long-Term Development of South Vietnam* (March 1966), at apps.dtic.mil, p. 53; Headquarters, US Military Assistance Command, Vietnam, *Handbook for Military Support of Pacification* (February 1968), p. 1.

94 Andrew J. Gawthorpe, *To Build as Well as Destroy: American Nation Building in South Vietnam* (New York: Cornell University Press, 2018), p. 12.

The prose of pacification during the 1960s and 1970s is replete with the language of modernization, but the classic text on the subject came from the economist Walt Rostow. In *The Stages of Economic Growth* (1960), Rostow argued that every society goes through five stages of economic development, with the most destabilizing and yet desirable of these being the transition to modernity. Modernization's destabilizing aspects mean that any society going through such change is susceptible to communism, and so capitalism's political administrators and social scientists need to carefully shape programmes to facilitate the 'take off' in those countries. For Rostow, modernization is not simply a model of historical development, but also a pointer to how the United States and other capitalist states might thereby shape the world according to that model: nation building. As Samuel Huntington put it in a 1968 article in *Foreign Affairs*, the answer to insurgency lies in a forced modernization.[95] This is modernization as capitalist ideology, as Michael Latham and others have shown, in the sense that the *revolution* of modernization is counter-revolution: countering resistance to the modernization process, countering insurgency and countering communism.[96]

On 28 June 1961, Rostow gave a commencement address to graduates of the 'Counter Guerrilla Course' at Fort Bragg in North Carolina. An economist speaking to graduates of a counter-guerrilla training course might appear rather odd, yet Rostow's speech had been discussed with Komer and reviewed by Kennedy. Moreover, the speech was published in a special issue of the *Marine Corps Gazette* in 1962, recommended by Kennedy as essential reading for the Marines, and then re-published in 1962 in an edited volume, *The Guerrilla – And How to Fight Him*. What makes Rostow's argument so compelling is the connection it makes between modernization and pacification, in effect offering *a political economy of pacification*. It is a political economy of building and growth. Rostow claims that 'the guerrilla force has this advantage: its task is merely to destroy, while the government must build and protect what it is building'. This stress on insurgency's destructive

95 Samuel P. Huntington, 'The Bases of Accommodation', *Foreign Affairs* 46: 4 (1968).

96 Michael E. Latham, *Modernization as Ideology: American Social Science and 'Nation Building' in the Kennedy Era* (Chapel Hill, NC: University of North Carolina Press, 2000).

character reinforces counterinsurgency as a constructive force, now undergirded by the most fashionable form of political economy. The destruction wrought by insurgents is clearly meant to be understood as fundamentally different to the destructive power of pacification, described above. It is also presumably meant to be different to that envisaged by Rostow when, in June 1961, he recommended to Kennedy the strategic bombing of Indochina, for which he continued to argue through the 1960s, and regardless of the fact that such a course of action might escalate into a full nuclear confrontation.[97] Pacification's destruction is aimed not to merely destroy, but is a constructive destruction, so to speak – a necessary part of the stages of growth, a modernizing destruction: 'Modern societies must be built, and we are prepared to help build them.' And, of course, this argument would not be complete without a description of the society as being treated like a patient. New orders are to be built, so that the people can be cured of the 'disease' of communism and other insurgencies.[98] Once more, the prose of pacification describes the need to treat the enemy: 'We have gotten to the position of the doctor faced with a strange disease.'[99]

The insertion of this hugely influential political economy into the prose of pacification meant that it then filtered into the arguments about pacification as nation building and social engineering. Manuals published during the 1960s described the world situation in terms lifted from Rostow's arguments to such an extent that Rostow's book, speech and subsequent work were considered by many to be essentially state policy. Much as the precise nature of modernization was, like the precise nature of pacification, never made entirely clear – economic take-off, a free market, the passing of traditional society, rationalization, secularization or bureaucratization (depending on which modernization theorist one was reading) – a *belief* in something called 'modernization' came to form the sine qua non of pacification, reinforcing the idea that pacification was a project to build the world anew. It is all too easy to see this as an 'American mission' pursuing the construction of an American

97 David Milne, *America's Rasputin: Walt Rostow and the Vietnam War* (New York: Hall & Wang, 2008), pp. 94, 179.

98 W. W. Rostow, 'Guerrilla Warfare in Underdeveloped Areas', in Lieutenant Colonel T. N. Greene, ed., *The Guerrilla – And How to Fight Him. Selections from the Marine Corps Gazette* (New York: Praeger, 1964), pp. 59–60.

99 Fall, *Counterinsurgency*, p. 111.

world order.[100] What was really at stake was a *liberal* and *capitalist* mission pursuing the realization of a *dream of world order*.

'Dream of world order' is a phrase from a televized speech given by President Johnson on 7 April 1965, titled 'Peace Without Conquest', in which Johnson compared the modernizing project taking place on the other side of the world with the achievements of the Tennessee Valley Authority (TVA). These achievements were being lauded high and wide to gain support for the 'Great Society' programme, launched by Johnson in 1964. Out of these, the idea of a 'TVA on the Mekong' took off, and the logic of a 'Great Society' programme carried over into building a new (and 'great') Vietnam.[101] However, just as the French pacification of Algeria was as one with the urban reorganization of Paris, going all the way back to the mid nineteenth century, so the pacification of Vietnam could spill over into building a new (and 'great') society back home. Oil can spill in different places and spread in different directions. 'To build greatness', Johnson argued, required 'fighting a war within our own boundaries', in which 'no man, woman, or child is really free from the hostilities' and 'nothing short of total victory can ever be acceptable'. We therefore need to consider this image of the 'Great Society' through the lens of the social wars of modernity.

That most ubiquitous of social wars, the 'war on poverty', was formally launched in the United States in 1964, and was heavily grounded on the general theme of 'development' and 'modernization'. It was formally recast a year later as 'a war on crime', based on the idea that 'the policeman is the frontline soldier'.[102] The two wars soon became one. There might be 'a war against crime in America', but 'poverty . . . is the real enemy', Johnson claimed. 'Strike poverty down . . . and much of the crime will fall down with it.'[103] This is one reason why race was, and

---

100 David Ekbladh, *The Great American Mission: Modernization and the Construction of an American World Order* (Princeton, NJ: Princeton University Press, 2010).

101 Chester L. Cooper et al., *The American Experience with Pacification in Vietnam, Vol. II: Elements of Pacification* (ARPA, 1972), p. 152.

102 President Lyndon B. Johnson, 'Statement by the President Following the Signing of Law Enforcement Assistance Bills', 22 September 1965, at presidency .ucsb.edu.

103 President Lyndon B. Johnson, 'Remarks to the Delegates to the Conference of State Committees on Criminal Administration', University of Maryland, 15 October 1966, at presidency.ucsb.edu.

remains, integral to this project, the war on poverty often narrowing down to a 'war on black poverty', and the war on crime to a 'war on black crime' – both then aligned with a war on 'black terrorism'. (In July 1969, J. Edgar Hoover announced that the 'greatest threat to the internal security of the country' was the Black Panther Party.)[104] But, as with all such wars, the war on crime and poverty expanded out into a generalized 'war on disorder', and in the early 1970s was folded into the 'war on drugs', to deal with what was seen as a 'crisis of governability' in the cities, often blamed on urban 'guerrilla warfare advocates'.[105] With a domestic agenda understood as being focused on poverty and race, new developments were launched in education, welfare, medical care and urban planning, reinforced by curfews, patrols, suspension of civil liberties, and arrest without warrants. The logic was always to *make people work*. Through work, patients could be cured of the diseases of poverty, criminality and disorderliness.

At the heart of this dream of world order and the war for the cities was the concept of pacification. 'It would be ironic, indeed, if we devoted so heavy a proportion of our resources to the pacification of Vietnam that we are unable to pacify Los Angeles, Chicago, and Harlem', observed George McGovern in the Senate on 25 April 1967. His view was commonplace. For example, on 25 August 1967, *Life* magazine featured on the cover a US marine helping a Vietnamese child walking with crutches, with the headline 'The "Other War" in Vietnam: To Keep a Village Free'. The article examined the work of a Combined Action Platoon of marines whose mission was said to be 'defending and befriending' the people in hamlets threatened by the Viet Cong. This was followed by an article titled 'The "Other" Pacification' – but *this* pacification referred to the combined actions being performed to manage the crisis in American cities. The reality of pacification as the 'other war' was becoming clear. The other war was to be fought across battlefields as diverse as the fields of Vietnam and the urban centres of America. Phrases emerged such as 'Great Society Pacification Program'

104 Cited in Joshua Bloom and Waldo E. Martin Jr, *Black Against Empire: The History and Politics of the Black Panther Party* (Berkeley, CA: University of California Press, 2013), p. 210.

105 House Un-American Activities Committee, *Guerrilla Warfare Advocates in the United States*, House Report No. 1351 (Washington: US Government Printing Office, 1968).

– this one used by Samuel Yette in a 1971 book called *The Choice*. Similarly, Robert Moss of the International Institute for Strategic Studies suggested in his book *The War for the Cities* (1972) that pacification was necessary in Washington and New York as much as Hanoi. And in *Low Intensity Operations* (1971), a book first published by British commercial publishers but with its copyright under Her Majesty's Stationery Office, implying a certain level of official status, leading British counterinsurgency expert Frank Kitson held that pacification was as much a domestic issue as it was to do with Britain's colonies, and needed to be exercised especially against 'industrial guerrillas', otherwise known as trade unions – despite the fact that their 'grievances' were 'genuine and serious'.[106] The task of the 'other war' was the task of all war, Kitson wrote: to produce 'order out of chaos'.[107]

The real secret of the other war is that it in fact encompasses the social wars through which we are forced to live our lives. These are the wars declared by the state on our behalf, and yet at the same time declared against us. They are the wars of pacification. They are also the wars through which the police power achieves its strength and status. For social war, read: social police.

Social police

In January 2023, in a policy announcement that passed largely unnoticed, the British state declared a 'new approach for tackling serious and organised crime'. This was to operate through a 'multi-agency' approach, at the heart of which was to be the professional police (specifically, 'common-sense policing') liaising with a range of 'local partners'. The approach? 'Clear–Hold–Build'.

The very use of the approach reiterates the way in which police and pacification coincide, but also serves as a salutary reminder of police power as a productive process. As the various British police forces made

106 *Life* magazine, 25 August 1967, cover, pp. 24–8, 30–4; Samuel F. Yette, *The Choice: The Issue of Black Survival in America* (New York: G. P. Putnam's Sons, 1971); Robert Moss, *The War for the Cities* (New York: Coward, McCann & Geoghegan, 1972); Frank Kitson, *Low Intensity Operations: Subversion, Insurgency, Peace-keeping* (London: Faber & Faber, 1971), p. 25.

107 Frank Kitson, *Warfare as a Whole* (London: Faber & Faber, 1987), p. 59.

clear in implementing the strategy through 2023, Clear–Hold–Build seeks not simply to tackle crime, but to 'reclaim and rebuild communities' through a 'relationship between residents, the police and statutory agencies'. Here is just one example:

1. Clear – interventions (arrests and relentless disruption) that target organised crime group members, their networks, business interests, criminality and spheres of influence . . . This creates safer spaces to begin restoring community confidence.
2. Hold – interventions, counter-measures and contingency plans to consolidate and stabilise the initial clear phase . . . Visible neighbourhood policing in hotspot areas provides continuing reassurance that police are still present.
3. Build – a single, whole-system approach to delivering community-empowered interventions . . . This improves living, working and recreational environment in the community for residents.[108]

The way the principle is formulated and explained is so close to those cited earlier in this chapter, from the war on terror and other contexts, that it is difficult not to think that this was the British state revealing that policing *is* pacification. In the context of a chapter on pacification as a process of building and construction, we therefore need to say a little more about the police power. Building on arguments I have previously made concerning police power as the *fabrication of social order*, I will develop a concept of *social police* to run in tandem with *social war*. This might help us make more sense of the liberal welfare state as pacification.

Open any official or semi-official text on pacification, and amid all the language of war and war again – small war, civil war, other war, guerrilla war, revolutionary war – one finds the police power in all its glory. This is no surprise, once we accept that the function of the war power is 'to pacify, and not to obliterate'.[109] We have already seen this

108 *Clear, Hold, Build – West Yorkshire Police and Merseyside Police Framework* (UK College of Policing, 25 April 2023), pp. 1, 3. The same language and formulations are used in all the documents from different British police forces and central government departments.

109 J. F. C. Fuller, *The Reformation of War* (New York: E. P. Dutton, 1923), pp. 200–8.

time and again in the prose of pacification, discussed in this chapter. For Gallieni, 'a well-organized police . . . will hold [the people] in respect'. For Lyautey, pacification requires the army to adopt 'a police role' in the broadest sense possible. For Galula, pacification is essentially an 'intensive police action', and the counterinsurgent 'has to engage in police work'. For Trinquier, 'internal warfare' is 'an extensive police operation' and, conversely, police work is 'actual operational warfare'. For Kitson, the various 'steps on the ladder' of war – subversion, insurgency (civil war), conventional or limited war, then all-out war – mean that many of the manifestations of war are police concerns. For political scientists such as Pye, pacification is equated with police work. Similarly, since the birth of counterinsurgency, the official field manuals have time and again stressed the police role and function, from the first army manuals in the early 1960s through to the 2006 Army and Marine *Counterinsurgency Field Manual*'s insistence that 'warfighting and policing are dynamically linked' and that 'the primary frontline COIN force is often the police'.[110]

In one sense, this plays heavily on the old trope of police fighting wars, cities as war zones, and police officers as frontline soldiers in the war on crime. But in another, more telling sense, it is often *community* policing that is stressed, no doubt to draw attention away from pacification's more explicit forms of violence. Instead, focus is placed on the idea of winning over the population, living among it, holding territory, gathering intelligence, and engaging multiple local stakeholders. Community policing is also intended to enable a distinction to be drawn between 'the People' and the insurgents who might seek to live among them and gain their support – and this is central to pacification. Take, for example, the 'Company Instructions' issued by Galula to his men in Algeria in October 1957, cited in the Introduction:

110 General Joseph-Simon Gallieni, 'Instructions' (1898), in Chauvet, *Gallieni Pacificateur*, p. 240; Lyautey, *Du Rôle colonial*, pp. 18–19; Galula, *Pacification in Algeria*, p. 119; Galula, *Counterinsurgency Warfare*, pp. 52, 87; Trinquier, *Modern Warfare*, pp. 5, 37, 41; Kitson, *Warfare as a Whole*, pp. 4, 56; Lucien Pye, 'The Roots of Insurgency', in Harry Eckstein, ed., *Internal War: Problems and Approaches* (New York: Free Press, 1964), p. 160; Headquarters, Department of the Army, *Counterguerrilla Operations*, Field Manual 31-16 (February 1963), pp. 37–48; Headquarters, US Military Assistance Command, Vietnam, *Handbook for Military Support*, p. 19; US Army/Marine Corps, *Counterinsurgency Field Manual*, Section 7–26, pp. 6–90.

1. EXTERIORLY. EVERY VILLAGER IS A FRIEND . . .
2. INWARDLY. EVERY VILLAGER IS A SUSPECT.

Make the people think you are their friend, but always think of them as the enemy. As we saw, this could be considered the very definition of 'community policing'.

Community policing is integral to pacification in being the perfect mode of the 'other war'. A cursory glance at three reports on pacification produced during the heyday of the war on terror makes the point. A typical pacification campaign, according to one 2008 RAND report on using the police power for 'war by other means', involves 'well-trained and well-led community police and quick-response, light-combat-capable (constabulary) police'. There simply is 'no substitute for local, community-oriented police'.[111] As another RAND report on policing and counterinsurgency published a year later puts it, 'Soldiers – especially military police – can make great advisors when embedded for community policing', because one of the key principles is to be as mobile as the insurgent, and this is equally important to community policing. This report argues that the predominant ways of utilizing police within counterinsurgency consists of 'the adoption of the community-policing approach'.[112] 'Pacification is best thought of as a massively enhanced version of the "community policing" technique that emerged in the 1970s', observes a RAND report for the US Office of the secretary of defense, called *On 'Other War'*, produced slightly earlier in the war on terror, in 2006. Community policing, the report argues, implies a broad concept of 'problem solving' by means of police officers working in a delimited area, with sensitivity to ethnic and other issues. This allows police officers to form a bond of trust with local residents and to work with local groups, businesses and churches to address the community's concerns. It states openly that 'pacification is simply an expansion of this concept'.[113] 'Community policing' has long been a crucial piece of police jargon for what is always an aggressively proactive style of policing, allowing it to blend with

111 David C. Gompert and John Gordon IV, *War by Other Means: Building Complete and Balanced Capabilities for Counterinsurgency* (Santa Monica, CA: RAND, 2008), pp. xlv, 290.

112 Joseph D. Celeski, *Policing and Law Enforcement in COIN: The Thick Blue Line* (Hurlburt Field, FL: Joint Special Operations University Report 09-2, 2009), pp. 52, 54.

113 Long, *On 'Other War'*, p. 53.

'paramilitary policing' in such a way as to make them nearly indistinguishable.

As those three RAND reports were being produced and circulated during the war on terror, Brazil launched a 'Favela Pacification Programme' in 2008. This was to be a cross-institutional strategy to 'clean up' the poorest of urban communities, known as favelas. The units charged with carrying out the task were called Unidades de Polícia Pacificadora (UPP): 'Police Pacification Units'. The UPP was expanded and intensified in 2014, when the city of Rio stepped up its plans for hosting the football World Cup, being held there that year, and the Olympic Games due to be held there two years later. By 2014, some thirty-eight Units had been established, involving around 10,000 'police pacification officers', often led by military personnel appointed by the Ministry of Defence. The UPP was invented as *police at war*. This became clear from the Wikileaks files: first, in September 2009, the state secretary for public security, José Beltrame, announced the reason for Pacification Units: 'we are at war'; second, a month later, the senior director for the International Committee for the Red Cross (ICRC) in Rio, Felipe Donoso, claimed that what was taking place in the favelas was, to all intents and purposes, an 'internal armed conflict'. In the light of my discussion in Chapter 1, we can say that the UPP makes clear the extent to which social wars are police wars.

The UPP was refined with the introduction in 2010 of the UPP Social (Social Police Pacification Units), revealing the expansive concept of police that was at stake. Their tasks included classic police operations such as clearing up vagrancy, administering street building and refuse disposal, and working with healthcare teams and NGOs. The aim, according to one of its documents, is 'the consolidation of the pacifying process and promotion of local citizenship in the pacified territories; to promote urban, social and economic development in the territories; and to execute the full integration of these areas with the city as a whole'.[114] In search of a form of social and urban

114 From the UPP Social website, this translation in Markus-Michael Müller, 'Entangled Pacifications: Peacekeeping, Counterinsurgency and Policing in Port-au-Prince and Rio de Janeiro', in Jana Hönke and Markus-Michael Müller, eds, *The Global Making of Policing: Postcolonial Perspectives* (London: Routledge, 2016), p. 89. See also Sebastian Saborio, 'The Pacification of the Favelas: Mega Events, Global Competitiveness, and the Neutralization of Marginality', *Socialist Studies/Études Socialistes* 9: 2 (2013), pp. 130–45.

reconstruction under banners such as 'hope and citizenship', the UPP Social organizes a wide variety of formal and informal educational activities. It conducts lectures on 'citizenship' issues such as drugs, runs essay contests, football games, jiu-jitsu, theatre classes, computer classes, day trips and Christmas parties, distributes toys, and participates in a 'Children's Day'. The UPP Social has declared a new social war: a war on Funkeiro, a style of music.[115] Literature has been produced to popularize the process, such as the 2012 booklet *UPP: A Conquista da Paz* ('The Conquest of Peace'), written and illustrated by Alves Pinto Ziraldo (creator of a classic children's book, *O Menino Maluquinho* – 'The Nutty Boy'), but overseen by the Rio State Department of Security. The booklet has been distributed in schools and used by teachers to explain the nature of citizenship, rights and obligations. The social nature of the police pacification process is illustrated in the booklet by an image of two police officers on one page, followed on the next pages by doctors, teachers, cleaners, lawyers and construction workers. In a sentence that could have been take straight out of the texts of Gallieni or Lyautey, the pamphlet announces: 'after [the police officers] will come education, health, more cleaning, more justice, more comfort and more security'.[116] Documents such as the *Manual de Campanha* stress the broad social work programmes that underpin so much of the 'building' phase of the pacification of the favelas. A cable from the US embassy in Rio, dated 30 September 2009 (revealed in the WikiLeaks files), notes that the UPP initiative utilizes 'Clear–Hold–Build' doctrine, and that this is explicitly because of how that doctrine had been carried out by the US and its allies in Afghanistan and Iraq. Unsurprisingly, a few years later, in 2015, the Brazilian state released a Field Manual, *Manual de Campanha EB20-MC-10.217: Operações de Pacificação*, at the heart of which is the principle of pacification in three phases: 'intervention, stabilization and normalization'. As the *Manual* makes clear, this is the Brazilian state's version of 'Clear–Hold–Build'.[117]

---

115 Luciane Soares da Silva, *Funk para além da festa: Disputas simbólicas e práticas culturais no Rio de Janeiro* (São Paulo: Ciclo Contínuo Editorial, 2021).

116 Alves Pinto Ziraldo, *UPP: A Conquista da Paz* (Rio de Janeiro: Unidade de Polícia Pacificadora, 2012), pp. 21–5.

117 Brazilian Ministry of Defence, *Manual de Campanha EB20-MC-10.217: Operações de pacificação* (2015), pp. 2–10, 42, 44, 48, at sgex.eb.mil.br.

As a means of attempting a social reconstruction around bourgeois notions of civilization, legitimized through the idea of working-class urban communities as centres of criminality and reinforced by the idea that this criminality is linked to their poverty, and hence that the people in such spaces are some kind of enemy upon whom war must be waged, the UPP captures the essence of pacification as a social war against the working class and marginalized groups, facilitating a smoother reproduction of capital, and remaking the state and the city for a brighter and nicer new life . . . for some.

Perhaps the real lesson of the UPPs is the lesson all states want us to learn: to acknowledge the state itself as a universal and absolute Police Pacification Unit. To acknowledge, in other words, the generalized *policing of the social* that is pacification, so general that it covers the whole range of social policy, and is itself a form of social work.

'Social work in civilised countries [is] the safeguard of society.' Without social work, there would be 'brigandage and even revolution'. So said Thomas Garrett Askwith, one time commissioner for community development in Kenya, and one of the more liberal colonial administrators in that country. For Askwith, social work was crucial to defeating the Mau Mau insurgency. Such 'disturbances', as he called the insurgency, were a result of 'maladjusted individuals' with 'mind-destroying diseases' such as a belief in communism or national liberation.[118] Askwith's view was far from being a peculiarity of that very peculiar thing known as the British colonial mind. We find the same idea throughout the prose of pacification. For example, when Trinquier describes pacification as an extensive police operation, its extensiveness includes a broad programme of social work. The US *Counterinsurgency Field Manual* claims that counterinsurgency 'can be characterized as armed social work'. To this end, the *Manual* cites a passage I have already cited from Galula's *Counterinsurgency Warfare*, which itself glosses comments from Lyautey to the effect that the soldier is a form of social worker. In similar fashion, COINdinista David Kilcullen describes counterinsurgency as 'armed civil affairs', including 'community organizing, welfare, mediation, domestic assistance, economic support . . . under conditions of extreme threat

118 'Memorandum from T. G. Askwith', 26 February 1953, cited in Caroline Elkins, *Britain's Gulag: The Brutal End of Empire in Kenya* (London: Pimlico, 2005), p. 108.

requiring armed support'. In other words, 'counterinsurgency is armed social work'.[119] This is why some commentators on the war on terror suggest that modern warfare turns out to be 'more like social work with guns'.[120] The idea of counterinsurgency as armed social work reminds us that, as social *policy*, social work is a means of *policing the social*.

In 1919, August Vollmer, the so-called 'father of American policing', gave a talk to the convention of the International Association of Chiefs of Police. The subject of his talk was the idea of police officers as social workers. So seminal was his talk that it was published in *The Policeman's News*, and then again in *The National Police Journal*. On the article's centenary, the international journal *Policing* published a special section on his arguments. Vollmer repeated most of the points in a speech in 1920, only this time to various social policy organizations in California, and his talk was then published in the *Social Agencies Bulletin* that same year. Aware that some might find the idea of the policeman as social worker problematic, Vollmer also toyed with phrases such as 'police social work' and 'social police work'. In classic police prose, Vollmer argues that 'dependency, criminality and industrial unrest have a common origin', which meant that the police role must extend beyond 'the mere apprehending and prosecuting of law breakers'. The police function was to produce 'decent, law-abiding citizens'. In that sense, policing was social work in the broadest of ways. This was why police forces operated alongside and through other organs that helped police the social, such as schools, churches, youth associations, public welfare departments, employment bureaus, hospitals, medical centres, psychiatric institutions and trades unions. To illustrate this, Vollmer offered examples of successful policing: a girl, arrested for stealing, found to have mental as well as physical disabilities, and so sent to a 'medico-Psychologist'; a boy, arrested for burglary, sent to relatives in the country for rehabilitation; a man, arrested for burglary, found to be a

119 Trinquier, *Modern Warfare*, pp. 5, 37; U.S. Army/Marine Corps, *Counterinsurgency Field Manual*, Section A-45, p. 299 and Section 2-42, p. 68; David Kilcullen, *Counterinsurgency* (Oxford: Oxford University Press, 2010), p. 43; David Kilcullen, 'Ethics, Politics and Non-State Warfare', *Anthropology Today* 23: 3 (2007), p. 20.

120 Andrew Bacevich, 'Social Work with Guns', *London Review of Books*, 17 December 2009.

'neurasthenic with morbid impulses' as 'the result of over work and financial worries'.[121]

What emerges from Vollmer's talk is the idea of the police power as a universal force responsible for a wide range of tasks, and working with all social agencies in a concerted and coordinated action, to the extent that police officers should not only liaise with all other agencies engaged in 'social work', but should themselves be considered 'social police workers'. As Vollmer later put it in *The Police and Modern Society* (1936), not only do police officers protect and defend the people in the area; they also function as a kind of parish priest, lawyer, medical adviser, social service, and even a counsellor.[122]

Arguments such as Vollmer's tend to jar with some of the engrained assumptions about the contemporary police function. But he was in fact merely reasserting some of the fundamental basics of police science in twentieth-century terms. We could approach this issue from the opposite direction. In June 2020, the chief executive officer of the National Association of Social Workers, the leading American professional organization in the field, was asked on TV to respond to the desire among some police abolitionists to spread some of the work of police to social workers. He commented that, in fact, the two fields already worked closely together: 'They [the police] love us . . . They have our backs as social workers, and we have their backs, so it's a very good partnership'.[123] As he explained, social workers are often stationed in police offices, going out with police officers in vehicles on callouts, and the two professions triage individuals in both directions: social workers frequently involve the professional police, and the professional police frequently involve social workers. We might add that both frequently involve teachers, medical professionals, mental health workers, welfare agencies and social housing institutions. When a social worker based in a school liaises with teachers to call in the cops, have a

121 August Vollmer, 'Policemen as Social Workers' (1919) and 'Tell This to Your Policeman' (1920), both in Willard M. Oliver, ed., *The Collected Writings of Police Chief August Vollmer, Vol. 1: 1914–1926* (Police History Academic Press, 2022), pp. 113–23, 141–4; August Vollmer, *The Police and Modern Society* (Berkeley: University of California Press, 1936), pp. 3, 196, 214.

122 Vollmer, *Police and Modern Society*, p. 216.

123 Cited in Cameron Rasmussen and Kirk 'Jae' James, 'Trading Cops for Social Workers Isn't the Solution to Police Violence', *Truthout*, 17 July 2020.

child strip-searched for drugs and then taken to a hospital for an involuntary mental health assessment, where does the police power begin and end?

The policeman as social worker takes us to the social work of police in the fabrication of order. It takes us to the idea of social police.

The idea of social police jars with the belief in policing as professionalized crime-prevention and law-enforcement. And yet, every single police theorist prior to the 'professionalization' of policing had a sense of something akin to 'social police', along the lines alluded to by Vollmer. This is why, to give a few examples, Patrick Colquhoun understood policing as part of the general project of political economy and the Poor Law, building on the work of Adam Smith, who understood political economy and the Poor Law to be part of the general project of policing. It is also why police reformers such as Johann Peter Frank in Germany and Edwin Chadwick in England understood medical power to be as fundamental to police science as the Poor Law, to the extent that they even considered good drainage to be a police function, and good sanitation as 'the gentlest of policemen'.[124] As I have shown in *A Critical Theory of Police Power*, this broad notion of social police was gradually dissipated, or even lost, in the professionalization of policing and the attempts to view policing solely through the lens of law-enforcement and crime-prevention that began with the emergence of 'new' police forces, following the creation of the Metropolitan Police in Britain in 1829. Through such professionalization, policing is said to have undergone a narrowing in focus, which essentially gave official sanction to a purported conceptual break between the 'new police' and the gamut of other services once understood as 'policing', but now increasingly seen as other forms of political administration. Key aspects of 'old police' – expressing an expansive idea of a science of government that embraced the fabrication of social order, the constitution of obedient subjects, and the governing of economic life – were now meant to be expressed in terms of a more general political administration, often taking the name 'social policy'. It has to be called 'social policy', because the liberal state's concept of 'police' would not admit to the reality of the situation of a *social police*, to which 'social

124 Christopher Hamlin, *Public Health and Social Justice in the Age of Chadwick: Britain, 1800–1854* (Cambridge: Cambridge University Press, 1998), p. 213.

policy' alludes in the most remarkable of ways. Yet the very term 'social policy' offers a clear hint that the original police remit has never been forsaken by the state.

Social police categorize and sort the population into various groups, some with official status but others merely part of the informal prose of pacification, to be policed in different ways by different parts of the system: 'vagrant', 'homeless', 'deserving poor', 'undeserving poor', 'habitual criminal', 'probationer', 'workshy', 'indigent', 'scrounger' – the list could go on and on. Each category oscillates in various ways around the question of labour, and opens its subjects up to different modes of social policing. The very process of such categorization is itself one of pacification's forms of power.

At the heart of the policing of the social lies an idealized notion of the family (as Jacques Donzelot has argued), in a way that makes pacification coincide with domestication (as Patricia Owens has shown). I will give just three examples. First, Galula, reflecting on potential allies among the people he sought to pacify, suggests that 'women, given their subjugated condition, would naturally be on our side if we emancipated them', but that this requires care 'so as not to antagonize the males too much'. Second, Kilcullen suggests that counterinsurgency must 'engage the women', because if you 'win the women . . . you own the family unit', and if you 'own the family . . . you take a big step forward in mobilizing the population'. Third, the COIN Manual holds that because 'women are hugely influential in forming the social networks that insurgents use for support', one must 'co-opt' them 'through targeted social and economic programs'.[125] This domestication is why the logic of 'protection' runs so deep in the social police.

This is precisely the pervasive nature of police power alluded to by Walter Benjamin. The critical analysis of such power encounters a kind of nothing that is everything, a formless power with an all-pervasive presence through our lives and relations. This *social police is pacification*: the policing of the social in the name of security through a series of tutelary institutions throughout civil society as well as the state. This

125 Jacques Donzelot, *The Policing of Families: Welfare Versus the State*, transl. Robert Hurley (London: Hutchinson, 1980 [1977]); Patricia Owens, *Economy of Force: Counterinsurgency and the Historical Rise of the Social* (Cambridge: Cambridge University Press, 2015); Galula, *Pacification in Algeria*, p. 105; Kilcullen, *Counterinsurgency*, p. 40; *Counterinsurgency Field Manual*, Section A-35, p. 296.

includes medicine and education along with social work, as we have seen. But more than anything it incorporates what were once Poor Law administrators and are now welfare officers. In pacification, policing and the Poor Law are always imagined as one and the same system of social policing designed to get people to work.

Work under capitalism requires us to build and exercise certain kinds of skills and abilities, and certain qualities such as motivation, resilience and self-discipline, and so the reproduction of labour requires qualitative interventions into these aspects of an individual's life. Social work encourages the view that failures are the responsibility of the individual. The 'presenting problem' will always be an individual problem, rooted in the individual's failure to 'be reasonable' and accept the strictures imposed on them through the regulation of their liberty determined by the demands of capital and the state. Through this, the individual must be reconstituted again and again, such that they will adjust to those strictures. Do not be indigent, incompetent or lazy. Do not have the wrong attitude, approach or focus. More than anything, do not be disaffected by life in capitalism, do not become belligerent about the very conditions that might make you disaffected, and do not take the seditious blockheads seriously. Signs of these tendencies in a collective turn the group into an insurgency that will need to be countered. In an individual, they turn the person into a 'case' to be treated, which is why the term 'casework' operates across the whole gamut of social police. Both processes together are central to pacification.

Pacification produces corpses, then, and plenty of them – but never only corpses, since it also processes us as 'patients', seeking to cure us of all manner of social illnesses and political diseases. Pacification's ultimate productive power is not only to build a capitalist social order, but continually to reproduce us as good subjects fit for such order.

In the process, we encounter one of pacification's further productive powers: its ability to induce political administration by bringing into being the very forms through which the social order is to be policed. New departments are created, new commissions established, new information gathered, new reports written, new files opened, all to police the social wars of modernity. Pacification's protracted social wars subsume social struggle into administrative forms, which it transforms into social policing.

This is why we need the expanded concept of police power (social police) to gain a full understanding not only of pacification's scope, but also of its productive capacities. Pacification as the power to clear and to hold, for sure, but also very much the power to build: houses, roads, villages, towns, cities, military bases, industrial bases, schools, clinics, bridges (literal and metaphorical), culture, support, trust, morale. Build the confidence of the people in the process of their pacification by reproducing them as good subjects. Above all: *build social order*.

The ultimate police message is, in effect, the message from God to Job, which, is why it is cited so approvingly by Hobbes, as we have seen: *Where were you when I laid the foundation of the earth?* Where were you when I built all this? Where were you when I brought good order? More to the point: where is your *acknowledgement* of this art of well building? You must acknowledge my power, just as you must acknowledge your darkness. Acknowledging these things will also put you in a better position to acknowledge your *containment* by the state and by capital, and your *debt* to both – subjects to which we will turn in the two chapters that follow.

4

Kettle Logic and the Fantasy of Containment

The power of the State sees something spill.
Something lies in the shit.
What's lying in the shit?
Something's lying in the shit.
There's something lying deadly still
– The People, why that's it!

Bertolt Brecht, 'Article One of the Weimar Constitution' (1931)

'Die Staatsgewalt geht vom Volke aus', claimed Article 1 of the Weimar Constitution of 1919: the power of the state proceeds from the people. But where is it proceeding to, asks Brecht:

Yes, where is it proceeding to?
There's some place it's proceeding to.
The policeman proceeds through the station gate.
– But where does he proceed to?

It is 1931. The police are proceeding rightwards. They are on the march. They are proceeding towards fascism. In the meantime, they have work to do, other marches to conduct. These are marches to be undertaken in the direction of 'something standing in a crowd'. What is it, this something in the crowd? It is something that must, by definition, be part of the people, and it has the audacity to query the demands being made on it by the state.

> Why should it query that?
> What cheek to query that!
> The State just shoots – for that's allowed –
> And something falls down flat.

The People: fallen, lying flat, possibly to become a patient, more likely a corpse. The People, lying in the shit.

Sometimes the state does not shoot, but employs other tactics and uses other weapons. Sometimes it prefers to charge people with batons, shields, dogs, horses or armoured vehicles. Sometimes it prefers to hold people in place, to keep them there as a crowd. We have witnessed this more than enough times to know how it works: a group of people held by police in a confined space, often for several hours, without food, water, access to toilets or protection from the elements, until the police grant permission to leave. The people have been *kettled*.

The police tactic known as kettling began to be used against protestors in the early 1980s. The 'Hamburger Kessel' of 8 June 1986, in which 861 demonstrators were held in the blazing sun for hours, is sometimes dubbed the 'mother of all kettles'.[1] Earlier examples can be found, such as the 'Battle of Orgreave' on 18 June 1984, when British police used kettling as a tactic against striking miners. Either way, kettling is now a standard police technique, as a few examples will show. In October 1995, disabled people were kettled in Parliament Square in London, during a disability rights demonstration, and a kettle was used against the N30 anti-WTO demonstrators in the city on 30 November 1999. Kettles were also used by the London Metropolitan Police during the May Day riots of 2001 to contain demonstrators (along with many bystanders, as it took place in the busy shopping area Oxford Circus), the G8 summit protests in 2005, and the G20 summit protests outside the Bank of England in 2009 (in which Ian Tomlinson was killed by being hit by a police baton as he sought to leave the kettle). Kettling was used again on 24 November 2010, during the student protests in London and elsewhere in the UK, and then again the following month to contain

1 Kai Von Appen, 'Die Mutter aller Kessel', *TAZ*, 8 June 2016.

student protesters in Parliament Square and Westminster Bridge. Kettling was also used three times in the UK in 2020, against Black Lives Matter protests. The technique is used across the world: anti-globalization protestors were kettled in Washington, DC in 2002, during Iraq War protests in Chicago in 2003, during the Republican National Convention in New York in 2004, against those protesting the repression of dissent in Hamburg in 2007, against Occupy Wall Street in 2011, during the inauguration of President Trump in 2017, and on 4 November 2020, when 646 protestors in Minneapolis were kettled while protesting against Trump's threat to challenge the US election. Kettling has also been used against those protesting the police killings – or acquittals of police officers accused of carrying them out – of Anthony Lamar Smith, George Floyd, Breonna Taylor, Daunte Wright and many more. Other examples can easily be found from around the world, from Australia to Canada to Denmark, France, Israel and Spain.

The kettle is as variable as it is universal. The kettled crowd can be held as a static mass, but it can also be forced to move by the police in what are referred to as 'mobile' or 'wander' kettles. There is also the possibility of a 'bridge kettle', where a bridge and a river help form part of the structure of the kettle, such as occurred on the Pont de la Guillotière in Lyon, France (20 October 2010), on Westminster Bridge, London (9 December 2010), and on Manhattan Bridge, New York (2 June 2020).

Discussions of kettling have mainly centred on the impact on civil liberties, the lawfulness of such arbitrary detention, and the appropriateness of the tactic's application given the incitement that the kettle produces. The same questions emerge time and again, reducing discussion to the tried and tested ways of thinking about policing: tactics and technologies, legalities and limits, and 'models of policing'. Others have treated kettling in terms of what they see as a rise in repressive police operations and a drift towards a more 'command and control' style of policing protests. It goes almost without saying that, in one sense, the kettle is an example of the 'show of force' that has been at the heart of police crowd control for some time – a precursor to the much later idea of 'escalated force' as a step up from 'confrontation management' or 'negotiated management'. But the 'models of policing' approach, which draws such a categorical distinction between 'communicative models' and 'repressive models' of policing, is trite and deeply uncritical. This distinction is a version of the type of dichotomy that comes up time and again, such as between the 'paramilitary police model' ('repressive') and the 'community police model' ('communicative'), or between 'coercion' and 'consent'. But, as we saw in Chapter 3, and as I have argued elsewhere, such distinctions are part of the mythology of the liberal state. Are not acts of repression, command and coercion also acts of communication? 'It wasn't politics', one of the French protestors of 2005 explained, 'we just wanted to tell the state something'.[2] Maybe the kettle communicates in the other direction: 'It isn't politics', says the state, 'we just want to tell the people something.' But what might be the message? Might it be that their containment within the kettle is a small-scale version of the much broader means of containment that is pacification? Might it be a warning that, if they carry on with such rebellious and insurgent behaviour, they will find themselves lying in the shit?

Protest contained

'A good metaphor is something even the police should keep an eye on', Georg Christoph Lichtenberg once observed.[3] 'Kettle' is one such metaphor. Symptomatic of how much the police keep an eye on this metaphor is the extent to which they repeatedly deny its very existence, for the 'kettle' exists in neither police discourse nor English law. Tellingly, what does exist is 'containment'. This can be illustrated by reference to several court cases.

In the case of a person who had been held in the Bishopsgate kettle in 2009, the divisional court in the UK (part of the High Court, but with 2 or more judges sitting) initially found that the actions of the police had been unnecessary and unjustified, but the Court of Appeal found the police actions were lawful. In this case, *McClure & Anon v Commissioner of Police of the Metropolis* (2012), the Court of Appeal held that:

2 Cited in Alain Bertho, *The Age of Violence: The Crisis of Political Action and the End of Utopia*, transl. David Broder (London: Verso, 2018 [2016]), p. 26.

3 Georg Christoph Lichtenberg, *The Waste Books* (1765–99), transl. R. J. Hollingdale (New York: NYRB, 2000), Notebook E, 1775–76, no. 91.

> the decision to contain a substantial crowd of demonstrators, whose behaviour, though at times unruly and somewhat violent, did not of itself justify containment, was justifiable on the ground that containment was the least drastic way of preventing what the police officer responsible for the decision reasonably apprehended would otherwise be imminent and serious breaches of the peace.

In the case of *Castle & Ors v Commissioner of Police for the Metropolis* (2011), three student demonstrators between the ages of fourteen and sixteen were kettled in Whitehall, London, and held for around seven hours in freezing temperatures, in conditions where the police themselves recorded witnessing theft of property and the burning of street furniture. The court held that being contained by the police in these conditions was 'justified by events occurring outside the cordon which required careful handling of those within the containment'. Similarly, in *Austin & Anon v Commissioner of Police of the Metropolis* (2009), concerning Lois Austin and three other people who had been kettled on Oxford Street in London in 2001, the House of Lords found that such containment was lawful when police resort to it in good faith, use it for a legitimate purpose, consider it proportionate to the situation, and enforce it for no longer than considered reasonably necessary. The Association of Chief Police Officers (ACPO) manual on public order tactics, called *Keeping the Peace* (2004), now uses the *Austin* decision to reassert the viability of the kettle. These decisions were upheld in March 2012 by the European Court of Human Rights.

This represents the familiar phenomenon of the law doffing its cap to the police power: the police invent a tactic; the law decides that the tactic is lawful. But the point is that the tactic in question is described not as 'kettling', but 'containment'. Why containment?

Following the policing of the G20 protests in London, the Metropolitan Police was challenged by a parliamentary committee in May 2009 about the tactic of kettling. It will be useful here to consider what the senior police officers had to say.[4]

4 The exchanges that follow are from the House of Commons, Home Affairs Committee, *Policing of the G20 Protests. Eighth Report of Session 2008–09. Report*, 29 June 2009.

One of the people who came before the House of Commons committee was Sue Sim, at that point lead officer for ACPO in the UK, here being questioned by Gary Streeter, a Conservative MP:

> MR [GARY] STREETER: Could you just share with us the ACPO guidelines for the policing of public protests like this? I am interested particularly in kettling . . .
>
> MS SIM: Firstly, I do not understand the term 'kettling'. Kettling is not a British policing public order tactic, it is something that has been created apparently in the media.
>
> MR STREETER: What do you call it when you group people together in this way?
>
> MS SIM: I would call that containment.

Note the disingenuousness of Sim's comments. She says she does not understand the term, but clearly knows enough about it to identify it as a media creation that refers to a specific police tactic. Unsurprisingly, this line of questioning went nowhere. But later in the discussion another committee member, Labour MP Karen Buck, returned to the point:

> MS BUCK: Going back to the issue of kettling as a term, as a concept, it is something that has entered discourse in terms of crowd control probably since the May Day demonstrations at the beginning of the decade. In an earlier answer you kind of rejected it as a term. Are you saying, really, that this is a media invention and that actually there has been no change in the tactics of crowd control?
>
> MS SIM: Kettling is not a term that is contained within any policing manuals or with any policing concept. The issue of containment . . . has been a tactic for a long time. On the issue of kettling, I do not actually understand how that has been come [*sic*] into the terminology because it is not something that we would accept; containment is.

Another Committee member, Bob Russell, a Liberal Democrat MP, takes up the issue:

> BOB RUSSELL: I wonder if you could give us the date when this system came in? . . . Like you, I have no idea where the term

'kettling' comes from, but the word 'kettle' does strike me as being very close to something that can boil over, and I suspect that this is what has happened.

MS SIM: Yes, but it is not within police terminology.

. . .

BOB RUSSELL: The point I am trying to get at is: is this a completely new method of policing? It strikes me as being something different from what it has been historically and I want to know at what point it changed to what we have got today?

CHAIRMAN [KEITH VAZ]: Mr Russell needs to know the date when kettling began.

MS SIM: We do not kettle, Mr Vaz.

CHAIRMAN: The date it began even though you do not do it. This is a media term, is it, the word kettling? It is not a police term.

MS SIM: I believe it to be a media term.

CHAIRMAN: You do not arrive on the scene and say, 'Let us kettle these people'?

MS SIM: No, we do not.

The same line of discussion continues in the Committee's questioning of Sir Hugh Orde, chief constable, and Duncan McCausland, assistant chief constable of the Police Service of Northern Ireland:

CHAIRMAN: Can you specifically tell us about what we have heard, which Mr Russell and others have raised, about kettling and kettles? Where does this term come from and what does it mean? Is it a recognisable police term or is this a Sky News term?

SIR HUGH ORDE: I have absolutely no idea where the term came from. Issues of containment are very clearly tactics . . . Duncan, do you want to touch on the tactics that we would use around containment?

MR MCCAUSLAND: We would not recognise the term 'kettling' . . . I believe it has been something created by the media about a kettle being on the boil. We would use clear containment tactics, that you heard and that Deputy Chief Constable Sims mentioned, but our role in terms of containment, Chairman, has been to potentially diffuse the situation and allow protesters and people to move away from the area that they are potentially wanting to get

> into. Sir Paul Stephenson [Commissioner of the Metropolitan Police] observed that 'we think that [kettling] is an entirely inappropriate term'.

In a following session a week later, on 19 May, the committee questioned Sir Paul Stephenson and Commander Bob Broadhurst, the 'Gold Commander' of the policing and security operation of the G20. Bob Russell again asked:

> BOB RUSSELL: Commissioner and Commander, this is the second session we have had where the term 'kettling' or 'kettle' has been used. I find it offensive. I do not know where the term has come from. The police have stated it is not terminology they use. I wonder if, first of all, you could tell us what your terminology is.
>
> CHAIRMAN: Are you implying that 'kettle' is not a British term?
>
> BOB RUSSELL: It is something, Chairman, that in my many, many years in public life, and as a former court reporter, I have never heard of until relatively recently. So I am just wondering where the term came from.
>
> SIR PAUL STEPHENSON: It is not a term we use; it is not a term we favour; we – and I think it is in the ACPO manual – use the term 'containment', and that is what we will continue to use because that accurately describes what the tactic is.

The law also follows this police insistence on referring to 'containment' not 'kettling', as can be seen in the numerous legal judgments on the issue cited above. One finds the same disavowal of the kettle far and wide: a sergeant testified that 'kettling . . . was not a practice with which he was familiar or had ever employed at NYPD'; a commissioner 'testified that he had never heard of the term kettling until after the protests began'; an NYPD spokesperson insisted that 'kettling is not a term known to the NYPD. It has never been referenced in our training or procedures. It is not a crowd control tactic for us. However a tactic known as "encirclement" is used.'[5]

5 The first two from New York State Office of the Attorney General, *Preliminary Report on the New York City Police Department's Response to Demonstrations Following the Death of George Floyd* (July 2020), pp. 30, 32; the third cited in Alice Speri, 'Ambushed by the Cops', *Intercept*, 2 June 2021.

One could consider this disavowal of the kettle by senior police officers in terms of the 'kettle logic' described by Freud in *Jokes and Their Relation to the Unconscious* and *The Interpretation of Dreams*. A man was charged by one of his neighbours with having returned a borrowed kettle in a damaged condition. The man's response? First, I didn't give the kettle back damaged; second, the kettle was already damaged when I borrowed it; and third, I never borrowed the kettle. The police version: first, nothing damaging happened to you in the kettle; second, you were already damaged when you entered the kettle; and third, we never kettled you anyway. What is not disavowed by the police, however, but in fact avowed quite openly and proudly, is containment.

The police use of the language and logic of 'containment' certainly has a history as long as 'since the manuals began'. It is found in key police texts of the 1960s, such as Raymond Momboisse's *Riots, Revolts and Insurrections* (1967) and Rex Applegate's *Riot Control: Materiel and Techniques* (1969), in key police manuals such as the FBI's *Prevention and Control of Mobs and Riots* (1967) and key army manuals including *Civil Disturbances* (1972). To take a more recent example, the British ACPO manual *Keeping the Peace* contains no reference to kettles or kettling, but plenty to a tripartite logic of 'containment, dispersal, arrest', various styles of cordoning as containment techniques, and how to use a 'Show-of-Strength' during containment (which includes, in practice, officers and mounted police charging at those being contained).[6] The British police thus use 'containment managers' to oversee a tactic of 'strategic incapacitation', a term now widely used to capture the process of spatial containment and the policing of protest, avoiding 'negotiation' with protesters and focusing instead on controlling and disrupting mobilizations, gathering intelligence on those incapacitated, and thus, more broadly, containing social movements.[7]

So important is this idea of containment to the state that we should observe two of its important features. First, the state takes it as read that

6 ACPO Public Order Working Group, *Keeping the Peace: ACPO Manual of Guidance: Public Order Standards, Tactics, and Training Manual* (March 2004), pp. 28, 52, 124–6, 190, 193, 198–9, 211.

7 Her Majesty's Chief Inspector of Constabulary (HMCIC), *Adapting to Protest: Nurturing the British Model of Policing* (2009), at assets-hmicfrs.justiceinspectorates.gov.uk, p. 43.

protestors can be regarded as having given their *consent* to being contained. In the case of *Austin*, Lord Neuberger made the argument that

> if imputed consent is an appropriate basis for justifying confinement for article 5 purposes, then it seems to me that the confinement in the present case could be justified on the basis that anyone on the streets, particularly on a demonstration with a well-known risk of serious violence, must be taken to be consenting to the possibility of being confined by the police.

In other words, 'consent to being confined could be *imputed to the people concerned*'.[8] Lord Neuberger's position was not quite that of the court. But the way he framed his view is in line with the court's, and this is telling because of his use of the legal notion of 'imputed consent' in the sense of consent between two parties who are treated in law *as if* they had consented. The use of 'imputed consent' in a public-law setting concerning a 'crowd' (and hence, by implication, involving a very different notion of voluntariness), is a means of insisting that *some* form of consent to be contained can be attributed to those contained. What this means, in effect, is that the disobedience of our protest is interpreted as a sign of our consent to *de jure* containment and *de facto* imprisonment; I use the term 'imprisonment' deliberately, for reasons that will become clear. To put this another way, the disobedience of our protest is interpreted as a sign of our willingness to undergo a lesson in obedience. This reading of consent is consistent with one of the fundamental features of the police power, which prefers to find a consent that it can interpret as *informally* expressed, and on grounds entirely decided by the police, rather than a consent *formally* expressed (especially through any kind of democratic process). Hence the notion of consent in the kettle replicates the police notion of consent more generally, which is always 'narrow and nebulous'.[9] The second important feature to note is that the state holds the view that the containment of people can take place simply on the grounds of 'a mere speculative danger', and thus containment can be used to prevent any *potential* disorder.[10]

8 Emphasis added.

9 Phil Scraton, *The State of the Police* (London: Pluto, 1985), p. 51.

10 HMCIC, *Adapting to Protest*, pp. 61, 89; ACPO National Policing Improvement Agency, *Manual of Guidance on Keeping the Peace* (London: ACPO, 2010).

We can thus begin to identify some of the logic of the kettle: the kettle is an act of pre-emptive containment to which those being contained are assumed to have given their consent. The kettle thus emerges as a microcosm of the state's wider fantasy of containment (to use a phrase of Wendy Brown's) to match the fantasy of building (see Chapter 3).[11]

'Containment' as a form of holding has a history that goes back to the seventeenth century. The *Oxford English Dictionary* (*OED*) offers a translation published in 1619 of an Ancient Greek text on wealth, with the sentence 'let us now see, if there be not as good meanes of vertuous containment, as well in the dayes of peace as of warre'. The roots of 'containment' lie in the older 'contain', from the Latin *continere*, meaning to 'to hold together' or 'enclose'. But 'contain' also gradually came to mean restraining someone, controlling oneself, or behaving in a restrained manner ('contain yourself!'). When the suffix 'ment' was added to 'contain', it acquired the sense of that suffix from the Latin '-mentum', indicating an action. 'Containment', then, gives us the action of holding together, enclosing in such a way as to restrain or control. The idea of containment gained some momentum in the seventeenth century. In political texts such as Hobbes's *Leviathan*, the move from the state of nature to the political state is designed to *contain* every person. Hobbes, the philosopher of motion par excellence – 'life it selfe is but Motion' – has us leave the state of nature to enter a civil society in which we remain, naturally, bodies in motion, so much so that the purpose of law is precisely to 'keep [people] in motion'.[12] But at the same time we are bodies to be *contained* and hence *restrained* by sovereign power. The logic of security lies in the sovereign's power to contain us, despite life (and, as we shall see, capital) being movement.

Regardless of this early history, the idea of 'containment' came into its own during the Cold War, which is one reason why it has at its core the concept of security. The *OED* cites a 1947 article in *Partisan Review* that used the word, but its most significant use by far in that year occurred in an article in the July issue of *Foreign Affairs*. The article was called 'The Sources of Soviet Conduct', and its author was listed as 'X', who turned

11 Wendy Brown, *Walled States, Waning Sovereignty* (New York: Zone, 2010), pp. 117–18.

12 Thomas Hobbes, *Leviathan*, ed. Richard Tuck (Cambridge: Cambridge University Press, 1991 [1651]), pp. 6, 239.

out to be George Kennan – one of the leading architects of the national security state and, by the time the article was published, head of the newly formed Policy Planning Staff. It was Kennan who gave 'containment' its meaning, and he did so by placing it at the heart of the emerging security doctrine. Both Paul Chilton and John Lewis Gaddis have shown that, from 1947 onwards, the fundamental outline of a strategy of containment received the endorsement of the highest authorities, was explicitly stated in many documents, conceptually presupposed in many others, and became a regular feature of discussion in intellectual circles. As Gaddis points out, what emerged was a veritable cottage industry among Cold War scholars and security intellectuals on the question of 'what Kennan really meant', and hence on the 'real' meaning of containment.[13] Although technically referring to American foreign policy from 1947, the idea of containment quickly came to permeate the whole discourse of security, filtered into the prose of pacification, and then came to undergird the idea of counterinsurgency when that term was coined in the early 1960s.

Despite the focus of containment on the military threat posed by the Soviet Union, the issue for the newly emerging national security state 'was not the containment by military means of a military threat, but the political containment of a political threat', as Kennan put it twenty years later.[14] Reflecting later still, Kennan added that the Soviet Union was at that time so utterly exhausted by the exertions and loses of the Second World War that 'there was no way that Russia could appear to me as a military threat'. In that case, why was 'containment' an appropriate term?

> When I used the word *containment* . . . what I had in mind was not at all the averting of the sort of military threat people are talking about today . . . What I *did* think I saw – and what explained the use of that term – was what I might call an ideological-political threat . . . There

13 X [George Kennan], 'The Sources of Soviet Conduct', *Foreign Affairs* 25: 4 (1947), pp. 566–82; Paul A. Chilton, *Security Metaphors: Cold War Discourse from Containment to Common House* (New York: Peter Lang, 1996), pp. 191–2, 213–14; John Lewis Gaddis, 'The Strategy of Containment', in Thomas H. Etzold and John Lewis Gaddis, eds, *Containment: Documents on American Policy and Strategy, 1945–1950* (New York: Columbia University Press, 1978), p. 37; John Lewis Gaddis, *Strategies of Containment: A Critical Appraisal of American National Security Policy During the Cold War* (Oxford: Oxford University Press, 2005), p. 25.

14 George F. Kennan, *Memoirs, 1925–1950* (Boston: Little, Brown, 1967), p. 358.

> seemed to be a danger that communist parties subservient to Moscow might seize power in some of the major Western Europe countries, notably Italy and France, and possibly in Japan. And what I was trying to say, in the article I am talking about, was simply this: 'Don't make any more unnecessary concessions to these people. Make it clear to them that they are not going to be allowed to establish any dominant influence in Western Europe and in Japan' . . . This, to my mind, was what was meant by the thought of 'containing communism'.[15]

Here we have a remarkable parallel to the explication of pacification we saw in previous chapters: first, think of it as political-ideological rather than straightforwardly military; and second, think of it is as dealing with the Enemy at home as much as the Enemy thousands of miles away. Containment as the 'keeping in place' of the Communist threat in the form of the Soviet Union was as much a 'keeping in place' of communism as a global anti-capitalist movement. Hence, despite containment doctrine having a long history in international relations – it was only in the 1980s that foreign policy circles started thinking of a doctrine 'beyond containment', in conjunction with major shifts in East–West relations – my interest is in its career as a security concept in general, and what this tells us about pacification. This was made clear in NSC 68 (1950), the most elaborate effort made by US officials during the early Cold War years to provide a comprehensive and expansive account of 'national security'. Officially referring to containment as 'policy', the message of NSC 68 was that, to demonstrate the superiority of the idea of 'freedom', freedom itself had to be carefully managed. In particular, 'dissent among us can become a vulnerability', it claims. 'Sometimes the dissent has its principal roots abroad in situations about which we can do nothing.' But dissent 'arises largely out of certain weaknesses within ourselves, about which we can do something'. People must therefore 'be asked to give up some of the benefits which they have come to associate with their freedoms'. That is, 'discipline will be demanded of the . . . people'.[16]

15 George F. Kennan, 'The Origins of Containment', in Terry L. Deibel and John Lewis Gaddis, eds, *Containment: Concept and Policy* (Washington, DC: National Defense University Press, 1986), pp. 25–6. Emphases in original.

16 'NSC 68: United States Objectives and Programs for National Security' (1950), in Etzold and Gaddis, *Containment*, pp. 392, 401, 404, 415.

What emerges from such a policy is two different meanings of containment, as noted by Andrew Ross, reflecting the two dimensions of pacification:

> One which speaks to a threat *outside* of the social body, a threat which therefore has to be isolated, in quarantine, and kept at bay from the domestic body; and a second meaning of containment, which speaks to the domestic *contents* of the social body, a threat internal to the host which must then be neutralized by being contained or 'domesticated'.[17]

The security of social order must therefore be achieved by the containment of domestic as much as foreign forces – just as the prose of pacification I have already discussed makes clear.

Thus, although the modern politics of containment started life in the Cold War, its real power lay in furnishing a rhetorical device to depict a world in which law and order are always already under threat from an *enemy within* (among the People) in league with the *enemy without*. The state acts as a container of power with both an inside and an outside, the powers of war and police being operationalized in both directions. For this reason, we find references in the literature to 'pacification and the containment of the enemy' in one and the same sentence, their unity lying in the need to control the movement of both people and resources.[18]

This is containment as a form of *holding*, in the sense denoted by the second term in the pacification doctrine Clear–Hold–Build. One of the earliest meanings of 'hold', according to the *OED*, is 'the action or fact of having in charge, keeping, guarding, possessing, etc', or 'keeping, occupation, possession; defence, protection, rule'. In early usage 'hold' also referred to a 'fortified place of defence'. A further meaning has 'holding' as confinement, custody, imprisonment, which the *OED* suggests is obsolete, but which in fact remains in the form of another meaning: 'the hold' as the police or prison cell. (The prison is the

17 Andrew Ross, 'Containing Culture in the Cold War', *Cultural Studies* 1: 3 (1987), p. 331.

18 Robert Thompson, *No Exit from Vietnam* (London: Chatto & Windus, 1969), pp. 155–6; Robert Thompson, *Defeating Communist Insurgency: Experiences from Malaya and Vietnam* (London: Chatto & Windus, 1967), p. 112.

ultimate in containment: a container containing cells, each of which is to contain prisoners, while the whole penal system is said to be necessary to contain crime.) 'Hold' also has a long history connoting 'contention, struggle, pulling opposite ways; opposition, resistance; chiefly in *hard hold*, strong or tough struggle', rather like the *stability* inherent in *stasis*. Holding also implies fixing people in space, and the etymology of the Latin *pax* is not only connected to pacification but also derived from *pango*, meaning 'to fix'. The unity between *pango* and *pax* lies in the pacified being *fixed in place* – that is, held – by the dominant force. A 'holding' is also a form of spatial possession, such as the hold of the ship, for the containment of slaves and other forms of property, thus offering a connection between the holding of property in the slave ship and the holding of prisoners in a police or prison cell. In taking possession and management of something, bringing it under one's control, holding connotes both security and property, which is one reason why the language of violence runs through discussions of the hold and why, in every 'holding', those being held are reminded of the power of life and death that the holders have over them – as those who have been kettled also testify.

Containment is therefore an operationalization of security logic and a key police category. When 'containment' rose to prominence in the Cold War, international communism was to be held in place by the 'four policemen' overseeing the international order of states, and engaging in 'police actions' in nations undergoing 'development' and 'modernization'. At the same time, the security of the capitalist order at home was to be administered through the policing of communist and socialist movements and groups, forms of organized labour, campaigns for sexual liberation, the women's movement, struggles for black liberation, and student radicalism – all of which were targeted in one social war after another. Even the most powerful weapon that emerged in the context of Cold War containment, the Bomb, was a technology that could be deployed in those social wars as much as in a potential nuclear war: the nuclear powers were engaged in a collusion that everyone agreed was 'MAD' (Mutually Assured Destruction), but which allowed them to stabilize themselves against threats emanating from their own subjects – a response to the social and political struggles within the polity, expressed through that most powerful of security concepts: the fear of violent death.

The process of containment in the social wars of modernity also made itself felt in becoming fundamental to new modes of urban pacification in the wars on crime, poverty and drugs. American cities such as Los Angeles implemented major redevelopment plans for the area known as 'Skid Row', covering fifty square blocks, and containing several thousand homeless, vulnerable and 'problem' people. The 'Containment Plan' was part of the police war on the urban poor and the vagrant. Low-income housing was to be concentrated in the containment area and managed through the mechanisms of social policing, facilitating the gentrification of other areas. Public spaces were redesigned to discourage 'loitering', while private spaces were redesigned with new forms of security architecture fencing them off, containing the wealthy in gated communities while the homeless were fenced off and contained in very different ways. During the same period, 'containment' was a key idea in the policing of the working class in the UK (see below).

The idea of containment frames the state as one of the most powerful agents of order: an active container of all social forces and political movements. Playing heavily on our everyday use of the terms 'security' and 'order', the logic of containment functions as a microphysics of power resonating through the personal as well as the political lives of citizens, right down to the health of the social body in the form of the 'containment' of viruses. Containment comes to be applied to everything from communism to Covid, functioning as a police operation par excellence.[19]

'Containment of social change is perhaps the most singular achievement of advanced industrial society', wrote Herbert Marcuse in 1964. In *One-Dimensional Man*, whose whole argument is structured around this idea of containment, Marcuse was grappling with perhaps the fundamental question of Marxist thought, with which this book began: How is it that capitalism and its technological rationality seem so capable of holding back the possibility of radical change? The answer appears to be that, in combining the powers of welfare and warfare, developing mechanisms of total administration, and finessing a system of countervailing powers that cancel each other out in such a way that defends the

19 Mark Neocleous, *The Politics of Immunity: Security and the Policing of Bodies* (London: Verso, 2022); Mark Neocleous, *Critique of Security* (Edinburgh: Edinburgh University Press, 2008).

status quo, capitalism manages to combat any historical alternatives that might emerge. To grasp this conceptually, Marcuse latched onto the idea that contemporary society seems to be able to contain any attempt at radical social change. He thereby applied and extended a category of Cold War strategy to achieve an understanding of the management of the capitalist polity in general: 'the foreign policy of containment appears as an extension of the domestic policy of containment'.[20] Marcuse thus grasped that containment is the dominant logic through which capitalist states protect and reproduce the capitalist order, conditioning subjects within the ideology of advanced capitalist society, and thereby forestalling any threat to the order it imposed.

In making this argument Marcuse was radically repurposing a key concept used among the ruling class and in security elites. Yet, oddly, he performed the opposite theoretical manoeuvre in relation to 'pacification'. For Marcuse, a new society built from radical 'progress' would enable technology to 'become subject to the free play of faculties in the struggle for the pacification of nature and of society'. He thus deemed the pacification of nature and society a positive outcome of demands for liberation and the notion of the 'abolition of labor':

> The term 'pacification of existence' seems better suited to designate the historical alternative of a world which – through an international conflict which transforms and suspends the contradictions within the established societies – advances on the brink of a global war. 'Pacification of existence' means the development of man's struggle with man and with nature, under conditions where the competing needs, desires, and aspirations are no longer organized by vested interests in domination and scarcity – an organization which perpetuates the destructive forms of this struggle.

He continues by suggesting that 'the more technology appears capable of creating the conditions for pacification, the more are the minds and bodies of man organized against this alternative'. The political fetters imposed by the status quo of 'mature industrial society' (that is, advanced capitalism) close society off against the *possibility* of pacification. A

20 Herbert Marcuse, *One-Dimensional Man: Studies in the Ideology of Advanced Industrial Society* (Boston: Beacon, 1964), pp. xii, 51.

pacified social order, in this understanding, would break the means-ends rationality of industrial society, including that of the communist East, and realize a society for the free development of human needs and faculties, which would include 'the pacification of existence'. This pacification of existence would be a liberating mastery of nature.[21] He repeats this argument in a 1966 'Political Preface' added to *Eros and Civilization* (1955), as well as in other essays and lectures from the period, in which he uses both 'containment' and 'pacification', yet treats them very differently. In 'The Containment of Social Change in Industrial Society', a talk he delivered in May 1965, and 'The Inner Logic of American Policy in Vietnam', a talk he gave a year later at a teach-in at the University of California, he pointed to the containment of opposition in whatever form it appears, noting too that whatever appears as an opposition to capitalism is now defined as communism, but then he simultaneously argued that technical progress increases the possibility that we ourselves might obtain a pacified existence.[22] For Marcuse, containment is the control of human needs and the subjection of human capacities by capital and the state – but pacification is the free development of human needs and capabilities. By 1975, with thousands more corpses produced in the name of pacification, and radical movements of all sorts contained on the same basis, Marcuse was still equating pacification with emancipation.[23] But equating freedom with pacification is *precisely what the state and capital want us to do*.

There is a sense, then, in which Marcuse gets containment absolutely right and pacification absolutely wrong. He adopts the idea of containment from the discourse of the security state, and uses it to grasp the

21 Marcuse, *One-Dimensional Man*, pp. 16–17, 53, 220, 224, 227, 235–6, 242–3, 251–3.

22 Herbert Marcuse, *Eros and Civilization: A Philosophical Inquiry into Freud* (London: Allen Lane, 1969); Herbert Marcuse, 'The Individual in the Great Society' (1966), and 'The Containment of Social Change in Industrial Society' (1965), both in Douglas Kellner, ed., *Towards a Critical Theory of Society: Collected Papers of Herbert Marcuse, Vol. 2* (London: Routledge, 2001), pp. 73, 85; Herbert Marcuse, 'The Inner Logic of American Policy in Vietnam' (1966), 'The Problem of Violence and the Radical Opposition' (1967), and 'Ecology and Revolution' (1972), all in Douglas Kellner, ed., *The New Left and the 1960s: Collected Papers of Herbert Marcuse, Vol. 3* (London: Routledge, 2005), pp. 39, 69, 175.

23 Herbert Marcuse, 'The Failure of the New Left' (1975), in *New Left and the 1960s*, pp. 190–1.

nature of capital's domination. But he simultaneously adopts the idea of pacification that plays such a key part in that same discursive universe, and indeed in the history of modern domination, while treating it entirely uncritically as emancipation. Marcuse's intellectual manoeuvres here are most likely an outcome of his problematic engagement with the security state itself, based on his work in the Office of War Information, as a senior analyst at the Office of Strategic Services, and then as a senior political analyst at the Central European Section in the Office of Intelligence Research. But I am less interested in the degree of Marcuse's collusion with capitalist imperialism and American intelligence (more cop than cop-out, as some within the 1960s radical movements put it at the time) than in the fact that he was seemingly unwilling to subject the concept of pacification to the same level of critical scrutiny as virtually every other concept he encountered in his intellectual career. Marcuse seems simply to take it as read that the 'peace' within the prose of pacification is somehow a 'real' peace, and thus aligns said 'peace' with freedom and *eros*. His argument is that we should break through the political technology of containment to create a world in which we oversee our own pacification. The question he was asking remains the most fundamental of all questions: How can the politically administered subjects of contemporary capitalism liberate themselves from their own mutilated lives as well as from their masters? To argue that such administration, mutilation and mastery constituted our containment was a major advance for critical theory. But to argue that our liberation from such containment would represent our 'pacification' was a mistake of the highest order. It is our masters who want us pacified, as well as contained. To put it another way, for our masters, the containment of social change is our pacification. But, if that is the case, then perhaps the kettle is a microcosm of a far wider containment of social movements. With that in mind, let us take another look inside the kettle.

Movement restrained

A remarkable feature of contemporary protests and counterprotests is the fact that they are configured as *battles*: the 'Battle of Orgreave' (1984), the 'Battle of Stonehenge' (1985), the 'Battle of Park Lane' (1994), the 'Battle of Seattle' (1999), the 'Battle of Genoa' (2001), the 'Battle of

London' (2010). Using the language of battle to describe a massive police operation is perhaps more appropriate than the protestors realize, given the long history of the kettle in military strategy.

Military thinkers have long held that one can win a battle by using force to control the environment within which the enemy is operating. This does not simply mean trapping them, but rather containing them within a particular space, restraining their operations, isolating them and shaping their decisions, to the point of exhaustion, surrender or death. The German word for this is *Kesselschlact*. The most famous example was the 'Battle of Stalingrad' between August 1942 and February 1943. In his book, *Stalingrad* (1999), Antony Beevor observes that, in Nazi strategy, 'the task of the panzer formations was to cut through and then encircle the bulk of the enemy's army, trapping it in a *Kessel*, or cauldron' (or as he later describes it, 'encircled area').[24] 'Encirclement' had itself been identified as an integral feature of counter-revolutionary warfare by Mao Zedong, who made clear in 'Problems of Strategy in China's Revolutionary War' (1936) that 'encirclement and suppression' represented one of the key problems faced by revolutionary armies and insurgents. Encirclement was also used by the Nazis as a key counter-guerrilla tactic, as well as in large-scale battles such as Stalingrad, and was adopted by other Western states too. As Andrew Birtle notes in his history of the US Army's pacification techniques, four important tactics were adopted from the Nazi practice. First, 'tightening the encirclement' – or, a more telling phrase, 'tightening the noose'; second, the 'hammer and anvil', a technique involving an advance by some of the encircling forces while the remaining forces wait for the insurgents to emerge; third, sending small numbers of forces into the encircled area to divide it, and then reducing each division further still; fourth, employing a powerful assault to overrun the insurgents.[25] The kettle, then, is a technology of war.

It has been said that 'the line between kettling and war is a fine one'.[26] In fact, there is no line. Just as the supposed line between war and

24 Antony Beevor, *Stalingrad* (London: Penguin, 1999), pp. 19–20, 269.

25 Andrew J. Birtle, *US Army Counterinsurgency and Contingency Operations Doctrine 1942–1976* (Washington, DC: Center of Military History, United States Army, 2006), p. 140.

26 Scott Sørli, 'The Political Aesthetics of Kettling', *Tripwire: A Journal of Poetics* 8 (2014), p. 149.

policing turns out to be a myth, so the kettle needs to be understood as a war tactic of the police power and a police tactic of the war power, constituting urban space as a permanent arena of police war. This is pacification through the containment of space.

The war to enclose space and declare the enclosure lawful is one of the hallmarks of capitalism. To seize and enclose common property as private property, thereby announcing the right to occupy and exploit it, requires the enclosure of space as well as bodies, the soil as well as the soul. Common land must be closed off to commoners, its fencing in as private property being the first act of police power. Through enclosure as containment, capital constitutes space anew. Such technologies of containment are themselves forms of movement: enclosure is the motion of enclosing and therefore of fencing, walling, bordering.

The production and perpetual reorganization of space is central to the sovereign power to pacify. Sovereignty implies space constituted by violence, against which violence is directed and through which violence is exercised. This is one way in which human beings are pacified and social movements contained. The insistence that the spaces of capitalist modernity are spaces of peace is undermined by the violence through which they are constituted, and by the perpetual declaration of one social war after another: spaces of peace are always already spaces of war. The 'peaceful' space of property cannot be established without a war of movement and enclosure to pacify that very same space.

The management of land and space is integral to the policing of security in capitalist modernity. Capital's desire to conquer the entire space of civil society is realized through the state's willingness to pacify such social space for capital. The outcome is a calculated policing of space in the name of security. Some mechanisms, such as the border, separate the sovereign inside from outside; others, such as kettles, temporarily prevent movement within the contained space of sovereign territory. Delimiting a zone or space or territory is itself a form of policing movement. The ideas of exclusion and inclusion on which so much of the literature on walls, borders and fences concentrates often fail to grasp the centrality of social movement.

Enclosure pacifies by containing and restraining movement, either across the technology of enclosure (wall, fence, wire, kettle) or within it. In Chapter 2, we saw Hobbes remark, 'Cities are compact with walls' – and I noted that the classic space of disobedience and rebellion known as the Garden of Eden is usually presented as a walled space. Historically, city walls 'served to overawe and hence bind and pacify the towns they encircled'.[27] As a technology of pacification, walls, borders and fences 'separate, differentiate, divide, filter, stratify and codify populations' – but they do so in order to 'homogenize, civilize, and pacify in order to smooth the workings of capitalism and responses to it'.[28] Walls help to constitute political space, which does not exist in the state of nature and must be constituted by the state. But, with my discussion in Chapter 2 in mind, we might ask whether political space is constituted as a site of security or of fear. Perhaps it is both.

There is a fundamental tension between freedom and movement in any kind of enclosure. Capital is a regime of motion, circulation, recirculation, flow, liquidity, expansion. Capital, by its very nature, drives beyond and strives to tear down every spatial barrier to its own development; that is, capital *annihilates space*.[29] Commodities, money, bodies, lives: capital is movement, its essence being money in search of more money, over and again, perpetually. For five hundred years, capital has therefore been the most unconstrained force in the world, moving everywhere, settling everywhere, reshaping the world in its own image as it does so: making the world anew.

This is one reason why liberalism, capitalism's chief ideology, is constituted as a political theory of mobility, and its concept of freedom attached to movement, and one reason why, as liberalism perfects its form of rule, the liberal state politically administers the spaces and flows. Capital needs to be mobile, and the capitalist state needs to ensure this mobility; but to ensure it the state does what the state always thinks it should do – namely, police it. Hence, to Hobbes's insight that cities are compact with walls we must add his stress on the importance of a good 'circulation' system within the body politic, including the flow of subjects and 'all commodities, movable and immovable' that 'accompany a man to all places of his resort'. In the words of Hobbes's friend and intellectual

27 Brown, *Walled States*, pp. 39–40.

28 Samantha Ponting and George S. Rigakos, ' "To Take an Accompt of all Persons and Things Going in and Out of the Citty": Walls as Techniques of Pacification', in Volker Eick and Kendra Briken, eds, *Urban (In)Security: Policing the Neoliberal Crisis* (Ottawa: Red Quill, 2013), p. 88.

29 Karl Marx, *Grundrisse*, transl. Martin Nicolaus (Harmondsworth: Penguin, 1973), pp. 524, 539.

heir, Sir William Petty, the compact nature of space provided by walls is the 'foundation of libertyes, securityes, and privilidges', because it facilitates the political administration 'of all persons and things going in and out of the Citty'.[30] Capital must be mobile; but commodities, including the human one, must be catalogued, tracked and administered – that is to say, policed. The wall (fence, barrier and, dare we say, kettle) is less about inclusion or exclusion than about the policing of movement.

The state's power to decide what objects and subjects are allowed to move and in what direction is integral to its regulation of circulation and flows. Professional policing was invented for this very purpose, to facilitate the security of the flow of goods through London's docks, and hence simultaneously control the movement of workers in those same spaces. Pacification requires that everyone knows their place, but also what movement is permitted to them. They must also know that they need formal permission from the sovereign power for specific kinds of movement (to hold a march, to leave the kettle, to leave the country). The wall, fence, kettle, border, and camp are thus reinforced through forms of political administration that operate as mechanisms for the containment of movement, such as passports, visas, ID cards and vaccination certificates. This also explains why nomads, hunter-gatherers, vagrants, travellers, homeless people, itinerants, migrants, runaway slaves and the other 'masterless' creatures we encountered in Chapter 1 constitute a perpetual police problem. With their seemingly autonomous movement, they engage in the wrong kind of flow, challenging the entrenched modes of political administration. Efforts to contain such people permanently are a perennial state project. In *Seeing Like a State*, James C. Scott suggests that the state always treats as enemies those people who move around, and his argument has been widely cited.[31] Yet, as we have seen, it is not quite right. The issue for the state is not movement per se. How could it be, when it exists to police a system that is itself movement? The issue is that the wrong people are moving in the wrong directions, or in the wrong spaces, or at the wrong time. From the perspective of police power, movement constitutes a problem only when

30 Sir William Petty, 'The London Wall' (ca. 1690), in *The Collected Works of Sir William Petty: The Petty Papers, Vol. 1*, ed. Marquis of Lansdowne (London: Routledge/Thoemmes, 1997), p. 32.

31 James C. Scott, *Seeing Like a State: How Certain Schemes to Improve the Human Condition Have Failed* (New Haven, CT: Yale University Press, 1998).

it is not overseen and administered by the police power: sustaining circulation while fabricating order requires an understanding of orderly flows as distinct from unruly movements. Movement that is antithetical to capital and beyond the grip of the state is chaotic, and must be stopped. This is also why viruses, from the plague to Covid, pose such a problem: quarantine – containment writ large – places the whole population under de facto house arrest, and thus immobilizes the very thing whose mobility reproduces capitalism.

Statistics, with its roots in state power, seeks to capture a moment at which movement can be measured, reminding us of *stasis* as the co-presence of mobility and immobility, movement and stability. *Stasis* as pacification is not non-motion, but, rather, captures a polity fighting a permanent *war of movement*, a war between the contradictory desire for simultaneous mobility and immobility. This is the dialectical contradiction of *stasis*: on the one hand, as in standing and status, *stasis* means stability, status quo, rest, quiescence, or *immobility*; on the other, as in political unrest, upheaval and revolution, *stasis* means movement, and hence *mobility*. *Stasis* thus denotes both movement and lack of movement. *Stasis* is *movement at rest*, to use Nicole Loraux's phrase.[32]

The state exists to police this very contradiction, which also lies at the heart of pacification. This is one reason why, for all capital's bravado about its ability to settle in every niche, about the 'freedom of movement' it brings to people, and about the orbit of liberty it imagines itself to enable, the world is nonetheless also the site of so many orbits of security in the form of walls, fences, barriers, bars, borders, cordons, fortifications, gates, wires and other paraphernalia, the history of each of which is a history of violence imposed on bodies and minds.[33] The logic of security allows such mechanisms of spatial ordering to be used imaginatively and productively for the purposes of pacification – purposes that vary according to the social and political nature of the groups being managed through them.

The containment of space can be seen in responses to the threat posed to order by moments when social movements seek to control space. Any

32 Nicole Loraux, *The Divided City: On Memory and Forgetting in Ancient Athens*, transl. Corinne Pache and Jeff Fort (New York: Zone, 2006 [1997]), p. 108.

33 Reviel Netz, *Barbed Wire: An Ecology of Modernity* (Middletown, CT: Wesleyan University Press, 2004), p. xii.

movement that goes by the name of, for example, 'Occupy', has in the mind of the state declared itself to be the Enemy, since it seeks to take control of public space, as determined by the state, or of private space controlled by capital. To seek to occupy the city or any part of it is, by definition, a form of insurgency.

Central to the history of insurgent power is the barricade. Through centuries of European history, the barricade was all but synonymous with 'revolution', which is one reason why the idea of the 'barricade' emerged during the same period as the idea of the 'insurgent'. Many claim that the term 'barricade' was first used to describe the response of the people of Paris on 12 May 1588 against the troops of Henry III, after the king had threatened to set up a garrison in the city and use it to arrest rebellious subjects. The event has become known as the 'Day of the Barricades'. But the word itself can be found a little earlier in the century. In Blaise de Monluc's commentaries on the pacification campaigns in which he had taken part, he stresses the necessity of destroying any barricades put up by rebels, and describes the siege of Mont-de-Marsan that he had overseen in 1569, commenting that 'the Enemy then made directly towards the Bridge, all along a great street where they had made a Barricado'.[34] The idea of the barricade was quickly absorbed into the English language as a verb in the early 1600s, and then as a noun by the middle of the century. It was the translation of Monluc's work into English in the 1670s that helped make 'barricade' part of the English language. The word also begins to appear in other European languages during the same period – as *barricata* (Italian), *barricada* (Spanish), *Barrikade* (German) and *barykada* (Polish).

Originating in the idea of an assemblage of barrels, from the French *barrique*, a barricade can be made from other useful objects: carts, paving stones, construction materials, discarded furniture, broken lampposts, vehicles. Its origin in the barrel is a reminder of the importance of using objects that could be rolled or easily moved from one position into another – a technique continued when the barrel was eventually replaced by carts, and then cars. Such use of everyday objects reinforces the idea of the barricade as a weapon of the people: an

34 Blaise de Monluc, *The Commentaries of Messire Blaize de Montluc, Mareschal of France. Seventh Book*, transl. Charles Cotton (London: H. Broome, 1674 [1592]), pp. 337–9, see also pp. 364, 368, 402–3.

invention of the crowd that, in its very building of the barricade, defines itself as insurgent and revolutionary. In his history of the barricade in France, Mark Traugott suggests that, in the three centuries from 1550, two-thirds of all 'barricade events' occur in years of concentrated insurgency.[35] In particular, the barricade dominated the revolutionary moments of the nineteenth century, reappearing in Paris and Belgium in 1830, and then through the 1840s, especially in the later part of that decade. On the one end of the political spectrum, thinkers like Alexis de Tocqueville condemned the 'instinct' for disorder and the 'taste' for revolution that the insurgent barricade represented.[36] On the other, Frederick Engels acted as 'inspector of the barricades' at Elberfeld, Germany. The year 1848 consolidated the barricade as a revolutionary technology with a range of practical functions: claiming turf, providing protective cover, barring passage, impeding circulation, isolating security forces, disrupting communications, testing support, fostering organization. 'Students, exiles, and itinerant workers were the groups primarily responsible for the proliferation of this technique during the nineteenth century', Traugott writes, adding that the spread of 'barricade consciousness' across international lines was one by-product of the internationalization of the revolutionary movement. The barricade then played a major role during the Paris Commune of 1871, and again in Russia in 1905 and 1917, Berlin in 1919, Barcelona in 1936, Paris in 1844, and Paris again in May 1968 – most notably on the 'Night of the Barricades' of 10–11 May.[37]

Despite his early role as inspector of the barricades in the revolutionary fervour of 1848 and 1849, Engels was later to claim that the barricade is more important for its moral than for its material effect, in the sense that it shatters the stability and assumptions of the forces of law and order, pits the people against the police, and stems the movement of traffic and commerce. It thereby pits the people against the movement of

35 Mark Traugott, *The Insurgent Barricade* (Berkeley, CA: University of California Press, 2010), p. 80.

36 Alexis de Tocqueville, *Recollections*, transl. George Lawrence (New York: Anchor, 1971 [1850]), p. 48.

37 Frederick Engels, 'Elberfeld' (1849), in Karl Marx and Frederick Engels, *Collected Works, Vol. 9* (London: Lawrence & Wishart, 1977), p. 447; Traugott, *Insurgent Barricade*, pp. 80–1, 110–12, 141, 175–7, 178–96, 222–4; Eric Hazan, *A History of the Barricade*, transl. David Fernbach (London: Verso, 2015 [2013]), p. 123.

capital itself, and becomes a means of people making themselves into *the People*. When the forces of law and order peer behind the barricade, however, they see not the People but 'rebels, subversives, plunderers, levellers, the scum of society'.[38] They see not the People, but insurgency; they see the People as the Enemy. For this reason, by the end of the nineteenth century the bourgeois class was rebuilding cities with a view to overcoming such obstacles to the circulation of capital. The most famous example, already noted in Chapter 3, is the redesign of Paris by Baron Haussmann in the second half of the nineteenth century, in such a way that the urban proletariat were forced out into the suburbs, while the streets were replaced with long, straight thoroughfares in order to secure the city against insurgency. As Walter Benjamin notes, Haussmann's 'strategic embellishment' of the city was also intended to make the erection of barricades impossible by widening the streets, and by adding new streets to shorten the route between the army barracks and working-class districts.[39] The strategic embellishment of the city took the form of the strategic incapacitation of insurgency.

The history of the barricade is thus part of the struggle for control over urban space, and of the movement and circulation so integral to the capitalist world. But the barricade thus also points to the permanent refinement of tactics for maintaining order and repression – which is why the security forces seek to eradicate the insurgent barricade and all of its traces as quickly as possible.[40]

Control of the streets is always regarded by the state as a function of its police power, which is why the barricade is a form of insurgency. But this cannot be the only way to imagine the barricade. Why? Because the barricade, for so long a feature of insurgency, was appropriated by the police power and repurposed for pacification: a technology of insurgency used to counter insurgency. Barricades establish the boundaries of containment zones, channel movement, block routes and control the

38 Frederick Engels, 'Introduction' [to Karl Marx's *The Class Struggles in France 1848 to 1850*] (1895), in Karl Marx and Frederick Engels, *Collected Works, Vol. 27* (London: Lawrence & Wishart, 1990), p. 518.

39 Walter Benjamin, 'Paris, Capital of the Nineteenth Century' (1935), in *The Arcades Project*, transl. Howard Eiland and Kevin McLaughlin (Cambridge: Belknap, 1999), p. 12.

40 Alain Corbin, 'Preface', in Alain Corbin and Jean-Marie Mayeur, eds, *La Barricade* (Paris: Éditions de la Sorbonne, 1997), pp. 1–2, 4.

size of the crowd. The police power has thus reinvented the barricade to help structure its zones of containment. In relation to the kettle, once one is formed the crowd is understood to be barricaded in. In effect, the insurgent barricade has given rise to a counter-barricade – or, better still, a counterinsurgent barricade: a weapon of the people turned against the people, a weapon of revolt become a weapon of containment, a weapon of revolutionary consciousness transformed into a weapon of pacification.

The movement of capital is reflected in the movement of struggles against it, and in the abstract notion of a 'social movement'. Communism is a problem for capital precisely because it is not a *state of affairs* to be established, but rather a 'movement which abolishes the present state of things'.[41] Any insurgency, protest or autonomous movement appears to the state to be part of a movement seeking to abolish the present state of things, and must therefore be contained. Ultimately, the greatest difficulty for the state is the 'social movement' itself, which becomes the basis of social wars and social police. One of Marx's contemporaries, Lorenz von Stein, sought to understand the idea of social movements as part of his understanding of 'the social movement' – a term he is widely credited with having brought into political and scholarly writing. In two books written during the revolutionary fervour of the late 1840s, *Socialist and Communist Movements Since the Third French Revolution* (1848) and *The History of the Social Movement in France* (1850), Stein argued that, aside from their range of social, economic and political demands, it was the *movement* in social movements that drove the state's desire to contain them. Alongside his analysis of democratic, socialist and communist struggles, and an account of the power of capital and the property-owning class to control the state, and hence the whole of society, one finds an argument that life is 'movement between opposing poles' – a form of motion brought about through 'movement and countermovement'.[42] The revolution is 'a law of the movement towards freedom', and thus a challenge to the very movement through which domination operates, and will in turn always

41 Karl Marx and Frederick Engels, *The German Ideology* (1846), in Karl Marx and Frederick Engels, *Collected Works, Vol. 5* (London: Lawrence & Wishart, 1976), p. 49.

42 Lorenz von Stein, *The History of the Social Movement in France, 1789–1850*, transl. Kaethe Mengelberg (Totowa, NJ: Bedminister, 1964 [1850]), p. 51.

generate counter-movement, resulting in a 'transition from latent to open social antagonism and to civil war'.[43]

If we consider the importance of the social movement qua movement, if we take as read the challenge posed by social movements to the state's control of movement and space, and if we momentarily look beyond the modes of political administration through which social movements are eventually co-opted into the regime of power, then we can begin to understand ruling-class power as permanent *counter-movement*: movement counter to the social movement, the latter being a 'continuous or free oscillation outside the limits of the dominant regime of social motion'.[44]

All of this takes us back to the kettle. There is a salutary tale from the Hamburg kettle of 2007, to contain those protesting against the repression of dissent. As a way of trying to deal with the likelihood of being kettled, organizers of the protest encouraged participants to remain 'on the move'. The response of the police was to ban walking on the pavement.[45] Such is the nature of police power that it can ban walking in the very space built by the state for walking. If 'walking can be understood as an elementary, phenomenological condition of freedom' (Patrick Joyce), and hence, by breaking the lines of ownership, as 'the antithesis of owning' (Rebecca Solnit), then the policing of such movement becomes a means of controlling freedom and reasserting the ownership of the territory by the police.[46]

Forcing people to remain in the same space turns the kettle into a police cell (or *holding* cell) on the street – a mobile prison whose walls are made from the actual physical bodies of the police, their shields, truncheons, dogs, horses and armoured vehicles, or from some fencing that they have brought with them for the very purpose of kettling. Recently added to this list is the mobile steel police cordon, around three metres high, which can be folded to create metal holding cells

43 Ibid., pp. 94, 409, see also pp. 230, 359.

44 Thomas Nail, *The Figure of the Migrant* (Stanford, CA: Stanford University Press, 2015), p. 159.

45 Amory Starr, Luis Fernandez and Christian Scholl, *Shutting Down the Streets: Political Violence and Social Control in the Global Era* (New York: New York University Press, 2011), p. 125.

46 Patrick Joyce, *The Rule of Freedom: Liberalism and the Modern City* (London: Verso, 2003), p. 211; Rebecca Solnit, *Wanderlust: A History of Walking* (London: Verso, 2001), p. 162.

enabling the police to kettle people into even smaller spaces. There is no exit from this prison other than with the permission of the police. The ultimate containment: since the crowd are not being officially detained, they cannot apply for official release. When the police grant people permission to leave, they are required to do so as individuals and not as groups; as individuals who have calmed down and express none of the excitement of the crowd, because they have accepted the police's 'show of force', at which point it becomes an offense to refuse. The 'permission' to leave the kettle is a command to move. Immobility once more unfolds into mobility, confinement into freedom – but *only at the command of the police*. Brecht again:

> The power of the State gives a piercing shout
> And yells: Get moving there!
> – But moving why and where?
> It yells: Get moving there!

But sometimes it also yells, 'Don't move!' Both 'moving too quickly' and 'moving too slowly' can count in the police mind as suspicious behaviour, and both can constitute grounds for a stop-and-search. But remaining stationary is also no solution for those subject to police power, since it can count as 'lingering' or 'loitering', and hence is equally suspicious, and also grounds for a stop-and-search – unless *one is forced to remain stationary by the police*. In giving unpredictable and contradictory commands sending people this way and that – 'Move!', 'Don't move!'; 'Move faster!', 'Slow down!'; 'No, you can't go home!', 'Go home!' – containment is not simply a holding, but also a channelling, moving, repositioning. People may or may not be permitted to move, but if they do move it must be *in the right way*, as commanded by the police.

Through such measures, the kettle is designed to demoralize. Yet it also appears designed to incite. But what does it incite? It incites the very irritability that is said by crowd theorists to be integral to the crowd. It incites fear. But it also incites fear's close cousin: rage.

Rage pacified

The kettle is a 'projection of police units in an efficient, effective and formidable manner which creates an atmosphere in the riotous mobs of apprehension and awe which could be close to fear'.[47] Such fear is to be experienced not only by those in the kettle, but also by those watching, for whom the kettle appears as a spectacle of absolute police power. As well as fear, those kettled also experience rage. The police kettle produces the very rage that the police need and want to police. It does so by creating a moment in which the rage of the pacified is required to receive the rage of absolute police power – thereby justifying the very use of the kettle. We need to pause here to make a couple of etymological points.

The first is that *kettel* comes originally from the Old English *cetel* or *cietel*, and in Middle English we also find *ketel* and *chetel*, influenced by an Old Norse word *ketill*. The Old English *cetel* is close to the West Frisian *tsjettel* ('kettle') and the Dutch *ketel*, but cognate with the Latin *catillus*, 'small bowl', diminutive of *catinus*, connoting 'deep bowl', or larger vessel for cooking or serving food, hence giving us not only 'kettle' but also 'cauldron'. Other terms also point in this direction: the Swedish *kittel* is closer to 'cauldron', as is the Russian котёл. *Kesselschlact*, which we saw is the German word for military encirclement, means literally 'cauldron battle'. The kettle as cauldron or boiler reminds us that kettles are containers in which things are heated all the way to boiling point. The senior British police officer turned academic police scientist generally credited with pushing for the use of kettling as a major police tactic, P. A. J. Waddington, likes to claim that kettling succeeds 'by using boredom as its principal weapon, rather than fear'; but the fact that he makes such a claim while also discussing the kettle as *bringing things to the boil* somewhat gives the game away.[48]

The obvious question arises: What exactly is being boiled? Brecht offers an answer: the People! The kettle, an apparatus of state, contains and immobilizes people in a small, cramped space in such a way as to guarantee to bring them to boiling point. But, conversely, and in the

47 Roy Henry, Commissioner of the Royal Hong Kong Police, being consulted in the 1980s by ACPO on colonial public order tactics, cited in Gerry Northam, *Shooting in the Dark: Riot Police in Britain* (London: Faber, 1988), p. 136.

48 P. A. J. Waddington, 'At Boiling Point', *Birmingham Post*, 21 April 2009.

words of the chief constable cited above, the very word 'kettle' indicates that it is something that might *boil over*. Thus, the kettle is meant to bring things to the boil, but also to prevent its contents from boiling over in a dangerous way; a lid must be put on the kettle, just as a lid must be put on the social cauldron. Here, as elsewhere, the language of police power resonates with the history of political thought on the right, which has long considered revolutionary politics as simmering away or ready to boil over. This connection takes us back once again to the social war, in that it is above all revolution that becomes 'manifested in the image of a gigantic process of boiling and liquefaction'.[49] We might not want to follow Freud's suggestion that kettles and other such vessels are representations of the womb, but the fact is that the forces of authority believe that something terrible may be being born from within such vessels.

If the kettle is a cauldron for boiling rage, then we might also note that the word 'rage' entered the English language around 1300 from the Old French *rage* or *raige*, meaning 'spirit, passion, rage, fury, madness', but also from the Medieval Latin term *rabia*, from Latin *rabies* ('madness, rage, fury'), related to *rabere*, 'be mad, rave', which is also the source of the Old English *rabbian*, 'to rage'. It quickly became a term to describe the multitude, the giddy people whose insane ideas about sovereignty too easily boil over into anger about their subjection: in *The Governor* (1531), for example, Sir Thomas Elyot expresses concern over 'the rage of a commonality, which . . . is most to be feared', and hence must be 'pacified and brought again into order'.[50] The idea of the multitude in a 'rage' suggests that there is a creature that needs containing, not just because it is angry or frenzied, but also because it is mad, contagious, rabid.

For this reason among others, the kettle involves treating people like nonhuman animals. The language of 'herding' people into 'pens' is common in police discourse. Containment is a tactic 'to herd the crowd into a pen, known as "the kettle"', observed one senior Metropolitan Police officer in 2010.[51] Herding and holding in pens is what humans do

49 Klaus Theweleit, *Male Fantasies, Vol. 1: Women, Floods, Bodies, History*, transl. Stephen Conway (Cambridge: Polity, 1987 [1977]), p. 238.

50 Sir Thomas Elyot, *The Book Named The Governor*, ed. S. E. Lehmberg (London: Dent, 1962 [1531]), p. 7.

51 Cited in Julian Joyce, 'Police "Kettle" Tactic Feels the Heat', *BBC News*, 9 December 2010.

to animals. So too is 'keeping'. Animals are kept in pens, cages and other spaces. Humans can be equally 'kept' in this way, held in place, contained. Those who run jails used to be called 'keepers', and Satan was once represented by theologians as a keeper. This is why the concept of 'keeping' is so important in bourgeois state theory: keeping the subjects in obedience, keeping them from discontent, keeping them quiet, keeping them from rebellion, keeping them in their place, keeping them in order and keeping them in awe are all rolled into the core principle of police theory: *keeping the peace*. From the police perspective, this is necessary. On the one hand, we might say that the kettle contains a human herd. On the other, herding people like this reminds us of the American police slang for police encounters with the kinds of social groups against which so many social wars are conducted: NHI – *no humans involved*. Once people are perceived as nonhuman animals, the pacifying techniques used to contain other species can be used against them.

The view of the crowd as some kind of wild beast, fundamentally at odds with the regime of sovereignty and property, is one that can be traced throughout the history of political thought, back to Plato's *Republic*, in which Socrates describes the *demos* as an unruly beast. 'Animal' and related terms such as 'beastly' are words used by those in power to describe a rebellious multitude – especially when they fear that their power is under threat, when they feel the need to ratchet up the levels of pacification. This view has remained integral to the contempt with which the ruling class and its ideologues have understood workers, the underclass, indigenous peoples, blacks, slaves, servants and many others. 'Political economy knows the worker only as an animal', notes Marx. Here too, political economy and police science converge: 'Man is always regarded by the police . . . as a species of wild animal and treated as such', a character comments in Friedrich Schiller's unfinished play *Die Polizey*.[52] Nowhere is this clearer than when the police deal with the crowd.

The idea of the crowd's beastliness became a mainstay of crowd theory and police accounts of crowd control. The outcome is a

52 Karl Marx, 'Economic and Philosophic Manuscripts of 1844', in Karl Marx and Frederick Engels, *Collected Works, Vol. 3* (London: Lawrence & Wishart, 1975), p. 242; Friedrich Schiller, *Die Polizey* (1799–1803), in *Schillers Werke: Nationalausgabe, Vol. 12: Dramatische Fragmente* (Weimar: Herman Böhlaus Nachfolger, 1982), p. 93.

remarkably consistent series of allusions found in police science, crowd theory, bourgeois political thought, colonial reason, the rhetoric of reaction and the prose of pacification: the crowd is an uncontrollable swarm, ferocious pack, stampeding herd, rabid mob, roaring mass, brutish creature, vicious beast. What is required is some kind of corral to contain them and hold them captive. These images came to be increasingly rationalized through studies of animal behaviour, as the sciences through which nonhuman animals were dominated and human crowds controlled came to learn from one another, generating a 'profusion of apparatuses for corralling, dispersing, tracking, and tagging "brute" biological bodies'.[53]

A common conservative refrain holds that man is the 'hardest of all animals to govern'.[54] When people are formed into a crowd, governing them is harder still. Being kettled communicates to the crowd the message that this form of governing is not only possible, but also sometimes necessary given their behaviour. It also communicates to them that, in the eyes of the state, they have *lost their humanity* – which is one reason why the crowd's assertion of their 'human' rights usually fails. The kettled are to understand that they have been *captured*. If the apparatus of capture is an apparatus of ownership and control, as Gilles Deleuze and Félix Guattari put it, then the state's subjects will learn that they are owned and controlled.[55] They must understand who their masters are. As the trope of animality makes clear, the containment produced by the kettle is part of the taming of the creature being held within – a training in how to accept their capture inside the cordon, their capture by the police power, and their ultimate capture by capital. The crowd are no doubt also expected to recall news items reporting what happens to animals that express an excess of rage or aggression: summary execution.

The guarding of the herd or the captured beast always implies the power of administering life and death. The police kettle thus contains the ultimate power of the master: the threat of death for any living creature within it. This is why police talk about *tightening the noose* around

53 Guy Scotton, 'Taming Technologies: Crowd Control, Animal Control and the Interspecies Politics of Mobility', *Parallax* 25: 4 (2019), p. 361.

54 Walter Bagehot, *Physics and Politics* (London: Henry King, 1872), p. 25.

55 Gilles Deleuze and Félix Guattari, *A Thousand Plateaus: Capitalism and Schizophrenia*, transl. Brian Massumi (London: Athlone, 1988 [1980]), p. 441.

those contained, like the hangman, the executioner whose actions in the name of sovereign justice we are expected always to remember with absolute fear. The death sentence might be suspended repeatedly, but we are never allowed to forget that it exists as part of the 'processing' that takes place of the objects being held. What we find in this exercise of violence over life and death is the reaffirmation of law itself in the form of the police power overseeing the kettle, which we might now want to consider as a kind of *kill box*.

In a memorandum to Secretary of Defense Donald H. Rumsfeld in February 2005, James A. Thomson, president of the RAND Corporation, suggested changes to traditional forms of coordination between air and ground support, in what he described as the 'long war'. The changes had at their core a system of 'kill boxes'. The technique had previously been used in January 1991, during Operation Desert Storm, but Thomson's memo suggested that kill boxes could be used 'for open terrain or urban warfare, and opened or closed quickly in response to a dynamic military situation'.[56] Within a few months, the US Army, Navy, Air Force and Marines produced a new field manual called *Kill Box: Multi-Service Tactics, Techniques, and Procedures for Kill Box Employment*, as a major step towards 'bringing the box into doctrine', according to one army monograph published in 2005 and regularly updated thereafter.[57] Kill-box management has since been central to the rules of engagement of twenty-first century warfare.

Everything said about the kill box might be said about the kettle. Any force using the box must have 'profound technological and logistical advantages over its enemy', including 'a sophisticated web of logistical, bureaucratic, and technological expertise to implement', as Scott Beauchamp puts it. The telling point, however, is a change in the arenas in which kill boxes are used:

56 James A. Thomson memo to Donald Rumsfeld, 7 February 2005, cited in Col. Howard D. Belote, 'Counterinsurgency Airpower: Air–Ground Integration for the Long War', *Air and Space Power Journal* 20: 3 (2006), p. 63.

57 Army, Marine Corps, Navy, Air Force, *Kill Box: Multi-Service Tactics, Techniques, and Procedures for Kill Box Employment* (June 2005); Maj. James W. MacGregor, *Bringing the Box into Doctrine: Joint Doctrine and the Kill Box* (United States Army Command and General Staff College, Fort Leavenworth, KS, 2004).

> In recent years, kill-box strategy has shifted: They are now used in conflicts that are not between two states, but rather within states against terrorists and fighters who aren't members of any particular country's military. With this change, two things have started happening. First, kill boxes have materialized in places the local population might not expect. And second, kill boxes have been used in conjunction with disposition matrices . . . to target people whose 'pattern of life' fit[s] the parameters of an algorithm, rather than specific individuals.[58]

Beauchamp claims that 'kill boxes are only used in places that are very different from the United States; military forces would never initiate a kill box in Manchester or Ann Arbor'. But, given the nature of the permanent social wars against 'patterns of life' considered subversive, insurgent or threatening of order, given that the central logic of the kill box is to *govern space*, and given the long history of liberal states killing their own civilians, Beauchamp's claim is more than a little dubious. The kill box is nothing less than a space defined as a target area over which violence can be exercised. At the heart of the kill-box technique is the combination of the control of the space of battle – especially from above, which is why the technique has been at the heart of the development of the drone – and an ongoing assessment of the degree of violence to be exercised over that space, and the attendant risks.[59] The purpose of the kill box is to *capture* and *trap* the enemy, *herd* it into a space, *hold* it there, *keep* it subdued, and *exert violence over it*.

What makes a trap a trap is the loss of mobility of whatever is trapped. As an act of containment, a trap literally 'arrests' people, stopping and containing them. It is an act of spatial power that obtains its force partly through the passage of time: being arrested and enclosed in a kettle entails being trapped for an indeterminate amount of time. This loss of mobility also always contains the threat of death.

The language of 'trapping' and 'herding' in the UK has historically been most commonly used in relation to the containment strategies

58 Scott Beauchamp, 'The Moral Cost of the Kill Box', *Atlantic*, 28 February 2016.

59 Grégoire Chamayou, *Drone Theory*, transl. Janet Lloyd (London: Penguin, 2015 [2013]), pp. 52–9; Elisabeth Weber, *Kill Boxes: Facing the Legacy of US-Sponsored Torture, Indefinite Detention, and Drone Warfare* (Goleta, CA: Punctum, 2017).

exercised over football supporters. At one point, this involved literally caging the crowd into pens in the stadium. During a match between Liverpool and Nottingham Forest football clubs at Hillsborough Stadium on 15 April 1989, overcrowding in the section of the ground allocated to Liverpool supporters was made worse by a police decision to order a further gate to be opened to allow in yet more supporters. The supporters were then unable to escape the overcrowding due to the cages in which they were contained. Consequently, ninety-six people were crushed to death, and another 766 injured, many seriously. This makes the event by far the worst disaster in British sporting history. The so-called 'Hillsborough Disaster' was due largely to the kettling of football supporters into cages. Subsequent inquiries, most significantly the report by the Hillsborough Independent Panel (HIP) led by Phil Scraton, have made clear that the deaths occurred because the operative police priority was the *containment* of fans rather than their welfare.[60] The submission to the inquiry by the Ambulance Service present in the stadium claimed that the fact that supporters were being crushed to death 'was evident to anyone whose mind was not conditioned by the need to *contain supporters* within the central pens'.[61] As Scraton notes, the police mindset throughout was that the supporters were a security problem.[62] This was yet another form of containment by police of a creature considered so uncontrollable that it had to be held in a cage. Only when it became clear that supporters were being killed did the police strategy move from containment to rescue – rescue, that is, from the police strategy itself – by which point it was too late. Either way,

60 Hillsborough Independent Panel, *The Report of the Hillsborough Independent Panel. HC 581* (London: HMSO, 2012), paras. 2.2.23–24, 2.7.102; Phil Scraton, *Hillsborough: The Truth* (London: Transworld, 2016), pp. 50, 412.

61 Hillsborough Independent Panel, *Report*, para. 2.4.72. Emphasis added. The containment being discussed here is but one example of the many ways in which the true nature of police power was revealed on that day, which might be itemized as follows: first, blame the victims; second, deny any negligence or liability; third, peddle lies to the media (about hooliganism, about fans stealing from the dead, about fans urinating on the dead, and many more); fourth, seek to pre-empt the findings of later inquiries; fifth, break police codes of practice concerning, for example, officers' statements; sixth, deny that any duty of care to the victims existed; seventh, show utter disrespect for the dead and their grieving families by eating chicken drumsticks in the same room as those families trying to identify the bodies of their dead loved ones.

62 Scraton, *Hillsborough*, p. 325.

whether corpse or patient, whatever was being contained in the cages at Hillsborough was considered the Enemy.

The Enemy? At a football match? In the fifteen or so years leading up to the events of 15 April 1989 – the very period when American cities were operating Containment Plans – the British state had been well aware that the construction of football grounds as a series of containment 'pens' or 'cages' was liable to lead to a disaster if supporters were not able to escape. The *Wheatley Report on Crowd Safety at Soccer Grounds* (1973) had recommended the required time for exiting a stadium as eight minutes or less, and specified the restructuring of entrances and exits to this end. This was updated in 1986 in the *Guide to Safety at Sports Grounds*, itself a response to the fire at Bradford Stadium in 1985, in which fifty-six people died having been unable to escape their containment in the stand that was on fire. The *Guide* recommended a metering system at turnstiles, intercommunication systems across grounds, and contingency plans for evacuation. Yet, as Ian Taylor and Phil Scraton have shown, all such recommendations with respect to architectural design and the welfare of supporters were overridden by the state's obsession with the containment of supporters and the wider penal disciplining of individual offenders. The extent of this obsession is most explicitly illustrated by the official inquiry into the fire at Bradford, chaired by Mr Justice Popplewell.[63] The report includes expert evidence on the dangers posed by accumulated litter, the velocity of fire, and technical aspects of ground construction. The report goes on to make a series of recommendations completely unconnected to fire and its hazards, instead proposing revision of the criminal law to ratchet up police powers over spectators entering grounds. The logic of the Popplewell report only makes sense, Taylor suggests, as an example of the ways in which issues of crowd safety and provision were displaced by a much broader logic of containment and penal discipline.[64] The more general point is that this was without question a product of the wider political moment, in which the Thatcher regime had defined organized working-class political movements such as trades unions in

63 *Committee of Inquiry into Crowd Safety and Control at Sports Grounds. Final Report. Chairman: Mr Justice Popplewell* (London: HMSO, January 1986).

64 Ian Taylor, 'Hillsborough, 15 April 1989: Some Personal Contemplations', *New Left Review* I/177 (September–October 1989); Scraton, *Hillsborough*, pp. 24, 54–5, 214–15.

no uncertain terms as the 'enemy within'. This language built explicitly on a new conservatism strongly inflected by racism, such as that found in the work of Enoch Powell, which connected racial minorities to radical students and socialist 'terrorists' in America and Europe, and on new liberal defences of dictatorship against the enemies of capital, such as that found in Friedrich von Hayek's defence of Pinochet's regime in Chile.[65] This enemy could take different forms in different contexts – the 'black criminal', the socialist agitator, the militant trade unionist – but it could also take the form of working-class gatherings for events such as football matches.

Against such an enemy, the powers of war and police had to be mobilized. This much is clear from the state's own report into Hillsborough: 'the ordinary law-abiding football supporter . . . is caught up in a police operation reminiscent of a column of prisoners of war being marched and detained under guard'.[66] For the Thatcher regime, football supporters, at that point so overwhelmingly working class that the figure of the football supporter could stand in for the class as a whole, so epitomized the 'national malaise' that they constituted part of the enemy within, along with other groups of workers, such as the miners who had fought in the Battle of Orgreave. Hence the official position on Hillsborough, held for a long time at the highest levels, including Thatcher and her close advisors, was the same as the official position on virtually all police violence during containment measures: such events were always the fault of a 'mob'.

What happened at Hillsborough was on a continuum with the assault on the culture and values of the 'enemy within' that began with the policing of the crisis of the 1970s, was ratcheted up with the authoritarian populism of the Thatcher regime, and was intensified with the miners' strike in 1984. The war on strikers coincided with the war on hooliganism, and both were rolled together with the war on crime. This is also

65 Hayek, speaking in Chile and referencing the Pinochet regime: 'At times it is necessary for a country to have, for a time, some form or other of dictatorial power. As you will understand, it is possible for a dictator to govern in a liberal way. And it is also possible for a democracy to govern with a total lack of liberalism. Personally I prefer a liberal dictator to democratic government lacking liberalism.' 'Interview with Friedrich von Hayek', *El Mercurio*, 12 April 1981, D8–D9.

66 *The Hillsborough Stadium Disaster, 15 April 1989: Inquiry by the Rt Hon Lord Justice Taylor. Final Report* (London: HMSO, 1990), p. 7.

one reason why undercover police were used time and again to infiltrate groups of football supporters as well as political movements – infiltration of the latter receiving far more coverage than of the former. As Gary Marx pointed out some time ago, such undercover police are also intended to 'serve as mechanisms of containment'.[67] Far from being a 'sporting disaster', what took place at Hillsborough was the result of the *physical containment* of an overwhelmingly working-class body of football spectators as an instantiation of the British ruling class's desire for the *political containment* of the working class. It is therefore unsurprising that, three decades later, this mass killing in the kettle at Hillsborough continues to generate a powerful rage.

Just as the kettle produces the space of violence that the police then claim needs kettling, so the kettle produces boiling rage – chiefly by producing the very crowd that will become enraged. Michel Foucault commented that, in bourgeois order, 'the crowd, a compact mass, a locus of multiple exchanges, individualities merging together, a collective effect, is abolished and replaced by a collection of separated individualities'.[68] Others have made the same point directly about the kettle: 'when the police talk about splitting up crowds and dividing different elements, they demonstrate their . . . sense of the crowd as merely a collection of individuals'.[69] This makes sense if, as David Correia and Tyler Wall tell us, 'cops are scared of crowds', for the crowd is, in the police view, 'always about to explode, always a riot about to happen'.[70] In one sense, this is true, and has its roots in the crowd as a source and symbol of popular sovereignty, from the *populus Romanus* in the Roman republic through to the long history of the crowd as a force for transforming power. Its truth is also evident in the prose of pacification, which insists that the crowd must be contained by the institutionalized sovereignty of police power, and in the fact that liberal constitutions, whatever their roots in popular struggles, can be read as manuals of

67 Gary T. Marx, 'Thoughts on a Neglected Category of Social Movement Participant: The Agent Provocateur and the Informant', *American Journal of Sociology* 80: 2 (1974), p. 403.

68 Michel Foucault, *Discipline and Punish: The Birth of the Prison*, transl. Alan Sheridan (London: Penguin, 1977 [1975]), p. 201.

69 Illan Rua Wall, 'The Open Crowd and the Kettle', *Critical Legal Thinking*, 16 June 2014.

70 David Correia and Tyler Wall, *Police: A Field Guide* (London: Verso, 2018), pp. 211, 213.

crowd control through their provisions for the suspension of all rights and liberties in the name of containment. Being scared of crowds would also place the police in a long tradition of classic crowd theory, which regards the crowd as evidence of the rise of the modern masses as a kind of emergent and insurgent force – an idea found in Gustave Le Bon's *Psychology of Crowds* (1895) and José Ortega y Gasset's *Revolt of the Masses* (1930).

But there is a sense in which saying that the police fear the crowd is to ignore a whole history of crowd mobilization by the state in the name of security, order, and even genocide. Under that ultimate security regime known as fascism, crowds were formed time and again *by the police* to hear the leader speak, watch him raise his hands, shout and sweat, be hypnotized by his aura and power, sing songs, and be libidinally charged. These were crowds *forged by the state* to celebrate the nation and its unity. That these crowds were also expected to offer tribute to the dead, singing to them and reciting their names, is one more reminder of the relationship between crowds and death.

Of course, the crowd created by the kettle is created not to worship the leader and declare allegiance to the state. Rather, it is created as an oppositional crowd. The question therefore remains: Why create a kettle? Why engage in a creative police practice that brings into existence the very thing that appears to abolish individualities and generate something that is always about to explode? After all, the threat contained in the kettle is a threat produced by kettling. Just as state and capital enclose and appropriate resources in the name of peace and security, creating the very wars, struggles, crimes and insurgencies that then need to be countered, and then representing the counterinsurgency that ensues as an entirely legitimate mode of governance, so we might say that the kettle performs the same task, bringing into existence the insurgent lawbreaker. The police offensive creates the offensive subjects, who then need to be policed. In provoking lawbreaking, the kettle transforms the protestor into a criminal, thereby creating the very figure against whom it conducts a social war. The kettle thereby produces the social enemy which is then used to explain why the kettle is needed. Kettling produces the violence which is used to justify the kettle. The kettle fabricates the very crowd, and thus the collective threat, that the police say must be contained in the name of security. Creating a crowd that is then presented to the public as angry and lawless offers evidence for the claim that the police are, literally, 'society's first line of defence' – and thus the perfect opportunity for the state to assert its powers of pacification. The question asked by Al Sandine in the chapter title of his history of the American crowd is always salient: 'Who Owns This Crowd?'[71]

The answer to that question will help us move towards an answer to the question posed at the beginning of this chapter, concerning the message of the kettle. What is it that the state wants us to acknowledge this time?

In *Crowds and Power*, Elias Canetti observes that the crowd always wants to grow, loves density, and needs a direction. The kettle, in contrast, is a crowd created through an act of police power, and thus its density, tendency and direction are always already controlled by the police. It is a *closed* crowd, whose closed nature is determined by the police. Of the space occupied by the closed crowd, Canetti writes that it 'can be compared to a vessel into which liquid is being poured and whose capacity is known'.[72] The kettle, having its contents poured into or out of it at the will of the police reminds us that it is a crowd built in order to be destroyed, fabricated in order to be dispersed, structured in such a way as to be dominated by the state, and ultimately *defeated in its very constitution as a crowd*. The kettle is *a crowd constituted to be contained* and exhibited as a *spectacle of pacification*. If this crowd possesses any 'destructiveness', it is a product entirely of the police power.

The police message carried by the kettle is clear, and it echoes the language of sovereignty stretching back to Hobbes, which wants the people to be *in awe* of the state, in the double sense of respectful and fearful. The message is: we own you. We own you because we own the streets. We own the right to the city. We can contain you like this, treat you like animals, carry out acts of discretionary punishment, identify you for police records, and then send you home humiliated, tired, hungry, and smelling of urine. The ultimate message, then, is that *this is what pacification can feel like if you protest*. You were hoping to

---

71 Al Sandine, *The Taming of the American Crowd: From Stamp Riots to Shopping Sprees* (New York: Monthly Review, 2009), pp. 117–40.

72 Elias Canetti, *Crowds and Power*, transl. Carol Stewart (London: Victor Gollanz, 1962 [1960]), pp. 17, 29.

change things, you say? Well, *this is what it feels like to have your hope disappointed.*

. . . and the hope of man disappointed

In the history of bourgeois thought, rage coincides with madness – the derangement of an unbalanced soul of the kind we have already encountered in *stasis*. For Hobbes, rage has its roots in excessive passion: excessive pride combined with anger is rage; an excessive desire for revenge becomes rage; excessive love combined with jealousy becomes rage; an excessive opinion of oneself combined with envy becomes rage; having one's vehement opinions contradicted by others becomes rage. But the excess is always in danger of becoming political, especially among the multitude. When it comes together and conspires, 'the Rage of the whole multitude is visible enough'. The madness of the enraged individual becomes 'Madnesse in the multitude', which then clamours, strikes, throws stones, and seeks to destroy *the very power that has offered it security*.[73] In a sense, the rage of the multitude is a sign that the multitude has lost its mind, has reached *ekstasis* to the point that it targets the sovereign power and security apparatus. The police power steps in to crush the rage, reassert the system's rationality, and thereby justify its own existence as police.

In Chapter 30 of *Leviathan*, Hobbes describes the desire to challenge the power that offers us security as a political sin against the sovereign equal to a breach of God's commands. 'This desire of change, is like the breach of the first of Gods Commandements: For there God says, *Non Habebis Deos Alienos*; Thou shalt not have the Gods of other Nations'. In truth, Hobbes is not really worried about people being tempted by the Gods of other nations. His concern is that people might start thinking that their prosperity could come from a change of regime from monarchy to democracy or some other form of popular rule. For Hobbes, 'the present [regime] ought always to be preferred'.[74] Preferring the present regime means nothing less than defending the claim that prosperity and good order come from 'the Obedience and Concord of the Subjects'. The

73 Hobbes, *Leviathan*, pp. 54–5.
74 Hobbes, *Leviathan*, p. 379.

most dangerous other 'nation', then, is the one which people think they can create through sedition, disobedience, insurgency and civil war. Such activities lead only to the dissolution of the state. To make this case, Hobbes describes the disobedient as exhibiting the stupidity of the giddy rabble, illustrating his point in several books by reference to the 'foolish daughters' in the fable of Pelias. Desiring to restore their old decrepit father to the vigour of his youth, the daughters are advised by that arch-rebel Medea to chop him into pieces 'and set him a boiling with I know not what herbs in a cauldron'.[75]

The image should not surprise us, because, despite the well-known portrayal of Leviathan that appears as the frontispiece of Hobbes's book, in which the sovereign is personified as a male figure standing tall, incorporating the subjects, and watching over the city, there is in fact a much longer and more established image of Leviathan. The image appears in the Book of Job as well as the history of demonology. It is of a creature with flames leaping from his nostrils. It is hard to imagine that Hobbes did not see in this image an expression of sovereign power. The social order becomes nothing less than a cauldron of fear, a kettle kept on the boil by the sovereign power, yet always in danger of boiling over into rage and revolt.

The kettle is expected to contain whatever is within it, however heated the contents become, even to boiling point – but it must never boil over. The kettle offers a *spectacle* of containment, and the important thing about such a spectacle, consistent with a society in which the spectacle is integral to pacified life, is how it *immobilizes* the spectators as well as those contained within the kettle. The bourgeois class loves to display whatever it has captured, as nonhuman animals know all too well. This need to display is the desire to make visible the victory of containment, and thus the power behind the capture. Those captured can be identified, surveyed, stopped from escaping, and held for as long as is necessary for their spirit to be crushed. The kettle thus becomes the spectacle of a fierce and absolute power. The protest is dead, and those watching are allowed, even encouraged, to gaze at the corpse. But as well as being

75 Thomas Hobbes, *The Elements of Law: Natural and Politic*, ed. Ferdinand Tonnies (London: Frank Cass, 1969), p. 178 – and, in different formulations, Thomas Hobbes, *De Cive* (1642), in Hobbes, *Man and Citizen*, ed. Bernard Gert (Indianapolis: Hackett, 1991), p. 255, and Hobbes, *Leviathan*, p. 234.

a corpse, the kettled also double up as patient, to be cured of their illness before being permitted to go home and engage in more humdrum activities: rehydrate, eat, shower, acknowledge their error in questioning the state, and get ready for work the next day.

The kettle is, in this regard, not only a containment of protesters, but a microphysics of our generalized political containment, in which the state wants us to face up to our strategic incapacitation and learn that resistance is not only futile but also unnecessary, to give up any hope that another way of life in a better society is possible. 'Hope is the opposite of security', observed Ernst Bloch in a conversation with Theodor Adorno.[76] In that case, says the security intellectual, abandon hope, embrace what we tell you is 'security', accept your pacification. Above all, steer clear of the seditious rebels.

According to Hobbes, there are three causes of seditious rebellion: discontent, the idea that there is a right to resist, and having some *hope* of success. 'The hope of overcoming' sovereign power is itself a seditious inclination, notes Hobbes in *De Cive*, where he goes on to insist that, however bad things are, rebellion will not happen 'if there be no *hope of having the better of them*'.[77] Kettle logic is thus the logic alluded to by the security intellectual, evident in Hobbes's citation of the verse in which God asks Job whether he thinks he could capture, control or even challenge the Leviathan (Job 41:8–9). 'Lay thine hand upon him, remember the battle, do no more.' Here is the power of the Leviathan state, its police power and security regime: try to lay hands on it, and you will never do it again, for upon Earth there is nothing like it, nothing to compare with its power. We are expected to lay low at the sight of such power and to dispel all hope of challenging it. The ultimate message, then, is that *the hope of man must be disappointed*. Think otherwise, and you will end up lying in the shit.

With that in mind, let us finish by turning to another form of containment, very different from the kettle, far more profound, and more successful too – not least because it is a form of capture from which we appear to have no hope of escape: debt.

76 In Ernst Bloch, *The Utopian Function of Art and Literature: Selected Essays*, transl. Jack Zipes and Frank Mecklenburg (Cambridge, MA: MIT Press, 1989), p. 16.

77 Hobbes, *Elements*, p. 168; Hobbes, *De Cive*, p. 252.

5

Debt as Pacification

Player 107, Kim Mi-ok, 540 million in debt. Player 118, Oh Yeong-uk, 1.02 billion in debt. Player 322, Jung Min-tae, 880 million in debt. Player 119, No Sang-hun, 1.39 billion in debt. Player 369, Park Ju-un, 900 million in debt.

All of you in this room are living on the edge, with debts you just can't pay off.

Squid Game (Netflix, 2021)

One of the stories told by Marx to his daughters was of a character called Hans Röckle, an impoverished magician who owned a toy shop full of wonderful things: wooden people, giants and dwarfs, kings and queens, workmen and masters, animals and birds, tables and chairs, carriages and boxes. Yet, as fondly recounted by Eleanor Marx, despite being a magician in possession of such a magnificent shop, 'Hans could never meet his obligations either to the devil or the butcher', and was therefore 'constantly obliged to sell his toys to the devil'.[1] The fact that a regular story in the Marx household concerned such a figure should perhaps not surprise us, since Marx was more than familiar with the ways in which indebtedness can shape a person's being: as well as

1 Eleanor Marx, 'Reminiscences to an Austrian Journal' (1895), in David McLellan, ed., *Karl Marx: Interviews and Recollections* (Totowa, NJ: Barnes & Noble, 1981), pp. 100–1.

suffering badly from boils and piles, Marx also suffered badly from debt. As Marx himself often observed, the more he wrote about money, the less of it he seemed to have, and so the more indebted he became. The debts are detailed in one letter after another. On 27 February 1852, he wrote to Engels that he was unable to get to the British Library to conduct his research due to his coat being in the pawnbrokers, adding that he could also not buy meat due to his outstanding debt to the butcher. On 15 July 1858, Marx recorded £6 owed to the school, £7 to the butcher, £6 to the baker, £2 to the greengrocer, £6 to the milkman, £9 to the previous milkman and baker, £10 to the doctor, £30 to the pawnshop, £9 in rates to the local authority, £3 to the tallyman, and several debts to friends. His debts were a 'chronically recurring state of affairs', he wrote on 18 June 1862.

The centrality of debt to Marx's personal life parallels its centrality in his analysis of capital. Debt was integral to the birth and development of capital and the modern nation-state, involving investments, financial speculation, a banking system, and international credit, all of which involve the expropriation of the masses. Being integral to the development of capital, debt is central to the history of capitalist violence. When Marx describes capital coming into the world dripping with blood, it follows a discussion of public debt, and makes debt one of the most powerful levers of primitive accumulation.[2] Marx is also aware of the impact this has on the lives of workers. Writing about the role of usurious interest rates in the subjugation of the European peasantry, Marx observes that 'the peasant only needs one of his cows to die and he is immediately unable to repeat his reproduction on the old scale. He falls prey to usury, and once in that position he never recovers his freedom.'[3] It is easy enough to see how Marx's comment about the peasant and his cow is replicated on an almighty scale for workers under capitalism.

Debt oozes from capital's every pore. On the one hand, debt is a mechanism for the appropriation of lands, exploitation of people, and privatization of the commons. On the other hand, debt is also a mechanism for the disciplining of people simply trying to get by. An analysis

2 Karl Marx, *Capital: A Critique of Political Economy, Vol. 1*, transl. Ben Fowkes (Harmondsworth: Penguin, 1976 [1867]), pp. 919–22; Karl Marx, *Capital: A Critique of Political Economy, Vol. 3*, transl. David Fernbach (Harmondsworth: Penguin, 1981), p. 572.

3 Marx, *Capital, Vol. 3*, p. 734.

of debt is therefore important in our understanding of capital's ability to capture and cage us, and the state's ability to police and punish us.

If it seems odd to find a chapter on debt in a book on pacification, consider two small etymological points. First, consider the fact that the origin of the verb 'to pay' stems from the Anglo-Norman and Old French words *paier, paer,* or *paiier,* which are generally offered in dictionaries of etymology as meaning 'to appease, to satisfy, to be to the liking of, to pacify'. The root of these words lies in the Latin *pacare* meaning 'to please, satisfy, or pacify'. In Medieval Latin, to pay a creditor was to satisfy them and hence 'make peace' with them, from *pax*, which is itself part of the root of pacify. This connection between 'pacify' and 'pay' has been lost in our contemporary understanding of 'to pay', but it points to something that we might at least want to consider. Second, consider Georg Simmel's observation that debt is integral to the history of 'partisan warfare'. In the sixteenth century, the loyalty of a citizen to the king could be measured by their being an owner of annuities to the sovereign. Simmel writes that 'the term "partisan" originally referred to a money-lender who was party to a loan to the Crown'.[4]

Beyond such minor etymological points, consider the far more substantive fact that inherent in the prose of pacification is the idea that 'money is ammunition'. This idea, articulated by Lieutenant General David H. Petraeus in an article in *Military Review* in 2006, made its way into the US Marine and Army *Counterinsurgency Manual* published the same year. Once it was formalized in the *Manual*, it came to be regularly repeated in COINdinista literature. As former soldier, and then professor at the US Military Academy, Isaiah Wilson III, tells us in *Thinking Beyond War* (2007), 'money is ammunition'.[5] Such views hark back to earlier counterinsurgency theory, such as Walt Rostow's *The Stages of Economic Growth* (1960), where it is claimed that one way to counter insurgents is to create a world in which people everywhere learn to 'enjoy the blessings and choices opened up by the march of compound

4 Georg Simmel, *The Philosophy of Money*, transl. Tom Bottomore and David Frisby (London: Routledge, 1978 [1907]), p. 501.

5 Lieutenant General David H. Petraeus, 'Learning Counterinsurgency: Observations from Soldiering in Iraq', *Military Review* 86: 1 (2006), pp. 3–4; US Army/Marine Corps, *Counterinsurgency Field Manual, No. 3-24/No. 3-33.5* (2006), Section I-153; Isaiah Wilson III, *Thinking Beyond War: Civil–Military Relations and Why America Fails to Win the Peace* (Houndmills: Palgrave, 2007), p. 132.

interest'.[6] Why not take these comments seriously? Why not believe the practitioners of pacification when they openly tell us that 'money is always involved', when they insist on the 'tactical use of money for security effects', or when they talk of 'Money as a Weapons System', and stress the centrality of debt to this system?[7] After all, these documents appear to be reiterating a point made by Marx, and by critical theorists ever since, albeit from a very different position – namely, that money is a social relation of power. Money disciplines. Money polices economic subjects in the name of sovereign authority. Money shapes the social order. The war machine is a money machine; the money machine is a war machine. Does not the very notion of 'Money as a Weapons System' or a slogan such as 'Money is Ammunition' remind us of capitalism as social war? If money is a weapon and ammunition, what is the target? Might the target be us? Might the strategy be to pacify? Might debt be understood as both social war and social police, and thus occupy a place at the very heart of our pacification?

Thinking of debt as pacification allows us to update and refine a wry observation of Ambrose Bierce's in *The Devil's Dictionary*, a wonderful book of cynical counter-definitions published in 1911, in which debt is defined as 'an ingenious substitute for the chain and whip of the slave-driver'. Debt, I want to suggest, is pacification's dirtiest little secret and its cleanest weapon.

Capital (it fails us now)

'The moment I was born I opened my eyes / I reached out for my credit card.' So begins a song by the Gang of Four. The ostensible message of the song was that we are bankrupt, that capital fails us, and that we should seize the moment and act. But the band were clearly not fully

6 Walt Rostow, *The Stages of Economic Growth: A Non-Communist Manifesto* (Cambridge: Cambridge University Press, 1960), p. 6.

7 Respectively: Sir Robert Thompson, *Defeating Communist Insurgency: The Lessons of Malaya and Vietnam* (Chatto & Windus, 1967), p. 81; *British Army Field Manual, Vol. 1 Pt. 10: Countering Insurgency*, Army Code 71876 (2009), sections 8-4–8-6; US Army, *Commander's Guide to Money as a Weapons System: Tactics, Techniques, and Procedures*, US Army, Handbook No. 09-27 (2009), pp. 17, 56–7; Headquarters, Dept. of the Army, *The Commanders' Emergency Response Program*, ATP 1-06.2 (2017).

convinced that we would seize the moment. The song's final lines offer a vision not of a non-capitalist future, but of a mechanism devised by capital to subdue us further still: 'One day we'll all be living on credit.' The song, called 'Capital (It Fails Us Now)', was released in 1981. That same year, household debt amounted to 30 per cent of GDP in the UK and 50 per cent in the United States. By the early 2000s it was comfortably over 90 percent in both countries, as well as many others, and it remains at historically high levels.

The same might be said for sovereign nations. In the post-war period, sustained growth meant that the high levels of public debt deriving from the Second World War were gradually reduced. But this tendency was overturned following the cycle of crises from the early 1970s. Between the mid 1970s and the mid 1990s, public debt rose on average from around 30 to 65 per cent of GDP, rising again from 2008 onwards in reaction to the financial crisis, and hitting 100 percent in 2015.[8] During this period, the corporate social contract that had existed between capital and labour in the post-war industrialized nations was gradually broken down as part of the statecraft of the neoliberal ruling class, which produced ongoing wage stagnation: the statecraft of political security was matched by a neoliberal crafting of economic insecurity. The increasing uncertainty of wages came to be paralleled by the increasing certainty of debt.

Such statecraft was implemented around the world through the system of loans and micro-lending programmes operated by international organizations such as the World Bank, the United Nations, the European Commission, the European Investment Fund, the Alliance for Financial Inclusion (established in 2008 by the Bill and Melinda Gates Foundation) and numerous NGOs. These integrated billions of people living in poverty into the circulation of finance capital. On a micro level, such loans are expected to facilitate, 'as with the stroke of an enchanter's wand' (the phrase is Marx's – one of the many he uses to allude to the magic that surrounds money), the appropriate (liberal bourgeois) financial and entrepreneurial skills among the indebted, in an attempt to not only bring all human activity into the realm of the market, but to turn that activity into the acts of indebted subjects, thereby reinforcing its

8 Cédric Durand, *Fictitious Capital: How Finance Is Appropriating Our Future*, transl. David Broder (London: Verso, 2017 [2014]), pp. 61–2.

disciplinary logic. On a macro level, the loans can then be bundled and securitized, enabling a trade in debt. The creditors can then decide on the conditions of repayment, policing the implementation of those conditions (that is, 'structurally adjusting' them), while the public debt becomes a stick with which to suppress and subjugate the working class in many nations. The appropriate term here is *debt bondage*. This is the incredibly revealing phrase that captures the mechanism by which workers are held in place in perpetuity. But the key point is that debt bondage has never ended:

> A person pledges him- or herself against a loan of money, but the length and nature of the service are not defined and the labour does not reduce the original debt. The debt can be passed down to subsequent generations, thus enslaving offspring; moreover, 'defaulting' can be punished by seizing or selling children into further debt bonds. Ownership is not normally asserted, but there is complete physical control of the bonded laborer.[9]

But does the phrase 'debt bondage' not have a much wider resonance, capturing a condition from which we can never free ourselves?

Even trying to list the various ways in which we are bound by debt is dizzying. First, graduates pay tens of thousands in interest on the debt taken out to get them through university, made worse by a dramatic increase in the cost of higher education, a decline in the relative salary level for graduate jobs, a decline in the number of graduate jobs, and the fact that graduates often get jobs that they could once have walked into without the degree. The undergraduate degree is now a promissory note, dripping in debt, from which one has little hope of redemption, as Richard Hall observes – adding that 'the promise of a degree and access to the elite has become an object of pacification'.[10] Second, the cost of wage stagnation, and then austerity, has meant that many workers have taken up debt to survive. Third, this is compounded by the massive increase in precarious forms of labour: short-term, fixed or zero-hours

---

9 Kevin Bales, *Disposable People: New Slavery in the Global Economy* (Berkeley, CA: University of California Press, 2012), pp. 19–20.

10 Richard Hall, *The Hopeless University: Intellectual Work at the End of the End of History* (London: MayFly, 2021), p. 117.

contracts; subemployment; underemployment; freelance work; contract work; gig-economy work; uber-jobs and microwork. All are part of the 'age of insecurity' and all help to erode older rights that were attached to the workplace. Unemployed, semi-employed and underemployed people are often forced to take out loans to cover periods without income. Fourth, there is the cumulative problem of rising housing costs, making decent housing without substantial debt a distant possibility for most, at the very moment when home ownership is foisted upon us as a key sign of one's status as a citizen. At one end of the scale, people take on debts that are inherently designed to leave them indebted for life in the form of the 'mortgage' – literally a 'dead pledge' (from the French *mort* and *gage*), about which I will say more below. It is also well known that workers who have a mortgage are less likely to strike. At the other, individuals and families are evicted in increasing numbers because of an inability to pay off a housing debt. Fifth, as the Gang of Four observed, it does indeed seem that, from the moment we are born, we are handed a credit card.

All told, we are now 'governed by debt' (Maurizio Lazzarato), and living in what is described variously as a 'giant debt machine' (David Graeber), a 'debtfare state' (Susanne Soederberg), a 'debt trap' (Brett Williams) or a 'creditocracy' (Andrew Ross).[11] The debt form is now as integral as the wage form in the imposition of the law of the market, built on a tacit acceptance that debt is now integral to survival, even for those also dependent on a wage.[12] Indeed, the wage form and the debt form come together within the temporality of debt, in that the possibility of present consumption generated by debt is only enabled by a

11 Maurizio Lazzarato, *Governing By Debt*, transl. Joshua David Jordan (South Pasadena, CA: Semiotext(e), 2015 [2013]); David Graeber, *Debt: The First 5,000 Years* (London: Melville House, 2011), p. 390; Susanne Soederberg, *Debtfare States and the Poverty Industry: Money, Discipline and the Surplus Population* (London: Routledge, 2014); Brett Williams, *Debt for Sale: A Social History of the Credit Trap* (Philadelphia: University of Pennsylvania Press, 2005); Andrew Ross, *Creditocracy and the Case for Debt Refusal* (New York: OR, 2013). See also Strike Debt/Occupy Wall Street, *The Debt Resisters' Operations Manual* (September 2012), and Debt Collective, *Can't Pay, Won't Pay* (Chicago, IL: Haymarket, 2020).

12 Midnight Notes Collective, 'The New Enclosures' (1990), reprinted in Midnight Notes, *Midnight Oil: Work, Energy, War, 1973–1992* (New York: Autonomedia, 1992); Silvia Federici, 'From Commoning to Debt: Financialization, Micro-Credit and the Changing Architecture of Capital Accumulation', Committee for the Abolition of Illegitimate Debt, 14 June 2016, at cadtm.org.

guarantee of future wage labour. (This, at least, is the theory – in practice, this is often disregarded by the creditor in order to capture the indebted person for life.) This is debt as an alternative mode of capture and containment, though very different in form and substance from the kind of capture and containment discussed in Chapter 4. Housing, education, healthcare, basic goods, and a myriad of other fundamental needs are for billions of people only satisfied through debt. Such debts colonize our lives, cause us to inhabit a vicious circle, and 'swindle' us, as Marx puts it, through a kind of 'secondary exploitation', along with the primary exploitation of work itself.[13] To invoke the series *Squid Game* cited at the beginning of this chapter, tweaked with a line from Jonathan Swift's poem 'The South Sea Project' (1721): we are all 'dipt over head and ears – in debt'.

Might this be a central aspect of our contemporary pacification?

We can perhaps begin to identify the underlying logic of the process via an observation of J. G. A. Pocock's concerning English national debt in the eighteenth century. The national debt was used by the British state to maintain and expand its power by mortgaging its future revenues – not least during the Seven Years' War, when the national debt almost doubled from £72 million to £140 million. The period was therefore one in which financial institutions consolidated their status as major political institutions. Unsurprisingly, the same period also saw a proliferation of pamphlets, books and tracts discussing the nature of debt in general. Pocock's observation is that national debt came to be a sign of confidence in the government at the very moment when debt in general became a *paradigmatic form of social relation*. The logic of an increase in the national debt coincided with the logic of a society increasingly accustomed to living through speculation and credit, and increasingly accepting of the powerful social role of money as the grounds for judging people and their likely future actions. Debt was becoming 'an expansive and dynamic social device' (indicated by the fact that usury had by then become increasingly accepted, as we shall see) that obliged capitalist society to develop as an ideology something that it had before then never possessed – namely, 'the image of a secular and historical future'. The speculative society was understood to maintain and govern itself by perpetually gambling on its own desires; but at the same time a new

13 Marx, *Capital, Vol. 3*, p. 745.

dimension was added 'in which not only was every man in debt to every other man, but every man was judged and governed, at every moment, by other men's opinion of the probability that not he alone, but generations yet unborn, would be able and willing to repay their debts at some future date'.[14] This is the 'promise of a future transfer' at the heart of capitalist debt, as Weber describes it.[15]

Pocock's observation points to the connection between the national and the personal, the public and the private, as the political economy of public debt coincides with a legal regime, a cultural formation and an ideological system. It is also undoubtedly the reason why eighteenth-century novels (and their successors in the century that followed) were so obsessed with debt. Hence, as well as grasping the ways in which the debts of working people are a fundamental part of the circuit of capital, we also need to understand them as an expression of a bewitched and distorted social, cultural and psychological universe. Take, for example, the Christian Lord's Prayer. When I was growing up, it was taught as follows:

> Our Father who art in heaven, hallowed be Thy name.
>
> Thy kingdom come, Thy will be done on earth as it is in heaven.
>
> Give us this day our daily bread; and forgive us our trespasses, as we forgive those who trespass against us; and lead us not into temptation, but deliver us from evil.

In fact, many translations of the relevant passages in the Bible from which the Prayer is taken, such as Matthew 6:9–13 and Luke 11:2–4, offer 'debts' instead of 'trespasses'.[16] The great eighteenth-century police reformer and founder of the Bow Street Runners, Henry Fielding, has one of the characters in his novel *Joseph Andrews* (1742) ask: 'How can such a wretch repeat the Lord's Prayer; where the word, which is translated, I know not for what reason, trespasses, is in the

14 J. G. A. Pocock, *Virtue, Commerce, and History* (Cambridge: Cambridge University Press, 1985), pp. 98–9.

15 Max Weber, *Economy and Society, Vol. 1* (Berkeley, CA: University of California Press, 1978), p. 81.

16 The King James version offers 'debts' in Matthew and both 'sins' and 'debts' in Luke.

original, debts?' (Book III, Chapter III). The key shift in the translations appears to have taken place gradually, during the slow emergence of commercial society between the late fourteenth and mid sixteenth centuries. John Wycliffe's translation of the Gospels in the 1380s contained what was by then the familiar 'debt', whereas William Tyndale's translation in the 1520s, which became part of the English Book of Common Prayer in 1549, offers 'trespasses' instead of 'debt'.

The shift from 'debt' to 'trespass' in translations of the Lord's Prayer is a reminder of three issues. First, debt speaks to an infringement on property: to trespass, a word that came into the English language in the fourteenth century from the Old French *trespasser*, means 'to go across or beyond, to traverse, infringe or violate'. In English, the word connoted transgression or the commitment of an aggressive offense. As the early capitalist enclosures increasingly came to place more tracts of common land into private hands, 'trespass' came to be associated with 'entering unlawfully'. Second, debt is not a 'spiritual debt' owed to God, but is understood as a sin. In Hebrew and Aramaic, the word for 'debt' and 'sin' are the same – translations of the Lord's Prayer sometimes offer 'sin' instead of 'debt' or 'trespass' – and this connection has been retained in Christianity's insistence that we must pay for our sins. When we die (in modern French *trépasser* has come to be used euphemistically for 'to die'), our sins are 'scored up', as one text on the Ten Commandments put it in 1624, adding that our sins, 'being registered in [God's] booke of accounts, stand in Record'. Without satisfaction in the accounts, the author continues, 'there is no remission'. The 'satisfaction' must be God's, as we seek 'a general release upon his satisfaction of the debt'.[17] There is, of course, a long tradition running through all the major world religions that conceives of God as keeping a book of accounts or ledger.[18] 'I saw the dead, small and great, stand before God; and the books were opened' (Revelation, 20:12). God is imagined as the Great Debt Collector. God has us on his books. God can call in our debts at any time. On death, we seek redemption from our debts and our sins, and our debts as sins. Third, it is notable that some aspects of the Lord's Prayer are often said

17 Peter Barker, *A Iudicious and Painefull Exposition Upon the Ten Commandements* (London: Roger Jackson, 1624), p. 75.

18 James Aho, *Confession and Bookkeeping: The Religious, Moral, and Rhetorical Roots of Modern Accounting* (Albany, NY: State University of New York Press, 2005).

to stem from the Old Testament, specifically the book of Leviticus (but also others, such as Proverbs). For the Israelites to whom that book was addressed, debt was a form of slavery, and Leviticus describes their degradation in terms of a denial of the proceeds of their labour, a denial of any other kind of wealth, a denial of any community between them, and their alienation from their own land.

What we have spiralling out of the Lord's Prayer, then, is the power of debt as *property*, debt as *sin*, and debt as *slavery*. That is, debt as an *economic power*, but also a *moral judgment* and an *ownership of the body*. Debt is a relation of power that has at its core the dialectic of master and slave, property and sovereignty, life and death.

Political economy and liberal ideology encourage the belief that personal debt is a simple device that financial institutions offer to working people – a voluntary exchange between consenting parties in which there is no power relation whatsoever, in which any interest and charges are contractual and hence fair. The voluntariness is reinforced by the supposedly 'non-political' nature of institutions such as banks, credit card companies, student loan systems, microfinance lenders and the plethora of other institutions that offer credit and loans. This idea of a simple and voluntary device harks back to a certain romantic and sentimental notion of the rich person giving credit to the poor person they have judged to be hardworking and honest. Marx picks up on this romantic and sentimental notion in an early essay on James Mill's political economy, highlighting the fact that behind the romance and sentiment there lies something deeply unromantic and very material: the capacity to *estimate the value of a person in money*:

> [T]he life of the poor man and his talents and activity serve the rich man as a *guarantee* of the repayment of the money lent. That means, therefore, that all the social virtues of the poor man, the content of his vital activity, his existence itself, represent for the rich man the reimbursement of his capital with the customary interest.

Hence, 'the death of the poor man is the worst eventuality for the creditor. It is the death of his capital together with the interest.' Credit, in other words, is chiefly an *economic* judgment on the *morality* of a person. 'Within the credit relationship', Marx notes, '*human individuality*, human *morality* itself, has become both an object of commerce and the material in which money exists'. In the credit relationship, 'it is my own personal existence, my flesh and blood, my social virtue and importance, which constitutes the material, corporeal form of the *spirit of money*'.[19] Credit *resolves the value of money into human flesh*, to the extent that the very life and body of the debtor acts as a guarantee of the legal compulsion to pay the debt: the creditors will have their 'pound of flesh', to use Shylock's phrase in *The Merchant of Venice*.

This phrase was meant literally. Roman law included 'the terrible law of the twelve tables', whereby 'the creditors might cut the debtor's body into pieces, and each of them take his proportionable share', and some 'inhuman laws' that allowed 'imprisoning the debtor's person in chains; subjecting him to stripes and hard labour, at the mercy of his rigid creditors; and sometimes selling him, his wife and children, to perpetual foreign slavery'.[20] Hence commentators as diverse as William Blackstone in his *Commentaries on the Laws of England* (1765–9), Benjamin Franklin in *Poor Richard's Almanack for 1758* (citing Proverbs: 'the borrower is a slave to the lender'), Friedrich Nietzsche in *The Genealogy of Morality* (1887) and Marx in his essay on Mill remind us that a debt could be recovered against the goods and chattels of the indebted, against the profits from their land, but also *against their body* and even *against their life*. The surety of the pledge, or the 'gage', could take the form of the actual human being, creditors being legally entitled to their 'pound of flesh'.

This is what Frederick Pollock and Frederic William Maitland call an 'animated gage', the debtor becoming 'a hostage delivered over to slavery but subject to redemption'.[21] In addition to becoming part of *mortgage*, *gage* also has a close etymological connection to *wage*. 'Gage, engagement, wage, wages, wager, wed, wedding . . . all spring from one root', observe Pollock and Maitland, and all are connected to that supreme concept of bourgeois society, *security*:

19 Karl Marx, 'Comments on James Mill, Éléments *D'économie Politique*' (1844), in Karl Marx and Frederick Engels, *Collected Works, Vol. 3* (London: Lawrence & Wishart, 1975), pp. 215–16. Emphasis in original.

20 William Blackstone, *Commentaries on the Laws of England, Vol. 2* (1765–69) (Chicago: University of Chicago Press, 1979), p. 472.

21 Sir Frederick Pollock and Frederic William Maitland, *The History of English Law Before the Time of Edward I, Vol. II* (Indianapolis, IN: Liberty Fund, 1968 [1898]), pp. 193–4.

> When a lord has seized his tenant's goods in distress they are in his hands a gage for the payment of the rent that is in arrear, and the sheriff is always taking gages from those who have no mind to give them. The notion expressed by the word seems to be that expressed by our 'security'; some thing has either been given or been seized, and the possession of it by him in whose hands it now is, secures the payment of money or the performance of some act by the person by whom it was given or from whom it was taken.[22]

One such 'security' could be the very life and body of the debtor as an 'animated gage' delivered into slavery as a guarantee of the debt's repayment, and reinforcing the general idea that a person's body could be substituted for money. In this, the punishment for non-payment of debt coincided with the punishment for vagrancy and idleness in many of the poor laws. The 1547 Act for the Punishing of Vagabonds in England, for example, held that anyone refusing to work should be sent back to their parish to work as a slave there, or condemned to be a slave to the person who had denounced him as an idler.

The debt system facilitates accumulation through a moral and economic judgment over the 'worth' of a person's entire existence, which becomes wholly dependent on this judgment and a reflection of the borrower's supposed status. This produces a 'distrustful calculation' (Marx's phrase) concerning whether the debt can be permitted, as the person without credit or with a low credit rating is pronounced not only poor, but also *untrustworthy*. This distrust prompts yet another form of distrust, in the guise of surveillance and intelligence-gathering conducted through various police powers, as the distrustful calculation employed by financial institutions, as one branch of the security industry, coincides with the distrustful calculative reason employed by the state. A distrust of workers is exacerbated by an absolute trust in the power of the law and the state to compel payment of the debt. Ultimately, of course, political economy assumes that the worker *owes a debt to capital* for the simple fact of their liberty, just as police science assumes that, for the same reason, the worker *owes a debt to the state* for their security ('the debt, that

22 Ibid., p. 123.

every man oweth to the Common-wealth for his defence', as Hobbes puts it).[23]

'How goes the world', Timon of Athens asks Flavius, 'that I am thus encounter'd / With clamorous demands of date-broke bonds, / And the detention of long-since due debts?' (*Timon of Athens*, II.II). Timon knows full well: it is necessary to pay one's debts. The Greek word for debt (*chreos*) was close to the word for necessity (*chreon*). The necessity of repaying a debt binds the person, which is why ancient texts such as Plutarch's 'Life of Solon' stress the extent to which the common people were in debt to the rich, pledging their persons for debts, and sometimes being seized and enslaved by their creditors. Later in Shakespeare's play, Timon's creditors and their servants come to collect. 'My lord, here is my bill', Titus says. 'Here's mine', adds Lucilius's servant. The servants of Hortensius and Varro demand the same. Timon responds: 'Knock me down with 'em: cleave me to the girdle.' Timon also knows perfectly well the extent of the power they possess over him: when Lucilius's servant points out that his master is owed five thousand crowns, Timon responds that 'five thousand drops of blood will pay that'. He knows they possess the power of life, of death, of servitude and of shares in his body. 'Cut my heart in sums', he insists, 'tell out my blood'. 'Creditors? Devils!'

There are plenty of reasons why Marx so loved *Timon of Athens*. The fact that our 'debts wither us to nothing' (IV.III), a chronically recurring situation, combined with the fear of the blood squeezed from us, literally and metaphorically, by our creditors, points to the way we are constituted as subjects, indebted and obedient to the financial rules and legal forces that confirm the power of our creditors: financial subjects subjected to the powers of finance. Through the threat of punishment and the power of law, the creditor always claims the *rights of the master*, as Nietzsche puts it in the *Genealogy of Morality*. Creditors? Evil Masters!

As indebted subjects, we internalize the distrustful calculation that is at play, learning how to engage in the very calculative reason and strategic relations that reproduce capitalist domination and our own pacification. By inculcating an indebted sensibility into our subjectivity and

23 Thomas Hobbes, *Leviathan*, ed. Richard Tuck (Cambridge: Cambridge University Press, 1991 [1651]), p. 238.

instilling a conception of ourselves as an indebted *Homo œconomicus*, debt has become capitalism's key mode of easing and teasing us into relations of obligation, and ultimately into a *dutiful submission* to capital itself.

Dutiful submission? Debt stems from the Old French *dete*, from the Latin *debitum*, the past participle of *debere*, meaning what is owed, a duty as well as debt, and hence connoting a state of being under obligation. The word 'duty', notes R. G. Collingwood, 'is formed by adding a common Romance suffix to "due", which represents the Latin *debitum*, "owed". "Duty" in the abstract is the state of something's being owed: "a duty" is a thing owed.' When the words 'due' and 'duty' appear in English in the late thirteenth and early fourteenth centuries, it is partly to capture this aspect of the state of indebtedness, in that they contain a reference to *debitum*, a past act of incurring a debt. Hence the idea of debt was associated less with the expectation of a money payment than with a payment in kind, in the form of a rendering of service to a 'lord' or 'master'. This was connected to the vernacular English expression of 'owe', which originally meant 'own' but which from the tenth century became a translation of *debere*. As Collingwood points out, etymologically the phrase 'it is my duty to do this' and 'I ought to do this' mean the same thing.[24]

To live a life in debt is to live a life weighed down by a duty to repay it. This is why the duty to pay one's debts is imagined as weighty (once again, like sin), pressing down on us: a massive 'weight on my mind', something 'one carries around all the time', an 'impossible weight', a 'heavy burden to bear'. Being indebted often means feeling weighed down by a burden so heavy that living a full life is impossible, encumbered by an obligation which seems to have captured us. The very idea of obligation is also revealing. The *Oxford English Dictionary* defines it as 'a binding agreement committing a person to a payment or other action', and a form of constraint or of being 'bound', either legal or moral. But part of its meaning is also 'an enforced or burdensome task or charge', and some of the word's earlier meanings are even more telling, even if they are now obsolete: obligation once connoted 'a bond by which a person is held captive'.

---

24 R. G. Collingwood, *The New Leviathan, or Man, Society, Civilization and Barbarism* (Oxford: Clarendon, 1942), p. 119.

'Man is no longer man enclosed, but man in debt', observes Gilles Deleuze of what he calls 'societies of control'.[25] But that is not quite right. Deleuze suggests that capitalism keeps three-quarters of humanity in such a state of poverty that they are too poor for debt and too numerous to be enclosed. In fact, capital has been encouraging indebtedness among even the world's poorest for a long time. We might rather say that *man is enclosed in debt*; debt *is* enclosure, which is perhaps precisely why, during the heyday of the historical enclosures, there was a body of literature connecting enclosure with high interest rates charged on loans to the poor, such as in John Lane's *Tom Tel-truth's Message* (1600), Gerard Malynes's *The Maintenance of Free Trade* (1622) and George Wither's *Britain's Remembrancer* (1628). As we saw in Chapter 4, there is an intimate connection between 'enclosure' and 'containment'. Debt as a form of containment – a capture, a holding or fixing of bodies, minds and lives – is now fundamental to the reproduction of pacified subjects. In fulfilling one's duties and obligations to 'pay one's debts', one learns obedience to capital. But one also learns obedience to law.

Law (it fails us now)

Nomos and *nomisma*: law and money. That they have the same root was first pointed out by Aristotle in the *Nicomachean Ethics*. Aristotle wants his readers to understand this as the condition of exchange in a community of equals, but what he does inadvertently is draw attention to the fact that both money and law are founded on violence. This feeds into the debt relation, which, like money in general, requires a consideration of sovereign authority and the political administration of subjects. 'The contractual relationship between *creditor* and *debtor* . . . is as old as the very conception of a "legal subject" ', Nietzsche observes.[26] Indebtedness is a legal condition; if debt is the credo of capital, then repayment is the credo of law. Law, like political economy, treats debt entirely neutrally, as a contract freely entered and based on equal exchange. Law thus regards

25 Gilles Deleuze, 'Postscript on the Societies of Control' (1990), *October* 59 (1992), p. 6.

26 Aristotle, *The Nichomachean Ethics*, transl. J. A. K. Thomson (Harmondsworth: Penguin, 2004), pp. 121–7; Friedrich Nietzsche, *On the Genealogy of Morality*, transl. Carol Diethe (Cambridge: Cambridge University Press, 1994 [1887]), p. 43.

it as right that the debt cannot be escaped: we must repay our debts. Herein lies the violence.

'Abstractly speaking, *nomos* is law and property', Carl Schmitt comments. But the Greek noun *nomos* derives from the verb *nemein*, and *nemein* is connected to taking or appropriating, dividing and distributing. As well as law, then, *nomos* is also appropriation, distribution and production. It is a word whose history is connected to colonization, conquest and land-appropriation.[27] This is the violence of enclosure and appropriation that is central to the development of capitalism. At the same time, we see a parallel development in the violence of punishment. During the development of capitalism, European law continued the Biblical tradition articulated in a parable reported by Matthew (18:23–35). In the parable, Jesus describes a king who wishes to settle accounts with his servants. As the king begins the reckoning, a servant who owes him 10,000 talents, the equivalent of twenty years of a labourer's wages, is unable to pay, and so the king orders that the servant be sold to repay the debt, along with his wife and children. The servant falls to his knees, begs for mercy, and the king takes pity and forgives the debt. When the servant leaves, he comes across a fellow servant who owes him a hundred silver coins, worth around a day's wages. He seizes the fellow by the throat and demands payment. The man also falls to his knees and begs for patience; but he is refused, and thrown into prison. When the other servants see what has happened, they are outraged and inform the king. The king calls the first servant in. 'Thou wicked servant,' says the king. 'I forgave thee all that debt, because thou desiredst me. Shouldest not thou also have had compassion on thy fellow servant, even as I had pity on thee?' In his anger, the king hands him over to the jailers until he pays back all he owes.

European law replicated this practice by allowing debtors to be jailed. Debtors' prisons were already common by the seventeenth century in countries such as England, and were then carried over to the American colonies and persisted in the American states. It was not always clear whether the imprisonment of debtors was an act of coercive punishment for non-payment, or a means of making them pay the debt (which

27 Carl Schmitt, *The* Nomos *of the Earth in the International Law of the* Jus Publicum Europaeum, transl. G. L. Ulmen (New York: Telos, 2003 [1950]), pp. 326–8, 341, 345–6.

they could rarely do, given that they were in prison) – but they were certainly being held as a security against the debt. Some of those imprisoned for indebtedness were wealthy individuals who were simply unwilling to release some capital to pay their debts; but most were from among the working poor, artisans and shopkeepers, and were often worse off than other inmates, not least because they had to pay for their 'accommodation' and food. In one famous case in 1551, concerning Thomas Maningham, it was held that 'he ought to live of his own, and neither the plaintiff nor the sheriff is bound to give him Meat or Drink . . . He ought to live of his own Goods . . . and if he has no Goods, he shall live of the Charity of others, and if others will give him nothing, let him die in the Name of God'.[28] One and a half centuries later, Moses Pitt, in *The Cry of the Oppressed*, tells of beatings and rapes of debtors by jailers, and of debtors and their families being made to sleep on the floor with no bedding, eating mice to survive, and sharing space with pigs.[29] The legal term used in some countries to describe such pitiful conditions was *squalor carceris*. As under Roman law, debtors were often forced to become indentured labourers to specific employers until their debt was paid off, which it often never was. Many debtors died in prison. When John Howard conducted his review of the state of prisons in England and Wales in the 1770s and 1780s, he found that debtors constituted almost half of all prison inmates (2,078 of the 4,379 inmates in 1779; 2,197 of 4,439 in 1782).[30]

Although the laws surrounding debt in the eighteenth century were undoubtedly an effective means of protecting propertied interests, incarceration for indebtedness was gradually abolished through the second half of the nineteenth century in industrializing and liberalizing states. This liberal abolition of a harsh law for non-payment of debts was but one small aspect of a restructuring of the forms of power through which debt was now to be managed, as well as an outcome of the shift in imprisonment towards correction and reform – that is, as a means to

28 Edmund Plowden, *Commentaries and Reports of Edmund Plowden, 1548–1579* (London: n.p., 1761), p. 68.

29 Moses Pitt, *The Cry of the Oppressed, Being a True and Tragical Account of the Unparallel'd Sufferings of Multitudes of Poor Imprisoned Debtors in Most of the Jails in England* (London: n.p., 1691).

30 John Howard, *The State of Prisons in England and Wales*, 4th edn (London, 1792), p. 492.

discipline and punish. During the same period, 'credit management' became increasingly institutionalized, and it became a 'respectable' part of an accountant's work to organize forms of 'respectable' credit for 'respectable' people. New systems of debtor–creditor relations and specialist accountants also emerged, advising on how to manage debt, increasingly reconceptualized as the more positive 'credit'.[31]

The restructuring of the forms of power through which debt was managed was but one aspect of a broader set of important changes in European penal systems in the middle of the nineteenth century (including, for example, the demise of transportation as a punishment). As George Rusche and Otto Kirchheimer point out, imprisonment remained the central point of the whole system, but as a form of punishment it was increasingly rivalled by the fine. The necessity for fines rather than imprisonment was partly a product of the general policy of the principle of 'proportion' in terms of punishment for 'minor' offences, but also of the introduction of ever more minor offences subject to police measures. The logic was that it was better for some offences to be punished by 'impoverishing' people with a fine rather than a prison sentence. After all, if, as bourgeois political economy had long argued, virtue is rewarded by wealth, then surely the 'reward' for vice should be the impoverishment that comes from a fine. As a result, despite all the difficulties in using the fine as punishment (calculating the size of the fine, establishing whether people had the means to pay), the system of fines came to form a core part of the apparatus of discipline and punishment. In this context we might pay heed to a sharp observation made some time ago by Anthony Bottoms, who pointed out that the fine is a remarkably neglected feature of contemporary penal practice, especially compared to all that has been written about the disciplinary nature of the prison. This is especially important given that the fine is a major form of punishment in bourgeois society, and plays a key role in the diffusion of discipline throughout the social body as a whole – and because one inevitable result of the rise of the fine as a form of punishment is that members of the working class have been imprisoned for non-payment of debts incurred as fines. To take the UK as an example,

31 Hugh Barty-King, *The Worst Poverty: A History of Debt and Debtors* (Stroud: Alan Sutton, 1991); Bruce H. Mann, *Republic of Debtors: Bankruptcy in the Age of American Independence* (Cambridge, MA: Harvard University Press, 2002).

by 1913 just under 50 per cent of male prisoners and just under 70 per cent of female prisoners were there for failing to pay fines. In effect, the extension of the fine as a routine form of punishment meant that ever more working-class people came to be imprisoned for debt incurred as punishment for non-payment of fines – despite the fact that imprisonment for debt was meant to have been abolished. This situation has not changed. Although incarceration for debt is illegal, then, imprisonment for non-payment of fines imposed by the court in cases of debt collection will usually lead to a charge of being 'in contempt of court', and a prison sentence. Once imprisoned, people are often denied parole until they pay their fines and any further fees incurred.[32]

One sees this most starkly in relation to the war on vagrancy. In the UK, while sections of the 1824 Vagrancy Act remain in place, vagrancy is also now policed through various measures that have come and gone in this particular social war, such as Anti-Social Behaviour Orders (ASBO), Criminal Behaviour Orders (CBO) and Public Spaces Protection Orders (PSPO). These new forms of spatial governance and mechanisms of containment allow local authorities to issue fixed-penalty notices and pursue criminal convictions for an extensive range of 'offences'. Note, these offences are determined by the social police operating through local authorities. PSPOs, for example, have criminalized people engaging in everyday practices such as feeding birds, making noise, napping in public, picking up stones, and climbing trees. Of more interest to us here are those offences connected to the policing of poverty, where we see bans issued on loitering, begging, and looking in bins. A pattern emerges in which hungry and homeless people are fined for begging or loitering, are unable to pay the fine, and are imprisoned as a result. Breaching one of the orders might lead to a fixed-penalty notice, which often cannot be paid, and then to additional fines, which in turn cannot be paid. An order might ban an individual from begging, even though begging is their means of subsistence, with the threat that violating that ban will result in five years in prison. If one follows a trail from the beginning of the process (such as begging) to the end of it

32 George Rusche and Otto Kirchheimer, *Punishment and Social Structure* (New York: Columbia University Press, 1939), pp. 166–9; Anthony E. Bottoms, 'Neglected Features of Contemporary Penal Systems', in David Garland and Peter Young, eds, *The Power to Punish: Contemporary Penalty and Social Analysis* (Aldershot: Gower, 1983), pp. 167–9.

(imprisonment), one finds that people are being imprisoned for trying to satisfy basic human needs. 'I will be sending a man to prison for asking for food when he was hungry', as a judge admitted during one case.[33] In fact, of course, he was sending the man to prison because of an *inability to pay a debt to the state.*

The case of this man offers a remarkable insight into the nature of how our social order moves people through categories of political administration as a means of pacifying the population. First, civil society is constructed in such a way that it fails to ensure its population is fed: a person is interpellated as a *beggar*. Second, the state fines people for begging, but their very status as a beggar means they cannot pay the debt: the beggar is turned into a *debtor*. Third, the non-payment of the debt-as-fine leads to imprisonment: the beggar-debtor has become a *criminal*. Finally, as part of their punishment, they become a *prisoner*. As an indication of the utter irrationality of our social order, we can also note that it is only when they reach the final category that the person finally receives what they wanted in the first place: a meal. A person seeking to satisfy a basic human need can thus find themselves very easily and quickly becoming a prisoner. Debt is central to the process.

There are other ways in which the series can be configured, such as through electronic tagging, which is increasingly used instead of imprisonment, sometimes used against those who have not been convicted of any crime (yet another reminder of one of my points in Chapter 4, where the tagged offender replicates a tagged animal). A tagged person must usually pay for the tagging, but often cannot do so as the costs are high, and so quickly becomes indebted to the company that manages the tagging process. The same process occurs through the US probation system, which has become a major source of profiteering, the effect of which is to send people to prison for non-payment of debts. A report by Human Rights Watch documents case after case of this. One concerns a man who pled guilty to stealing a can of beer from a convenience store. He was fined $200 and sentenced to a year on probation. Unable to pay the 'start-up' fee required by the probation company, he went into debt, and then to jail for a month, being released only when someone paid the fee for him. But the fees for being monitored by the probation company

---

33 Cited in Patrick Greenfield and Sarah Marsh, 'Hundreds of Homeless People Fined and Imprisoned in England and Wales', *Guardian*, 20 May 2018.

still amounted to $260 per month, while his income was $300 (which he earned by selling his blood plasma). In the end, he fell behind with the payments and into debt with the company, eventually being imprisoned once again for non-payment of that debt. He thus went from probationer to debtor to criminal to prisoner.[34]

Such developments have boosted the exponential rise in imprisonment for non-payment of all sorts of other debts arising from an inability to pay fines, associated court fees and other legal costs, including lawyers' fees, surcharges, interest on the original fines, and fees for treatment imposed by the court. One can follow the same pattern in trial after trial, as attempts to satisfy basic needs at the beginning of the process lead to imprisonment at its end. In the UK, we can find tales such as one concerning a single mother unable to work and receiving benefits due to illness, given an eighty-one-day jail sentence after building up arrears of £4,742 in Council Tax. A court had initially ordered her to pay £10 a week towards the arrears, which she did for a few months, but then defaulted. Despite her making a last-minute payment of £100, police officers and bailiffs went to her home, where they arrested her and took her to be detained in prison.[35] The pattern is now so common that, in March 2011, the *Wall Street Journal* ran an article titled 'Welcome to Debtors' Prison, 2011 Edition', and the same claim about the continued existence of 'debtors' prisons' has been made by campaign groups in the UK.[36] Even judges have been known to comment that the system 'could reasonably be characterized as the operation of a debtors' prison.'[37] The whole problem is compounded by the growing use of private debt collectors and their increasing tendency to use the courts to enforce private debt obligations. Again, plenty of examples could be

34 Human Rights Watch, *Profiting from Probation: America's 'Offender-Funded' Probation Industry*, February 2014, at hrw.org. On tagging, see Chrysse Haynes, 'Lawsuit Confronts Extortion of Prisoners by Electronic Monitoring Firm', *Equal Justice Under Law Report*, 6 August 2018.

35 Frances Perraudin, 'Woman Jailed for a £4,742 Council Tax Debt', *Guardian*, 12 April 2019.

36 Jessica Silver-Greenberg, 'Welcome to Debtors' Prison, 2011 Edition', *Wall Street Journal*, 17 March 2011; Chris Daw QC, *Unfair, Ineffective and Unjustifiable: The Case for Ending Imprisonment for Council Tax Arrears in England* (London: Social Market Foundation, 2019), p. 5.

37 Cited in Adrienne Roberts, 'Doing Borrowed Time: The State, the Law and the Coercive Governance of "Undeserving" Debtors', *Critical Sociology* 40: 5 (2014), p. 672.

given, but one will suffice, such as the person sentenced to 'indefinite incarceration' until they paid a $300 debt to a lumberyard. Related practices, such as forced eviction for non-payment of debts, have likewise increased. An entire 'subprime' population governed through intensified and punitive police measures has generated yet another 'problem' group from among the working class.[38] As for the servant in the parable recounted by Matthew, the punishment for non-payment of a debt can result in years of penal servitude.

The extent to which indebtedness and incarceration now work together is a reminder of the prison as a form of class power that is expected to have its impact outside as well as inside the prison. The 'industrious' and 'respectable' representatives of capital, whose 'insolvency' is treated as one of the downsides of their industry, are said to deserve the lenient treatment they receive for their indebtedness – treatment seen not only in individual cases, but also in the massive bailout of the global finance industry following the 2008 crisis and the state's willingness to 'socialize' that debt. But supposedly less industrious, less respectable and 'undeserving' debtors, whose inability to manage their indebtedness is seen as entirely their own fault, must be punished accordingly. The policing of the indebted poor reinforces what we know about the policing of the working class in general: it is an expression of coercive political power in a world colonized by capital and law. The threat of imprisonment for non-payment of debt is an expression of the ways in which the police power is mobilized against the working class; the class system is secured and reproduced through social relations of debt and the threat of punishment for indebtedness. Members of this class then become *legitimate objects of the entire apparatus of police power*: government, courts, police, prisons, credit agencies, debt collectors, bailiffs, housing officers, social security offices, social workers – all jointly engaged in the social reproduction of the class. This is total enclosure through political administration, and the range of powers just listed, when considered as a unity, is truly terrifying for anyone caught in the trap they represent.

All of this is a reminder of the complex ways in which the working class is policed. It is also a reminder that the working class is time and

---

38 Annie McClanahan, *Dead Pledges: Debt, Crisis, and Twenty-First-Century Culture* (Stanford, CA: Stanford University Press, 2017), p. 121.

again being taught a lesson (Pay your debts!), that bourgeois society is organized around the notion of *punishment as debt collection*, and that those being punished are paying the biggest debt of all: their 'debt to society'.

To say that a prisoner 'pays their debt to society' is to reiterate the link between debt and sin (as crime), but also as guilt, as noted by Nietzsche in *The Genealogy of Morality* and Freud in 'Dostoevsky and Parricide', where he wrote that Dostoevsky's sense of guilt had taken the form of a burden of debt. This is what Walter Benjamin refers to as the 'demonic ambiguity' that exists in Germanic languages between *Schuld* (guilt) and *Schulden* (debt), and, in other Indo-European languages, between *owe* and *ought*. (This is why defeated nations are often forced into indebtedness, their guilt for their earlier crimes and misdemeanours being transformed into financial debt; and it is also why countries are punished by international organizations such as the IMF, their punishment being justified by their guilt of being in debt.) If, as Benjamin puts it, capitalism is a cult that creates guilt, such guilt also reminds us that capitalism is also a cult organized around debt, and our obedience to the law through which debt is regulated.[39]

To think that a person imprisoned is *paying* their debt to society is to treat time as money. As Evgeny Pashukanis puts it,

> Deprivation of freedom, for a period stipulated in the court sentence, is the specific form in which modern, that is to say bourgeois-capitalist, criminal law embodies the principle of equivalent recompense. This form is unconsciously yet deeply linked with the conception of man in the abstract, and abstract human labour measurable in time.[40]

Just as control over a worker's time is at the heart of capitalist order, so control over a prisoner's time is at the heart of carceral power, which

39 Water Benjamin, 'Capitalism as Religion' (1921), transl. Rodney Livingstone, in Walter Benjamin, *Selected Writings, Vol. 1: 1913–1926*, ed. Marcus Bullock and Michael W. Jennings (Cambridge, MA: Harvard University Press, 1996), pp. 288–9; Émile Benveniste, *Dictionary of Indo-European Concepts and Society*, transl. Elizabeth Palmer (Chicago, IL: Hau, 2016 [1969]), pp. 143–4; Elettra Stimilli, *Debt and Guilt: A Political Philosophy*, transl. Stefania Porcelli (London: Bloomsbury, 2019 [2015]).

40 Evgeny B. Pashukanis, *Law and Marxism: A General Theory*, transl. Barbara Einhorn (London: Ink Links, 1978 [1929]), pp. 180–1.

includes carefully regulated schedules for socializing, exercise, meals, visits and work. The outcome is a new form of distrustful calculation, in the guise of prison regulations that calculate prisoner time in a way that gives the prison file a remarkable resemblance to the financial document. Miranda Joseph cites a handbook of instructions, worksheets and template forms issued by the California Department of Corrections and Rehabilitation, which specifies ways of calculating a prisoner's time, such as 'Pre and Post Sentence Credit', 'Vested Credit', 'Dead Time' and 'Time Imposed'.[41] Such technical calculation of time brings together financial accounting and criminal justice around a prisoner's indebtedness. Herein lies the self-evident character of the prison as the historical twin of the wage-form, as described by Pashukanis, pursued further by Rusche and Kirchheimer in *Punishment and Social Structure* (1939), and elaborated by Michel Foucault in *Discipline and Punish* (1975).[42] By demanding the *time* of the prisoner, imprisonment expresses the idea that the offender has injured society in general, and that a punishment that takes the form of days, months and years is both economically and morally self-justifying in a capitalist order. Hence the expression that the prisoner must 'pay their debt to society'. In punishing the prisoner through the deprivation of *time*, the implication is that the offence has injured *society as a whole*, and not just the victim. The transformation of individuals through the disciplinary apparatus of the prison takes the form of debt in both the abstract ('paying one's debt to society') and the concrete ('doing time'), thereby reinforcing the pacificatory nature of debt more generally.

At the same time, however, the more we are *pacified by debt* and *pacified through debt*, the more the debt relation itself takes on the form of a total institution, like the prison. It is the prison of debt, and not simply the imprisonment of debtors, that so neatly matches most standard definitions of the goal of the prison as a total institution: acceptance of the hierarchy of power, construction and maintenance of order within the working class, inculcation of obedience, salvation of one's soul, and rationalization of one's personality.[43] We are incarcerated in the money

41 Miranda Joseph, *Debt to Society: Accounting for Life Under Capitalism* (Minneapolis: University of Minnesota Press, 2014), pp. 36, 41.

42 Despite Foucault's complete lack of interest in debt as a form of discipline and its relation to imprisonment.

43 John Bender, *Imagining the Penitentiary: Fiction and the Architecture of Mind in Eighteenth-Century England* (Chicago: University of Chicago Press, 1987), p. 31.

machine and imprisoned by debt, with little chance of parole. The outcome is that we are policed as indebted subjects and encouraged to police ourselves in the same ways – even unto death.

And so, while it may feel as if I have already said plenty on the subject in this book, let us conclude by thinking just a little more about death – this time in relation to debt.

'Death has us by the scruff of the neck' II: debt

Pacification is always already directed towards the future, towards cutting off alternatives, blocking threats to the social order, crushing hope. The containment of future possibilities demands the fabrication of political subjects in such a way that they will manage themselves with such containment in mind – with no hope for anything beyond the present. In this, pacification coincides with the temporality of debt.

Neoliberal financialization has sought to make the creditor–debtor relation permanent, with the growth of 'rolling' or 'interest only' debts, in which debt persists despite the interest payments far exceeding the original loan, and even a small debt can end up being unpaid. The debt is permanently *serviced*, rather than paid off. The question asked by financial organizations is now less, 'Does this person earn enough to repay the loan in full?' than, 'How much profit will their servicing of this debt bring us?' This rewriting of the relationship between debt and income is evidenced in loans and mortgages designed to outrun not only the working lives of those in debt, but their entire lifespans.[44] The selling point offered by financial institutions is that this allows households to transfer resources from the future to the present. This is one reason why Marx was so keen to stress the importance of the credit system to capital, because it points to the essentially speculative nature of the process, and hence to capital's futurity. Here, however, we can note that, on a personal level, it also commits us to an always-indebted future, for the rest of our lives and even beyond. This is an indebtedness with no prospect of release: debt as another kind of life sentence. More

44 Lisa Adkins, 'Speculative Futures in the Time of Debt', *Sociological Review* 65: 3 (2017), p. 456; Richard Dienst, *The Bonds of Debt: Borrowing Against the Common Good* (London: Verso, 2017), p. 58.

and more, debts are treated this way by a financial system that seeks to retain us as indebted subjects. If there is one person the credit card companies hate, it is the person who pays off their debt at the end of every month. We are of little use to the system if we have paid off all our debts: their profit depends on our indebtedness. Hence Marx's comment that the death of the poor man is the worst eventuality for the creditor. Capital wants us alive because it wants us to service the debt.

Servicing the debt implies financial payment, of course, but it also connotes *submission* and *obedience*. Capital wants us *in servitude*, the servile nature of wage labour being reinforced and even supplanted by the servile nature of indebtedness; the *bond* of indebtedness indicates our *bondage*. For this servitude and bondage to be engrained in us, embedded in our psyche, debt must become habitual, precisely matching the way that capital and the state like us to make a habit of all the other mechanisms of obedience through which pacification occurs. As a *bad habit*, debt becomes an *addiction*.

The roots of our idea of 'addiction' lie in the Latin *addictio*, but the 'disease model' of addiction is relatively recent, emerging in the late eighteenth century. In Roman law, *addictio* was the legal term for the act by which a debtor was handed over as a slave to his creditor. A sentence was pronounced by a judge, or *praetor*, according to the ancient law of the Twelve Tables. The *addictus* could be physically handed over to the creditor and held for sixty days, or until the debt was paid. As I have noted, failure to pay the debt rendered the debtor a slave to be kept, used, or sold as property. This sense of 'addiction' remained in place during the rise of capitalism, connoting, the *OED* tells us, the 'formal delivery of a person or property to an individual, typically in accordance with a judicial decision', 'the binding of a person to another as a servant' and 'the state of being so bound'. But, in the light of our contemporary state of habitual indebtedness, along with our other multiple addictions, we are all 'debtor-addicts', to use Mark Fisher's term, bound to this (bad) habit, and thus bound as servants to the forces that manage it.[45] If the message from capital is that there is 'no exit' and that of the security state that there is 'no hope', then these messages are delivered in a package of debt, and marked by the habitual ways in which we submit to the endless

45 Mark Fisher, *Capitalist Realism: Is There No Alternative?* (Winchester: Zero, 2009), pp. 25–6.

fabrication of servile subjects, with no vision of a future beyond debt: debt now, debt in the future, debt for life, debt to death.

There is something very peculiar about the relationship between debt and death. Since debt and sin were once so close, and since 'the wages of sin is death' (Romans 6:23), then perhaps this should not surprise us. Consider the mortgage, often the biggest debt incurred by most people, but obscured by the profound sense of property ownership that it is meant to entail (the label 'homeowner' usually being a euphemism for 'heavily indebted person'). The mortgage is literally a *death pledge*. Dictionaries of etymology inform us that the 'mortgage' was originally so called because the debt becomes void – that is, dead – when the pledge is redeemed, or that, should the borrower default on the payments, then the property pledged as security is lost, becoming 'dead' to them. In Part I of his *Institutes of the Lawes of England* (1628), Sir Edward Coke makes the following observation:

> It seemeth that the cause why it is called mortgage is, for that it is doubtful whether the Lessor will pay at the day limited such sum, or not; and if he doth not pay, then the land which is put in pledge upon condition for the payment of the money is taken from him for ever, and so dead to him . . . And if he doth pay the money, then the pledge is dead.

Coke's comment is in fact more or less an exact quote from *Littleton's Tenures*, one of the first books on English law, written in French by Sir Thomas Littleton in the late fifteenth century.[46] But as a way to describe a debt taken on for decades, the exact amount of time being based partly on a calculation of one's expected death, the etymology rings remarkably true for other reasons, too. Yet this aspect of the mortgage points also to broader issues, which pertain to death.

'[E]veryone owes nature a death and must expect to pay the debt', wrote Freud in an essay written during the First World War called 'Thoughts for the Times on War and Death'. He attributes the line to

46 Sir Edward Coke, *The First Part of the Institutes of the Lawes of England, in Three Volumes, Vol. II. Fifteenth Edition* (London: E. and R. Brooke, 1744 [1628]), Part I, Section 332 (no pagination); Eugene Wambaugh, ed., *Littleton's Tenures in English* (Washington, DC: John Byrne, 1903), pp. 156–7.

Shakespeare, in *Henry IV*, but in that play the talk is of our debt to God: 'Why, thou owest God a death' (V.I) – providing a reminder of the point made above concerning God's book of accounts, and that we must in the end satisfy our debt to him. With the secularization of modernity, 'God' was increasingly replaced by 'nature': 'To *die*, is the great debt and tribute due unto nature', Laurence Sterne observes in *Tristram Shandy*, one of Freud's literary influences. Picking up on some of these connections, Jacques Derrida observes that it does not really matter whether the debt is to God or to Nature, because the point is that, once our death corresponds to the payment of a debt, we die indebted; and because we are indebted, and therefore in some sense, guilty, so every death is like a retribution, or the execution of a verdict, or compensation for damages. The dead person disappears as a subject of rights and obligations, and is thereby liberated from being a debtor. It is for this reason, I think, that death figures in so many books on debt. A life debt 'pledges allegiance to the absolute sovereignty that is death', observes Michel Aglietta in his history of money.[47] It is also for this reason that, so often when debt is discussed, the topic of suicide as a means of liberating oneself from the burden of it is never far away.

Herein lies the significance of Pollock and Maitland's reference to redemption, cited above, with its roots in *redeem*, meaning to buy oneself out of slavery. Coming into the English language in early modernity, roughly in the mid fourteenth century, redemption is 'deliverance from sin and spiritual death', from the Latin *redemptionem*, meaning 'a buying back' or 'releasing', and *redimere*, 'to redeem'; and then from the Old French *redimer*, 'buy back'. 'To redeem', in the sense of 'making amends' for something, dates from the early sixteenth century. The idea of debt redemption is a reminder of debt's religious connotations, and of the fact that money, far from being essentially secular and rational, is in fact sacred to the core. But it is a reminder more than anything of the

47 Sigmund Freud, 'Thoughts for the Times on War and Death' (1915), in Sigmund Freud, *Standard Edition of the Complete Psychological Works, Vol. 14* (London: Vintage, 2001), p. 289; Laurence Sterne, *The Life and Opinions of Tristram Shandy* (Harmondsworth: Penguin, 1985 [1759–67]), p. 349; Jacques Derrida, *The Death Penalty, Vol. 2*, transl. Elizabeth Rottenberg (Chicago: University of Chicago Press, 2017 [2015]), pp. 32, 70; Michel Aglietta, *Money: 5,000 Years of Debt and Power*, transl. David Broder (London: Verso, 2018 [2016]), pp. 60–1.

fact that true redemption comes with death. The recalibration of debt requires the calculation of death, which turns out to be our final payment: our final release – from debt.

Pollock and Maitland observe that, in addition to its connection to the gage and the wage, the mortgage was originally thought of as being close to usury, and the usurious nature of such 'gages' was a matter of some importance in the transition from feudalism to capitalism. The concept of usury has a long and complicated history, not least because its meaning was never entirely clear. Sometimes it has been distinguished from 'interest', sometimes conflated with it, and sometimes conflated only with high or excessive interest. But it also eventually came to be known in common law and colloquial English as 'compound interest' (*anatocisme* in French, *anatocismo* in Italian and Spanish). A further reason why the concept of usury is so complicated lies in the fact that it was once widely condemned as immoral and unlawful, but was gradually legalized, losing its moral stigma. It is this shift that interests me here.

'There must be no lending at interest', Plato announces in *The Laws*. In *The Politics*, Aristotle describes usury as 'the most hated' sort of money-making.[48] For Aristotle, usury is unnatural because it undermines friendship, one of the core themes of his political thought: 'a creditor . . . is not a friend; for, if a man is a friend, he gives and he does not lend.'[49] But Aristotle also regards usury as unnatural because it seeks to 'make a gain out of money itself', which encourages the belief that money can breed money – a point to which we will return. Usury was also prohibited in Republican Rome. In his letters to Atticus, Cicero tells the story of having to deal with Brutus, who had been using his administrative post in Cyprus to extort money from the people at high rates of compound interest, sometimes as high as 48 per cent:

> If Brutus thinks that I ought to have allowed 48 per cent, when throughout my province I have recognized only 12 per cent, and have fixed this rate in my edict, with the approval of the most grasping

48 Plato, *The Laws*, transl. Trevor J. Saunders (Harmondsworth: Penguin, 1975), p. 211; Aristotle, *The Politics*, transl. T. A. Sinclair (Harmondsworth: Penguin, 1992), p. 87.

49 Aristotle, 'Problems', in *The Complete Works of Aristotle, Vol. 2*, ed. Jonathan Barnes (Princeton, NJ: Princeton University Press, 1984), p. 1493.

usurers . . . well I shall be sorry that he is angry with me, but I shall be far sorrier at discovering he is not the man I imagined he was.

The term Cicero uses for this is *anatocismo*, a word he apparently introduced into Latin from the Greek ἀνατοκισμός (*anatokismós*), which itself stems from *ana* ('above') and *tokos* ('a product'), though Cicero appears to have meant 'interest again'.[50] The *anatocism* is an agreement whereby a debtor repays a debt along with the interest accrued, but with the interest calculated on both the original loan and the interest accrued on it. The interest is 'compounded', so to speak. What this means is that the debt can produce 'interest again', on an ongoing basis, 'above the product'.

As well as being condemned by the Greeks and Romans, the usurer was also a despised figure in the major religions. In Old Testament books such as in Exodus (22:25), Deuteronomy (23:19–21), Leviticus (25:36), Ezekiel (18:7–9, 22:12) and Psalms (15:5), usury is a grave sin, and New Testament reports of Jesus's injunction to 'lend, hoping for nothing again' (Luke, 6:35), are often taken to be a Christian injunction against usury. The commandment in Deuteronomy, the Old Testament book that formed the foundation for the morality of the Hebrew brotherhood, is: 'Thou shalt not lend upon usury [*neshek* – also sometimes translated as 'interest'] to thy brother . . . To a stranger thou mayest lend upon usury; but unto thy brother thou shalt not' (23:19–20). The condemnation of the usurer was for multiple reasons. Usury was an indication that one was seeking to make a profit without working, thereby undermining the Biblical injunction that only 'in the sweat of thy face shalt thou eat bread' (Genesis 3:19). Usury was also a sign of avarice, and that one was worshipping Mammon rather than God, and no one can serve two masters (Matthew 6:24). At the same time, usury was seen as theft (of time as well as money) – an unjust and shameful act. All in all, it was regarded as a grievous sin.

Such condemnation continued through the centuries. In the fourth century, in 'Homily 12: A Psalm of David against Usurers', Saint Basil described usury as an act of 'the greatest inhumanity'. Thomas Aquinas, citing Aristotle in his *Summa Theologica*, written between 1265 and

50 Cicero, *Letters to Atticus, Vol. I*, transl. E. O. Winstedt (London: Heinemann, 1919), pp. 408–9, 423.

1274, stated the position clearly: 'To accept usury for the loan of money is itself unjust.'[51] The Lateran Councils of 1139, 1179 and 1215, the Second Council of Lyons of 1274, and the Council of Vienne of 1311–12 all sought to contain a growing wave of usury. The Council of 1179, for example, noted: 'Nearly everywhere the crime of usury has become so firmly rooted that many, omitting other business, practise usury as if it were permitted, and in no way observe how it is forbidden in both the Old and New Testament.' To withstand the increase in the practice, the Council denied usurers communion and Christian burial. The Council of Lyons declared that usury 'devours souls and swallows up property', encouraging authorities to expel usurers from their territories and deny them Christian burial.[52] Meanwhile, the Council of Vienne declared that any ruler or magistrate who sanctioned usury would be excommunicated. This was the reason Dante, in *The Divine Comedy* (1308–20), put usurers in the seventh circle of hell, along with sodomites and blasphemers. Usury was also considered contrary to Islam, the Quran asserting: 'God has permitted trading but made usury unlawful . . . God has laid His curse on usury' (30:39).

Beyond the theological context, usury was also widely understood to be contrary to the good of the people. The condemnation of usury found in the later socialist tradition was part of the wider condemnation of injustice in economic exchange from centuries before, and hence part of a broader argument about the just society, evident in the popular hatred of usury that Marx thought could be easily seen among the people. Hence the innumerable fables concerning the usurer who goes to hell, or whose money turns to withered leaves in his safe, or who is crushed by a stone on entering the church on his wedding day. As R. H. Tawney notes, the power of this combination of popular consciousness and religious doctrine is reflected in the fact that cities that were the commercial hubs of Europe, such as Florence, often fined bankers for usury in the fourteenth century, while others, such as Coventry, decreed that no usurer could become mayor or councillor.[53]

---

51 Aquinas, Summa Theologica, in A. P. d'Entrèves, ed., *Aquinas: Selected Political Writings* (Oxford: Basil Blackwell, 1954), p. 173.

52 Third Lateran Council – 1179 A.D.; Second Council of Lyons – 1274 A.D. Both at papalencyclicals.net.

53 Marx, *Capital, Vol. 3*, pp. 730, 735; Marx, *Capital, Vol. 1*, p. 267; R. H. Tawney, *Religion and the Rise of Capitalism* (Harmondsworth: Penguin, 1938), pp. 49–50.

Usury, then, was considered contrary to the world's major religions, contrary to Aristotelian philosophy, contrary to nature, and contrary to popular notions of justice. To make sense of how this situation changed, how even exorbitant (that is, usurious) interest rates came to be an accepted feature of capitalist society, and the role this development has played in making debt integral to our pacification, we need to consider the old debate about the relationship between religion and the rise of capitalism.

The starting point for analysing that relationship tends to be Max Weber's thesis in *The Protestant Ethic and the Spirit of Capitalism* (1904–05). To stress his case for discerning the spirit of capitalism in the Protestant ethic, Weber rather downplayed the role of the Catholic Church. Identifying the drive and effort expressed by an individual that is characteristic of both the ethic of Protestant salvation and the spirit of capitalist accumulation, Weber essentially dismissed Catholicism as a kind of pre-modern magic – 'magic' being one of the key concepts in his sociology of religion – and the Catholic priest as a 'magician' seemingly able to perform the miracle of transubstantiation, holding the key to eternal life in his hands, and thereby able to relieve an individual of personal responsibility for planning and calculating their lives. Weber admits that this characterization of Catholicism enacts a certain violence to the historical reality, but his overall argument has entrenched the idea that the Catholic Church had little to do with the rise of capitalist modernity, which needed the ideology of Protestantism to bring it properly into being. For this reason, the idea of a dense entanglement between the 'spirit of capitalism' and the 'Protestant ethic' became the prevailing view for generations of scholars.

In *Der Bourgeois* (1913), a book translated into English two years later as *The Quintessence of Capitalism*, Werner Sombart challenged this prevailing view. Rather than seeing the Church as essentially opposed to the new type of profit-seeking creature that came into being in the capitalist age, Sombart reminds us that 'the origins of capitalism made their appearance at a time when the Church held sway over men's minds in all their activities'. Capitalism was brought into being in Renaissance Italy some two centuries before Martin Luther announced the Ninety-Five Theses, and found significant ideological support within the Church's teachings. Sombart also asks us to bear in mind that it was the economic imperialism of Catholic rather than Protestant powers that opened up the world economy, and that the first commercial capitals of Europe were predominantly Catholic. In Florence, 'the Bethlehem of the capitalist spirit', the rising class of merchants were devoted Catholics – albeit ones who sought to synthesize their 'religious zeal' with the teachings of Roman thinkers such as Cicero, Seneca and Livy. The same was true across Tuscany, including that citadel of security and policing discussed in Chapter 2, namely Siena, as found in the writings of figures such as Bernardino of Siena.

Three points emerge from this. First, the scholastic notion of *liberalitas* was especially important, seeking to find a way between the two extremes of prodigality and avarice (one of the 'evils' of bad government in Lorenzetti's frescoes in Siena, as we saw). Second, on the other hand, Church ethics condemned idleness. This condemnation applied to humans, obviously, in that people must work. But it also began to be applied to money, which was expected to be equally 'active'. From this idea of money being active, a distinction emerged between borrowing for unproductive purposes (in a simple loan) and borrowing for productive purposes (as capital). In the first case, money is barren; in the second, it is productive, 'possessing in that capacity not merely the character of money or of a commodity, but something more – the power of creation, which we term "capital"' (as Bernardino of Siena put it, cited by Sombart). In this conception of money, Sombart argues, the Schoolmen had a better understanding of capitalism than the later Puritans. In fact, Sombart goes so far as to suggest that, in their conception of money as productive, in motion, and in need of creativity, the Catholic scholars understood capital in ways that political economy has more recently had to relearn from Marx. The third point, and the most important one here, is that the Schoolmen's notion of money as productive meant that they sought to liberate it from restrictions, and thereby to allow borrowing and lending. This had an impact on the question of usury, since it encouraged the view that borrowing and lending money were ways of allowing it to be fruitful.[54]

The point of this discussion is not to mediate between Weber and Sombart, or to weight their respective influence over our understanding

54 Werner Sombart, *The Quintessence of Capitalism: A Study of the History and Psychology of the Modern Business Man*, transl. M. Epstein (London: T. Fisher Unwin, 1915 [1913]), pp. 228–48.

of capitalism. Rather, if we take them together and consider them in terms of the normative pacification inherent in Christianity's social power, then perhaps a significant part of this pacification can be found in the loosening of strictures concerning lending, usury and high interest, and hence the gradual legitimizing of the condition of indebtedness.

In Medieval Latin, the idea of *interesse* shifted from being something about which I am concerned – that I have an *interest* in – to a compensatory payment for a loss. There was a Roman legal concept of interest that provided for a penalty to be paid by a borrower who was slow in repaying a loan. The 'interest' was not part of the loan agreement but was a kind of penalty, in that it referred to a payment which was to correspond to the difference between, or the amount that came 'in between' (that is, *quod inter est*), the present financial position of the lender and the position he would have been in if he had not made the loan. Lewis Hyde puts it as follows: '[I]f someone loses something of mine, something I have an "interest" in, then he pays me my *interesse* to make good the loss (and he pays me nothing if I have no interest)'. The word thus came to refer to what might be considered 'lost' when capital was loaned, and so a debtor who defaulted on a loan was obliged to pay a fixed amount described in his contract, namely the *interesse*. Such payment was supposed to differ from *usura*, meaning a direct charge for the use of money, but, in practice, the difference was not that great. *Interesse* and *usura* overlapped in both theory and practice, and the condemnation of the latter often implied a condemnation of the former, which is why they were widely considered to be one and the same practice, and impossible to differentiate in a systematic way. A distinction gradually emerged between interest and 'excessive' interest, usury being identified with the excess. By the time capitalism came fully to accept and justify 'interest' on loans, a social order grounded in the general doctrine of *self*-interest helped make *financial* interest more palatable.[55] Capital wants us to have an interest in interest, and by the early seventeenth century each notion of interest had come to reinforce the other. This is the context in which we can begin to understand the usurer as central to the birth of capitalism, to grasp properly why debt has become so prevalent to capitalism's

55 Lewis Hyde, *The Gift* (Edinburgh: Canongate, 2007), p. 125; Albert O. Hirschman, *The Passions and the Interests: Political Arguments for Capitalism before Its Triumph* (Princeton, NJ: Princeton University Press, 1977), pp. 31–44.

contemporary shape, and gain a better sense of why this draws our attention to what it is that has us by the scruff of the neck.

In *Capital*, and in the notes made during its writing, Marx points to usury as one of the first forms in which capital confronts landed property, helping to form the preconditions for industrial capital.[56] This is part of his wider argument about the importance of debt to the rise of capitalism. The fundamental shift in the status of usury lies in the rise of bourgeois order. The increase in chartered burghers and the first elements of the bourgeoisie in growing urban areas, the slow decline of feudal corporate forms, the increase in commerce and growth of manufacturing, the discovery and colonization of the Americas, maritime trade, peasant revolts – all were parts of a massive revolution in economic and social relations that effected a shift in consciousness, not least in the consciousness of money and practices associated with it. Usury came to be tolerated so long as it was confined to the kind of contracts within which high interest rates were more easily accepted. Marx points out that those rates often hit 100 per cent in Charlemagne's time, and even 216 percent at Lindau im Bodensee in 1344.[57] In this context, some of the subtle phrasing in decisions of the Lateran Councils took on a new significance. The Third Lateran Council (1179) singled out 'notorious' usurers, for example, while the Fourth Lateran Council (1215) singled out usurers whose practices were 'heavy and excessive'. This enabled scholastic arguments to emerge offering excuses for practices that would once have been condemned as usurious. High interest rates were deemed appropriate for delayed payments, for example, and usury was increasingly justified in terms of the risk being taken, in the sense that one might lose the capital that one had lent. Likewise, usury was also sometimes described as payment for certain kinds of 'labour', including what might have been seen as the 'labour' of the usurer.

Usury received further legitimation with the birth of purgatory. Like most religions, Christianity imagined two destinations in the afterlife: Heaven and Hell. Between the year 1000 and the thirteenth century, this distinction came to be seen as a little too simplistic, and for many unbearable, in that it did not seem to allow space for

56 Marx, *Capital, Vol. 1*, pp. 247, 267, 740, 914; Marx, *Capital, Vol. 3*, pp. 515, 728–32, 745.

57 Marx, *Capital, Vol. 3*, p. 732.

redemption after death. Might there be a place where the dead could be redeemed? From this question, the concept of *Purgatorium* emerged. According to Jacques Le Goff, the idea of Purgatory points to an intermediary position which helps to identify those who are neither totally good nor totally evil, meaning that it is unclear whether they are destined for Heaven or Hell. To avoid being condemned to Hell for eternity, they go into Purgatory, suffer the kind of punishments associated with Hell, but can come through such ordeals as a kind of purifying trial, after which they can be saved and go to Heaven. This created the opportunity for people who were not entirely evil eventually to be saved. What this means is that the invention of Purgatory created a way for those who once would have been destined for Hell to escape that fate, make restitution for their sins, and eventually take a place in Heaven. After all, the Church loves nothing more than a repentant sinner. The argument made by Le Goff is that one of the functions of Purgatory was to save from Hell certain types of sinners once condemned as totally evil, but increasingly less so given the new material and commercial conditions. One such sinner was the usurer. In this sense, the invention of Purgatory, as a space and time through which the salvation of the usurer became possible, can be seen as a further element of the Church's assistance in the birth of capitalism.[58] By creating the possibility of escaping Hell by going to Heaven via Purgatory (or via the 'suburbs of hell', as Protestants sometimes described it), the Church eased the pressure on acts previously regarded as sinful.[59] Maybe the usurer was not so bad as to go straight to Hell. Maybe the usurer could in fact go to Heaven, albeit via Purgatory. In legitimizing the practice of usury in this way, the Church helped to facilitate the rise of what was to become a central practice of capitalism, and 'one of the complicitous winks that Christianity sent the usurer's way during the thirteenth century'.[60]

John Maynard Keynes once commented that it was perhaps no accident that those people who did most to put the promise of immortality into the heart and essence of religion were the same ones who

58 Jacques Le Goff, *The Birth of Purgatory*, transl. Arthur Goldhammer (London: Scolar, 1984 [1981]), pp. 76–7, 93, 305.

59 John Hartcliffe, *A Discourse Against Purgatory* (London: n.p., 1685), p. 10.

60 Jacques Le Goff, *Your Money or Your Life: Economy and Religion in the Middle Ages*, transl. Patricia Ranum (Massachusetts: MIT Press, 1988 [1986]), p. 92.

stressed the 'dizzy virtues' of compound interest.[61] It was certainly the case that forms of interest previously condemned increasingly came to be regarded as legitimate. The Deuteronomic distinction between foreigner and brother was now taken to imply that *some* degree of usury/interest was acceptable; as the distinction became ever less relevant with the idea of 'universal brotherhood', so the Deuteronomic injunctions against usury/interest bore increasingly less weight. By the sixteenth century, the question of the usury 'offence' was a common topic among theologians and canon lawyers. Martin Luther interpreted Biblical passages about usury and interest simply as calls to act generously. In a 'Short Sermon on Usury' (1519), which became part of his treatise *On Trade and Usury* (1524), Luther argues that usurers commit a sin when their actions violate more general Christian principles, such as that one should not worship Mammon and that one should treat others in the way one wishes to be treated. But those who participate in only a little usury are not to be treated as gross extortioners.

John Calvin pushed this argument much further, which is one reason why he looms so large in the 'protestant ethic' thesis. In a series of essays and letters (most notably 'On Usury' in 1545, and a letter to Claude de Sachin the same year), Calvin argued that the Deuteronomic precept to lend without usury applied only to Jewish society, and was by no means a universal injunction. Otherwise, why would God have allowed the Hebrews to practise usury in their relations with the Gentiles? God permitted many things 'for the policing of the Jews' that did not need to be extended to others, and the specific laws given to the Jews could be overridden: '[T]he situation in which God placed the Jews and many other circumstances permitted them to trade conveniently among themselves without usuries'. For Protestants today, the situation was different. 'Therefore, I do not feel that usuries were forbidden to us simply'. For Calvin, so long as it remained within a general sense of 'equity or charity', usury was neither sinful nor unlawful. According to him, the scriptures forbade only the practice of excessive usury against the poor. Indeed, the scriptures can and should be read as suggesting that we should lend to the poor to help them. In other words, if the poor

61 John Maynard Keynes, 'Economic Possibilities for our Grandchildren' (1930), in *Essays in Persuasion* (London: Macmillan, 1931), p. 371.

need to go into debt to survive, why not allow them to do so? Better still, why *not* charge them interest?

Here, the Protestant ethic really was important in the rise of capitalism, albeit in ways that built on developments within Catholicism, since the position was one in which capital and credit were seen as indispensable. The financier was a useful member of society, and lending at interest was part and parcel of God's injunction to industrious labour (so long as the interest rate was not 'unreasonable'). In effect, Calvin's exegesis of the Deuteronomic distinction brought about its demise, helping to justify one of the key practices of an emerging and increasingly powerful social class that needed a new Gospel to preach: the Gospel of Interest.[62]

Given England's place in the rise and development of capitalism, it is unsurprising to find this position articulated most clearly there. In 1545, parliament had passed an Act establishing 10 per cent as the legal rate of interest for the reign of Henry VIII, supplanting the common-law notion of usury, only for that Act to be repealed in 1552 under Edward VI, when interest was made illegal again. In 1571, the merchants with an interest in interest mobilized to achieve the abrogation of the Usury Act of 1552. The parliamentary debate that ensued had little to do with economics, and everything to do with questions of God's will. Hence one finds debates in parliament concerning the books of the Bible in which usury is discussed, the work of Aquinas and Augustine, the nature of the Devil, and forms of excommunication.[63] Some parliamentarians argued that God did not absolutely forbid usury, which he would have explicitly done if he thought it that bad, while others held that it made sense to permit a little usury rather than damage the commerce that depends on it. Others made the additional claim that would be repeated time and again through the centuries: *We do this to help the poor.*

By the end of the sixteenth century, an increasing number of people were arguing that the question of usury be left to the state rather than to religion, since even if usury was a sin it should still be up to state officials to decide how it was to be regulated. By 1610, the Bishop of Bangor,

62 Benjamin Nelson, *The Idea of Usury: From Tribal Brotherhood to Universal Otherhood* (Chicago: University of Chicago Press, 1949), pp. 73–4; Tawney, *Religion and the Rise of Capitalism*, pp. 116–17.

63 Norman Jones, *God and the Moneylenders: Usury and Law in Early Modern England* (Oxford: Blackwell, 1989), pp. 25–46, 163–4.

Henry Rowlands, could write: 'A bastard child borne, usury is taken now to be almost legitimate' – a view confirmed through the early seventeenth century.[64] In 1624 the English parliament passed a new Usury Act that overrode religious strictures. A year later, Francis Bacon added an essay on usury to the 1625 edition of his *Essays*, which noted the multiple ways in which usury is condemned yet still argued that usury must be allowed: first, because otherwise people would not lend freely; second, because it encouraged commerce. And in a book on money and law written in the late 1620s, Sir Robert Filmer argued that the debate over usury was 'a mere popish question . . . usury is no where in Scripture forbidden to Christians'. Likewise, Hugo Grotius, in his well-known work *The Rights of War and Peace* (1625), suggested that the laws against usury denied the idea that man had made things to be fruitful rather than barren, and this included money.[65] For these writers, usury is a matter of contract and conscience – a matter of economic expedience rather than a sin – and necessary for the new world of commerce.

To put it bluntly, between roughly the 1570s and 1620s, a key period in the development of capital but also in the debate about the pacification of the social order in which capital was going to thrive, usury was liberated from religious restrictions and legitimized as a secular political ideology and commercial practice. In 1570, many people were still looking back at the power of the Old and New Testaments and the strictures against moneylenders. By 1630, most were looking forward, towards the power of finance capital and removal of restrictions on money being lent, so that more could be made. To be sure, strong condemnations of usury could still be found in works such as the anonymously authored *Usurie Arraigned and Condemned* (1625) and Nathaniel Holmes's *Usury Is Injury* (1640); but the powerful commercial interests, along with political and theological thinkers, were finding it increasingly easy to ignore them. By the middle of the seventeenth century usury – once considered the opposite of charity; close cousin of idolatry; damaging to the commonwealth; detested as a vice by all major religions; associated

64 Cited in ibid., p. 145.

65 Francis Bacon, 'Of Usury' (1625), in *Essays* (London: Dent, 1972), pp. 123–6; Sir Robert Filmer, *Quæstio quodlibetica, or, A discourse Whether It May Bee Lawfull to Take Use for Money* (London: n.p., 1653), Preface (a date of composition of the 1620s is suggested by the editor, Sir Roger Twysden); Hugo Grotius, *The Rights of War and Peace*, ed. Richard Tuck (Indianapolis: Liberty Fund, 2005 [1625]), p. 759.

with sorcery, magic and necromancy – came to be seen as acceptable, even respectable and necessary, albeit 'regulated'. A man suspected of being a usurer was once 'taken for a devil in the likeness of a man', his house seen as the home of the devil, shunned by men and women, barred by priests from the Holy Supper, observed Philip Caesar in *General Discourse against the Damnable Sect of Vsurers* (1578). But now? 'Good Lorde, howe is the Worlde chaunged?'

Quite how much the world had changed is evident from the work of a range of thinkers through the seventeenth and eighteenth centuries, which culminated in the abolition of usury laws in the nineteenth century. When usury was gradually being legalized in the sixteenth century, legal limits of 10 per cent had been introduced, gradually reduced to 6 per cent in 1651. In the 1660s Sir Josiah Child published two pamphlets advocating a reduction of the legal rate of interest to 4 per cent, to match that of commercially successful Holland. This debate saw the intervention of John Locke, soon to become the grandfather of liberal thought. In 1668 Locke produced a manuscript, 'Some of the Consequences that Are Like to Follow Upon Lessening of Interest to 4 Per Cent', written as a reply to Child and possibly at the behest of the chancellor of the exchequer, Lord Shaftesbury. Locke argued that charging interest was necessary to facilitate trade, and explicitly placed the figure of the usurer in that role.[66] This fed into Locke's work in the years that followed, culminating in *Some Considerations of the Consequences of the Lowering of Interest and the Raising the Value of Money* (1692):

> The first thing to be consider'd, is, Whether the Price of the Hire of Money can be regulated by Law. And to that I think, generally speaking, one may say, 'tis manifest it cannot. For since it's impossible, to make a Law that shall hinder a Man from giving away his Money or Estate to whom he pleases, it will be impossible, by any Contrivance of Law, to hinder Men, skill'd in the Power they have over their own Goods, and the ways of Conveying them to others, to purchase Money to be Lent them at what Rate soever their Occasions shall

66 John Locke, 'Some of the Consequences that Are Like to Follow Upon Lessening of Interest to 4 Per Cent' (1668), in John Locke, *Locke on Money, Vol. I*, ed. Patrick Hyde Kelly (Oxford: Clarendon, 1991).

> make it necessary for them to have it. It will be a prejudice to none, but those who most need assistance and help; I mean widows and orphans, and others uninstructed in the arts and management of more skilful men.[67]

Locke was making some significant claims. Money is 'subject to all the same laws of value' as commodities and land. Money is 'a universal commodity'. Money is 'as necessary to trade as food is to life'. Money does not need regulating by law. Money can and should be lent at whatever interest people will pay:

> My having more Money in my Hand than I can, or am disposed to use in buying and selling, makes me able to lend: And another's want of so much Money as he could employ in Trade, makes him willing to borrow. But why then, and for what Consideration doth he pay *Use*? For the same Reason, and upon as good Consideration, as the Tenant pays Rent for your Land. For as the unequal Distribution of Land, (you having more than you can or will manure, and another less) brings you a Tenant for your Land; and the same unequal Distribution of Money, (I having more than I can or will employ, and another less) brings me a Tenant for my Money: So my Money is apt in Trade, by the Industry of the Borrower, to produce more than Six per Cent. to the Borrower.

To push the point, Locke openly acknowledged that this was usury:

> The Usurer's Money would bring him in no Yearly profit, if he did not lend it, (supposing he employs it not himself) and so his Six per Cent. may seem to be the Fruit of another Man's Labour, yet he shares not near so much of the profit of another Man's Labour, as he that lets Land to a Tenant.[68]

All of this reinforced the point first made in Locke's 1668 essay: that borrowing money at interest is necessary for some, unavoidable for

67 John Locke, *Some Considerations of the Consequences of the Lowering of Interest and the Raising the Value of Money* (1692), in *Locke on Money, Vol. I*, p. 211.
68 Ibid., pp. 250–1.

others, lawful, and fundamental to the 'constitution of humane society'.[69] This was a point of principle Locke also used in his personal life: whenever he lent his friends money, he made sure to take it back with interest. In 1676 he lent Lady Windham £600, and took £36 a year in interest; and in the 1690s he lent David Thomas £600, repayable at 5 per cent interest. So important to Locke was the principle of charging interest that when Thomas died, his son received a letter from Locke expressing condolences and then detailing the money that he was owed from Thomas's estate.[70]

One finds similar arguments through the following century and into the nineteenth. In his *Commentaries on the Laws of England*, William Blackstone argues that religious strictures against usury are in essence political. The enemies of interest, he argues, make little distinction between it and usury, and do so 'by the law of Moses among the Jews', from Aristotle's teaching, and from canon law. Yet he argues that the law of Moses was a political rather than moral precept, in that it 'prohibited the Jews from taking usury from their brethren the Jews', but 'permitted them to take it of a stranger'. This, Blackstone argues, 'proves that the taking of moderate usury, or a reward for the use, for so the word signifies, is not *malum in se*, since it was allowed where any but an Israelite was concerned'. These comments occur just before Blackstone states that the bodies of debtors can be taken and used by those to whom they owe money. The position is restated over and over: in Montesquieu's *The Spirit of the Laws* (1748), Anne Robert Jacques Turgot's 'Reflections on the Formation and Distribution of Wealth' (1766), Richard Price's *Observations on the Importance of the American Revolution* (1785) and Jeremy Bentham's essays on usury in 1787, written while he was visiting Russia to assist his brother Samuel in establishing a factory system for Catherine the Great, and later published as *Defence of Usury* (1837). The extent to which opinion about usury, compound interest, and interest charged on debts in general had changed is clear from a major work published in London in 1807, called *The New Encyclopaedia; or, Universal Dictionary of Arts and Sciences*, which offers an entry for *anatocism*. Initially described as 'the accumulation of interest upon interest' and

69 Locke, 'Some of the Consequences', pp.182–3; *Some Considerations*, p. 251.

70 Maurice Cranston, *John Locke: A Biography* (Oxford: Oxford University Press, 1985), pp. 115, 377, 393.

'a species of usury generally forbidden', the *Encyclopaedia* goes on to equate *anatocism* with compound interest, adding that it is ultimately 'difficult to discover, wherein the injustice lies'.

By the nineteenth century, then, the road was clear for exploitative loan arrangements, excessive interest, predatory financing, unjust lending rates, and the kind of loansharking that continues to this day. The road was marked out initially by the theological and political arguments I have outlined, but it was paved by the law in capitalist states. Usury laws were repealed in England in 1854, Denmark in 1855, Spain in 1856, Sardinia, Holland, Norway, and the Swiss Canton of Geneva in 1857, Oldenburg in 1858, Bremen in 1859, Saxony and Sweden in 1864, Belgium in 1865, Prussia, the North German Confederation, and parts of Austria in 1867. As the increasingly liberalizing states abolished usury laws, so too did the Church develop a highly convenient 'elasticity' (the term is Weber's) concerning its supposedly eternal prohibition against usury: priests were encouraged by the Vatican to refrain from inquiring during confession about infractions of the prohibition against usury, and to grant absolution for any confessions to the practice.[71] With all the old condemnations of usury now abandoned, the capitalist system could proceed on the basis of its express recognition.

Usury, then, became consolidated as a form of liberal rationality, and the idea of 'high interest rates' became bourgeois society's more neutral term for what was once universally despised as usury. Indeed, in terms of the combined power of law, financial organizations, corporations, a generalized culture of indebtedness, and the willingness of politicians to turn a blind eye to practices which would have once seen lenders cast into Hell, usury has in fact become a major weapon in our pacification. Critics occasionally write about 'excessiveness' or the 'abuse' of high interest rates to condemn the extortionate rates of interest sometimes charged: 'abusury', as some have called it.[72] The rulers of the universe simply tut and look the other way. We remain captured.

Is there any escape from this captivity? One option is forgiveness and a jubilee. In Deuteronomy (15:1–6), it states: 'At the end of *every* seven years thou shalt make a release. And this *is* the manner of the release:

71 Weber, *Economy and Society. Vol. 1*, p. 562.

72 Alexander X. Douglas, *The Philosophy of Debt* (Abingdon: Routledge, 2016), xiv, pp. 58–9.

Every creditor that lendeth *ought* unto his neighbour shall release *it*.' This is part of the pretext for the sabbatical year, which sees an end to both debt and servitude, as well as a period of rest, and the jubilee. As described in Leviticus, the jubilee is a year of emancipation and restoration, proclaimed by the blast of trumpets throughout the land, during which fields are to be left uncultivated. One advanced modern translation offers Leviticus 25 under the title: 'Jubilee, the Priestly Solution for Economic Injustice'.[73] Henry Schaeffer suggests that the idea of the jubilee in Biblical books such as Leviticus is really a compromise measure designed to bridge the gap between the early 'communism' of the old Hebrew clan brotherhoods and the later institution of private landownership. Robert Yelle has likewise commented on both the jubilee and the sabbath as 'fruitful metaphors for the idea of an egalitarian foundation of polity', invoking 'a preference for solidarity over utility', and a utopian idea of equality and redemption.[74] The jubilee eventually came to connote a time of restitution, remission or release, such as the remission from the penal consequences of sin, or release from the bondage of slavery. The jubilee thus contains a major injunction: 'proclaim liberty throughout all the land' (Lev. 25:10), but also a moment at which debts are 'forgiven'. The emancipation of slaves coincides with an emancipation from debt. This is one reason why the idea of the jubilee continued to resonate through the centuries. Eighteenth-century workers and peasants invoked the term 'jubilee' to demand an end to enclosures, and enslaved people used it to demand their emancipation. Many modern campaigners have used this idea to argue that 'we are long overdue for some kind of Biblical-style Jubilee' (Graeber), or that 'every struggle against enclosure and for the commons inevitably becomes a call of jubilee' (Midnight Notes).[75]

There is indeed much to be said for such an argument, but it is not without its difficulties. Debt forgiveness leaves the whole foundation of

73 Jacob Milgrom, *Leviticus, 23–27: A New Translation with Introduction and Commentary* (New York: Anchor, 2001), p. 2145.

74 Henry Schaeffer, *Hebrew Tribal Economy and the Jubilee, As Illustrated in Semitic and Indo-European Village Communities* (Leipzig: J. C. Hinrichs, 1922), pp. iii, 91–5; Robert A. Yelle, *Sovereignty and the Sacred: Secularism and the Political Economy of Religion* (Chicago: University of Chicago Press, 2019), pp. 140–1, 144.

75 Graeber, *Debt*, p. 390; Midnight Notes, 'New Enclosures', p. 332; Éric Toussaint, *The Debt System: A History of Sovereign Debts and Their Repudiation*, transl. Snake Arbusto (Chicago, IL: Haymarket, 2019 [2017]).

the system of debt in place, and hence the premises of the money system itself completely untroubled. The language of debt forgiveness is a recognition of the power of the creditor, with the debt 'forgiven' not in the name of justice but in the name of power: it is within *our* power to forgive *you*. The theological background is a reminder that to be forgiven our debts would require some kind of supplication, transforming forgiveness into another mechanism for submission. It would also in turn reinforce debt management as another form of political administration.

A second option is abolition. This is a political demand linking debt abolition to abolitionist politics in general. Despite the depth of his argument and the strength of his claims, abolition is only of interest to Graeber in relation to slavery – despite the abolitionist tradition within anarchism within which Graeber situated himself. When Errico Malatesta and his comrades seized control of Lentino in 1877, announcing that the king had been deposed, they carried out what had become a standard anarchist ritual of burning the state archives concerning property holdings, tax payments, and debts.[76] They did not ask for forgiveness. They abolished the debt. To seek the abolition of debt is to align struggles against the power of debt with other forms of abolition, including police abolition.[77] This would mean nothing less than the abolition of debt as pacification, and hence the abolition of pacification per se. It would, in the end, be to make the one abolitionist demand which unites and combines all others: Abolish capital! Some have therefore suggested that debtors might come to seem like a potentially revolutionary class.[78]

But we must be honest: the mechanisms of capture and containment make this feel distinctly unlikely. Moreover, such calls fail to address the broader issue at stake, beyond the simple fact of exploitation and extortion. This is the issue with which this book will conclude: what is really at stake is the *life of money* in our pacification.

The ultimate achievement of debt, interest and usury is the absolute triumph of the money form over our lives. We have seen how much of the argument against usury emerged from Aristotle's idea that money is 'naturally barren', and that it should not be considered as something that

76 James Joll, *The Anarchists* (London: Eyre & Spottiswoode, 1964), p. 122.

77 See The Anti-Security Collective, *The Security Abolition Manifesto* (Ottawa: Red Quill Books, 2024).

78 Ole Bjerg, *Making Money: The Philosophy of Crisis Capitalism* (London: Verso, 2014), p. 256.

could breed, as though it were itself a form of life. Similar arguments were repeated time and again, with barrenness specified as part of the essential nature of money. When, in the fourth century, Saint Basil condemned usury in the 'Homily' cited above, he suggested that money-lenders were trying to make us imagine money as able to give birth to yet more money, like a highly reproductive animal:

> They say that hares bring forth and at the same time both rear young and become doubly pregnant. So also with moneylenders, the money is lent out and, at the same time, it reproduces from itself and is in a process of growth . . . There is interest upon interest, the wicked offspring of wicked parents.[79]

The increasingly dominant arguments over the centuries against usury laws, and thus for the freedom to charge as much interest as possible, dismissed such concerns by rejecting the idea that money is 'a barren thing' producing nothing. In stark opposition to the Deuteronomic principle, the new position was closer to that of Genesis: the injunction 'go forth and multiply' applied as much to money as to any living thing.

Interest on loans thus reveals the same truth as is revealed by the debt system of which they are part – the inner truth that capital wants us to grasp in order to accept our pacification: that, far from being barren, money is a living and creative thing. Capital wants us to imagine money 'like the growth of trees', observes Marx. In the light of death having us by the scruff of the neck, capital wants us to think of money as life itself, the very blood of the body politic. Interest encourages this. Interest is akin to 'the property of a pear tree to bear pears'.[80] The term Marx commonly uses for this is *Naturwüchsigkeit*. This is often translated into English as 'spontaneous', but, as Kojin Karatani points out, a better translation, if a little awkward, would be 'natural growing'.[81] Money, the

79 St Basil, 'Homily 12: A Psalm of David Against Usurers', in Saint Basil, *Exegetic Homilies*, transl. Sister Agnes Clare Way (Washington, DC: Catholic University of America Press, 1963), p. 187.

80 Marx, *Capital, Vol. 1*, p. 267; Marx, *Capital, Vol. 3*, pp. 515–17; Karl Marx, *Grundrisse*, transl. Martin Nicolaus (Harmondsworth: Penguin, 1973), p. 334.

81 Kojin Karatani, *Architecture as Metaphor: Language, Number, Money*, transl. Sabu Kohso (Cambridge, MA: MIT Press, 1995 [1983]), p. 177; Kojin Karatani, *Transcritique: On Kant and Marx*, transl. Sabu Kohso (Cambridge, MA: MIT Press, 2005 [2001]), p. 218.

supreme fetish, wants us to believe that it is natural, able to grow like a living thing, in a way that makes interest-bearing capital its most fetish-like form, and money 'the religion of everyday life'. In the face of this, all other life loses its value, and capital claims the right to dissolve all non-monetized ways of living.[82]

It is in this desire to be the lifeblood of community, to be the only community, that we can detect capital's desire itself to become the subject to which all other life must submit, remain obedient, be pacified. Or, to put it in the terms used in previous chapters: any resistance to the power of money must be countered; any movements challenging it must be contained; any hope that we might live differently must be disappointed. Money giving birth to money produces the *most insane form of a society replete with many insane forms*.[83] Money lives, money rises, money grows, all while our debts capture and contain us, becoming ubiquitous and total – which is how capital wishes them to be, until the end of our lives and even beyond. We owe a debt and feel owned by it. We live in debt, and in the face of a life in debt. Money lives, and all the while debt, like death, has us by the scruff of the neck.

82 Marx, 'Comments on James Mill', p. 212; Marx, *Capital, Vol. 3*, p. 969.

83 Marx, *Capital, Vol. 3*, p. 596. I have tweaked this translation slightly, picking up the alternative in Karl Marx and Frederick Engels, *Collected Works, Vol. 37* (London: Lawrence & Wishart, 1998), p. 463.

Index